TILL KINGDOM COME

TILL KINGDOM COME

Medieval Hinduism in the
Modern Himalaya

LOKESH OHRI

Till Kingdom Come: Ritual Politics and Reflexivity in Mahasu's Himalayan Realm by Lokesh Ohri was first published by Permanent Black D-28 Oxford Apts, 11 IP Extension, Delhi 110092 INDIA, for the territory of SOUTH ASIA.

This publication was accepted as a dissertation in the year 2017 under the title "The Kingdom Comes: Ritual Politics and Reflexivity in Mahasu's Himalayan Realm" in the subject anthropology at the Faculty of Behavioural and Cultural Studies of Heidelberg University.

Not for sale in South Asia

Cover image: The temple official from Khaniyasini, Rupin Valley, in full regalia, climbs the spire at Shiraji, as the pinnacle is bedecked with white cloth in a show of unity. Image courtesy of the author.

Published by State University of New York Press, Albany

© 2019 Lokesh Ohri

All rights reserved

Printed in the United States of America

No part of this book may be used or reproduced in any manner whatsoever without written permission. No part of this book may be stored in a retrieval system or transmitted in any form or by any means including electronic, electrostatic, magnetic tape, mechanical, photocopying, recording, or otherwise without the prior permission in writing of the publisher.

For information, contact State University of New York Press, Albany, NY
www.sunypress.edu

Library of Congress Cataloging-in-Publication Data

Names: Ohri, Lokesh, author
Title: Till kingdom come : medieval Hinduism in the modern Himalaya / Lokesh Ohri, author.
Description: Albany : State University of New York Press, [2019] | Includes bibliographical references and index.
Identifiers: ISBN 9781438482552 (hardcover : alk. paper) | ISBN 9789781438482576 (e-book)
Further information is available at the Library of Congress.

10 9 8 7 6 5 4 3 2 1

To
FAMILY AND FRIENDS
*who permit switching tracks
and tolerate long absences*

Contents

	Acknowledgements	ix
	Glossary	xi
	Note on Transliteration	xix
1	Introduction: Kings Divine	1
2	Ritual Longevity	32
3	Journeying Sovereignties	88
4	Stranger Kings	128
5	Being Young	167
6	Emerson Emerges	198
7	Duty Bound	234
8	Tribal Caste	287
9	Rites and Rights	321
10	Conclusion: Change and Continuity	353
	Bibliography	361
	Index	379

Acknowledgements

THOUGH I HAD TRAVELLED through Jaunsar Bawar earlier, in 2009 when I commenced fieldwork for this book, I was determined to stay at Hanol, a small settlement on the banks of the Tons River, where the temple of the deity, Bautha (seated) Mahasu, is located. However, I soon realised that my understanding of Jaunsari society would not be complete unless I walked with the palanquin processions of Chalda Mahasu, the constantly journeying deity at that point halting in Shiraji in Himachal Pradesh, and the other divine kings. Keeping track of the Chalda palanquin, and those of the others, was a constant challenge and people in remote locations in the Western Himalaya provided information as well as warm hospitality. I am indebted to all of them.

This work is part of my doctoral thesis submitted to the Faculty of Behavioural and Cultural Studies, University of Heidelberg. I am thankful to the SFB 619, Ritual Dynamics, Department of Anthropology at the South Asia Institute, University of Heidelberg, Germany, for generously supporting this research. The staff and colleagues all deserve my heartfelt thanks.

I am grateful to Professor William S. Sax for his support and guidance. Without the benefit of his deep insights on the social life and history of these mountains, this dissertation would not have been possible. I am also grateful to various scholars: Hans Harder, Klaus Peter Zoller, Shekhar Pathak, Peter Sutherland, Erik Moran, Ute Hüsken, Eric Venbrux, Christoph Bergmann, Jürgen Schaflechner, Niche-Ann Schröder, D.R. Purohit, Harish Naraindas, Karin Polit, Johannes Quack, Borayin Maitreya Larios, Eva Ambos, Justus Weiss, Hassan Ashraf, O.C. Handa, R.K. Singh, and several others, for inspiring discussions on my research. I must appreciate the meticulous record keeping at the India Office Records, British Library, London, where I spent long hours.

I am grateful to the ministers of Mahasu moieties, Jaipal Singh and Diwan Singh, and friends in the region, Raghubir Singh Rawat, Radhey Shyam Bijalwan, Jaisi Ram Jodhta, Mahesh Rajguru, Prahlad Rawat, Nandlal Bharti, and Lakshmikant Joshi for their support. Also of great help was Jayendra Dutt Dobhal, who accompanied me on field trips.

I am also grateful to Wendy Doniger for supporting this work, to John Keay for his encouragement, to Rukun Advani of Permanent Black, and to Christopher Ahn of SUNY Press – for their support.

Finally, I would like to thank my family and friends, whose forbearance allowed me to dedicate several years to this research.

Glossary

annas	Old currency coins, replaced in the late 1950s; one anna was one-sixteenth of a rupee.
badi	Carpenter, usually denoting an occupational caste.
badshah	Ruler of the land.
bajgi	Drummer bards of Mahasu. Usually also messengers and singers of genealogies.
bali, balidana	Sacrifice, in propitiation or offering, to a deity.
barabasha	The twelve-yearly tour of Mahasu to either bank of the Tons.
barah beesi	The 240 Rajput clans who fought under the parasol of Chalda Mahasu.
bhaat/bhat	Singers and keepers of genealogies, usually denoting a caste.
begar	Compulsory labour provided by subjects to their rulers.
bethu	Serfs or persons who provided free agricultural labour, having no claim over the land they tilled, and bonded to their master's land either ritualistically or for debt repayment.
bhandari	Storekeeper of the divine king, a temple official who assisted priests.
Bhothu, Buatha	The seated divine king.

bir	Demigods, deputies to the deity.
Bolanda Badri	Incarnation of Vishnu, Badrinath. The Raja of Tehri (formerly Garhwal) claimed the title; it proclaimed him as the mouthpiece of Lord Badrinath.
Char Dham	The four holy sites of Hinduism in Uttarakhand, namely Badrinath, Kedarnath, Gangotri, and Yamunotri.
chatra	Ceremonial parasol of Chalda Mahasu; it accompanies his palanquin.
chatrai	Warrior groups that take pride in marching under Chalda Mahasu's parasol.
chauntroo/chauntru	Council of clan elders.
cheriya boli	The high-pitched utterances of a possessed oracle.
chowki	Police or military post.
dalit	Members of the lowest and most oppressed castes.
Dastur-al-Aml	A legal document and proclamation of land settlement and revenue laws, initially promulgated by Mughal emperors.
damru	Bifocal membranophone with beads attached to both ends with strings. Shiva's hand-held drum.
dand	Fine or levy imposed by a divinity.
dangra	A hand-held axe.
devta	A deity.
dev karya	The work of the deity.
deopujya	Priests of the Brahman caste belonging to clans allotted time to worship and collect offerings at Mahasu temples.

GLOSSARY

devta raja	Divine king.
devta raja ka kaam	Work of the divine king.
dewal	Drummer bards deputed to duties at the cult centre, the Mahasu temple at Hanol.
dhakeur	The outer threshold of the Mahasu temple, inside the courtyard.
dhanti	Out-married daughter.
dhandak	Public demonstrations and protests against officials of the human kings; through these, peasant communities, owing to their democratic character, believed they were enabling rulers to restore order.
digvijaya	Conquering of quarters through journeys undertaken.
dhiyan	Out-married daughter.
dhumh	Rebellion, insurrection, non-cooperation by peasants against rulers and their agents; refusal to accept orders from the ruling class.
dolacra	Tribute in the form of gold or silver offered to Mahasu.
dos	Retribution of Mahasu on account of offence caused by the inadvertent breaking of rules or disobedience.
donriyan	The cylindrical silver receptacle that serves as Mahasu's symbol.
gaddi	Seat of power, throne.
ganadhish	A general in Shiva's body of attendants.
ghat (ghat lagana)	To ensnare someone through a magic spell.
ghee/ghi	Clarified butter.
gotra	Patrilineal clan name.
harul	A ballad from Jaunsar.

jal	Water, usually referred to in political discourse as a resource.
jajmana	A patron performing a sacrifice conducted by a priest.
jati	Caste or subcaste.
kalash	The metal pinnacle of temples that represent the potentialities of life.
Kanet, Kanait	A revenue term used to denote the landowning peasantry of pre-British times. This term, extensively employed by the British in earlier times, became contentious later.
kanphata jogi	Mendicant followers of Gorakhnath, who are said to have lived in India in or before the twelfth century. *Kanphata* literally means "split ear", and these ascetics who venerate Shiva can be identified with the large rings they wear in their split ears.
khat	An administrative and revenue unit consisting of a number of villages.
khanda	Long double-edged sword carried by Mahasu warriors.
khukri	A Nepalese (Gurkha) knife with a curved blade, similar to a machete, used both as a tool and a weapon.
khumri	A general assembly of all heads of families of a clan or village.
khund	The warrior groups of Mahasu, the Rajput.
Kolta	The most depressed of the social groups in the Mahasu cult, condemned to performing menial tasks.
kot	Fortress.
kut	Share of the crop, given away as tribute to the divine king.

lakshagriha	The lacquer palace from the epic Mahabharata, built by the Kauravas, gifted to their siblings the Pandavas and their wife Draupadi, with the intention of getting rid of them by setting it on fire.
maharaj	Great king.
maiyat	Mother's home or natal home, usually for out-married daughters.
mali	Oracle of the divine king, a human, through whom the divine kings speak.
mandaan	A possession ritual in Garhwal.
maya	Illusion, magic.
mauff	Revenue-free land granted to individuals or deities. Often hereditary, when given to individuals, but not essentially including claims on *begar* (bonded labour).
maund	A varying unit of weight in some Asian countries; an Indian unit of weight equivalent to about 37 kg.
Muhammadan	Muslim, follower of Islam.
munshi	A keeper of accounts, an assistant.
nath	Followers of Gorakhnath.
naubat	Honorific drumming, usually at palaces and temples.
nisan	Object as symbol.
pamvara	Ballads of war and valour.
pancva dham	The fifth significant pilgrimage destination.
panchayat	A village-level self-governance institution and unit in village India.
pansi	The moiety on the upper bank, tracing their descent from the Pandavas.

panti	Period of duty at the Mahasu temples, where priests perform rituals and receive offerings.
param bhakta	Topmost devotee, as kings were wont to project themselves in relation to the presiding deity of the kingdom.
pargana	Revenue and administrative unit until British times.
patti	Narrow strips of land in the Himalayan rivers' watersheds, organised as revenue units.
Paush	Tenth month of the Hindu calendar corresponding to December/January. Winter.
phaslana	Share of the crop offered as tribute to Mahasu's perpetual kitchen.
praja mandals	Citizens' groups leading movements for independence, towards the end of British rule in India.
prasad	Food constituting a Hindu religious offering.
puchvai	The task of making an offering and consulting an oracle.
puja	Ritual worship.
rakshasa	Demon.
rajguru	The Nath yogi, as chief preceptor of the divine king.
rajinama	An agreement, written down and signed. A legal document.
Raghunath	Another name for Mahasu, also sometimes commonly used for deities across the mountains; has associations with the god Krishna.
sadr sayana	Elder in a group of clan councils.
sakti	Primordial cosmic energy usually depicted as female.

sathi	The moiety on the lower bank, tracing their descent from the Kauravas.
Sanatana Dharma	Literally meaning "eternal religion", the term usually refers to mainstream Vedic Hinduism.
salwar-kameez	Women's attire, including long shirt and loose trousers, popular in the Punjab region.
sanca	An ancient text, probably from Kashmir, used to make astrological predictions in Mahasu country.
sanskriti	Culture.
sayana	Leader of a clan, and its representative in relations with the state and other clans.
Tamasa	The dark and angry river, as the Tons is usually referred to.
tamasik	One of the three *gunas* or attributes that signifies disorder and imbalance.
tantra	Esoteric traditions of Hinduism and Buddhism that co-developed most likely about the middle of the first millennium CE.
tehsil	A revenue and administrative division, smaller than a district.
thakurai	Principalities or clan territories that were somewhat developed to consider themselves as states; petty hill states.
than	Sacred space.
thani	A tax collector from Mahasu's temple.
tihar	A practice by which lands could be appropriated by a king in the absence of a male heir to property.
tikke	Principalities.
upar ka pani	Water emanating from a spring upstream, reserved for higher castes.

vakil	Attorney, agent, or ambassador.
vazir	Minister to the divine king; chief administrator; top official of the ruler in the hill states.
vazarat	The ministership or power to adorn the seat of *vazir*.
vikas	Development, a term commonly used to indicate improvement in living conditions.
wajib-ul-urz	Record of rights; an important appendix to land settlement documents which listed the rights of various stakeholders to land and other natural resources.
yatra	Pilgrimage.
zameen	Land, usually denoting land as a resource.

Note on Transliteration

I HAVE ADOPTED A minimalist approach when transliterating, especially in relation to diacritical marks – which I have omitted on the assumption that most readers know the words. A glossary is provided for those not familiar with them.

All place names (e.g. Hanol, Maindrath), deity and caste names (e.g. Bijat, Kolta), and mythical figures or other divinities (e.g. Mahasu, Karna) appear in the normal way, the only consistent modification being a substitution of "sh" for both palatal and retroflex sibilants.

Some Jaunsari and Hindi words appear in the text either because they are important terms (e.g. *sathi*, *pansi*) or because they indicate an original phrase. I have not used the initial capital on these words and have italicised them to flag them as foreign-language terms. Here, for the sake of simplicity, I have not rendered the palatal and retroflex sibilants as "sh". I have often used the English plural marker "s" in lieu of the Jaunsari or Hindi plural forms (e.g. *khunds*, *khashas*).

Though I have tried to be consistent in the representation of local terms, some arbitrariness may be visible to those familiar with my terrain.

1

Introduction: Kings Divine

JAUNSAR AND BAWAR are twin mountain regions situated in the north-west of the district of Dehra Dun, interim capital of the Indian hill state of Uttarakhand. With the two principal hill regions in Uttarakhand – Garhwal and Kumaon – dominating electoral politics and constantly bickering over the spoils of development, Jaunsar and Bawar seem to have been left out of the race for material progress. Even though picturesque, these regions attract few visitors as compared to the neighbouring hill station of Mussoorie or the pilgrim centres of Haridwar and Rishikesh. The region's natural resources are exploited in good measure, for there are several hydroelectric projects and timber-collection centres, but the absence of roads, the poor communication networks, and the lack of educational facilities point towards long-term neglect on the part of successive governments. Historically, too, Jaunsar and Bawar, owing to their strong social and political system of village councils under the tutelage of deities (which inhibited the emergence of human rulers), have remained isolated from the neighbouring regions that have been ruled more conventionally by human kings. During colonial times and thereafter, access to the Jaunsar-Bawar region was restricted, with the British setting up a military base at Chakrata, the entry point to the mountains from the United Provinces. Even now, foreign nationals are not permitted into the Chakrata Cantonment. Appellations such as "tribal" were attached to the traditional Hindu caste society here – despite its social structure being not very different from other mountain communities around it – after the government of independent India decided on affirmative action aimed towards giving greater opportunities for education and employment to people from this region. This proved counterproductive, leading to even more seclusion.

The region's social particularities, such as the practice of human sacrifice and head-hunting, have fascinated scholars for long, even as local anthropologists and sociologists themselves, following the peculiar traditions of anthropological research in India, have contributed to notions of the region's peripherality by focusing almost entirely on specific matrimonial practices here, such as polyandry, *dhanti* marriage (marriage of a divorced woman), and bride-price.

Jaunsar-Bawar is bisected by the River Tons, which has carved out largely inaccessible river valleys and deep gorges, creating a densely wooded landscape. Once the Tons joins the Pabbar and flows into the plains at Dehra Dun, it is referred to as the Yamuna. While the river is considered sacred in the plains – poets and saints have eulogised its banks as Krishna's playground – in these parts it is usually referred to as Tamasa, "the dark river". Ancient texts refer to it – in stark contrast to the Ganga as the river that washes away sins and grants immeasurable merit to those who bathe in it ritually – as Karmanasha, "the destroyer of merit". These uncharitable connotations have ensured that the river flows through the mountains largely undisturbed. Few temple towns – other than the small township with the Yamunotri temple at the fountainhead, set up to complete the pilgrimage circuit of Char Dham, the four sacred sites within the state – appear on the banks. There are no bathing ghats dotting the mountainous course of the Tons, and the few temples that may be found by the river, established next to cremation sites, are considered cursed. Water from the river is rarely used for purificatory rites and ritual bathing.

In Dehra Dun, the administrative headquarters of the hill district where I grew up, mention of the region in conversations usually fed into notions of otherness. Jaunsar-Bawar was often referred to as a land of magical spells (especially those cast by women to ensnare unsuspecting men from the plains!), the land of heroin cultivation, the land where home-brewed rice-beer flowed free.

I first arrived in Jaunsar in 1995 as a college student, after the successful conclusion of an international youth convention that I had helped organise. So pleased was the district administrator with the success of the event that he arranged an official jeep for me and my friends, who were part of the organising team, to travel through the region as a reward for our efforts. We were quite excited at the prospect of venturing into what was to us until then unknown territory. However, our spirits were somewhat dampened when he asked us to keep our ears to the ground for instances of women trapped into bonded labour and prostitution. This had been increasingly reported to him in recent times, a matter that could not be investigated "officially" without ruffling political feathers. His strange request and the hidden agenda behind our reward holiday greatly added to our misgivings about the region and the trip.

As we drove up the narrow gorges and down the steep valleys carved out of the mountains by the Tons, we arrived at the temple of Hanol by the river bank. The temple did appear different from those we were accustomed to in the Dehra Dun valley and the plains beyond. Situated in an area of vast fields, a rarity in these parts, the temple made quite an impression on us. Owing to the open space around it, the shrine was visible from a distance despite being situated much below road level. With a pagoda-like roof covered with black slate tiles, wooden pendants hanging from the eaves, and intricately carved wall panels, the shrine was quite unlike any other temple we had seen. Though bedecked with Hindu iconography, the images carved on its wood panels were interestingly rustic, some of them illustrating warrior-like divinities combating demons to establish their supremacy.

Upon entering the courtyard, we were sternly warned against carrying leather inside the sanctum lest we invoke the displeasure

Photo 1.1: The Mahasu Devta Temple at Hanol.

of the presiding deity, Mahasu. We had to leave our waist belts, wristwatches, wallets, and footwear outside the courtyard boundary. After a fleeting glimpse of the idol in the dim light of a solitary pine twig burning like incense, this being twirled around by the priest for a few seconds before the door of the sanctum was slammed shut, we came out of the temple. The images inside were shrouded in secrecy and no photographs were permitted. We emerged into the courtyard – only to see a goat being sacrificed. A man wearing the traditional village cap and jacket had decapitated the goat with a small axe called a *dangra* and was holding the beheaded animal upside down, while another collected the blood dripping from its neck in a bowl. A few men waited around, as if to collect their share of the kill. For some of us in the group, unused to bloodletting, it was quite a revolting sight.

As we went around the shrine, we noticed another smaller but shiny new temple across the river. This temple, we learnt, was also devoted to Mahasu, albeit with a different first name for the deity: while the temple at Hanol was dedicated to Bautha Mahasu, the one on the other bank was dedicated to Pabasik Mahasu. The gods were siblings and of the same form (*ek rup*), we were told, their devotees at times allies, at others competitors for grazing rights, and in certain ways adversaries too. Pabasik was a localised form of the deity who "ruled" over the north bank, while another deity, Basik, held jurisdiction over the south bank. The seated deity, Bautha (*lit.* sitting) Mahasu, provided a kind of axis for the cult to revolve around, and it was Chalda (*lit.* walking) Mahasu who tilted the spatial balance of political power within the cult, constantly travelling in a palanquin carried by his officials and militia over a large area across both banks of the river.

Since we were travelling in a jeep fitted with official plates, it was presumed that we were government officials from the administrative headquarters at Dehra Dun. One of the priests at Hanol, while offering us a cup of tea, complained that the new shrine commissioned in Thadiyar, on the opposite bank, was a challenge to the authority of their deity, also pointing out that the river marked

Photo 1.2: In the foreground, the temple at Hanol, with the Pabasik Mahasu temple in the distance, at Thadiyar, across the river.

the boundary of the Dehra Dun district. Across the river, the temple had been built in the district of Uttarkashi.

The political significance of what at the time appeared to be an instance of unremarkable rivalry between two shrines competing for devotees was revealed several years later as a full-blown religious and political battle. That happened when I returned to Hanol, almost a decade and a half later, in 2009, to commence field research. My work on the implications of religious rituals on social and political life in the Mahasu cult revealed to me that religion and politics commingled in more ways than one could imagine. Now, when I looked at the two temples across opposite banks of the Tons, I was at once reminded of the priest's objection to the new temple. The two shrines facing each other, the new one erected in fairly recent times as an act of defiance, seemed to offer an insight into the political effects of religious ritual in these mountain communities. But before one delves into the politics of temple-building, it is perhaps essential to comprehend the nature of divine politics at work in these valleys.

This is quite a task, for the political control of deities extends over vast territories much beyond the limits of Uttarakhand and into the neighbouring state of Himachal Pradesh. During the course of fieldwork I travelled through valleys and over ridges spanning these two hill states where Mahasu is worshipped and where grand temples to him keep springing up, usually with active financial support from politicians, those in office looking for divine support to continue, and those out of it seeking intervention. I walked with the deity's processions to understand what it was that made the devout invest substantial financial resources and time to the organising of ritual tours and festivals. I also observed politicians, firmly entrenched in echelons of power, visiting temples and seeking allegiances with the deity. Observing Mahasu's influence closely, I came to realise that rituals which at first glance appeared religious ("blind superstition" to some administrators) were politically quite significant. Mahasu, even though a deity in a temple – or an image concealed inside a box-like palanquin – was in fact political master to the people of Jaunsar-Bawar and their neighbours. I witnessed Mahasu oracles delivering verdicts towards the choosing of candidates for elections, saw temple officials endorsing electoral candidates, and received hints from temple managers on how even British officials had capitulated to Mahasu's authority. That these incidents pointed towards how religious ritual translated into powerful political effects gradually became evident to me over successive trips. But whether, in a country described by its constitution as a secular democracy, Mahasu ritual stood its ground as an agentive force, i.e. an influence strong enough to significantly alter social lives, and whether it represented a unique "system" of divine kingship which probably pre-dated human kingship, seemed to require further inquiry.

Political secularism has for long been considered a necessary aspect of modernisation. Modernisation theory, with its roots in Enlightenment ideals of progress, gained strength ever since Marx formulated his notion of class analysis corresponding with the growth of modern capitalism. The notion that new forms of production bring in unprecedented change within modes of human living – including the idea of a gradual separation of religious activities from those of the state – gained currency with the growing influence of Modernisation theory.

Building upon Marx's ideas almost five decades later, Weber introduced the concept of rationality to explain how society had shifted from a mystic or traditional orientation to a more rational one. Rationalisation, to Weber, was the process of replacing traditional and emotional thought with reason and practicality. He believed that most societies were throughout history governed by tradition, and that the most significant trend in modern times was the increasing rationalisation of every aspect of daily life. The rise of scientific education, the development of capitalism, and the introduction of bureaucracy into government over the last two centuries were, according to Weber and several subsequent thinkers, examples of this trend towards secular living (Lerner 1957; Luckmann 1967; Weber 2002). These social scientists and intellectuals, influential at the time of India's independence, predicted the gradual demise of religion as a political factor.

The idea central to this belief had been that the onset of modernity would lead to a complete break from the past, an ontological break as it were, and that the dominance of science would force human society to change drastically, making it tread a path where ritual and religion would find no place in political and social life. Sax (2009: 235) has pointed out that in the 1950s and 1960s modernisation theory was enthusiastically supported by many newly liberated states that believed they would be strengthened when pre-modern loyalties – to ethnic group, regional language, tribe, caste, and above all religion – which they collectively designated "primordial loyalties", were abandoned for secular, democratic, and national, i.e. thoroughly modern, loyalties, values, and ideas. In post-colonial times India, like other newly liberated states, found it hard to resist the allure of secularism. Leaders like Jawaharlal Nehru and others after him harboured the belief that a forward-looking society with a socialist state at the helm should progressively distance itself from religion. This belief was widely shared by the educated classes responsible for running influential institutions. In the first decades of independence, India seemed to be progressing steadily on this path, its rulers focusing on economic and social development towards the building of a "Nehruvian State" (Brass 1990; Nayar 2001). However, even during those times, there were forces opposed to Nehruvian secularism that were constantly working in favour of the religious impulse as a means to political dominance.

Nehruvian secularism, as espoused subsequently by leaders from within his political party, the Congress, has a complex lineage, quite distinct from the Western notion of a secular state. Rather than aiming towards a complete separation of religion from the state, as in the USA, the secularism of post-colonial India has based itself on the idea of equal treatment of various religious communities by the state while safeguarding the interests of minorities. This definition of a secular state required the upholding of "personal laws" among Muslims and other minorities alongside the civil law of the country. A liberal pluralism, where the state itself was seen as not invoking any religion, was an ideal that the likes of Jawaharlal Nehru and B.R. Ambedkar aspired towards, and it was on their insistence that the word "secular" was added to the preamble of the Indian constitution – some would say as an afterthought, since this most detailed constitution of the world did not really define the term. The practice of this notion of secularism in post-independence India indicates that a complete separation of state and religion has never happened, and that in fact it has never been on the national agenda. Frequent acts of mass violence in the name of religion, the lack of an ecclesiastical structure within both Islam and Hinduism, as also communal tensions in the aftermath of Partition required the Indian state to frequently intervene in religious matters. Optimally, the secularism of India denotes the obligation of the state to ensure the well-being of all religions. The foundations of this liberal pluralism in the guise of a secular outlook were laid on privileging minorities with constitutional provisions in order to safeguard their religious practice.

This divergence in viewpoints on secularism between India and the West, between Nehruvian, dalit, and right-wing politics, comes from the diversity and multiplicity within India and, especially, within Hinduism. Hindus historically did not all share what was supposed to constitute a religion, such as creed, deity, ritual, or text. Those that wished to promote a Hindu identity, consequently, had a problem that appears the reverse of Christianity's in secular times. They had to assert the existence of a common religion and give it an overarching status when, for more than a millennium, there was little that linked the various sects and faiths in the subcontinent. For instance, there was no thread that united "caste Hindus" and the so-called untouchable castes.

Meanwhile, external threats, such as missionaries, "secularists", and above all "Muslims" took time to invent. To bring together all the disparate elements under the umbrella of a Hindu identity was a time-consuming project.

Over almost two decades after the end of British rule, Nehru's popularity and dominance ensured some distancing between politics and religion. But, as Berglund (2013) has pointed out, this secular model began to crumble in the 1970s when the Congress Party was challenged for the first time and new identities based not on ideology but on religion and ethnicity began to emerge (Jaffrelot 1996; Madan 1997; Gupta 1985; Kohli 1992). Various forces mobilised these identities, resulting in political unrest and separatist claims within several states. Followed in 1975 by the Indira Gandhi "Emergency", they resulted in a further reorientation of national politics whereby political parties, especially the Bharatiya Janata Party (BJP), began to draw political inspiration increasingly from religion (Malik and Singh 1995; Ghosh 1999). The rise of the BJP parallel with what are projected as the leitmotifs of modernity – globalisation, economic growth, the spread of education and industrialisation – confirms the failure of modernisation theory. The most significant aspect of the BJP's success, as of now, has been the party's ability to make religion and nationalism compatible in the eyes of large sections of the educated Hindu middle class.

In India's 2014 general election, almost seven decades after independence, the notion of a modern secular government not relying on religious mobilisation for political gain, and not employing religious symbolism to win political support, suffered a body blow with the BJP, inspired by its right-wing "Hindutva" worldview, sweeping the polls. The BJP had constantly criticised the ruling United Progressive Alliance (UPA), led by the Congress, of practising what it called "pseudo-secularism", which it argued the UPA had achieved by privileging Muslim interests (i.e. the constitutional privilege given to Muslim personal law) above the interests of the nation's Hindu majority. This, the BJP argued, was "vote-bank politics", and in 2014 it won them an absolute majority. Narendra Modi, who had led the tirade against his hapless adversaries – with his party people coining the oft-repeated phrase "sickular" to berate the Congress – swiftly overcame a semblance of opposition within his own party to become prime minister. With the swearing in of Modi as the country's sixteenth prime minister (his party had an absolute majority after decades of coalition governments), the secular dreams of India's founders – as well as of those who thought decades of material progress, industrialisation, and global flows would enfeeble the claims of ethnicity – seemed to have been shattered. The ideal of equal understanding and respect for all religions was now effectively replaced by the rule of a majority that could choose how tolerant it wanted to be of other faiths. In the various interpretations of secularism that have prevailed in India, religion, rather than disappearing from political discourse, has remained centrestage – even if in varying degrees.

These markedly divergent standpoints on how to interpret secularism, culminating in the BJP's ascension, point towards the growing rather than diminishing significance of religion in political and social life. Modi's victory has merely reaffirmed the fact that advocates of modernisation were incorrect in their assessment that religion would vanish from public life and politics. Modi, more than anyone else, has been responsible for bringing religion to the foreground by arguing that if one is a devout Hindu, one is by default secular. Sax (ibid.) has pointed out that modernisation theory has been criticised for its "explicitly teleological orientation (that is, its assumption that there is a single universal form of modernity toward which all societies tend to progress) and for its assumption of a universal rational subject." Empirically, it is evident that the spread of education, the expansion of democratic institutions, and increased economic opportunity have in no sense diminished claims to ethnic diversity and religious practice.

India's ethnic and religious diversity is evident from the manner in which the cult of Mahasu in Jaunsar-Bawar is still living out its particular customs and ritual organisation, practising its ancient rites, and carrying on its ancestral traditions. None of this seems to conflict with the cult's robust participation in Nehru's or Modi's democracy, even if at times this is done through seemingly archaic rituals of oracular possession and royal processions. For these inhabitants of the mountains – for whom the main occupations have for centuries been transhumant pastoralism and subsistence agriculture – the political, the religious, and the economic are so enmeshed that they defy segregation. For instance, Mahasu, the deity worshipped in the temple at Hanol, is also the political figurehead, a divine king who controls territory and collects taxes through a bureaucracy appointed by him, while holding court through his designated oracles. His temples also double as spaces of healing. In them oracles "cure" possessions afflicting Mahasu's subjects, and pronounce punitive measures against those violating the codes of Mahasu citizenship. For a society gradually moving from pastoralism to agriculture, it was imperative to protect lands from competing groups, and thus Mahasu also maintained a militia to protect pasture and farm, and in turn the economic interests of the temple and the community.

Mahasu represents a unique political and social system. Here, a presiding deity, an idol, is accepted as divine king. The system has not only survived the arrival of modernity but also adapted to it in a manner that is *sui generis*. Even today, the divine king travels constantly, carried in elaborate processional rituals to habitable spaces that come under his jurisdiction. The travel is undertaken by carrying idols in box-like palanquins, locally referred to as *palqi*. The palanquins are carried on the shoulders of the divine king's possessed subjects and oracles, at which time the deity is said to be in procession. Divine kings, being idols, speak to their subjects indirectly through these oracles, who are specially appointed to articulate the wishes of the divine king, while possessed. The lands that a divine king can traverse, overcoming challenges from neighbouring deities, are considered to have been annexed to the kingdom, and people have been socialised over generations to think of themselves as Mahasu subjects. Sax (2006) and others have pointed towards the existence of a widespread "system" of Western Himalayan kingship where the small mountain kingdoms are either ruled by humans acting as "managers" to sovereign state deities, or are territories "ruled" by deities whose ritual processions create and define the territory over which the deity rules. This form of politico-religious organisation, referred to by Sutherland (1998) as "government by deity", could have preceded the polities where human kings ruled over kingdoms.

Divine kingship is still current practice in these mountains, with the two temples across the River Tons indicating a continuing political tug-of-war between "ruling" deities. The four Mahasu siblings – two minor ones on either bank (Basik and Pabasik) serving as opposing forces with Bautha Mahasu as the fulcrum; one sitting in the cult capital at Hanol; and the forever journeying Chalda Mahasu – are allied to each other when facing challenges from other divinities, human kings, colonial officials in the past, and modern governments now. However, conflicts among the four are not uncommon, owing largely to the loyalties of clansmen on opposite banks of the Tons who consider themselves descendants either of the Kauravas or the Pandavas (the squabbling cousins from the Mahabharata) and describe themselves as belonging alternatively to the moieties of the *sathi* and the *pansi*.

In 1998, while Chalda Mahasu was touring the remote Himalayan region of Duni-Bhitri on the north bank of the Tons, the deity decided – the decision was articulated through his oracle – to extend his stay to three years, against the customary halt of a year, at Bhitri. As the new millennium approached, his oracle announced that Mahasu would need a new palanquin. These palanquins are usually gilded with pure silver, and smiths had to be invited from neighbouring Kumaon to mould a vehicle befitting the divine king. Money for the several kilogrammes of silver metal required had to be raised. Once the royal mount was ready, the deity, rather than proceeding to the destination next on the itinerary, i.e. to a hamlet called Kashdhar in Himachal Pradesh, decided to travel towards Thadiyar facing the temple at Hanol, the procession eventually arriving there in the year 2000. This was the year the state of Uttarakhand (then Uttaranchal) came into existence.

Chalda Mahasu now set up camp at a spot overlooking the temple of Hanol on the other bank, at Thadiyar, and ordered the construction of a temple. The deity made it amply clear that his procession would not travel further until the temple was ready. The reason given for this was the deity's desire to check the misappropriation of temple finances in the temple at Hanol.

Most temple officials were tight-lipped, but when I persisted in my efforts to know what financial improprieties had been committed at the Hanol Temple, an elder from the village council of *pansi* agreed to speak. Historically, both factions had equal rights over the offerings made by pilgrims in the temple at Hanol. The

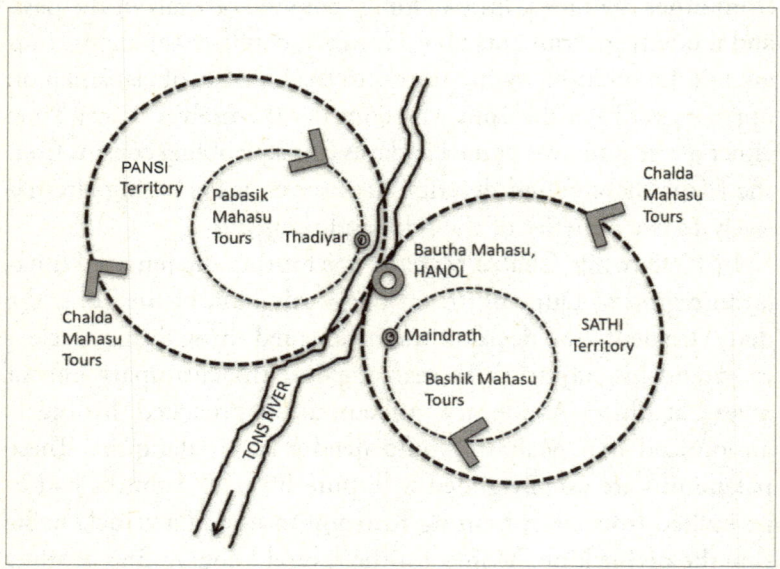

Fig. 1.1: Mahasu territories as described by tours of the divine kings.

Mahasu council at Hanol had, in accordance with the oracle's pronouncements, contributed ingots of gold from the divine king's treasure to the Indian war effort during the Indo-China conflict in 1962. This act typified Mahasu's kingly demeanour – like a king coming to the aid of an ally, Mahasu had gifted wealth to the Government of India to avert a crisis that could harm both. By the time the gold was delivered, the war had ended and the Indian government duly returned the gold. While people had seen the gold go out of the deity's treasure, they had not seen it return. The administration of temple treasures is the responsibility of the Mahasu-appointed minister, the *vazir*, one on each bank. The responsibility of returning the gold, in this instance, fell on the minister of *sathi*. Following remonstrations from the other faction, the *sathi* declared that since the divine king's temple lay in their territory, the *pansi* had no right to question grants and receipts. They went to the extent of installing locks on the treasure chests where the devout made offerings at the temple of Hanol, to prevent the *pansi* from collecting their share. When the *pansi*'s patience ran out, they installed their own treasure chests for pilgrims from their region to make offerings at the temple. As a counter to this move, the chieftains of the *sathi* got together and decided to assert their rights over the temple at Hanol. They rolled the *pansi* chests over the mountainside and tossed them into the river.

The *pansi* were at their wits' end. They could not muster enough numbers to retaliate against the aggression of the opposite faction, nor was violence a feasible option under the democratic government's administrative dispensation. They knew that filing a law suit to restore their rights would enrage the divine king. Even if they did file a law suit in a civil court, it would take years to get a decision. If they decided to seek divine justice at the Hanol temple, the oracle from the opposing faction would be the medium of adjudication. The choices were uninspiring and wider consultations were needed to save face.

A large council of elders, with delegates from as far as Shimla and Kinnaur in Himachal Pradesh, was called, and they decided to meet the district magistrate of Dehra Dun, the government administrator, with a list of complaints against financial irregularities at the Hanol Mahasu Temple. Also appended was a list of malpractices, such as animal sacrifice and the exploitation of lower castes by officials at the Hanol Temple, practices that had been declared unlawful by the administrative machinery in the past. The *pansi* also lobbied with the district administrator of Uttarkashi. The two civil servants met and decided that the law of the land needed to be imposed on the temple. At the opportune moment, delegates from Shimla presented to the civil servants copies of the temple management laws enacted by the government of the neighbouring state, Himachal Pradesh. These laws outlined a mechanism for the utilisation of temple funds for the welfare of pilgrims by temple committees. Soon, government officials brought the Hanol Temple under a new temple management committee, the *pansi* further earning the ire of their brethren on the opposite bank.

On the banks of the Tons, meanwhile, the moment Chalda Mahasu arrived, his oracle expressed the deity's desire for the construction of a new shrine, within sight of the temple at Hanol. The divine king's bureaucracy, and the clan heads or elders, the *sayanas*, not too enthused at the prospect of further aggravating an already tense situation, offered the excuse that there was no abode suitable enough for the deity to stay in this little settlement. The carriers of the palanquin of Chalda Mahasu, almost on cue, moved into the home of Jai Pal Singh Panwar, the divine king settling down in the home of his minister, which was instantly vacated and converted into a shrine. Chalda Mahasu's insistence and intent gave his subjects the courage to go ahead with the challenging project of building a temple overlooking the imposing shrine at Hanol. The divine king had taken upon himself the task of restoring the dignity of one group of subjects, violated by the other, even as both groups claimed his tutelage. But was this going to be *pansi's* Hanol, a new power centre asserting the political will of the *pansi*? Whatever the fate of this new shrine, divine politics was at work with a view to restore the delicate balance of power between the two factions.

Very soon, the temple had reached plinth level and wood was now needed for the columns and the roof. Residents petitioned the officials of the government forest department to grant permission to fell trees in the nearby forests. The official responsible, the forest ranger, cited the ban on tree felling in the forests and refused permission. Chalda Mahasu's devotees, however, entered the forests in violation of the ban and brought the requisite wood. The forest ranger, providentially, was called away for a meeting to Dehra Dun. On his return, the ranger noticed the missing trees, made inquiries, and issued legal notices to the offenders. Very soon, inexplicable mishaps in the ranger's family forced him to seek the help of Chalda Mahasu's *mali*, the oracle, to resolve his domestic crisis. The oracle struck a deal and the notices were quietly withdrawn. This is a familiar pattern in Mahasu country and in this manner, with the divine king's wrath often afflicting government officials, the Mahasu polity manages to evade and trounce the legal system, retaining its political and social relevance.

The foundation stone of a Mahasu temple is laid at the command of the oracle and the temple, once finished, is consecrated in a grand ceremony that resembles a coronation. The allies of the divine king, human and divine, are all present in state and, as is usual with political pageants – who sits where, who arrives when and how close one can get to the deity – defines political power. For the Thadiyar consecration, Chalda Mahasu, because he was in Pabasik Mahasu's territory, involved the divine king and his bureaucracy in the organisation of the event. As the temple neared completion in June 2003, invitations were extended to all major and minor divinities within the realm. Several came in their palanquins, brought to the ceremonial site in processions by their subjects. However, the ones that were invited and yet preferred to stay away caught everyone's attention. The reasons for their absence were debated throughout the ceremony.

Both Chalda and Pabasik Mahasu received the invited divinities at the doorway of the temple courtyard. When it was the turn for the palanquin of the deity Kaul Kedari of Village Salra, Chalda Mahasu refused to come forward for the welcome. The affront was registered instantly and Kaul Kedari decided to pitch his tent away from the temple quadrangle, aloof from where all the other deities were settling to witness the ceremonies. Once the temple consecration was over and all the deities had left, Chalda Mahasu recommenced his processional tours. Buli Das, the drummer-bard of another deity, Raja Karna, in the neighbourhood of the Mahasu kingdom, observed that in their invocations, recited like genealogies of Chalda Mahasu, his drummer-bards had begun to omit Kaul Kedari's name. The deity was definitely out of favour!

When the officials of the Mahasu siblings on the other bank from Hanol received invitation cards for the consecration, the divine kings announced through their oracles their disinclination to participate. They clearly perceived the ceremony as a challenge to their authority. Priests and other officials raked up the issue of how the faction on the other bank had once sought a share of the offerings from the temple at Hanol, forcing them to say, "We will not grant you a share, for the temple lies in our territory. The capital of the kingdom is ours and we shall not give up our rights over it." And then, tongue in cheek, adding insult to injury, "This temple is ours. Create another Hanol for yourselves, if you can!"

Thus, the consecration of a new temple across the river was being seen, between the rival factions the *sathi* and the *pansi*, the sixty Kauravas (as in local folklore) and the Pandava siblings, as a challenge to the age-old *sathi* domination of the cult, an attempt to create another power centre. As a result of the rivalry, Basik Mahasu, rather than himself travelling to the ceremony, sent only his officials, that too to Hanol and not the consecration site. The officials remained in Hanol on the other bank, witnessing the consecration from across the river. This was also done in order to honour the convention of Basik Mahasu not violating Pabasik Mahasu's territory. On the other hand Bautha Mahasu, who is seated and does not travel, sent only his emblem, his *nisan*, against the customary silver coin sent by the Mahasus to each other's temple consecrations.

On 5 June 2003, at the consecration, the emblems of Bautha, and the palanquins of Pabasik and Chalda Mahasu, were ceremonially brought to the temple site and placed on a pedestal under the direction of the Mahasu minister. The oracles of the three deities also sat next to the emblems, possessed by the deities. During the ceremonies, the oracles assured the large audience of their resolve to protect the region, stressing unity. They consecrated the temple as a place of devotion to all four Mahasus.

Once the ceremony was under way, with several deities in attendance, its ritual framework became a bone of contention. While Pabasik Mahasu, the host, had announced his intentions (through his oracle) of honouring the government diktat on animal sacrifice and would henceforth desist from it, Chalda Mahasu would not accept this proposal. Another deity from further upstream, Serhkuriya of Duni-Bhitri, announced through his own oracle that animal sacrifice (*bali*) would indeed be essential for the consecration to be efficacious. However, he also announced that the wishes of the host ought to be taken into consideration in deciding upon the course of action. With Chalda Mahasu insisting on the performance of rituals according to his secret knowledge of *tamasik puja* and the rituals of animal sacrifice, the palanquins of Chalda Mahasu and the deities that accepted animal sacrifice, including Serhkuriya of Duni-Bhitri, got pride of place inside the inner sanctum. On the other hand, the vegetarian deities, including the host, remained seated outside the shrine even as several goats were sacrificed on the temple roof.

Rituals such as these, where stately protocol meets pomp and pageantry, and where groups within communities confront each other over "reform", such as the giving up of animal sacrifice, clearly point towards their contemporary political gravity. Folklore and records from the neighbouring kingdoms tell us that in pre-colonial and colonial times too, the Mahasu cult was associated with powerful polities, with the divine king sharing borders with other divine or human kings. The kingdom was created through the performance of mass rituals of possession and procession, organised on behalf of the deities by officials appointed for the purpose. While Chalda Mahasu is constantly travelling in processions organised by his temple officials, the other siblings too move – once they are invited to host villages. Their visits are needed, even as evil spirits come to possess people. This is when the divine kings, to exorcise the possessed, possess the Mahasu oracles.

It was these rituals, including blood sacrifices and caste segregation – even head-hunting until not very long ago – that negotiated social and political boundaries and translated into acts that would fall within the ambit of Sutherland's (ibid.) "government by deity". Even though practices such as head-hunting have long disappeared and new modes of living – owing to education, roads, mobile phones, and commercial agriculture – have been adopted, Mahasu retains power over his subjects. The subjects still consider it obligatory to participate in his rituals of divine kingship, and unquestioningly accept the power of the deity to alter their world. It is these strong allegiances that translate into political power for the divine kings.

Despite the fact that many disputes between the deities and their officials are now being adjudicated in law courts, the divine kings' subjects continue to converge to their shrines, seeking justice delivered by possessed oracles under the watchful eyes of temple officials. Healing by exorcism of people possessed by spirits is a common sight in all Mahasu shrines. In fact, such is the strength of belief that – given the volatility of the political situation in the state – when in 2016 former Uttarakhand chief minister Harish Rawat faced a crucial vote of confidence in the state assembly, he was seen carrying sacred rice blessed by the divine king in his left palm throughout the legislative debates. His fist remained tightly clenched until the vote had been won. Though he was severely criticised by rationalists for superstitious conduct, the incident of the clinching of rice, and the chief minister's subsequent visit to the divine king's shrine to give thanks, reveal the influence primordial loyalties exert even now.

Charles Taylor (2007) has criticised modernisation theory for its universal assumption of new modes of living subsuming the traditional world of spirits and divinities. According to Quack (2014), the idea of a secular age was opposed by Taylor who preferred an "enchanted world" in which spirits, moral forces, things, and words can transform independently of human beings, and where the line between personal agency and impersonal force, as well as between the physical and the moral, is not impermeable. Taylor argues that certain boundaries in an enchanted world – for example between "humans and things" and between "mind and world" – are experienced as porous and diffusive. He thus offers a description of people as "porous selves" inhabiting an enchanted world rather than "buffered selves" living in a secular world, as is made out. To those looking at the Mahasu kingdom from the outside, the divine king may appear just an idol, an object venerated and shrouded in mysterious secrecy. To his subjects, however, he is an integral part of their enchanted world. To the observer he may appear an inanimate figure, a "thing" treated as a king. To the Mahasu subject the kingship of Mahasu is a part of his very being, the divine king being a non-human agent intrinsic to community life.

Much before Taylor criticised modernisation theory for its "a-cultural" assumptions, McKim Marriott (1976, 1990) had suggested that any inquiry into a culture must apply categories derived from that culture itself. In other words, Marriott opposed the universal application of Western analytical terms to cultures within countries like India, arguing for an indigenisation of theory and the employment of an alternative social science distinct from inherited concepts such as those of Marx and Weber. In this context, the clear difference between interpretations of secularism in India and the West is important.

In *We Have Never Been Modern* (1991), Bruno Latour argues that modernity, rather than being an ontological fact, is an ideology. This ideology allows so-called progressive people to claim superiority over those of their brethren who are less fortunate in terms of scientific and economic advancement. Latour is critical of modernity's separation of nature from culture, of the self from the other, and of science from religion. Opposing these dichotomies, he insists that their mutual entanglements cannot be separated. These inseparable entanglements he terms networks – of agency, technology, humans, etc.

Today, given the broad acceptance of the notion of people as universal rational subjects, belief in a non-human agent as a political and social entity appears counterintuitive. Despite "development" such ideas are apparent from the fact that people desire subjecthood to a non-human king, Mahasu Devta, even as they participate in the citizenship protocols of modern India. The archaic cult of Mahasu, though at such extreme variance with contemporary secular norms, retains its vitality, with its mass rituals performed on an ever-growing scale of kingly pomp and pageantry. The lives of almost every individual born into the cult revolve today, as in the past, around *devta raja ka kaam* (the work of the divine king). Mahasu processions move across the kingdom, dispensing justice and performing ritual functions significant to his subjects. Grand temples, referred to as *kot* or fortresses, hitherto unimaginable in scale, continue being built for these divine kings, with considerable financial support coming from the community as well as the political class. Divine kings wield considerable clout in political and bureaucratic circles, in the Himalayan state capitals Dehra Dun and Shimla. Though some of the divine kings' functions have been usurped by the state and the government sometimes meddles with the rituals of divine kingship, Mahasu's writ still runs large over his subjects. These divinities continue to retain agentive power over their subjects, even as they help their subjects negotiate their identities.

Mahasu subjects are deeply influenced by the state's discourse of progress and development, referred to commonly as *vikas*. According to Sax (ibid.), though there is little consensus on what *vikas* is, it is thought of as "an unqualified good that brings greater prosperity, increased literacy, and a better functioning democracy." And in this sense there are signs of progress, with many people of the region shifting from agro-pastoralism to apple horticulture, exporting high-quality apples grown here to foreign markets. Apple prosperity has generated a huge demand for "English-medium" schools, and income from tourism is now very considerable and rising. However, when I raised this issue with the divine kings' subjects – of Mahasu's continuing dominance despite the material progress all around – people appeared confounded. Many did not see a contradiction between the practice of ritual as prescribed by their divine king and material progress. Several, in fact, attributed material progress to the grace of the divine king rather than to democratic institutions, and felt that, owing to the new-found wealth and opportunities for education, the onus fell on them, now even more than earlier, to offer goats to their divine king, to go on processions with his palanquin, to build grand temples to him, to consult the *sanca* (an ancient text used for making predictions), or simply "protect our *sanskriti*" (lit. culture).

As we shall see during the course of this book, even when voices are raised for "reforming" ritual practices – such as ending animal sacrifice and permitting entry to women and the lower castes into temples – change that seems quite radical to the cult and questions the absolute authority of Mahasu, is never directly challenged by the oppressed. It is usually Mahasu officials that are attacked for being corrupt and intransigent, it is as if the divine king can do no wrong.

Mahasu's agentive power is not a matter of as immediate concern to his subjects as it is to the anthropologist. To his subjects the divine king's ritual regime is simply life as they and their ancestors have always lived it. However, it has become a matter of interest for academia and of practical concern to officials of the state. In conversations, the reasons usually proffered for the cult's extraordinary longevity and for the survival of its ancient ritual systems are geographical enclosure and remoteness. The explanation offered is that divine kingship has survived owing to the region's distance from the mainstream, and, since the long arm of the state and its development efforts have not reached the cult, it remains mired in ritual and (as colonial records sometimes suggest) "superstition" (Williams 1874; Walton 1911). The claim, of course, is not true since the mountains, even though they represent a climatic divide, have always seen migration and movement. The state has made deep inroads ever since the British arrived. In fact, British officers like Young (political agent for Dehra Dun in the 1830s) and Emerson (1881–1962, colonial administrator and scholar) engaged deeply with the divine king, ritually as well as politically.

After India gained independence in 1947, parts of the Mahasu realm within Jaunsar-Bawar came into sharp focus owing to indicators of endemic poverty and belief in rituals that seemed incomprehensible to state officials. At the behest of influential local politicians, a committee was set up to enquire into the reasons for "backwardness". The politicians, instrumental in the constitution of the committee, influenced its findings too. The state began efforts towards assimilation by granting the status of a "scheduled tribe" to the entire population in Jaunsar-Bawar, despite the fact that the subjects of Mahasu were only a differentiated Hindu group. Mahasu subjects, and those of other divine kings in regions with identical cultural practices around Jaunsar-Bawar, were left out of the tribal appellation. Scheduled tribe status brought special benefits, such as job reservations in government and a regular inflow of development funds into the region, notwithstanding the fact that most state doles were cornered by an elite "creamy layer" of the upper caste, dominant Rajputs and the Brahmans. The affirmative act of granting reservations has thus proved counterproductive to the creation of an egalitarian society.

Today, the functioning of democratic institutions and material progress are visible in the form of roads, schools, hospitals, banks, national parks, and horticulture and tourism development projects. They are also manifest in democratic elections, as keenly contested as anywhere else in India, notwithstanding the fact that divine kings have a role in choosing candidates and none can hope to secure a win without their endorsement. Several individuals born into the cult have adopted professions such as medicine and the law, or joined the bureaucracy and the police force. They live in cities and yet continue to owe allegiance to the divine kings, returning periodically to participate in temple rituals. Mahasu subjects, thus, seem to have adapted to change within their unique matrix of material progress without adhering to a defined and linear modernity.

Despite the fact that Mahasu subjects continue to be deeply connected to their rituals, they also aspire to be modern citizens in a democratic state. Modernity, for Mahasu subjects, as Sax and Nair (2014) have pointed out for another group, seems to be a state that no-one can define, but to which everyone seems to aspire. For the subjects of the divine king, their proximity to religious power centres is as much a matter of belief as a tool for advancement in the tumult of social politics. Temple priests and Mahasu officials have easy access to powerful bureaucratic and political circles. Political figures in the hills, even from regions other than the Mahasu realm, owing to the fear of Mahasu being a divinity easily offended and very difficult to propitiate, grant special privileges to those close to Mahasu. In the capital of

Uttarakhand, Dehra Dun, I have more than once accompanied the Mahasu temple priest who, owing to his proximity to the divine king, carrying the temple *prasad* as a kind of passport, gained easy access to the inner chambers of the chief minister's residence. In an article on the neighbouring region of Kullu, Berti (2006) has discussed the "modern" political uses to which the king of Kullu puts his identification with the local deity, Raghunathji.

In a society where religious associations pay political dividends, belief, rather than going out of circulation, is likely to gain greater currency. For Mahasu subjects – as Tambiah (1989) has pointed out for contemporary times more generally – religion, rather than fading into insignificance, has gained in importance and claims of ethnic diversity here have become louder rather than being muffled. This is evident in campaigns by other Mahasu subjects in neighbourhood regions of Jaunsar who emphasise their "backwardness" and archaic ritual practices in the hope of acquiring the coveted tribal status.

Throughout this text I grapple with the issue of continuity amidst change. Rituals emerge as a potent political force in Mahasu's continuing dominance, even as the state makes its presence more emphatic. Every time advocates of reform from within or from the outside threaten Mahasu's ritual regime, the community rallies around their divine kings and tradition is reaffirmed. The divine kings allow contesting groups to argue until finally enforcing the will of the community. This not only points to an ingrained conservatism within rites and rituals but also to their potential for innovation. Rituals, in the cult of Mahasu, prove potent forces of cultural and political continuity as well as social change. Kertzer (1988) has dwelt on this aspect and argued that as societies grow complex they become even more encrusted in symbol and myth: "Because ritual is usually identified with religion and, since modern Western societies have presumably separated political affairs from religious life, there is an assumption that ritual remains politically significant only in less 'advanced' societies." Arguing against this assumption, he asserts that politics is essentially expressed through symbols. Even though material resources are crucial to the political process, their distribution and use are largely shaped through symbolic means. To understand a political process, therefore, it is necessary to understand how political actors consciously and unconsciously manipulate symbols and how this symbolic dimension relates to the material bases of political power.

The ability of ritual to constitute political ideas is often underplayed in modern "secular" discourses. Geertz (1980), in his analysis of Negara (the Balinese theatre state), claimed that rituals and rites did not in fact imitate social reality as much as they imitated themselves in socially recurrent repetition. Through repetition, rituals created an idea of the state as something transcending the individuals in charge of the state, while also in a way constituting the state. This idea has influenced much of the writing on ritual in modern political thought, perhaps giving rise to the notion that ritual, expressed in terms of pomp, pageantry, procession, and repetitive ceremony, has no place in modern democracies. Kertzer has offered a counterpoint and underlined the significance of ritual, claiming that ritual is absolutely central to modern politics – as central as it was in the theatre state of Bali, and not merely in relation to creating permanence.

In order to achieve solidarity and allegiance, politics employs what Kertzer refers to as polysemic symbols. He equates polysemic symbols with ritual or symbolic behaviour that is socially standardised and repetitive. In order to emphasise the meaning of ritual, Kertzer brings into focus the Durkheimian idea that ritual is a symbolic activity through which, within a society, mutual interdependencies are sacralised. For him, ritual is behaviour that is formalised as well as repetitive, with the emotional and psychological underpinnings of dramatic effect. He says three attributes of ritual symbols are especially important – condensation of meaning or the interaction of different meanings and their synthesis; multivocality or the understanding of the same actions by different people in different ways; and ambiguity or the multiplicity of meanings for one single action. Rituals, he believes, are those actions that can create a sense of solidarity and allegiance even when a consensus is difficult to achieve.

In Mahasu country the phenomenon of a modernity polarised by belief, rather than one that denies belief, underlines the fact that there is no single path to modernity, and that each cultural and denominational tradition contains the possibility of leading to an internal elaboration of its own democratic and pluralist approach to it. In the Mahasu context, the citizens of a democratic nation-state also remain, simultaneously, the subjects of a divine king. Change occurs within the matrix of self-differentiation in modernity as each village attempts to outdo the other in displaying devotion to their divine king by constructing shrines reflecting an unmatched grandeur, and with contributions coming in from "development funds" given by government ministers who represent the very state whose officers sometimes treat divine kingship as a primitive form of social life. Divine kings in fact play decisive roles in politics, negotiating with state leaders for development projects.

Theorists like Gaonkar (2001) have attempted to revive parts of modernisation theory under the rubric of "alternative modernities". This is modernisation theory devoid of both the teleology and the universalism. It holds, as Taylor (2001) has pointed out – referring to what he describes as a "cultural theory" – that modernity always unfolds within a specific cultural or civilisational context and that different starting points for the transition to modernity lead to different outcomes. Under the impact of modernity, all societies will undergo certain changes in both outlook and institutional arrangements. Some of those changes may be similar, but they do not amount to convergence. Different starting points ensure that new differences will emerge in response to relatively similar changes. A cultural theory, as opposed to an "a-cultural theory", directs one to examine how "the pull of sameness and the forces making for difference" interact in specific ways under the exigencies of history and politics to produce alternative modernities at different national and cultural sites. In short, modernity is not one, but many. The political theorist Sudipta Kaviraj (2005) has argued "that there is a logic of self-differentiation in modernity" such that the more it expands to different parts of the world, the more it becomes "differentiated and plural".

For Mahasu subjects, this constant struggle between change and continuity is usually explained away as a deficient modernity stemming out of remoteness and the enclosure of the community within the deep valleys of the Western Himalayas. This is perhaps not a correct assessment since even though the community is situated at a somewhat distant and inaccessible location (from our standpoint, not theirs), history provides abundant evidence of the divine king's active engagement with the British and postcolonial regimes. The ballads of the Mahasu drummer-bards, recited for centuries in Mahasu shrines and processions, indicate contact and engagement with precolonial regimes such as the Mughals as well as proximate kingdoms. Thus, remoteness does not explain the extraordinary longevity of the Mahasu ritual regime *vis-à-vis* secularising forces. The community, in fact, deployed its intransigent and particularised rituals as bargaining chips to extract preferential treatment from the Mughals, the British, and the government of newly independent India. It is this extraordinary conservatism of Mahasu rituals, accompanied by their potential for innovation that this book seeks to explore. The persistence of the ritual in the face of modernity points towards a path hitherto not trodden, leading to an unknown destination.

In the chapters that follow, I trace the steps of the Mahasu subjects' tryst with contemporary politics, charting out the community's constant struggle to retain a ritualised way of life while also embracing progress. Given the arguments of modernity theorists, seemingly archaic ritual practices should have been long discarded whereas they are employed within the community for the divine kings to achieve harmony amongst several contradictions intrinsic to the cult. I show that the cult is organised into several oppositions along narrow strips in the mountains. Mahasu subjects living on either bank of the river insist that they belong to rival moieties: the *sathi* and the *pansi*. Like the ever-squabbling cousins in the Mahabharata who decimated their respective bloodlines when fighting at Kurukshetra, the moieties of the *sathi* and *pansi* are engaged in a constant tussle over the right to extend hospitality to the travelling divine king. Democracy has compounded the conflict by dividing Mahasu territory between two modern states, Himachal Pradesh and Uttarakhand. Mahasu has to constantly negotiate administrative controls when crossing these lines drawn by modern-day administrators and cartographers – for the divine king borders are conceptualised differently, not as lines on a map but as negotiated settlements between the rulers to whom allegiance is owed. Mahasu kingship is established through ritual visiting, gift giving and receiving, and by demonstrating the efficacy of ritual through performances such as controlling the weather and exorcising evil spirits that possess subjects. To the outsider, these rituals may appear questionable. For the Mahasu subject, they are life itself as lived for centuries on these ridges. The term "ritual", therefore, reflects a problem of our modern world and not of those who perform rituals. To subjects of the divine kings, rituals are efficacious in terms of binding their society together, ratifying collective decisions, sanctifying spaces, and even marking territory.

The resilience of the divine kings' rituals comes from their inherent capacity to adapt. Mahasu's encounters with two British administrators, almost a century apart in time, reflect a trend that reveals more about how attitudes in the external "secular" world towards the possibility of a non-human agent, and as a political ruler, have hardened into considering such beliefs as blind faith or superstition. They indicate how those living in a secular age have gradually chosen to become inflexible in relation to alternative cosmologies. Mahasu, owing to adaptability to changing social and political realities, continues to thrive as an agent with the capacity to alter lives and endure change. Meanwhile, a Mahasu subject participating in rituals and living by a tradition is not concerned with whether to the external observer what he does is meaningless repetitive activity or efficacious action. Such an individual is just going about the business of living; he embodies the normal behaviour that has helped his ancestors and his contemporary kinfolk to negotiate through the rough and tumble of life. His performance may appear mere ritual to an observer, yet, for him it is nothing but life; in this sense, ritual is a category invented by the social scientist, not the practitioner.

This book hopes to reveal that indigenous cultures are not deficiently modern, but rather that modern cultures which have encountered the ritual regime of Mahasu – as well as similar indigenous native social organisations – have progressively lost the ability to comprehend and accept alternative modes of thinking and living.

2

Ritual Longevity

POST-INDEPENDENCE, IN 1947, India was faced with the task of reorganising itself into a federation of states. Nehru and others in power, keeping in view the vast ethnic diversities that made up India's social fabric, and the strife that religious fundamentalism was causing in the subcontinent, ruled out ethnicity as the factor determining statehood. Linguistic difference was to be the main factor on the basis of which the states of India were to be organised. However, when in regions like the Punjab ethnicity became too strong a factor to be ignored, religion and ethnic difference were sneaked in under the garb of language to force a split. In other regions such as north-east India, where a common religion could have acted as a uniting force, language and ethnicity were employed in order to divide the region into small "manageable" states.

In the Western Himalayas, ethnic and linguistic differences were never strong enough to merit separations. Even though there was a demand in some quarters for the merger of the little Himalayan kingdoms adjoining Punjab with it, it was utterly opposed by the hill states' erstwhile rulers and people at large. Praja Mandals – the organised workers' groups that had led the freedom struggle in the hill kingdoms – as well as the rulers of kingdoms reinstated by the British after they had defeated the Nepalese armies to win over the region, held divergent views on the future of the hill states. After brief negotiations with the rulers and the Praja Mandals, the small Shimla Hill States were consolidated into a district named Mahasu. They were then made a part of the chief commissioner's province and later part of a union territory under the name "Himachal Pradesh". The erstwhile kingdoms *per se* were not directly under central control in independent India until Himachal Pradesh was finally granted statehood in 1971. On the other hand, the hill kingdoms in adjoining Uttar Pradesh (called United Provinces under the British), with the exception of Tehri Garhwal, had come under direct colonial rule immediately after the Anglo-Gurkha War of 1815. As recently as the year 2000, after a protracted protest by residents of the hill regions of this state, the state of Uttarakhand (at the time of its creation called Uttaranchal) was created. Kumar (2011), tracing the events of the agitation for separation, says that the protest movement was centred on developmental regionalism and had little to do with ethnic difference. His view is that it was a manifestation of political and economic deprivation in the hills, with the community demanding a restoration of its control over *jal, jungal, aur zameen* (lit. water, forest, and land), resources widely seen as rightfully owned by highlanders but exploited by plains' people.

Religious and ritualistic beliefs did not figure prominently in the demands for redrawing boundaries and the creation of Uttarakhand. The driving force behind the demand for a separate state was the lack of participation of hill people in policies and plans that governments made for them. According to Sax (2010), once severed, given the "logic of statehood", ethnic differences between plains and hills had to be identified and invented. For instance, the goddess Nanda Devi, the divinity revered in Garhwal as the daughter outmarried to the god Shiva, was adopted as a unifying symbol despite the fact that, earlier, the goddess had been a bone of contention between the hill regions of Garhwal and Kumaon, the two regions that principally constituted the new state. In the seventeenth century, the king of Kumaon had taken away the Garhwali idol of Nanda Devi, believing that the possession and worship of it would guarantee his victory over the armies of Garhwal. Later, the Kumaon armies adopted the battle cry, "Victory to Nanda Devi!" (Atkinson 1884, II: 566; Sax 1991: 167–8), causing much heartburn in Garhwal. One of the rulers of the earliest known local dynasty, the Katyuris, styled himself the *paramabhakta* (greatest devotee) of Nanda Devi in the mid-ninth century (Kielhorn 1896: 179, 183; Sircar 1956: 179, 282, 287–8).

Against the background of animosities over the abduction of the *dhiyan* (daughter of Garhwal) by the Kumaon kings, this projection of the goddess Nanda Devi as a unifying force in the new state was significant. The Nanda Raj Yatra, the twelve-yearly ritual procession in which the goddess is escorted back to her husband's abode in the mountains, which was primarily a pilgrimage of the Garhwal region, has in recent years been reinvented in the new state as the prime cultural event not just of Garhwal but of the entire state. In 2014 the pilgrimage, in fact, officially commenced at the temple of Nanda Devi in Almora, Kumaon. Only when a large contingent of Kumaoni pilgrims, bearing the parasol of Nanda Devi, arrived at Nauti in Garhwal did the procession proceed further. The pilgrimage thus became a meeting ground; the very deity that was once the cause of a rift between the two hill regions was now uniting them by symbolising their new-found apparently singular cultural identity. Regions like Jaunsar and Rawain that were ruled by their own local deities were also forced to identify with the goddess in some ways, sending parasols to accompany the procession.

In a country described by its constitution as secular, it would be easy to look at deity processions as mere pageantry, as politically meaningless activity. In fact, the pageantry around divine kings like Mahasu undergirds a very significant political culture. Though their prime purpose is social cohesion, their performance (or non-performance) can lead to contestations, sometimes resulting in mass violence. Rituals with such powerful social effects cannot be divorced from political life.

Hill people invest substantial time and money visiting deities and accompanying their processions, the ritual being the essence of social life. Sax (ibid.) believes that in contemporary social formulations the "symbolic" is generally relegated to the "merely symbolic". What this means is that, usually, religion and ritual are treated as merely an expression or reflection of more fundamental realities. We often commit the error of imagining rituals as merely mirroring and symbolising political or economic realities but not actually creating them.

Rituals like the Nanda Devi and Mahasu processions have immense political significance for communities since they are intended to integrate a social group even as the movement of deities appears to define territory. Closer examination reveals that the prime purpose of the processions, more than a marking of territory, is to test the subject's faith. The divinities' physical presence helps in itself to define their influence. What seems a symbolic act has immense political consequence because it is these rituals that reveal a society in conversation with itself, confronting issues that really demand attention. Modern states governed by "secular" constitutions may find it inconvenient to recognise rituals as constituting significant political agendas – they are attuned to thinking of election rallies and canvassing tours as the essence of contemporary political processes. Ironically, this is notwithstanding the fact that present Indian electioneering is also completely definable as a ritual. So, ritual is seen only as an aspect of religious life, because the requirements of genuflecting to secular and constitutional imperatives cannot easily permit seeing ritual as constituting political power and economic substance; to admit this would seem to project the state as deficiently modern.

In fact, in the South Asian context rituals, religious processions, and pageantry are an intrinsic part of politics. After independence, with princely states subsumed by the democratic state, election rallies and public meetings became the new norm. During the freedom struggle, Mahatma Gandhi redefined politics with new forms of protest rituals, such as the public burning of foreign goods, salt marches, and the mass spinning of cotton on spinning wheels, with the *charkha* becoming the leitmotif of the freedom struggle. For the princely states, on the other hand, the restrictions democracy imposed on kingly ritual, pageants, and holding of titles led to the dissolution of their political power.

With independence, these erstwhile kingdoms were absorbed into the dominion and the royalty left to the mercy of privy purses, which too were withdrawn in due course. Ruling dynasties were now reduced to the status of common citizens, left to eke out a living from their properties and palaces. With territories and riches taken away, many chose to retain their former hold over political power by jumping into the rough and tumble of electoral politics, an implicit acceptance of the end of their dynastic reigns. While the political power of human kingships such as Tehri, Jubbal, Sirmaur, Rampur, Mandi, and others in the Western Himalayas continued to dissipate during colonial rule – their remnants subsumed by democratic politics in independent India – divine kings such as Mahasu, Shirgul, and Bijat continued tenaciously to hold on to power and legitimacy in their territories. How did these divine kings manage not only to retain control over their subjects, but also to actively engage with the state?

Divine kings like Mahasu, perhaps owing to the ambiguities of their legal personhood, were largely ignored by colonials as well as the Indian state. Their rituals puzzled the British, who chose to grant special status to a large part of the Mahasu territory. A similar policy was adopted in free India and the state designated parts of Mahasu territory, i.e. the Jaunsar-Bawar region, "tribal", with the natives largely left to their own religious devices. The state did not realise that concealed within the non-human agent's religious ritual lay the kernels of political longevity.

Hocart (1927) put forward the case that kingship, and with it government, was originally merely a ritual activity directed towards a "collective regeneration of life" and that only subsequently did kingship acquire governmental functions. In other words, rituals gained primacy over politics in Indic and classical traditions, and kingship was primarily a matter of ritual on to which the more mundane aspects of governance were added. Hocart argued that caste originated in royal courts when a system of ritual offices centred on the king. Ethnographic accounts from South Asia tended to support Hocart's somewhat simplistic argument, but the issue was complicated by Dumont's (1962) influential representation of Hindu kingship as secular, but encompassed by the ritual role of the Brahman. According to Dumont, India distinguished religion and politics centuries before the West, and this distinction manifested itself in a form of kingship that was more purely "political" than the forms of divine kingship found in the West. Raheja (1988) critiqued Dumont with a new understanding of kingship – of the god as a divine king at the centre of his realm, with the various castes ranged around him as in a royal court, these caste relationships defined on the basis of proximity and distance from the centre and actualised through gift-giving and receiving. The centre–periphery models of kingship, advocated by Dirks (1987) and Raheja (ibid.), were inconsistent with the opposition Dumont posited between secular kingship and sacred priesthood, but are more reflective of the political reality in the courts of the Western Himalayan divine kings.

Sahlins (1985) also drew on Hocart and suggested the representation of kings as strangers or outsiders, which is quite consistent with the Mahasu myth (outlined later) of divine kings having been invited from Kashmir by a Brahman to kill the tyrant demon Kirmir and establish their kingdom. Sahlins points towards a different conception of kingship, focussed on political power, as something which may not be embedded in society but is inherent in individuals and can only be dealt with once represented as having arrived from outside the normal. Taking the power concept further, Benedict Anderson (1983) has argued of Indic kingship that the task of a king was to demonstrate the concentration of power at the centre, often paradoxically through inactivity, and to transform the world with the exercise of power. This leads to a significant point of departure between the Western conception of classical kingship and what we know as South Asian kingship. Amongst pre-modern South Asian social groups, as Galey (1989) has indicated, kings may have disappeared but representations of kingship are pervasive in inter-caste relations within villages and in ties of patronage with political leaders. This would indicate that even the idea of mass politics as conceptualised in the West may be subtly different from that in South Asian societies.

A pre-modern society within which a non-human entity also exists as divine king offers a unique opportunity for examining the conception of power in a polity focussed on a moving centre rather than on borders and boundaries – as is the case within most modern nation states. Tribal nomadic states, in fact, have for centuries made good use of the idea of a moving centre. For instance, between 1556 and 1739 the Mughals are believed to have spent over forty per cent of their time in royal camps. Many large tribal states in India were not defined territorially, their sovereignty depending on a moving axis.

However, in present times, territory refers in an intuitive sense to people living within the confines of lines on a map and things that a border envelops. So deeply ingrained is the idea that even when I represent Mahasu territory in this book, I have to do it with a map, despite there being no evidence of any map pre-dating the land records of the British. Mahasu kingship manifests a pyramidal social structure centred on the divine king. This centre, owing to the presence of several divinities – the four Mahasu siblings, their mother, their deputies or *birs*, their networks of allegiance and fealty owed directly to the elders or *sayanas*, through them to the regional elders or *sadr sayanas*, and through them to the divine king – can be both mobile and ever expanding. The ordinary individual in this social system owes allegiance to the village elder, who in turn pays ritual homage to regional elders that swear fealty to the divine king. In this manner, divine kings emerge as moving ritual centres that hold power over their subjects, this power being exerted through the winning of loyalties performed by subjects through ritual – as against the power invoked by modern Western theory, acquired through the marking of borders on maps after military conquests. Through this book I explore the possibility of the central–peripheral model of kingship – mindful of the dangers of essentialising Mahasu subjects as deficiently modern or trapped in tradition – and creating thereby a cultural vision of the political. Through ideas of what constituted a kingdom in ancient Indian thought, I explore the notion of a moving ritual centre in the context of the Mahasu kingdom.

The Mahasu realm in democratic India today is spread over the two Himalayan states of Uttarakhand and Himachal Pradesh. In Uttarakhand it extends to the western area of Dehra Dun district and is the "tribal" region known as Jaunsar-Bawar. In Himachal Pradesh it extends into "non-tribal" parts of Upper Himachal

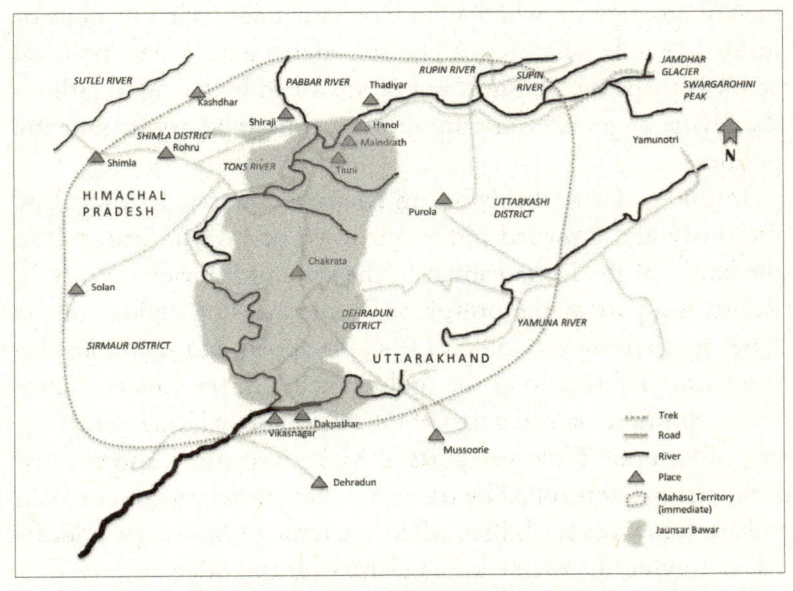

Fig. 2.1: Mahasu territory.

and falls in the districts of Rampur, Sirmaur, Shimla, and Solan. Mahasu processions crisscross the region, often over state boundaries, testing allegiances and dispensing justice, in the course of performing and thereby creating divine kingship.

This freedom of movement for Mahasu, who moves in state with drummers, goats, and militia in attendance, does not mean that the divine king still rules over the region. The question remains whether Mahasu, despite the officials, treasure, fortresses (as the temples are known), retinue, militia and territory, can legitimately claim, politically and sociologically, to be a king, and whether the domain, described as a pre-colonial polity, continues to function as one. My fieldwork suggests that Mahasu wields substantial political clout across state boundaries. But is the Mahasu phenomenon a mere instrumentalisation of the deity by a few to retain their hold over power (as generally understood by the Indian bureaucracy), or does it translate into far-reaching political effects for the entire community? This brings us to another fundamental question on whether an idol, either concealed in a box or inside a temple sanctum, can be considered a legitimate political actor. Perhaps the question can be answered by trying to fathom the divine king's relevance in terms of contemporary democratic politics.

In 2009, during fieldwork in Mahasu country, I stopped by the dusty and crowded mountain town of Rohru. Situated on the banks of the River Pabbar in the state of Himachal Pradesh, Rohru is a part of the prosperous apple-growing regions of the state, specialising in Golden Delicious apples and therefore also sometimes referred to as the "golden belt". In pre-independence times, Rohru remained a part of the territory of a human king, the raja of Rampur. However, parts of Mahasu territory also abutted into territory controlled by the raja. I was on my way to one such village, known as Kashdhar, where a temple to Mahasu was located, signifying the divine king's claim over the ridge.

My visit to Rohru coincided with elections to the state legislative assembly, where the contest seemed straightforward, as witnessed in most parts of the country, between candidates from the two national parties, the left-of-centre Congress and the Hindu right-wing BJP. In such contests it is not difficult to predict the results, keeping the national or the regional mood in mind. But Himachal Pradesh is different. The state's population is overwhelmingly Hindu, with Muslims constituting less than two percent of the population. Even though the national communal agenda usually fails to cut much ice with the electorate, local issues, including the influence of divine entities, dominate the political discourse. Himachal Pradesh, after its formation, quickly embarked on a policy of developing horticulture as the mainstay of the agrarian economy. The six northern districts of the state, Kullu, Mandi, Sirmaur, Solan, Kinnaur, and Shimla, together constitute what is generally referred to as Upper Himachal. These apple-growing regions have traditionally been a Congress stronghold. Lower Himachal, on the other hand, grows the orange-like citrus fruit called kinnu. The BJP controls the kinnu-growing regions. The politics of the state are thus polarised between apple and orange (kinnu), the economic interests of the two lobbies divided between the two mainstream national political parties.

A substantial part of Himachal's apple belt also happens to be Mahasu territory, where the boundaries of erstwhile human kings meet those of the divine king. In these parts, where economics as well as religious ritual combine to form a significant part of social life, the erstwhile raja of Rampur, Virbhadra Singh, held the Rohru constituency ever since the state was formed. In 2009, what made the contest interesting was that the raja was not contesting for the state chief minister's position, having already been given a minister's rank in the Indian government. He had proposed his wife's name as a contestant and even begun campaigning, but the proposal did not find favour with the central leadership. The Congress decided to field a new candidate. This had given renewed hope to the opposition, the BJP, whose present candidate had lost his deposit in his five previous electoral outings against the raja. Losing your deposit in elections signifies a humiliating defeat, entailing forfeiture of the security money deposited with the Election Commission, on account of the failure to secure even one-sixth of the total votes cast.

In Rohru, politicking was at its peak. Most election banners and posters, despite the Election Commission directive against the use of religious symbols for electioneering, bore an invocation to Mahasu. Perhaps the Election Commission of India, usually quite strict when it comes to the use of religious symbols, was also perplexed over whether Mahasu was a political or religious figure. I soon realised how significant the election was to both parties because I could get no accommodation in any inn or government guesthouse. They were all packed with political workers, out to ensure their party's victory. Having found no room in Rohru, I was forced to move ahead to my ultimate destination, Kashdhar, a three-hour uphill drive from Rohru.

Here I found shelter in the village headman's home, himself out on the campaign trail. As evening drew, it became known in the hamlet that both candidates for the Rohru seat would call on the divine king, Mahasu of Kashdhar, the next day, seeking his blessings for their campaigns. By next morning, the banners had all been put up in the village. The white ones with the Congress symbol and the saffron-green from the BJP proudly declared "Victory to Mahasu" along with the candidate's name. Later in the day, the Congress candidate's retinue arrived in the village. The candidate was a Rajput, the dominant upper caste in these mountains. The warrior-like Rajputs commission the divine king's rituals, own most of the land, and are his officials. The Brahman priests are subordinate to them in some ways, as are the lower castes that constitute the working class. The Congress candidate arrived in a cavalcade of jeeps; he asked for the chief priest and instructed him to open the temple sanctum. While inside, he consulted the divine king's oracle, in camera, about his chances in the election. Emerging from the temple, he addressed a group of people who had gathered in the temple courtyard, invoking the support of Mahasu.

The BJP candidate, on the other hand, belonged to a caste lower than his opponent. He chose to walk up the slope to the village, supporters in tow. He did not attempt to enter the sanctum because most low-caste men pay obeisance from outside. He too invoked Mahasu's blessings while addressing almost the same set of people in this small, remote hamlet.

It was quite evident that the divine king's endorsement was a crucial factor in the election since both candidates were claiming to have been blessed. The contest was quite crucial for the BJP candidate, for the raja had defeated him comprehensively on all five previous outings. This was also his last chance to contest the seat, for the government had declared Rohru a reserved seat for the scheduled (lowest) castes after the present election, and he would consequently not qualify as a candidate. India has a delimitation commission constantly engaged in redrawing the boundaries of constituencies, based on demographics. The commission also suggests that certain seats be declared the preserve of underprivileged communities, and once such areas are so notified only individuals from these communities are permitted to contest them. Many in this constituency believed that reserving the seat was a move by the ruling BJP to curb the growing clout of the raja in Himachal politics, notwithstanding the fact that it affected the BJP's own candidate. In this case, it would be left to the community to vote, considering the crucial question of keeping the raja out of the equation.

Having seen the election frenzy at close quarters, I followed the results carefully. This time the BJP candidate came up spades, defeating for the first time ever in the constituency's electoral history a Congress candidate. The Congress, it was clear to all, had been the victim of a vengeance vote, having failed to secure the candidature of the Mahasu ally, the raja, or his chosen one. In fact, even though the Congress had lost, most people saw the verdict as a personal victory for the raja who had been sidelined by the Congress. For most voters I spoke to, this expression of allegiance towards the divine king and his ally was a significant gesture on their part. It became quite evident that despite the democratic process and its provision of a secret ballot, the divine king's subjects expected their political masters to owe ultimate allegiance to him. For Mahasu subjects, it was important that the power of their elected representative emanate from the divine king. In fact, the question of an idol, a non-human agent, stationary or mobile, retaining the loyalty of a large social group kept on returning. Usually, a king accumulates political power and then distributes it amongst subjects to earn their allegiance. How do divine kings manage to gain allies?

A few days later, I reached the town of Tiuni on my way to Hanol. Tiuni, situated not very far from the point where the Tons and Pabbar rivers meet to enter the plains as the Yamuna, is a convenient night halt. It was once a significant spot connecting the hill station of Mussoorie and the bustling military station of Chakrata with the summer capital of British India, Shimla. Now the town of Tiuni has lost its importance owing to the construction of shorter routes.

Entering the government guesthouse, an idyllic colonial bungalow on the banks of the Tons, I saw government jeeps parked outside. Knowing that officialdom would be given preference in a place that belonged to them, I began to doubt if I would manage accommodation even though I had made advance bookings. Having travelled on a dusty and hazardous mountain road for close to fifteen hours, I was not enthused at the prospect of looking for another place to stay. The attendant confirmed that a room was indeed booked in my name and showed me to it, commenting on my good fortune in being able to occupy it. There were only two suites in the guesthouse, and the SDM (subdivisional magistrate), the administrator of the region, occupied the one next to mine. The guesthouse attendant mumbled under his breath to the effect that he had taken quite a bit of trouble to accommodate the SDM's assistants in other places because of me.

Electricity is quite erratic in these remote hills and life comes to a halt soon after dark. By the time I had unpacked my bag and left the room, the electricity had failed once again. It was pitch dark and I had to walk to the Gurkha eatery uphill, on the main road. Most roadside restaurants in this town are run by Gurkhas, the hardy people from Nepal whose ancestors were rulers of this region before the British occupied it. It was still open, thanks to the gastronomic demands of the SDM's entourage. I was delighted at being able to treat myself to a private candlelit dinner with the rushing waters of the Tons within earshot. But in these mountains, home to close-knit communities, one cannot hope for too many moments of solitude. The minute I dug into my plate, the person on the nearby bench wanted to know where I came from and what brought me to Tiuni. It turned out that he drove the SDM's official jeep and was a native of Jaunsar. We started a conversation and when he learnt of my interest in Mahasu, he began to tell me his own story.

In the year 2005, Sadhuram Sharma, head priest of the Mahasu temple at Kuna, was posted to do "duty" to his *devta-raja*, the god-king Mahasu. Priests in Mahasu temples, as in most Hindu temples, are drawn from the Brahman caste. Only men from a specific lineage, and within clans only a few men who follow strict rules of priesthood – vegetarianism, celibacy during "duty", wearing no garment over the legs during temple duty, eating only self-cooked meals once a day – are entitled to what is commonly described as *panti*, meaning simply "duty". The duties include a series of secretive rituals performed before sunrise and until sunset, all preceded by a ritual bath.

It was winter and the priest had just finished his bath in the icy waters of the spring close to the temple. Mahasu temples usually have springs reserved for the ritual bathing of priests and the king's regalia – his jewels, parasols, cauldrons, and weapons. The spring is usually referred to as *upar ka pani* (elevated water). The king's militia as fiercely protect this source of water as the temple itself. In the days of feuding between communities, poisoning or defilement of the enemy's water source was a standard tactic, and hence the need for protection. The springs at lower ground levels are, however, open to public use.

As the scantily clad barefoot priest – who goes into a trance once he is proceeding for the ritual – climbed up the steep path leading to the shrine, he was heralded by an assistant calling out aloud for everyone around to clear the path, especially low-caste men and menstruating women lest they defile the priest with their unclean presence. If they came in his way or if their shadow fell upon him, he would have to turn back for another purificatory bath, delaying the ritual worship. This would annoy the divine king no end and the offenders would have to face severe punishment. The village was Kuna, isolated and away from the gaze of the government administration, where this traditional form of calling is still practised. Untouchability is forbidden under Indian law and so in these more mainstream temple precincts, where government officials or their informers are likely to be present, the practice has been replaced by the subtler one of ringing a bell to signal that the path needs to be cleared.

When the priest arrived at the temple courtyard, a messenger from the SDM confronted him. The SDM also heads the revenue department of the district. Mahasu territory has been governed via revenue officials ever since the British wrested it from the Nepal armies. Colonial officials realised the difficulties of administering an inhospitable terrain and refractory people, restricting their administrative objectives to the realisation of revenue. They did not establish a police force, and foreseeing no criminal activity that the divine king could not adjudicate upon, left the region under the charge of their revenue officials. The Indian government retained this arrangement after independence. With the creation of the hill state of Uttarakhand in 2000, the footprint of the government has enlarged and the authority of the state often comes into direct conflict with that of Mahasu.

The SDM's messenger was a powerful officer, locally known as the nayab-tehsildar, doing his rounds, recovering loans taken out by people from the government. My current informant, the driver on government duty, was accompanying him at the time. The priest, who was about to enter the sanctum for ritual worship, had borrowed money from the government and was listed among those defaulting.

Some temple officials preparing for the ritual, along with the driver himself, advised the officer – who hailed from the plains and was therefore unaware of local custom – that he should wait until the priest had fulfilled his "duty". But the officer was under pressure from his bosses to realise the bad debts and decided not to heed their advice. He went ahead and served the priest with court summons. Amid loud protests from several temple officials and visitors, the priest was taken to the police jeep to be driven off and produced before the civil courts. As the jeep started on its journey on the narrow winding road to Tiuni, the administrative headquarters, the driver lost control of the vehicle. "It was as though I was driving on flat tyres!" he insisted.

Finally, when he could bear the strange and strong tug on the wheel no longer, he let go and the jeep carrying the priest and the government officials veered off the narrow road, colliding with a parapet that overhung a deep gorge. The passengers, including the officer, were grievously injured, but the priest miraculously escaped the near-fatal crash. Since the priest was unhurt and under arrest, government orders on his prosecution had to be carried out. An ambulance was brought in for the injured while the defaulting priest was sent to the administrative office, the *tehsil*, to be kept in confinement until he paid up.

But before the party could reach the *tehsil*, a group of people had arrived to pay the priest's debts and bail him out – to prevent interruption of the temple worship. He was reinstated to his duties at the Mahasu temple. But the government official, the SDM, who had dared to abduct Mahasu's priest, disrupting his ritual worship, was not going to be let off as lightly: he would have to pay dearly for the zeal with which he had done his "duty".

In a few days' time this SDM suffered a paralytic stroke, the doctors giving him neither diagnosis nor hope of recovery. It was then that my informant of this entire saga, the driver, came forward to advise the magistrate's family that they ought to seek forgiveness by visiting the Mahasu shrine at Kuna, the site of the priest's arrest. He attributed the family's sufferings to Mahasu's wrath (*dos, prakop*) arising out of the divine king being deprived of his priest's services. The hapless family brought the crippled official to the temple on a stretcher. The oracle was consulted, followed by the ritual of untying the knot of the offence (*bandh kholna*).

Once an individual is seen as conceited enough to defy the divine king, every misfortune that may happen to befall him is attributed to his defiance. His misfortunes are considered inexplicable, causing either physical or psychosomatic harm, and largely incurable by medical science or recourse to legal measures. Explained as *dos* (affliction) of the divine king, usually by his oracle in a state of possession, the remedy, if sought, is also prescribed in the form of rituals, including sacrifices.

In the case of the SDM, the entire clan was asked to arrive and seek forgiveness by facing the divine king and offering him a sacrificial goat. Once the punishment was served and the prescribed sacrifices made, the official recovered and another Mahasu ally was gained in government. My informant was emphatic in his conclusion: "Mahasu, you should be aware, is the unforgiving god of immediate justice. If you offend him, he will make you pay – with interest!"

In Mahasu country, such conflicts with the state and its "secular" subjects are the stuff of legend as well as common conversation. During my research I encountered several instances of government officialdom at loggerheads with divine kings. It is at these points of conflict that we can best examine whether this unique system can be understood as a particular form of South Asian kingship. They allow us to go beyond the oft-held notion that Mahasu rituals of possession and procession are merely religious ceremonies. At these points of intersection the traditional and seemingly archaic Mahasu ritual regime, frequently dismissed as superstition, crosses the path of modern government and allows an examination of the political dimensions of Mahasu rule. Mahasu's encounters with officialdom, whether Mughal, British, or Indian, display a pattern of political power being defined differently for the divine king, as compared to other polities. For the political entities that came in contact with Mahasu, territory has usually been a matter of prime significance, control over land translating into political power. For the divine kings, however, it is the community and the subject's fealty – establishing a relationship with the soil and binding subjects into a cycle of rituals – that defines territorial sovereignty. Finding justice and redressal for life's problems in temples becomes the reason for faith. The Mahasu processions that seem to mark territory for the divine kings not only test the waters of political faith but are also aimed at creating ever-expanding circles of allegiance. So for Mahasu processional tours are not just a ritual marking of territorial boundaries but a renewal of a relationship with the soil. Mahasu subjects renew their own and Mahasu's relationship with the soil, all land considered as having been owned by the divine king and entrusted to tillers by Mahasu – once they bring the soil or its produce (rice from their granaries in most cases) to the divine kings' temples, and seek the divine king's blessings and adjudication. Thus, the kingdom is constructed not by marking territory on maps or setting up outposts but is won by the process of a ritual binding of the comity of groups that accept subjecthood. These allegiances are won through a disruption of the social order – through epidemics of disease or possession, social discord, drought or deluge, attacks by wild animals or fire – followed by the restoration of normalcy, with Mahasu considered the chief agent of such restoration. Once normalcy is restored, allegiances gained through sacrifice and the unconditional acceptance of Mahasu's supremacy lead to control over territory as a ritual outcome. Thus, even in cases where territory is controlled by governments, Mahasu kingship coexists owing to the divinity's control over people and communities rather than over land and revenue. The extraordinary longevity displayed by Mahasu can be mainly attributed to this factor.

However, as evident in the previous vignette, conflicts between the divine king and contemporary rulers arise all too often. They are not just a recent phenomenon, the outcome of clashes between the modern and the pre-modern, for the narratives of the Mahasu temple bards, the *bajgis*, indicate that conflicts occurred in both the mythical and the historical past. By looking at them from an ethno-historical perspective, we can comprehend how even now Mahasu subjects, while retaining their primordial loyalties to king, clan, caste, and soil, also claim citizenship of the secular nation-state. This brings into focus the persistence of the Mahasu regime in the face of colonialism and subsequently, democratisation. A study of these civilisational intersections also reveals that even as the Mahasu realm has displayed rare tenacity, the outside world gazing at the cult has indeed transformed much more radically. Colonial attitudes towards Mahasu kingship show interesting con-trasts over the course of the centuries, pointing to a trend of growing intolerance towards this alternative form of political organisation.

The kingdom of Mahasu survives partly because the ballads about it were composed and entered the substantial genealogical literature on Mahasu in an ancient past regarded with veneration. The ballads continue to be sung now by *bajgis*, the Mahasu temple bards and drummers. Emerson (1911), a British officer, reports a story in his unpublished ethnographic manuscript that he most likely heard from one of the divine king's musicians, across

RITUAL LONGEVITY 51

the Tons, in the regions collectively known as the Shimla Hill States:

> There is an obscure connection between Mahasu and the city of Delhi, which may have originated through the loot of one of his temples by Muhammadan invaders of the hills. At any rate, he [Mahasu or the divine king's idol or image] is supposed to have been kept in prison for some years, and incense from the hills is said to be still burnt there in his name in certain seasons. The offering may be one of thanksgiving for the return of his idol, or as the following legend puts it, of his deliverance from bondage.
>
> In the days of Akbar there lived in the Simla [Shimla] Hills a Rajput whose wife was a witch, a familiar of the goddess Kali, to whom she owed her powers. Two sons were born to them, one of whom was called Katanya and the second Dum. While they were still youths, they set out to seek their fortunes, coming at last to the court of the Great Moghul, where they begged for employment in the court of the king. But, when the emperor saw them, he laughed aloud. "You are mere striplings," said he, "and I have need for men." But his ministers had been looking closely at the boys, and astounded by their beauty, intervened on their behalf. "Observe their eyes, how large and bright they are," they said to Akbar, "Surely these youths are the sons of some wise man. Be pleased to test their powers." "So be it," laughed the emperor in jest, "let them lift this iron block, weighing a thousand *maunds* and place it on top of yonder wall." "Your majesty has given us a task unworthy of our strength," the boys remarked and putting one hand each to the block, lifted it lightly on the wall. Akbar was much astonished, for, only a little time before, his army had tried to move the iron and failed.
>
> "Let these youths graze my herds of cattle," he commanded, "and as pay let the steward give them as much as they can eat." So the boys went off to graze the royal herds. A few days later, the steward reported to the emperor that Katanya and Dum were eating three hundred weights of flour, and half that weight of butter at every meal and still complained of being hungry.
>
> "Summon the youths hither," commanded Akbar, "and bring from my storehouse three hundred weights of wheaten flour and three

hundred weights of butter. But first have the flour kneaded into dough." So the food was brought and spread before the youths, and the Emperor commanded them to eat it up.

"The wishes of your Majesty shall be accomplished," answered they, and set about their task. First they piled the dough together in a heap; then they made a large hole in the middle and put inside the butter. This done, they started the feast – Dum sat on one side of the heap and Katanya on the other. Pushing first the right and then the left hand through the outer crust, they brought out handfuls of dough and butter mixed, swallowing them so quickly that in five minutes the heap had disappeared.

"Bring us more to eat," they cried, "for our bellies are still empty." But the eyes of Akbar were opened and he would not give them any more. So then they showed their skill in archery, stretching their bows so taut that the arrow pierced seven iron griddles placed one behind the other. When Akbar saw their skill, he trembled, for he feared lest when they grew to manhood, they would rob him of his kingdom. So he resolved to send them off without delay. "Ask what reward you will," he said to them, "but depart to your own country." "Give us yonder cauldron," replied Katanya and this the Emperor gave them, glad at their moderation. "Now be pleased to grant us men to bear the cauldron to our home," asked the brothers. But this the Emperor could not do, for the vessel was many tons in weight, and so huge that an army could not lift it from the ground.

"Since you cannot spare us men," said Dum, "then give the god Mahasu who is now captive in your dungeon and he will take the cauldron for us."

Then Akbar, glad to save his honour, granted their request, and gave an order to the captain of the gaol to bring Mahasu forth. So the gaoler brought Mahasu and at the bidding of the Emperor unloosed his chains. Thus the youths accomplished their design, and the god, grateful for his deliverance, asked what service he could do in return.

"Carry us and this cauldron to our home," they answered.

Mahasu bade them sit inside it and he himself sat on the rim. When all was ready, he gave a whistle, and, forthwith, the vessel flew through the air, while the goods and the chattels of the brothers flew in its wake. Straight and true flew the cauldron, Mahasu whistling all the while, until the confines of the village were reached where the brothers lived. Then he brought the pot to rest on an adjacent hill, where the people of the countryside came out to greet them. Mahasu and his comrades talked with them for a little while, and then casting off their mortal shapes vanished from their sight. So the peasants knew that they were gods, and have worshipped them ever since.

We may choose to question the historical veracity or the rationality of this episode, but we need to take into account its significance from the standpoint of a powerful figure in the colonial administration recording the narrative. This episode, read with Emerson's other accounts, indicates an attempt, even though at times mocking, to rationalise and explicate a system that he found difficult to comprehend and restrain.

Even though folklore is replete with instances of Mahasu's conflict with human kings, there are numerous instances too of the *devta-raja* building alliances with neighbouring kingdoms, and occasionally even with the colonial rulers and the nation-state. For instance, in Himachal Pradesh, tiny kingdoms like Dhadi Rao and Tharonch were allied to Mahasu. Kingdoms like Sirmaur, Jubbal, and Rampur-Bashahar made contributions to his temple in the form of tribute, reserved rooms in their royal palaces for the divine king to stay on his tours, and gave land grants.

In contemporary politics, Mahasu's political clout is considerable. Zoller (1985: 150) documented the performance of the possession ritual of *mandaan*, performed publicly in New Delhi at the behest of Hemvati Nandan Bahuguna – a Congress politician whose son was a few years back chief minister of Uttarakhand – in order to win favour with Indira Gandhi, prime minister at the time. That such ritual practices from the remote mountains can find contexts in mainstream politics, in the national capital, point to the continuing links between ritual religion and the nation-state.

In 2011 Mahasu's oracle from Hanol, Jagdish *mali*, was invited to the home of the chief minister of Uttarakhand, Bhuvan Chandra Khanduri, for a consultation. Along with the oracle came Pandit Kanchand Pandey, a well-known priest and authority on the *sanca vidya*, an ancient tantra text from Kashmir commonly used in Mahasu country for astrological predictions. A consultation such as this ritually involves participation of the seeker's clan, in the presence of the priest and the oracle. The priest conducts the ritual as he is the custodian of the text, the *sanca*, and the divine king's *nisan*, a ritual object charged with divine power. The oracle, possessed by the divine king, examines rice brought from the seeker's hearth, if grown in the seeker's fields, in order to answer questions about misfortunes that have befallen the seeker in the past and the future prospects of his clan. If the seeker has not grown the rice and has bought it from a store, he is permitted to place the rice under his pillow for a night before bringing it to the oracle. The grains are placed before the oracle alongside an offering of money. Then the oracle begins to question the seeker and his family in the *cheriya boli* (the possessed tone) of the divine king. Tossing the rice into the air, catching it, and observing carefully the number and pattern of grains that land in his palm, the oracle interrogates the seeker publicly, assessing the reasons for the seeker's complaints. The interrogation leads to an apportioning of responsibility and the announcement of a ritual solution prescribed to end the complainant's misery.

The elected chief minister of the state's secular government and his wife sat through the traditional ritual of worship and *puchvai* – the process of seeking answers from Mahasu through his embodied oracle. The answer the couple were seeking was whether a grandson would be born in the family to carry forward the lineage. The chief organiser of the ceremony informed me that the divine king was quite forthright in his response to their question. "We are both kings – do something for my kingdom, visit my temple, improve it, and you shall have a grandson."

The chief minister soon laid out plans to visit the shrine and announced that Hanol, Mahasu's capital and main temple, would be developed and projected by the government as the *pancva dham*, the fifth main pilgrimage centre in the state (in addition to the four

Photo 2.1: The Mahasu oracle prepares to examine a pile of rice.

well-established Hindu pilgrimage sites of Badrinath, Kedarnath, Gangotri, and Yamunotri). He also ordered the construction of a helipad close to the temple, probably for his own future visits. As with many other government plans, these temple development plans got entangled in red tape. Uttarakhand's volatile politics soon took over. Not only did the grandson not arrive, the chief minister himself was forced to resign a few months later. Whatever the cause of the decline in Khanduri's fortunes, Mahasu subjects are convinced that he earned their divine king's wrath because his promises to the deity were not fulfilled. And indeed there is a commonly held belief that all chief ministers who come to the Mahasu shrine and make promises that they have no intention of fulfilling soon lose their hold over power. Most state chief ministers therefore avoid visiting the Mahasu temple at Hanol.

The question remains whether, for all his political clout, Mahasu's rule can still translate into genuine kingship. The question seems preposterous to his subjects, for in their eyes he is the genuine article – his rule protects them by keeping intruders as well as inclement weather at bay, by exorcising ghosts, settling disputes, restoring social parity and balance. Besides, he metes out punishment to wrongdoers, diagnoses misfortune, heals sickness, welcomes brides, blesses first-born males, settles legal disputes, removes illegal squatters from public property, and collects taxes – in short he is the celestial pole connecting the earthly and the higher realms. The organisation of his realm and rituals points to his centrality to life in the region, his power diffusing from the centre towards the periphery. As king, Mahasu is addressed as Maharaj, Devta Raja, and at times Raghunath, all titles denoting divine royalty.

But Mahasu is not a monarch seated on a throne. He has forever been concealed from his subjects in a dark chamber inside his temple. His subjects only get a glimpse of his image when they bring a sacrificial goat for their king, when the priest, for one brief moment, illuminates the idol with an ignited pine twig. His expansive territory is marked by his travels within a silver box atop a palanquin, his subjects carrying him across great distances over high mountain passes with several men in attendance. In some ways he represents a power centre by being a mobile Mount Meru – capable of moving in the four directions, tracing the pattern of a mandala (Sutherland 1998: 96). This pattern is visible in the construction of his palanquin and temples. Mahasu's centrality to the cult is because his power emanates from the centre, the Bautha Mahasu at Hanol, with other power centres distributed through the peripatetic Chalda, the siblings, and deputies wielding power in the extended territories. The organisation of his personal invisibility in tandem with his visibility in the shape of his unusual mobility is calculated to ensure that Mahasu never stops being regarded as a divine king.

In his description of South Asian kingdoms Tambiah (1985: 254) refers to a mandala – of the organisation of a kingdom corresponding to a "galactic polity". Quoting Shamasastry (1960), he says that the ancient Indian political theorist Kautilya, in his *Arthashastra* (date disputed, while Trautmann [1971] dates it to early centuries CE, some historians propose the text was composed a date closer to post-Ashokan, Mauryan time. *c.* 200 BCE–200 CE), proposed the mandala as a geopolitical concept to represent the spatial configuration of friendly and enemy states from the perspective of the royal centre. It describes circles of friendly and enemy states surrounding the king's state.

In historical, social, and political senses, the term "mandala" is also employed to denote traditional South East Asian political formations (such as a federation of kingdoms or vassal states). It was adopted by twentieth-century historians from ancient Indian political discourse as a means of avoiding the term "state" in the conventional sense. Not only did South East Asian polities not conform to Chinese and European views of a territorially defined state with fixed borders and a bureaucratic apparatus, they also diverged considerably in the opposite direction: the polity was defined by its centre rather than its boundaries, and it could be composed of numerous other tributary polities without administrative integration. Empires such as Bagan, Ayutthaya, Champa, Khmer, Srivijaya, and Majapahit are referred to as mandalas in this sense. The concept of mandala alludes to a cosmos constituted of Mount Meru at the centre, surrounded by oceans and mountain ranges. Such radial constructs are also referred to in Geertz's (1973) description of the Indic kingdoms' exemplary centre, representing a graded spirituality in a theatre state where the king is seen as a pivot of the polity, the *axis mundi*.

This form of political organisation has evolved, according to Tambiah, not because of any rational or practical considerations or even because it constitutes a prior ontology: "What the Western analytical tradition separates and identifies as religion, economy, politics may have either been combined differently, or more likely constituted a single interpenetrating totality." The Mahasu polity also probably evolved as a result of events contingent on history and ecological factors. The realm, with factions inimical and yet bound by common allegiance to their divine king available through defined territories, appears to have assumed the form of a mandala, defining a centre with expanding spheres of power spreading out in several directions.

For Mahasu's neighbouring divine kingdom, the *mulq* (allegiance-based territory) of Raja Karna, Sax (2000a; 2002) has shown that the tiny territorial/political/cultic unit is indeed a kingdom. Sax (2006b: 121) also refers to Kautilya's *Arthashastra*, describing the "seven limbs" of a kingdom as comprising king, country, minister, army, fortified town, treasure, and ally. Taking these defining features as a touchstone, we can examine how the Mahasu realm acts as a centre of ritual power around which fealties were created without the notion of a boundary marking the kingdom. The true nature of Mahasu's divine kingship and its extraordinary longevity can also be explicated by going into folklore and ethnographic detail relating to the "limbs".

Mahasu's kingship and his journeying sovereignty force a second look at conceptions of a kingdom, as distinct from the Western view of territorial sovereignty. As pointed out by Bergmann (2016) in reference to another Himalayan community, this sovereignty is claimed through multiple and shifting articulations, positioned in a complex geography of graded and partially overlapping shades of political and cultural authority.

In the Mahasu realm, politico-territorial boundaries were established through rituals rather than cartography and physical delimitation. While in a modern political context rivers separating land masses are usually construed as border markers, here they are meeting grounds instead of lines demarcating and excluding the other. It is on the ritualised crossing of the rivers that shifts in power and mutual exchanges are witnessed. Distinctions between populations are usually upland and lowland, or on either bank, each referring to the other territory with the expression *aar ke paar* (on the other bank to mine), denoting a sense of the other but always with a ritual reciprocity. This means that even though people from river banks, like *sathi* and *pansi*, may be inimical to each other in some ways, there is mutual agreement in relation to the performance of rituals such as hosting the divine king, feuding, stealing the other's sheep, abducting women, and headhunting – all rituals that give rise to political power within their own communities. After all, if you want to quarrel you need an enemy. Ritual that is simultaneously reciprocal and antagonistic emerges as the central paradigm defining kingly power through shifts across regions and communities. Through it Mahasu's rule establishes spaces in which competing local politics are waged and rival agendas advanced, defended, mediated, and transformed. If we consider all these elements as constitutive of the Mahasu kingdom, how the realm is constituted in Kautilya's limbs of the state becomes clearer.

For the Mahasu kingdom, let us first consider the king, the pivot and the conceptual centre, the source of sovereign authority. To Mahasu subjects, the divine king manifests himself in layered multiplicities – god, tutelary figurehead, *devta* or divinity, king, healer, rainmaker, adjudicator, even a tyrant afflicting people with misfortune if offended. Interestingly, the term *devta*, the common form of address for Mahasu, has completely different connotations in Hindi and Persian-Arabic. Just as several other colloquial terms in the Mahasu realm, for instance *vazir* for minister and *mali* for oracle, have Persian-Arabic origins, the term *dev* in Persian-Arabic connotes a demonic entity. In Hindi usage the term *dev* usually describes a divinity. Mahasu, therefore, is a tyrannical protector, a presence that is at the same time a bulwark against misfortune, but easily offended.

To be an effective king, and win allegiance, Mahasu must visit and assist subjects in times of need. The divine king wins their devotion only if the power attributed to him proves efficacious in times of dire need. Folklore is replete with instances where Mahasu expanded territory, winning over divinities and humans, becoming an agentive force by causing disruption, and then restoring order. In the little settlement of Kashdhar, a village that was once a part of Bashahar, I came across a small abandoned hut which, I was told by the village headman, was once a police outpost of the Tehri king. Kashdhar, it turned out, was given away to the raja of Tehri, the neighbouring state and principal kingdom of Garhwal, by the king of Bashahar, Raja Padam Singh, as dowry following a matrimonial alliance. Oblivious of the terrestrial exchanges caused by the compulsions of matrimonial politics, the tutelary gods were also engaged in their own give-and-take in an effort to establish divine sovereignties.

The ruling deity of Kashdhar was Peje Nag, the serpent-headed god. Once administrative control of Kashdhar was handed over to the raja of Tehri, he established a *chowki* (outpost) on the edge of the village. A venerable figure in Kashdhar was the local chief, octogenarian *vazir* (minister) to Peje Nag, Bhagmal Mahta. The soldiers of Tehri, known for their imperiousness, decided to display it in this remote outpost at Kashdhar. When the village women went out to the mountain spring for their ablutions, the Tehri soldiers followed and molested them. As word reached the *vazir*, he decided to visit the scene of crime with his faithful servants in toe. The wronged women narrated their plight to Bhagmal. As the enraged minister questioned the soldiers, who proudly owned up to the crime, the men accompanying Bhagmal took out their scythes and hacked the Tehri soldiers to death. The outpost was ransacked and burnt to ashes as retribution for the outrage.

The king of Tehri had to take cognizance of the killing of his soldiers and the torching of his symbol of authority. An armed party was dispatched with express orders to arrest the offenders and bring them back to Tehri town. As the armed party entered Kashdhar and began to make enquiries, the chief, following the true dharma of a Rajput, and as a receptacle of his own people's allegiance, accepted the blame in an effort to save his loyal servants from certain beheading. Bhagmal, the wizened *vazir* of Kashdhar, was put into heavy chains and asked to march towards Tehri. The trip was a gruelling mountain trek lasting almost a fortnight.

As they dragged and shoved the old man across precipitous ridges and sharp rock faces, he stumbled along, the possibility of his survival becoming bleaker by the minute. It was at this point that he saw a palanquin procession passing by in all its regal splendour. "I will establish a shrine to this deity if at all I return alive," he promised to himself.

The arduous trek finally ended and he was thrown into a prison cell in the Tehri jail, notorious for housing prisoners, regardless of their crime, who never emerged alive from it. Here, Bhagmal was offered coarse rice (*china ka bhat*) as food. In spite of his considerable appetite owing to the rigours of his journey, he kicked the plate aside, saying that even his pet dog would not excercise his teeth on such gross victuals. News of the audacious captive reached the raja of Tehri, who grew curious to meet him. He also asked for Bhagmal's pet dog to be brought from Kashdhar, with strict orders that the animal be deprived of all food and drink until it reached Tehri.

The famished dog was brought before a large audience with the king announcing publicly that the dog would be offered coarse grain, as offered to Bhagmal, to eat. Should it refuse the food, the prisoner would be set free. If it even licked the food, the prisoner would be skinned alive. The dog was released even as the starving animal circled around the plateful of rice. Finally, the dog moved towards the plate, sniffed it, and urinated decisively into the rice. The Kashdhar chief was a free man.

Presumably on his way home he fed his dog a sizeable bone; speculation apart, on his return journey Bhagmal enquired about the deity whose palanquin he had vowed to honour. Coming to know it was Mahasu, he visited the divine king's shrine and brought along a symbol charged with Mahasu's power, establishing it in his home as a deity. He performed his devotions to his new divine king secretly, usually in the middle of the night, for his own village belonged to Peje Nag, while he was the village god's earthly representative. The serpent-headed god, he knew, would not tolerate the presence of a rival.

But soon, strange noises began to emanate from his home. Village folk began accusing Bhagmal of having brought to their village a ghost or evil spirit. He hid Mahasu's symbol, the *nisan*, in a box and placed it in the house of a loyal subordinate, and stopped worshipping it. Soon, the entire village was afflicted with misery and disease. In due course, it was Peje Nag's oracle that finally diagnosed that it was Mahasu's affliction, *his* curse that was the cause of general suffering. However, it was argued that Bhagmal bringing in the deity's symbol was justifiable since Mahasu had come to Bhagmal's rescue. So, the snake god himself declared that henceforth both deities would be worshipped with equal reverence. Mahasu's shrine was thus also established in the village, and his palanquin granted the freedom to move about as and when the god desired. In this way Mahasu established his presence and expanded his territory into Kashdhar. Through his timely assistance to Bhagmal, the divine king not only acquired Kashdhar's loyalty in this remote Tehri outpost, he also succeeded in undermining the authority of his rival, the human raja of Tehri.

As in this village now, across the rest of his kingdom Mahasu subjects subscribe to their king's ritual, seek his advice and justice, and organise their lives around his ritual calendar. His kingship decentralises and distributes power, establishing more or less horizontal relations between power holders and subjects engaged in ritual practices, along with pastoral, artisanal, and agricultural folk. Kingship in these regions presents a history of power structures interacting in processes of articulation, competition, and superimposition, all these being a part of processes contingent upon events such as the one in Kashdhar.

As the Mahasu realm interacts with other power structures – divine kingships similar to his own, human kingships, or powerful forces such as the British colonials and the Indian state – it employs varying degrees of agency depending upon the people it interacts with. For instance, in the context of current confrontations with a democratic state that seeks to intervene in Mahasu ritual practices – such as animal sacrifice and temple entry for low-caste dalits and women – when the region's political representatives refuse to speak out in support of the ritual practice the divine king, through his officials, employs methods such as the media to reach out. Even as constitutional laws obstruct him, his contentious rituals continue unabated in line with the will of the community, away from the public gaze. It is now generally accepted that political leaders owe their electoral success to votes cast by the divine king's subjects. These leaders, for fear of losing support, refuse to interfere in his ritual practices and help keep the state at bay. In colonial and pre-colonial times too, while dealing with power centres, it was the *mali* (oracle) and the *vazir* (chief minister) who emerged as interlocutors for the *devta*. In ritual confrontations with other divinities, it is the *birs* (deputies), ritual drummer-bards, and performances of trickery (like transforming sand to gold) that help establish Mahasu supremacy.

Just as a traditional kingdom is ritually constructed by the presence of a powerful human on a throne, a non-human political entity seems capable of acting as an agent, employing to varying degrees the agentive powers of the community. Multiple collectivities are represented in the process: at times the entire cult, at times the subjects of individual *devtas*, at times clans or caste groups, at others opposing factions on either bank of the river. These collectivities, in fact, afford greater flexibility than human kingship and show almost unparalleled potential to deal with transforming political landscapes. Agency, in anthropological discourse, is often ascribed to individual persons (Taylor 1995). Sax (2010b) suggests that this human-centric approach is an outcome of the pervasive but unexamined individualism in Euro-American social theory. Writing about divine kingships in the Himalayas, he says, "If we define it [agency] in a straightforward way, as the capacity to effect changes in the external world, then it is perfectly reasonable to ascribe agency to groups, organizations, even to non-human entities."

This argument enables a recognition of the non-human agency of divine kings. The king is capable of accomplishing collective purposes. This is also in line with Inden's (1990) notion of the complex agency of early-medieval Indian political formations which include individuals as well as the collective institutions of deities (Sutherland 1998; 2003; 2003-4). Mahasu, in similar vein, represents a form of religious and political organisation that articulates the collective agency of his subjects. The collective agency of the community manifests itself in various forms – in community events such as temple consecrations, the divine king's processions, and even rivalries between clans of the divine king's militia.

If country or territory is the second "limb", the Mahasu realm represents a kingdom, albeit with a complicated federation-like structure that distributes political power through allegiances among not one but four forms of the same king. The Mahasu kingdom is a complex royal formation constituting four divine brother-kings: Basik, Pabasik, Chalda, and Bautha, three of whom define their territories through processional movements, with the fourth being stable as the enduring centre. Mahasu is a grouping of these four divine kings, collectively referred to as the Mahasu kingdom. The four Mahasus are, first, Basik, who circulates perpetually on the left bank of the Tons in a small area; second, Pabasik, who circulates perpetually on the right bank of the Tons; third, Chalda (from the Hindi word *chalna*, to move), who travels for twelve years on one side of the river, then for twelve years on the other, and whose area is therefore the largest by far, encompassing those of all his brothers; and, finally, Bautha (from *bauth*, "sitting"), who sits at the cult centre of Hanol, on the left bank of the Tons, facing the direction of the flow.

Mahasu's origin myth, recited for me by Madan Das of Maindrath, his official musician-bard (*bajgi*), devotes considerable attention to the arrival of the divine kings from Kashmir, their battles against earlier rulers and, after they had established sovereignty, the procedure followed for distribution of territory. Before they could establish themselves as kings over this territory, they had to defeat the demon Kirmir. Chalda Mahasu and his deputies chased the demon over mountain ridges and finally managed to slay him. Then they decided to divide their kill into equal parts for each to share. The division was attempted thrice, and every time they came up with one extra piece of flesh, the whole always greater than the sum of its parts. Finally, this extra piece escaped their clutches into the snowbound unknown, shouting out advice to the Mahasu kings to the effect that they would do well to retain whatever territory they had won, leaving the uninhabitable upper reaches to the demons. Once this was done, the actual division of territory was accomplished. This story is clearly intended to mark out the territorial limits for the Mahasu kings – in terms of the snowbound higher reaches. Beyond the pastures is the land of the demons, which the Mahasus may not covet.

During the division of the kingdom, now won by the four brothers and their deputies, Bautha Mahasu – because he injured his leg while appearing before his subjects – demanded that he be established at the cult centre at Hanol. This pivotal position ought really to have gone to the oldest brother, Basik Mahasu, following the established convention of primogeniture. In order to avoid dissension amongst the siblings, Chalda persuaded Basik to accept the territories of Bawar, Deoghar, and Jaunsar, the region collectively referred to as *sathibil* (or just *sathi*). In order to compensate for the loss of privilege of being at the centre, he was awarded Chalda's parasol, which is displayed prominently in his processions. Pabasik was given charge of lands across the Tons, in the regions of Bangan and parts of the Shimla Hill States, referred to as the *pansibil* (or just *pansi*). Even the Mahasu deputies who assisted in the battles were granted territories. For instance, Serhkuriya was asked to govern territory further up in the mountains, in the region known as Fateh Parvat. The myth talks of Chalda's

Photo 2.2: Chalda Mahasu's palanquin and parasol arrive in village Bhotanu.

dissatisfaction at the arrangements, since no specific territory was left for him to govern. When he threatened to return to Kashmir, the land from where the Mahasus came, he was given the privilege of proceeding through the entire territory, as well as the task of mounting campaigns for territorial expansion.

The integrity of these territories is honoured to this day. While Mahasu processions correspond to *digvijaya* – marking territory, performing and creating kingship – visits by divine kings impose considerable expense on the community. Every single individual in the village is mobilised to host the large retinue accompanying the palanquins. These visits often assume the form of sacrificial rituals performed collectively by the entire village. Everyone contributes and therefore derives merit with the return grant of protection. The processions serve to constantly renew spatial networks through a renewal of allegiances within the realm. For instance, Basik, who rules over *sathi*, has four *thans* or divine stations in his territory, where he spends a year each (from the month of *jeth* to the next *jeth*, that is, from June to June). They include Hanol, Bagi, Kuna, and Rarhu. These places form his itinerary, known as a *barabasha*. At times, the divine king may be requested to take a detour and travel to an unscheduled destination for a night, provided a written request is made to the minister along with the necessary fee. The elders mobilise the villages under their control to contribute to the divine king's tour, with the lower castes being the porters, the drummer-bards the ritual musicians, the Rajput the bearers of arms, and the Brahman the priests and cooks. The collective sacrificial ritual of hosting the divine king's procession is an emotional moment that renews Mahasu's relationship with the soil of the kingdom, as much as it is an opportunity for the *sayanas* (elders) to renew codified relations with the villages under their tutelage.

Indian law recognises some divinities as legal persons and permits them to own lands. Basik owns a large tract close to the village of Bagi, where the king's temple is also situated. The land is cultivated by lower castes; these lands are under the control of the Brahman chieftain of the village, held on the divine king's behalf. While the cultivators get a third of the produce, two-thirds goes to the storehouse of the divine king and the landowner. Thus, divine kings exercise rights over land by virtue of being kings as well as landlords. Not only do the Mahasu kings own vast tracts, they zealously protect their territory from incursions. Chalda covets neighbouring kingdoms and is feared as an expansionist tyrant, often in the past coming into conflict with his rival neighbouring divine kings Chasralu, Someshu, and Karna.

As kings, the Mahasus also appoint regional councils of elders comprising Rajput men – referred to as the *sayanas*, the most powerful central council being called the *chauntru* – who take decisions pertaining to the governance of the realm. The council usually convenes in the courtyards of Mahasu temples that are described by his subjects as *kot* (fortified palaces). The council consults the Mahasu oracle before arriving at a decision. Mahasu has the power to appoint and dismiss officers, confiscate property, and levy fines. The king hears civil as well as criminal cases (though increasingly rarely), and then, through the oracle, enforces judgment, usually compelling the disputants to compromise.

The third significant limb of a kingdom is the minister who, in the case of Mahasu's kingdom, is the *vazir*. The *vazirs* too break the traditional mould of high-ranking officials. Outwardly, their dress or lifestyle does not reflect the trappings of high office. They are plain and rough highlanders, but they are also quite powerful, socially and politically. Even as the king emerges as the axis around which the realm revolves, the task of running the kingdom is assigned to a minister. Berti (2006: 39) and Luchesi (2006: 62) have shown that human kings in the neighbourhood of the Mahasu realm also acted as ministers to the gods. In Mahasu kingdoms, however, the divinities have themselves become kings and assigned administrative tasks to their ministers. A hierarchical bureaucracy headed by a minister governs the realm. The *vazir* is always chosen from a named exogamous lineage segment, which is in turn associated with an overarching clan. Even though the agency of the god is distributed amongst various other persons, especially his oracle, priests, and militia, it is the *vazir* who emerges as the most influential human figure in the realm.

The power and authority of the minister's office is expressed through the term *vazarat* – a caste-based, hierarchical, and hereditary system. The *vazarat* is a delegated authority, inherited but never absolute or irrevocable. Mahasu has not one but two ministers, one each for *sathi* and *pansi*, both constantly involved in inimical reciprocity since both are under pressure from the community to ensure the divine king's visits and favour. Forced to ensure the king's processional time in their own regions, they are often pushed to adopt a confrontationist stance against letting go of him once the king is in their area. While the ministers of the *sathi* come from the Rana clan, those of the *pansi* come from the Panwar clan. Both clans belong to the dominant Rajput caste. By virtue of this office, the Rana ministers on the right of the Tons become ministers to the divine kings Bautha and Basik Mahasu. They also look after the affairs of Chalda Mahasu while he is on tour in their territory. On the other hand, the Panwar *pansi vazir* remains minister to Pabasik, as well as Chalda during his tour.

Photo 2.3: The *pansi* minister, with the Mahasu palanquin in the background, carried by Rajput boys in a trance-like state.

The ministers have traditionally been responsible for managing the divine king's lands and the large sums of money received as donations in their temples. They are capable of mobilising the entire community and wield considerable political clout. In fact, the divine king's ministers can easily tilt the scales in favour of candidates during state elections and are wooed by political parties. The *vazir* remains in office at the pleasure of the divine king, and as long as he retains the confidence of the community. The office of minister has witnessed several intriguing battles of succession during colonial and contemporary times, since the minister is in effect the executive agent of the king.

The Mahasu *vazir*'s centrality to the polity became evident to me during the final phase of the river-crossing ritual, when the Mahasu palanquin was to cross over the Tons, from the *pansi* to the *sathi*. The significant event, where the divine king comes to spend the next twelve years travelling amongst his subjects on the other bank, was in fact occurring after a long wait of nineteen years – the usual twelve, and added to it a delay of seven. The subjects that host Mahasu are reluctant to let their divine king leave, while the prospective hosts are always impatient to receive him.

Chalda Mahasu's oracle would not announce the date of the crossing and caused delays on one pretext or the other. Finally, when the divine king did make up his mind and travelled all the way to the village on the riverbank for the final crossing over, Chalda Mahasu again employed what many saw as a dilatory tactic. By this time a large number of people had gathered on the other bank to welcome their divine king, creating an almost riotous situation. Government machinery, forced to deal with large expectant crowds, began breathing down the *pansi* chief minister's neck, pushing for the declaration of a firm date for the event, even as the divine king's oracle appeared non-committal. The chief minister, though categorical before government officials as well as Mahasu subjects that only Chalda Mahasu could decide on the date of departure, also appeared a little concerned at the turn of events. Knowing that Chalda Mahasu does not as a matter of convention travel during *paush* (the winter months after the solstice) he knew that even a day's postponement would mean that the river crossing would be delayed by several months.

After the divine king, riding on his oracle's back, had performed several exorcisms and taken a tour around the border village of Bhotanu, the *vazir* approached the possessed oracle, carrying Mahasu's palanquin on his shoulders. He asked for the *mali* to announce a specific date. The divine king would still not commit himself. Then the minister, in a rare gesture of supplication, removed his cap and inverted it like a begging bowl before the oracle and the palanquin. In India, the upturning of the cap is a gesture of complete supplication, and in Mahasu shrines it is usually performed only by the lowest castes. Headgear often indicates social position and rank. Removing it is a stepping down, and upturning it or placing it on the ground shows a complete surrender of social rank for the achievement of an objective. The result once obtained, the headgear can be promptly placed on the head again!

What was significant was that the minister had approached the divine king while in procession, in full public view, near the threshold of the temple. While this gesture indicated his helplessness, it also displayed a subdued belligerence, a kind of rebellion against the norm of the minister as always instrumental in bringing the divine king, here obstructing the divine king's path, asking him to leave. The Mahasu oracle still seemed non-committal and continued to skirt the issue, whining that perhaps the *pansi* did not want to host him any longer and were therefore asking their chief minister to coerce him. The chief minister stood his ground, cap upturned obstinately before his king, silent and waiting for the final response. After a few moments of awkwardness, the divine king had to relent as the oracle announced that he would indeed proceed for the crossing the next day.

The *vazir* thus has a pivotal role to play in the Mahasu kingdom. As the earthly representative of a divine king, he is the dominant power broker, even though he does not wield power himself. Had

Photo 2.4: The Mahasu oracle tosses rice, even as he carries the palanquin, with its gilded tiger-headed silver handles, on his shoulders. Flanking him, the chief priest on the left and an official carrying the cylindrical box-like symbol, the *donriyan*, on the right. In the background is Mahasu's parasol.

the divine king, through his oracle, refused to proceed for the river crossing, the *vazir* would have had to yield to him, whatever the consequences. The situation could easily have flared up into a violent skirmish, with the *sathi* desperate to receive their divine king's palanquin. While this wielding of absolute power points towards Mahasu being a king, it also points to the unique distribution of agentive power in the Mahasu realm amongst minister, priest, oracle, and drummer-bard. Each exercises a degree of ritual control and contributes to Mahasu divine kingship.

Though the position of *vazir* is inherited and decided by primogeniture, history points to the fact that, given the significance of the position, succession has never been smooth. What also points to the political importance of Mahasu *vazir*s is that, in the past, human kings from realms in the vicinity of Mahasu's kingdom, the kings of Tehri, Tharonch, Jubbal, and Sirmaur, often manipulated *vazir* appointments to serve their own interests. British courts also sat in judgment over *vazir* succession disputes. The *vazir* of the *pansi* has in his possession a document issued in favour of his ancestors that ratifies his clan's rights to the position of minister. The king of Jubbal had issued the document under his seal.

The *sathi vazir*, by virtue of governing a larger area and the capital of the Mahasu realm falling under his jurisdiction – as does the temple of Bashik and the Mahasus' mother, Deoladi, at Maindrath – is the most influential figure in the realm. However, a bitter battle of succession to the role of *sathi vazir*, with both claimants lobbying the powerful elders, has granted a greater leverage to the *vazir* of *pansi*. This had, as many people in *sathi* told me, emboldened the *pansi* to detain Chalda Mahasu for more than the stipulated twelve-year tenure in their territory. The *sathi vazir* comes from the clan of Rana Rajputs, referred to as *vaziraiyik* (or of the *vazir* clan), located at the village of Bastil. Bastil's geographic proximity to Hanol and its strong affinal connections with the influential elders of Bagi, Kuna, Binnar, Chausal, and Koti villages of Bawar, account for its strong position in the Mahasu matrix. Most significantly, the villages from whence come the *deopujya* priests of Mahasu – the Brahmans of Chatra, Puttarh, Nenus, Baaghi and Maindrath – all fall under the *sathi* jurisdiction. Political power, in the Mahasu realm, like in any other social group, emanates from a number of factors that could catapult individuals or clans in positions of proximity to the divine powers.

For instance, on the other bank in the Mahasu kingdom, the *pansi vazir* is a Panwar Rajput. The kings of the neighbouring human kingship of Tehri have also been Panwars. While the Panwar *vazir* from *pansi* derived support from the ruling Panwar kings in neighbouring Tehri, the Rana of *sathi* on the other bank was politically close to the Sirmaur rulers. Two rival human kingships extended support to Mahasu *vazirs* on opposite banks of the Tons. Folklore suggests that the dominant Ranas of *sathi* employed Una Bhat, the Brahman priest responsible for fetching the Mahasu kings from Kashmir. On the other hand, the Panwars served Vishnu, a divinity that was tricked into vacating his palace at Hanol by the Mahasu divine kings. The Mahasus were four siblings, invited by the Brahman Una Bhat to defeat the demon Kirmir, who lived midstream of the Tons near the village of Maindrath. When the Mahasus had rid the region of the demon's terror and asserted their right to rule over it, they found the Maindrath territory inadequate. Una Bhat led them to the neighbouring territory of Vishnu, who ruled from Hanol. The Mahasus challenged Vishnu to a bout of ritual magic, to turn the sands on the river Tons into gold. Vishnu lost to Mahasu and was forced to abandon his throne. When Mahasu assumed power, and embarked on a relentless campaign of territorial expansion, the Panwars refused to let go of their powers owing to their proximity to Vishnu and negotiated for their own clan a position that gave them some control over the realm as *vazirs* of *pansi*. They were given exclusive rights over the affairs of Pabasik Mahasu and the privilege of hosting Chalda Mahasu for his twelve-year sojourn in the region of *pansi*. The power structure emerged in such a manner that the Ranas, owing to their hold over Una, retained *sathi* as well as exclusive rights over Bashik and Deoladi. Traditionally and historically, the Ranas of *sathi*, owing to the factors mentioned above, have been the dominant group. Apple wealth and political empowerment that came with the regions under the *pansi* after becoming a part of the state of Himachal Pradesh, formed much earlier than Uttarakhand, has tilted the balance in favour of the *pansi* somewhat. The balance of power between the two regions still shifts periodically and the seesaw battle to wrest control has witnessed violent conflict and bloodshed. At the time that Chalda Mahasu had completed his long overdue sojourn in one region and was expected to cross over into another, tensions were once again simmering.

At the time of Chalda's river crossing in early 2013 – which happened when the elder chief minister had died and his brother and son were locked in a battle of succession, with each side's claim supported by one faction within the cult – I sought an influential Rajput politician's opinion on who would succeed as the next *vazir*, now that Chalda was coming to their territory. He smiled and responded, "In our region, conventionally, the *vazir*'s son seldom succeeds him!" He was making an oblique reference to his own support to someone other than the logical successor through the principle of primogeniture – described in local parlance as *jethang* – suggesting that it was the community rather than the divine king that, finally, had power over the minister's appointment. Also, he was referring to the fact that minister succession was seldom a smooth affair.

The divine king, I have observed in more instances than one, owing to his multiple manifestations and stress on negotiated allegiances, has the ability to bring the community to a point of consensus and then merely pronounces it. As Chalda Mahasu crossed over, within a few days' time, the king confirmed the appointment of the elder, Diwan Singh, to the position of *vazir*.

While *sathi* and *pansi*, the two factions on either bank, check and balance each other's power in a struggle presided over by Mahasu, several small and parallel Mahasu territories have emerged, as with Lakhwar where the Chauhan Rajputs are *vazir*s, while further up the slopes in Thaina the Tomar Rajputs have assumed

Mahasu ministership. These smaller groups consider Mahasu the overarching divine king, establishing shrines around idols charged with his essence, their gods often journeying to the temple at Hanol. However, their own processional calendars and festivities are independent of the larger Mahasu complex, their rituals less demanding and more attuned to the demands of contemporary realities, exhibiting a kind of schismogenesis.

Mahasu temple complexes, usually referred to as *kots*, conform to the description of Kautilya's fortified towns. Mahasu shrines are different from traditional Indian temples. Mahasu temples have fortifications and are generally constructed out of wooden logs with dovetail joints used to bind walls of stone. They follow a style of architecture usually referred to as the *kath-kunni* style or the Koti-Banal (after a village in Garhwal) type. In fact, the Panchpura,

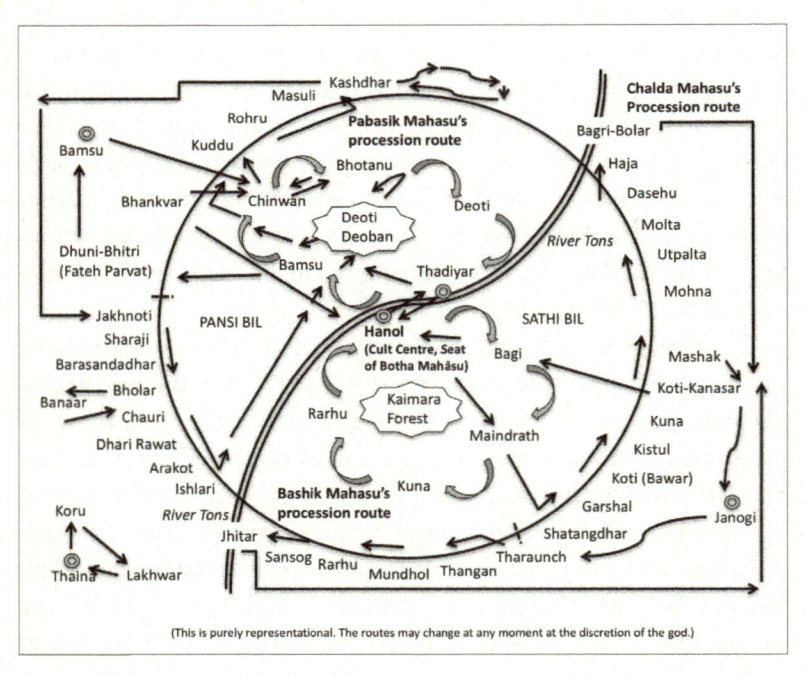

Fig. 2.2: Tours of the Mahasus, with minor Mahasus depicted on the left, bottom.

a five-floored tower at Koti-Banal village, its façade pockmarked with dents from cannon balls, is a fortress in its design. The inner sanctum of these *kots* is usually dark and small with the idols placed in perpetual darkness and secrecy. Many fortress-temples in the region are three- to five-floored towers with space for the idol, the divine king's treasure, and the weapons. Warfare and feuding were so endemic to this region that many temples, and most of the storehouses adjacent to the temples, were fortified and built so that in times of war or feud their defenders could lock the doors and withdraw to the upper levels, where weapons were stored along with rocks that could be hurled at their enemies. The lower floors were designated for living and the lowest for storage of livestock and foodgrain. The upper floors could only be approached through a steep ladder fashioned out of a single log. In case of an attack, the ladder could easily be pulled up, limiting access to the upper floors. Anyone trying to climb could be attacked with rocks and arrows from a height, inflicting maximum damage. Larger temple complexes, like Hanol, converted from earlier usage, were more spread out, following a courtyard design and keeping in mind the ritual function.

The temples, where the divine king's idols or objects charged with the deity's power are kept, serve as significant nodes in the circles of allegiance. Whenever a new temple is constructed, or an old one refurbished, the kingdom is ritually performed, the ceremonies helping establish, ritually, the centrality of Mahasu to existence within his realm. Divine kings use these occasions to test people's commitment to their rituals. They also offer opportunities for the socially and politically powerful to renew allegiances to the divine kings and to the community by making financial contributions and adding to his display of power through their physical presence.

When Chalda Mahasu's processions travel through a particular territory, the *chatrai* or the warriors that march under his *chatra* or parasol lead them. Mahasu armies are referred to as the *barah-beesi* (twelve-twenty) *khund*, once again borrowing from the Persian-Arabic *khun* (blood). A *khund* is a warrior and a fighter, someone willing to spill blood, either his own or that of his enemies, in defence of his divine king and his territory. They are volatile warriors and form his militia.

Mahasu's wealth and regal splendour, in comparison to other minor divine kings, as perceived by his subjects, have earned him the appellation of *deban-ro-raja* (king of gods). His treasure is often alluded to in ballads and, as mentioned earlier, large sums of money are collected in his temples. When the processions move from one village to another, the divine king's jewels, his silver and his gold, are carried in large copper coffers designed for the purpose. For a deity wealthy enough to offer a loan to the Indian government during wartime, wealth and treasures often become a bone of contention for the subjects.

Finally, let us talk about the allies. Mahasu is by far the most powerful of the divine kings in the region, successfully forging alliances with divine as well as human kings. These alliances were also in the form of pledges of allegiance made after Mahasu's help was sought in averting natural calamities, especially drought. Mahasu was adopted as the *kul-devta* (deity of the lineage) for the human king of the state of Tharonch. Within the precincts of the royal palace of Tharonch stands a temple dedicated to Chalda Mahasu. In the palace of the raja of the kingdom of Dhadi, a chamber on the top floor is reserved for Mahasu's palanquin to stay and rest during his tours. During the temple consecration at Shiraji, by far the biggest congregation of Himalayan kings, divine and human, Basik Mahasu – the oldest among the Mahasu divine kings – rather than arrive straight to the temple, chose to lead his procession to the palace of Dhadi close by. This led to widespread consternation at the ceremonial site since the eldest sibling's presence was essential for the consecration ritual. When Chalda's representatives rushed to the palace to placate the divine king, he took up the issue of his ally, the Dhadi king, complaining that even though Chalda's temple was in such close proximity to the Dhadi palace, and the raja had contributed his wealth to the building of the temple, he had been ignored in the ceremonies. "A raja that has established a *gaddi* (seat) of Mahasu in his own palace must not be treated in this manner," was the command his oracle articulated.

The scion of the hill state of Rampur Bashahar, Virbhadra Singh, who was not long ago the chief minister of Himachal Pradesh, was in attendance at Shiraji and regularly visits the Mahasu shrine at Hanol, adequately displaying his alliance with the divine king for the benefit of his voters, a large section of whom worship the deity.

Mahasu fulfils the criterion of all the "seven limbs" set forth by Kautilya – king, country, minister, army, fortified town, treasure, and ally – and qualifies for the description of a kingship, even though unique in terms of being a moving ritual centre rather than a stationary monarch. The defining central figure in this kingship is the non-human entity, the divine king Mahasu, around whom the lives of the subjects revolve. His kingdom is a pre-modern polity focused on a ritual centre, as against the Western or modern conception of a kingdom defined by physical boundaries. Political power, in this kingdom, is based on what Brughart (1996) referred to as pyramidal ties of overlordship and fealty, where the ordinary Mahasu subject recognises the ritual centrality of the elder (*sayana*), who in turn offers ritual tributes to the *chauntru*, the regional elders closer to the centre, with the king holding power at the axis. The powerful *sayanas*, however, are generally subordinated to the community owing to the strong democratic structure of mountain village society.

The literature on South Asian kingship points towards two poles of argumentation, the proponents of each engaged in a protracted debate. On one pole are Dumont and others who have defended the conceptual and empirical separation of religion and politics in the classical polities of South Asia, and who have tended to underplay the importance of ritual in defining kingship. According to Sax (ibid.: 51-2), Dumont (1962: 75) argued that India distinguished religion and politics centuries before the West, and that this distinction manifested itself in a form of kingship that was more purely "political" than the forms of divine kingship found in the West. His argument was based upon a dichotomy of "spiritual" versus "temporal" and on the view that the politico-economic domain "necessarily emerges in opposition to and separation from the all-embracing domain of religion and ultimate values, and that the basis of such a development is the recognition of the individual."

Dumont (1966) proposed that South Asian kings and priests existed in a logical and structural complementarity, that their roles mutually defined the terms of the caste system. He could not see that power may be culturally constructed and ideologically central. His views were in keeping with the post-colonial milieu where sovereignty was systematically interpreted as a matter of economic relations, without considering ritual significance. Dumont has been widely critiqued for representing South Asian polities as fundamentally static, his analysis freezing king and priest in an unalterable hierarchy as part of an immutable inflexible system. Kings and for that matter ministers and priests in the Mahasu realm, rather than being locked in a totalising hierarchy owing to a logical play of binaries such as pure/impure, spiritual/temporal, Brahman/Kshatriya, are part of a dynamic process where, keeping social and historical circumstance in view, each role, whether of king, minister, priest, militia, or drummer-bard, has to be embodied, performed, and negotiated. The Mahasu complex, like most kingships in these mountains, reflects the inseparability of the religious and the political, the "magico-religious" and the "secular", especially since for all matters of state policy Mahasu's receptacle, the *mali*, who embodies the divine king, is consulted.

Dumont insisted that in the Indic world of caste it was the Brahman priest, rather than the king or the cultivator, who was the ideological point of reference. The Brahman was seen as "religiously" superior, while the king was "temporally" superior. The Brahman was seen as more knowledgeable, but as always seeking the king's favour, who in turn would always be characterised as a giver. Raheja (ibid.) refers to Dumont and others, saying that they maintained Hocart's characterisation of the ritual centrality of the king as relevant only to the pre-history of caste and not to contemporary observable relationships in an Indian village or to the historical record of Hindu kingdoms.

On the other argumentative pole, Dirks (ibid.) has criticised Dumont's model, based on a hierarchy of caste, arguing for a model focused on centrality and peripherality. Rather than a "spiritually" superior Brahman who ranks higher than the king, but is nevertheless materially dependent on him, the centre-periphery model places the king at the centre of a system of exchanges or transactions in which other actors derive their power and rank mainly through transactions with him. According to this model, rank in the system of castes is not rigid, dependent on an immutable structure based on purity and impurity, but is rather the outcome of human actions and transactions. Rank is conditional, negotiable, and transitory, a more accurate description of the social reality. Such a model invites us to look specifically at ritual transactions and examine to what degree they create or transform political and social identities and power relationships.

For instance, the Nath or *kanphata jogis*, who live close to the Mahasu shrine at Hanol, present themselves and are addressed as *rajguru* (teacher-preceptors) to the divine kings. They are assigned specific and important ritual roles in the temple courtyard. They are accorded the ritual privilege of the offering of *phaslana* (alms of grain) at the time of each harvest. Despite this, access to the Mahasu temple is for them limited to the *dhakeur* or the first threshold at the entrance beyond which women and the lower castes are not permitted. Even though the Nath are not untouchable, the Rajput and the Brahman maintain ritual distance from them. Mahasu musician-bards, the *bajgis*, who otherwise occupy the lowest rung in the hierarchy of Mahasu officials, are custodians of the divine king's lore and no rite of passage can be performed in their absence. Even though the social order is very strictly hierarchical, with Rajput hegemony clearly evident, there is ambivalence and constant negotiation between caste positions.

Geertz (1980) kindled the debate on the role of ritual in South Asian monarchies. He argued that Balinese kingship revolved entirely around ritual and had very little to do with political administration. His argument that "power served pomp, and not pomp power" is also invalidated to an extent by the Mahasu realm where the divine king has a significant role even in contemporary democratic politics. Ritual is definitely central to Mahasu kingship, even as ceremony and pomp translate, in Bourdieuan terms, into "cultural capital", but are not the only essence of kinghip. In fact, the political effects of rituals are significant. Ritual in the Mahasu realm, unlike the usual attribute of being rigid and repetitive, is adaptable. The unlikely longevity of the Mahasu regime, even as most human kingships in the region have folded up, points towards a certain efficacy embedded in it, explaining the strong allegiance to divine kings.

With the essence of debates on kingship in South Asia boiling down to the question of degree – of whether kingship was substantially or completely about ritual – one needs to perhaps adopt a position that lies somewhere in the middle, where, for the Himalayan divine kings, ritual power translated into practical political power. Ritual does account for Mahasu's power and, while the state's imposition of restrictions on certain rituals has led to some corrosion of the divine king's control and authority, the community is often seen to respond by disregarding the law, or tempering it in a manner that does not offend contemporary sensibilities.

Mahasu kingship, in a sense, represents a centre-periphery model resting on the edifice of ritual since there is no visible human presence as the axis of power. The roles and prominence of castes emanate from proximity to this axis. Kingship, caste dominance, and power structures are maintained and legitimised through the elaborate system of ritual gift-giving and receiving. Mahasu combines spiritual and temporal powers, intrinsically mixing kingship and divinity, more so than human kings that claim a divine connection since Mahasu, as an invisible divinity, can always be embodied in the oracular *mali* and consulted on matters of statecraft. The divine king's behaviour and ideology is unforeseeable, and therefore Mahasu becomes a permanent source of dynamism and political innovation.

The Mahasu kingdom presents a religio-political system with the potential of playing on different registers, depending on social and political circumstance. Two systems – divine kingship and *sayanacari*, the system of elders – where a believing, influential, and intervening peasantry connects through its chosen elders with a divine, non-human, imported monarch, without the need for chiefs as intermediaries, lends the social organisation longevity. This idea of kingship does away with the need for the transmission of incarnation to each generation of kings. It focuses instead on managing an immanent figure, the secrecy surrounding him lending a certain opacity to the realm, within which decisions taken democratically can be finally ratified as the will of the divine. Power to decide on crucial matters rests only with the divine king, even though the kingdom is organised into localities and Mahasu is seen as taking decisions after carefully considering the views of the council of elders – in the end, usually espousing consensus and compromise. Inden (1990: 209) has commented on this model of "dual sovereignty" as implying that the king's royal sovereignty at the higher level is "merely" a matter of ritual, and therefore less real than pragmatic, lower-level, clan- and territory-based chieftainship. The ability of this abstract non-human king to create the largest common consensus between opposing groups headed by chosen elders points towards a unique system of community-centred monarchy.

Often – for instance, in the case of Chalda Mahasu's stay at

Shiraji extending much beyond the stipulated twelve years even when subjects on both banks of the river want the divine king to cross – Mahasu exercises the option of deciding otherwise. Of course, some influential sections in the *sathi* construe this as a dilatory tactic on the part of the king's oracle and minister on the other bank, both of whom had gained considerable influence and wealth owing to their proximity with the deity while in their territory. Despite this being discussed frequently in private, it was never openly articulated, nor were the oracle's pronouncements ever questioned for fear of the divine king's wrath.

As the river crossing became imminent, with palanquins visible on the other bank, one of the influential Rajput politicians from *sathi* remarked to local elders in a meeting that they should not commit the mistake of relying only on one oracle. "We must be careful not to depend completely on the pronouncements of one *mali*. We do not want a *pansi*-like situation here," he cautioned, clearly referring to his belief that the delay had little divine approval. However, on the other bank, the chief minister and the council of elders, even though much concerned at the delay, could not have pushed the case beyond a point. In fact, the entire realm had waited patiently for an extra seven years for the divine king to make his next move.

Staying equidistant from models that advocate centrality of caste, as well as pre-state kingship societies, this book looks at the Mahasu realm as representing a history of community power structures interacting with each other, with the divine king as pivot. These processes, however, have been contingent upon change in the larger socio-political environment of India. My empirical evidence suggests that the Mahasu kingdom, despite its interactions with external forces, largely remains a sovereign polity for Mahasu subjects.

The sovereignty of divine kings like Mahasu has traditionally been defined by their establishing a relationship with soil and territory. For instance, only Chalda has the right to traverse the entire territory. The Basik and Pabasik palanquins never violate each other's territories. In the realms of the four Mahasu siblings, animosities amongst moieties and neighbouring kingdoms are based on relations to the soil. Consubstantiality with soil emerges as the primary factor in social organisation, where the king as the centre defines the territorial connection based on which boundaries amongst groups are constantly negotiated.

In the Mahasu realm the centre-periphery model is visibly at work, not simply as a matter of centralising political power but also as a social system leading to the ritual maintenance of ordered life. Indigenous conceptions of polity, sovereignty, dominance, and kingship clearly preceded the caste orientation of society here. The Mahasu origin myth corroborates the view that it was the divine king who distributed caste roles upon his ascension to the throne. It is the king who has the pivotal ritual capacity and is perceived as the royal protector of territory. It is his landholding or control over territory and the soil, and through it over people who inhabit it, that forms a precondition for this ritual centrality. Proximity to the divine kings, articulated through various forms of ritualised exchange, is a crucial guarantor of rank. This makes life in the Mahasu realm nuanced, multiplex, and semiotically constituted. The king firmly remains at the centre of a system of transactions with human actors deriving rank and power through their dealings with him and his bureaucracy. Sax (2010a) has this to say about this centre–periphery model:

> According to this model, rank in the system of castes is not determined in once-and-for-all fashioned immutable structure based on purity and impurity, but is rather the outcome of human actions and transactions. Rank is contingent, negotiable, and impermanent – adjectives that are far better descriptors of social reality than a notion of transcendent structure. Such a model invites us to look specifically at ritual transactions, and examine to what degree they create and/or transform political and social identities and power relationships.

The Mahasu kingdom does not conform to a description of the unitary state, nor is it an acephalous organisation. A reference to the Mahasu realm as a kingdom is not an interpretation but a literal translation of local cultural understandings. Despite being subject to several invaders, to human and divine kings in the neighbourhood, the Nepal armies, colonial rulers, and the Indian nation-state, the kingdom has displayed an impressive durability and penetration. The survival of the Mahasu kingdom partially answers Dirks' (ibid.: 404) proposition of a "totalising analysis" in which the complex ritual-symbolic forms interweave with the so-called actual mechanisms of state power: "kinship, caste, territorial organisation, temple worship, and the growth of protection networks and local chiefship were all variably but powerfully inflected by a discourse of order, control, dominance, and power; this discourse was in turn expressed through, and in, these gifts, offerings and related social and political processes."

Kertzer (ibid.: 8) brings to light the centrality of ritual in politics, pointing to what he considers the "fallacious view that modern politics is governed by rational action." He argues that with increasing complexity in any society, politics becomes more and more constituted by symbol and myth. Since ritual is usually identified with religion, and since Western societies presume a separation between political affairs and religious life, it is often assumed that ritual remains politically significant only in the less "advanced" societies. This, he says, is nothing more than a self-serving myth. Weaving together examples from around the world and throughout history, he shows that the success of all political groups, whether conservative or revolutionary, is linked to their effective use of ritual. His work seeks to correct what he regards as the widespread tendency among social theorists to see political institutions as "simply the outcome of different interest groups competing for material resources." As an insightful corrective to more conventional interpretive views, he says ritual can enhance solidarity even without creating shared meanings or beliefs. Thus, in the Mahasu realm, even the so-called rationalists who believe that it is the oracles that instrumentalise Mahasu possessions, or that animal sacrifice rituals violate animal rights, must still be subjects of Mahasu. In relation to the isolated survival of such ritual-centred theism, Barth (1969) has questioned the idea of isolation, and, looking in this case within the realm at the outward signs of modernity and change – communication networks, education, apple horticulture – there seems no difficulty in discounting the notion that the subjects of the divine king are deficiently modern because of their remoteness.

Sax (2009: 231) has dealt with the idea of modernity and criticised its teleological orientation that attributes to it a universal rational subject. Referring to Kertzer's descriptions of political party meetings, he states that it is only during the carefully staged dramatic mass meetings for live television audiences that "the *Party*" as a concrete thing comes into existence. The same could be said about divine kingship. It is when we describe South Asian kingship as such – a kingship, a cult or anything else that describes the mass rituals – that Mahasu materialises as a ruler with subjects engaged in something unusual. Public rituals represent and legitimise the relations that constitute our social life, and in doing so they create them. Firth (1967) says that indigenes never refer to what we describe as "ritual" (alluding to meaningless, repetitive activity) as such, but use expressions such as dancing, healing, or simply "work". According to him, "what we see as a ritual, they see as technique." In the Mahasu realm this translates simply into *dev karya*, the work of the gods.

3

Journeying Sovereignties

HISTORY TRULY BELONGS to victors, since it is they who write it. It became a preserve of the colonial archive in Mahasu country after the Anglo-Gurkha battles in 1814–15, when the British arrived in the Western Himalaya and began recording their own impressions of the mountain people of Jaunsar-Bawar, referring to Mahasu as a "religious scarecrow" (Williams 1874). Colonial officers, from whose dispatches the first written records of the Mahasu kingdom come to us, perhaps saw Mahasu's divine kingship through the prism of their own political strategies and social categories. They generally portrayed the divine kings as tyrannical figureheads devised by castes they considered hegemonic – the Brahman and the Rajput – to exploit gullible countrymen. Their assessment was no doubt influenced by the stereotypes they acquired in the plains of India through observations of mainstream Hindu religious practice. While the early British administrators of the region had no qualms engaging with the divine kings, even visiting their temples and seeking divine justice in irresolvable disputes, the ones that arrived towards the beginning of the twentieth century betrayed a gradually "secularising" mindset, adopting a patronising attitude towards the divine kings. They were not willing to cede governmental and administrative roles to a divine king while themselves ruling over territory they had fought hard to win. Whilst the new rulers attempted to confine the divine kings to the realm of religion, active political engagements with them became imperative in order to establish control over the region. Colonial records indicate that Major Fredrick Young travelled to the temple of Mahasu at Hanol in 1829, seeking adjudication in a long-standing land dispute between the chieftains and the human king of Tehri state. In 1911 H.W. Emerson, administrator of the Simla Hill States, more sceptical of divine kingship than his precursor by a century, also felt obliged to directly interact with the divine king in matters of revenue and temple-building. While the British remained suspicious of the Mahasu tours, they still used the divine king's juridical authority to fulfil their own ends. In general, they were unhappy at any loss of revenue on account of tributes collected by the divine kings. Their early dispatches indicate attempts at a deliberate misrecognition of the political effects of Mahasu as mere ritual – to borrow from Bourdieu (1977) – of the divine king's territorial power, branding Mahasu tours as meaningless ritual practice, even though they had no difficulty harnessing Mahasu's political agency to further their own political agendas.

This misrecognition enabled the institution of divine kingship to survive the colonial state. Galey (1989), in his description of the Garhwal Himalaya, points to the continuing reality and efficacy of kingship in the region. He makes a crucial distinction between kingdom and kingship, stating that rather than discussing the idea of a kingdom without a king, it would be more relevant to focus on "the reality of kingship without a kingdom" (Galey 1989: 181). He therefore points out that even though kingdoms in the mountains may have dissolved and are long gone, the institution of kingship remains a significant aspect around which life revolves. In the neighbourhood of Jaunsar-Bawar, in Garhwal, for instance, the descendants of the Tehri royal family have until now contested the general elections successfully, without much exertion required in canvassing for votes. The raja, Manvendra Shah, remained a member of the Indian parliament throughout his life (a seat now occupied by his daughter-in-law) and won his subjects' support, even though he chose not to mingle with his electorate. During electioneering he refused to alight from his car for fear of being rendered impure by the polluting touch of low-caste commoners. It is common knowledge in local political circles that once offered a minister's position in the national cabinet by the prime minister of the day, Atal Behari Vajpayee, he famously turned down the offer, stating that a raja – the regal personage through whom Lord Badrinath spoke (*bolanda badri*) – could never accept a minister's position. He could only be king.

The kingdom too persists, albeit not in the manner modern states might like. As noted earlier, the retinue arrives, the divine king being carried in a box-like palanquin on the shoulders of possessed oracles or Rajput headmen. This usually happens when certain "reforms" challenge his regime or when there is discord within the community. In such situations, influential actors aim to mobilise the community's support and get the divine king to their village to seek a resolution. Is journeying, therefore, the idiom through which divine kingship has emerged as a resilient institution that has survived social change over the centuries?

In his conception of the Balinese theatre state of Negara, Geertz (1980) describes the kingdom not as a form of oriental despotism but rather as an organised spectacle. Kingship was created through a dramatisation of rank through grand public ritual and ceremony. Such cultural processes did not support the state, he argues, but *were* the state itself. The abstract model of a theatre state developed by Geertz created, particularly in the institution of kingship, the most visible manifestation of political life. The whole of Negara – court life, organisational routines, collection of taxes and dues (extractions that supported it), and accompanying privileges – was essentially directed towards the articulation of control and order.

> Particular kings came and went, "poor passing facts" anonymized in titles, immobilized in ritual, and annihilated in bonfires. But what they represented, the model-and-copy conception of order, remained

unaltered, at least over the period we know much about. The driving aim of higher politics was to construct a state by constructing a king. The more consummate the king, the more exemplary the centre. The more exemplary the centre, the more actual the realm. (Geertz 1980: 124)

Geertz uses the Balinese case to develop an abstract model of the theatre state applicable to South East Asian Indic polities. He argues that state ceremonials in Negara were a kind of "metaphysical theatre", that is, a theatre designed to express a vision of the ultimate nature of reality that at the same time tried to shape current conditions to match that reality. Ritual events re-created social relations of *jero* ("inner", to whom one surrendered power in the ritual event, thereby making them powerful) and *jaba* ("outer", a provider of services to those who are *jero*), between chieftains and their subordinate chiefs. Every ritual performance reproduced *jero–jaba* relations as both symbolic ideal and pragmatic reality, thereby reinforcing social order. Thus, although the state was cross-cut by the conflicting jurisdictions of temples, hamlets, and irrigation societies, they all came together for mass state rituals in which the ideal social order of the state was made real.

Though Geertz's analyses of mass rituals as constituting elements of the kingdom and ideal social order may help to describe Mahasu processions, his depiction of the kingdom as a rather static institution invites contestation. His overarching analysis can be termed ahistorical, and, as Barth (1993: 222) says, it has "depoliticized" a political institution and emphasised only the cultural but ignored the political aspects of kingship. Tambiah (1985: 319) notes that Geertz presents the Indic king as the focus of a ritual theatre that creates the exemplary centre as being "immobilized into passivity and reflective trances" whilst simultaneously acknowledging the presence of "virtually continuous intrigue, dispute, violence and an enormous amount of micro-upheaval." Tambiah believes that Geertz does not transcend the break between expressive and instrumental action, or between power as pomp and power as control of people and resources. The state thus remains an illusory representation where kingship is neither credited with governmental functions nor rituals seen as creating or legitimising power.

In another paper, Geertz (1977) examines the idea of kingly charisma and its legitimising forces, comparing the splendour and hierarchical display of Indic kingship to processions in Queen Elizabeth's England, which he finds representative of virtue and allegory. He compares this to the Moroccan ruler Hasan's moving centre, representing mobility and energy, a relentless searching out for contact. In elegant prose Geertz compartmentalises these different cultures, once again relegating the political to the background. His contention that political authority requires cultural contexts to define it ultimately leads to fragmentation. As is evident from the ethnographic evidence, Mahasu kingship constantly breaks through such cultural frames and shows how rituals of departure, movement, and arrival directly translate into political power and its legitimisation.

One dimension of Mahasu, to use Geertz's terminology, is an exemplary centre, manifested in the seated Mahasu, the divine king referred to as Bautha, consecrated in the temple at Hanol. All stable and organised societies probably have a political centre. According to Geertz, political centres have both a ruling elite and a collection of symbols that legitimise those who rule. Essentially, rulers must justify themselves, and as Geertz (1979: 15) puts it, "they justify their existence and order their actions in terms of a collection of stories, ceremonies, insignia, formalities that they have either inherited or, in more revolutionary situations, invented. It is these that mark the centre as centre and give what goes on there an aura of being not merely important but in some odd fashion connected with the way the world is built."

Conceptually, the movements of the four brothers and their corresponding territories trace a kind of mandala, with the king as the pivot of existence, an organisational system that answers the description of Tambiah's (1977) "galactic polities", a pattern that recurs at various levels, from the construction of palanquins to the temples and the organisation of the realm with the temple of Hanol at the centre. Hanol thus continues to be the main locus of Mahasu's agency. The two factions that alternately host the divine king are situated on either sides of this central axis.

Within the Mahasu realm, mountain rivers like the Tons at Hanol bisect the kingdom, with the downstream half composed mainly of the region associated with the Kauravas of the Mahabharata, and the upstream half with the Pandavas. The moieties, *sathi* and *pansi*, get to receive and host their divine king for a period of roughly twelve years. During this period the divine king either holds court in his temples or proceeds through his territories. Mahasu temples, as in Hanol on the banks of the Tons, are usually located where these sub-districts or land divisions come together, from where both regions are accessible.

Taking a cue from Galey (1989) about the continuity of kingship in the Himalayas, I would argue that in Mahasu's realm kingship is alive not just as a trope but also as a political reality. In fact it never disappeared despite several state regimes, including the British and the modern Indian, claiming the divine king's territory. What do the royal processions, organised like communal journeys involving immense logistical challenges, represent? Why do they retain their significance in a region now governed by a secular and democratic government? Do these arduous journeys contribute to the longevity of a social system that has survived centuries of incursions?

Sax (2000b: 54), while examining the processional aspect of *digvijaya* (the conquest of quarters), refers to it as the most important Indian concept with regard to sovereignty, a phenomenon that was always both religious as well as political. A term for the conquest of the whole earth – the heroic and idealised aspiration of ancient Indian kings – refers to a venturing out to claim territory. Processions, even today, are a very significant aspect of political practice in India (and indeed in the world). According to Sax (ibid.), "as lord of the earth (*bhupati*), a king had physically to traverse the land, to mark it with his footsteps, and thus establish a physical relationship with it and the people who lived upon it. The process did not end with military conquest." This suggests that marking with footsteps has to be a continuous process. Various state actors may have included the region in their maps and cadastral surveys post-military conquest, or through logical succession, but there was one actor, the divine king Mahasu, who actively engaged in establishing this physical relationship with his subjects and the soil of the kingdom. To understand whether these journeys "translate power into authority" – to use Galey's (ibid.) expression – we need to look at their genesis and present form.

The elaborate origin and arrival myth of the four Mahasu brothers as kings into this region forms the ritual repertoire of the divine kings' drummers and bards who have inherited this knowledge orally through the generations. The drummer-bards are genealogists and record keepers for their divine king. According to them, the inauguration of the Mahasu realm was marked by the appearance of the Mahasu siblings in a field at a village called Maindrath, after their journey from Kullu-Kashmir, a day earlier than they themselves had prophesied. Their arrival was a direct result of the epic journey undertaken by a Brahman named Huna Bhat to rid the region of the terror of a cannibalistic demon, Kirmir. The deities, after agreeing to help tame the demon, had instructed Huna that they would appear on the seventh day, following the usual trope of the *utpatti murti*, or an image that self-manifests.

Either due to a miscalculation of the exact time of the divine king's arrival or on account of impatience induced by the demon's excesses, the plough was put into the field on the sixth day. This ritual error led to one of the Mahasus being struck by the plough and born with a walking disability. Though not the eldest, owing to his handicap, he was stationed at the capital or centre of the cult at Hanol as the Bautha, or the sitting Mahasu. The eldest and the middle-born, Bashik and Pabasik Mahasu, were also impaired and allotted territories on both sides of the river, covering smaller parts of the realm for their touring. The able-bodied and youngest, Chalda Mahasu, adept in the knowledge of magical ritual, intuitively knew that their arrival had been marked by ritual failure or inauspiciousness. Chalda Mahasu therefore opted not to settle at one place and retained a peripatetic role for himself. It is this ritual journeying, as a constant quest to reconcile with the ritual failure accompanying the appearance of the stranger kings, that is the crux of the processional cycle. The concept of a stranger king developed by Sahlins (2008) to highlight the imposition of colonialism – not as the result of the breaking of the spirit of local communities by brute force, or as reflecting an ignorant peasantry's acquiescence in the lies of its self-interested leaders, but as a people's rational and productive acceptance of an opportunity offered – also helps explicate the acceptance of Mahasu as divine king. Mahasu's arrival corresponds in some ways to Sahlins' (1985) depiction of Latin kingship, wherein the accession of the king is equated with a recreation of the universe, with rulers invariably not springing from the same soil as their subjects.

Once the gods had arrived, their immediate task was the slaying of the demon Kirmir who had terrorised the region with his cannibalism. The deities chased the demon on the ridge that marks the boundary between the two regions of Jaunsar and Bawar and dismembered him serially as he fled across the entire range. Then they proceeded to the cult centre of Hanol where they forced the local deity, king Vishnu, out of his temple-fortress and occupied it.

This inauguration of the realm through a disruption of the existing order is described by Sutherland (2003–4) as "the primary *introjection* of wild power from the forest that, at regular intervals, is reversed in a secondary *projection* of power (emphasis by the author), now in its ritually reordered form as the divine, in a movement of collective agency – typically by feuding – the raiding and looting of sheep and goats, and, in earlier times, also of women, from a neighbouring martial group or *khund* for the temple consecration sacrifice." Sutherland refers to narratives of this "government by deity" being shaped by a double figure of reversal: the immobilisation of wild forest power as a god in a temple, and its subsequent remobilisation as a roving ruler in ritual practice. This is why, he believes, many origin myths begin with disruption and end with a similar trope: the construction of a palanquin as the deity's ritual vehicle. The palanquin and the procession thus become the primary means of projecting power in ritual when the deity, as a king, tours his domain.

Villages group together and send written applications to the divine king's minister with a request that the divine king visit them. The minister consults the deity's oracle to take time out of his schedule and make a detour. The request, if granted on the appointed date and time, means all able-bodied men from the host villages appear at the temple to escort the deity and bear his palanquin out. They also carry the royal paraphernalia, the royal sword, sceptres, parasols and whisks, cooking cauldrons, tents, and heralding trumpets. The deity's bureaucrats from the main shrines and the Rajput men from the host village walk alongside, guarding against any violation of the strict rules of conduct. It is the dominant Rajput and the oracles that take turns in carrying the palanquin on their shoulders. Well ahead of the procession walk the drummers and trumpeters, heralding the arrival of the royal vehicle but never coming close enough lest they render unclean the divine king. The lowest of the castes, the Kolta, serve as porters. The priests and upper-caste women, meanwhile, prepare to welcome and host the divine king upon his arrival in the host village.

These royal processions are a logistical nightmare for the organisers. Though there are no written records of the ritual journeys from pre-colonial times, descriptions gleaned through the writings of British authors, mainly colonial administrators, on both sides of the river give us a glimpse of what the processions were like at the turn of the nineteenth century. G.R.C. Williams (1874), referring to the year 1827, writes that Major Young, the British Resident and administrator of the region, found Mahasu and his processions a great nuisance during the early settlement operations in the district. Referring to Mahasu as "a deity of pernicious influence and exactions", Walton (1911), the author of the Gazetteer of the region, says:

> The god when on circuit, observed both state and etiquette. His palanquin was invariably accompanied by a train of sixty to seventy men and dancing girls, but he never visited a village unless he received an invitation through his vazir (minister).
> The terror inspired by the god, however, always procured him the necessary invitation. If a village has suffered a misfortune, the god was requested to pay a visit. He attended, seated in a palanquin, surrounded by silver vessels followed by his own retinue to which all chance-idlers invariably attached themselves. The throng was fed for one day by the inviting village and kept for six months by collections levied on the *khats* (land administration units) in the division, who are also obliged to furnish their quota of *ghi* (clarified butter) and goods.

These exactions, Walton remarks, "ruined the superstitious inhabitants; so much so that they were unable to pay the revenue" due to the colonials, and the administrator, Major Young, "interdicted the levy of contributions within British territory and ordered the *vazir* (the minister) to accept no more invitation from a village." He further notes that perhaps this ban on Mahasu journeys across his realm was honoured more in the breach.

Though Major Young, as a colonial administrator out to assert his claim over Mahasu territory, tried to restrict the deity's movements, he also actively engaged with the deity. For instance, in a land settlement dispute with the neighbouring human king of Tehri – a dispute he himself could not pronounce judgment on as a magistrate since no documentary evidence could be produced in order to legitimise the landownership claims of each side – he travelled all the way to Mahasu's temple at Hanol to seek the deity's divine justice (see chapter 5).

Almost a century later, on the other bank of the river, in the princely state of Rampur Bashahar, of which Emerson was the colonial administrator, something even more intriguing happened. Emerson, who has extensively described the region and its people in his unpublished ethnographic manuscripts, organized durbars or assemblies inviting processions of various local deities. On one such occasion, when King George V and Queen Mary visited India and held a durbar of subordinate regional kings in Delhi in 1911, the divine kings were asked by the governor of the Shimla Hill States to assemble with their regalia and retinues in the British Raj's summer capital, Shimla. According to Emerson, the palanquins arrived in their processions and circled around a portrait of the royal couple in a display of allegiance. Mahasu, however, either did not care to come or was not invited to these assemblies. Emerson (1911), separated in time from Young by a century and therefore more secular in his outlook, describes Mahasu processions as follows:

> The spheres of influence have long since been demarcated, and there is generally a code of honour among the gods forbidding one to intrude upon another's territory. But Mahasu's conduct is regulated by no such scruples. His relentless energies allow him no repose, he admits no boundaries to his dominions, and his trespasses bring him into constant conflict with his rivals.
>
> He chooses the richest and the most pleasant villages to halt in, which have to bear the burden of his exactions. But the neighbouring villages do not escape scot-free. Every family in the districts through which he passes has to contribute one-rupee eight annas towards his expenses, the rupee being kept by his priest and the eight annas paid into his treasury. In addition, the peasants have to furnish instruments of music and ornaments of silver in honour of the god, and grain and other contributions in kind to feed his following. Happily for them, these visitations are followed by long periods of rest, for Chaldu (Chalda Mahasu) having finished his progress, takes his ease for the next twelve years in his temple, situated not far from Hanol where his brother Bhothu (Bautha) lives.

It is presumably to this order that Chaldu now owes his twelve years of rest from travel. He, however still tours in the Simla (Shimla) States adjacent to Garhwal, sometimes staying so I was told, for twelve months in a single village. The rapacity of his priests is notorious. If they see a peasant wearing clothes or ornaments of more than ordinary value, they demand them in the name of the god, threatening his wrath if they were not handed over. And such is the popular estimate of his powers that few dare refuse the request; but they cut their losses by wearing little of value when Chaldu is about.

Fortunately for the peasants, this member of the Mahasu family visits only a few villages in the Bashahar State, where, however, several of his brothers have obtained a firm footing.

If we go beyond the general tone of colonial disparagement, the narratives do indicate a grudging acceptance of how Mahasu continued to exercise sovereignty over his dominions. The officers, too, appear to be assiduously attempting to comprehend the Mahasu phenomenon. The imposition of restrictions and references to the deity accepting exactions also indicate that even though the territory traversed by Mahasu processions was now under British control, the deity continued to enjoy a sovereign right over his subjects through these ritual journeys.

Bergmann (2016: 91) underlines the need to distinguish between territoriality and sovereignty. Referring to confluent territories and overlapping sovereignties as the key to understanding imperial frontiers, he proposes that at many sites different actors claimed control over the same sort of thing, for instance trade. While these claims are often imagined as inherently territorial, their articulation is often marked by uncertainty over control. Mahasu's sovereignty, rather than emanating from cartography and revenue collection, was embedded in assemblies at temples and in processions; it was expressed in religious ceremony, even though the purpose was political. Depending on when the gaze of the state was focused on the divine king, the subjects could foreground the religious and obscure the political.

As was the case then, Mahasu processions continue to criss-cross the region today. They involve even greater expense and human mobilisation. In an age of roads and jeeps, they entail the sheer difficulty of walking barefoot over the rough and sometimes snow-bound terrain for several miles a day, for days on end. While on tour, the divine king also expects subjects to follow strict codes on food, hygiene, and sleep. Food is cooked communally, is quite frugal, and most men accompanying the procession sleep on the floor, wherever they find space around the palanquin.

Besides closely knitting the areas of Mahasu influence spatially, socially, and politically, these processions perform the specific role of reassuring Mahasu subjects of the divine king's tutelary presence. They also serve to send out a stark reminder that Kirmir, the oppressive demon who ruled the territory before the Mahasus arrived as saviours, is down but not out. This is also explained in the Mahasu origin myth through the conundrum of dividing conquered property, in the elaborate myth of the slaying of the demon.

The Mahasu siblings, as is well known to all the kings' subjects, employed their assisting demi-gods, the *birs*, in slaying the demon Kirmir in order to inaugurate their kingdom. Finally, it was Kailu, one of the demigods, who managed to kill the demon at Kuddu, midstream of the Pabbar River. Nineteen warriors, including the four Mahasus, accomplished this task and they decided to divide the demon's body amongst themselves as trophies. Every warrior attempted to achieve an equitable distribution but they always ended up with twenty pieces. The whole was always more than the sum of its parts. At this point, Kailu, a Mahasu deputy, decided to claim an extra trophy for his efforts while Chalda Mahasu decided to have another go at dividing the corpse into nineteen pieces. Instantly, the twentieth trophy managed to slip out of his grasp, crossed the river, and climbed atop the nearby hill. As the warriors ran to claim it, the other trophies, body parts of the dismembered demon, cried out saying that the deities must accept happily what is their right and leave the extra bit for the *rakshasas* (demons).

Thus, once again, the river was accepted as a boundary with the lowland region to the left, referred to as the Mausat or Mahasu territory, while the land beyond the mountains was Rakshasan, the land of the demons, unknown but a constant threat. In order to keep the demons at a safe distance, Mahasu subjects have to periodically display their allegiance to him, as much as the deity needs to renew his claim to the kingdom. In this context, the twelve-yearly cycles of travelling also have a social and juridical significance since, according to the Hindu code, a person loses ownership rights over property if it remains unclaimed for over twelve years. Perhaps the periodicity of the Kumbha Mela, the Nanda Raj Jat Yatra (the principal pilgrimage of Garhwal) and the *yatra* of Parsuram in Nirmand, Kullu, are therefore all linked to this twelve-yearly routine.

Undoubtedly, places on the divine king's itinerary indicate the space over which Mahasu exercises religious influence. However, they are also markers of his political domination. But what does it mean for the average Mahasu subject to host or accompany a Mahasu procession? Sax (2002), referring to them, says, "As shamanic performance, these processions heal, as legal performance they bind, as political performance they ratify and as a religious performance they serve to sanctify." Most significantly, while renewing Mahasu's connection with the soil, they serve to create power and legitimise the divine king's right to rule over subjects.

Mahasu is not just limited to a centre but also translates himself, through folklore recited by drummer-bards, into allegorical virtue. While Mahasu has an exemplary centre in the seated form in Bautha, the other form of Mahasu, the moving form, Chalda Mahasu, traverses the entire realm, marking territory and performing governmental as well as spiritual acts. The journeying form of the divine king is thus about mobility, contact, and search for fealty over a vast mountain terrain. The collective mobility of these three brother gods, complemented by the stability provided by the centre, translates into effective kingship.

Mahasu kingship therefore surpasses all of Geertz's cultural frames alluding to different parts of the world – exemplary centre to Indic kings, allegory to the West, and mobility to the African and Central Asian – and encompasses actions that account for a stable and organised political structure. To comprehend the divine king's transcendence of such pigeonholing, one needs to observe Mahasu on tour through his realm. These journeys lead Mahasu and the divine king's subjects across the boundaries of the Indian mountain states, Uttarakhand and Himachal Pradesh, where the divine king claims allegiances and retains a delicate balance of power within the state communities. Ritual activities are adopted on these journeys to reinforce hierarchies, solve subjects' personal problems, build consensus within the community, and retain political control. The crowds sometimes swelling into several thousands are part of the procession, as are armed warriors – now increasingly carrying rifles rather than pickaxes and bows – drummers, and other musicians such as trumpeters. Frequently, the divine king is called upon to perform exorcisms and make forecasts. In such situations the oracle must be at the head of the palanquin, resting it on his shoulders, possessed by the divine force, while in others it is usually the Rajput men who take turns to carry it.

The palanquin is never placed on bare unconsecrated earth. For a night's rest or a halt it is either placed in a temple, or enters the home of a devoted Rajput family, or is placed in a special tent when in the wild. One of the divine king's priests, carrying his symbols (*nisan*), always walks a day ahead, giving advance notice of his arrival to villages that the divine king has agreed to visit, whilst also sanitising the space the divine king will traverse. These days, almost all those walking with the procession carry a mobile phone and, therefore every village in this vast region is well informed about the *devta*'s movements.

Several male mountain goats lead the processions as an integral part of the divine king's entourage. Owing to the former pastoralist livelihoods of Mahasu subjects, goats are considered the ultimate offering one can make to the divine king. Despite the fact that religious offerings are nowadays increasingly being made in the form of gold or currency, many people, even if they do not follow a pastoralist lifestyle any more, buy male goats and offer them to Mahasu. When the entourage is granted hospitality by a village, these royal goats are allowed to feed nonchalantly on crops and kitchen gardens, wherever the procession halts.

Today, the processions attract increasing media attention, and administrative arrangements are made by the state government to maintain order. Amongst the most arduous processions I experienced was Chalda Mahasu's tour from the newly consecrated temple at Shiraji in Himachal Pradesh to the cult capital at Hanol in Uttarakhand. The expedition took almost forty days, everyone usually walking at the command of the deity, given through his oracle. On the last leg of this exhausting expedition, as we crossed the snowclad ridge to get a clearer view of the remote Himalayan village of Bhotanu, I heard the faint beating of a *dhol* (the mountain drum), accompanied by loud shouts from a large group of men proclaiming their king's victory. Bhotanu is an outlying high-altitude village in a region known as Bangan, located on the boundary of two major Mahasu territories. From past experience I could tell that the men were probably also carrying firearms as they rallied round a silver palanquin. The group had gone ahead even as I lagged behind because of exhaustion caused by days and nights of mountain hiking. I had been hiking with the procession of the divine king Chalda, the walking Mahasu, from remote high-altitude villages of Himachal Pradesh to the banks of the River Tons in Uttarakhand. The crossing of that river is a ritual that can only be witnessed once in twelve or more years, as one cycle of touring on either of the two banks of the Tons is completed.

We had already crossed over into Uttarakhand, but crossing this boundary mattered little to the large number of Mahasu subjects. I deliberately use the expression "days and nights" because Chalda Mahasu's royal procession usually camped during the day and walked through the night, on very hazardous trails, with progress only aided by a few dim flashlights and the entranced intuition of the palanquin bearers. Most times, we blindly followed those ahead of us with no inkling of where the next step in the treacherous terrain would lead. Perhaps Mahasu wanted to test his subjects' resolve to bring their divine king back, forcing the subjects into these nocturnal adventures.

For Chalda Mahasu's subjects, the destined boundary was the bank of the River Tons at Thadiyar, the traditional dividing line between the two factions tracing their ancestry to the rival cousins from the Mahabharata. Subjects of the divine king on opposing banks of the river divide themselves into constantly hostile factions, each hosting their divine king for what the other hopes will be a twelve-year period. We were presently in Pandava territory, or *pansi*, while on the other bank of the Tons stood the *sathi* – the land of the sixty Kauravas.

Throughout our expedition, once the travelling party had set up camp in a village or a clearing in the forest, we were left clueless about the divine king's plans. Members from Chalda Mahasu's council of elders, part of the entourage, constantly deliberated and advised the divine king's *vazir* about the duration of a halt or rules regarding the divine king's itinerary. However, precedent mattered little to Chalda Mahasu and the progress of the procession depended entirely on his *mali*, in a state of possession, announcing it was time to proceed to the next village. It was only then that the advance party, with the priest bearing the Mahasu insignia, was asked to proceed to the next halt. Chalda could announce a sudden change in the route or extend our stay indefinitely at a particular place.

During one such tour, seven years ago, Chalda Mahasu had decided to divert his processional route and announced, for the first time in living memory, that he would set up camp at the village of Shiraji. Shiraji is a small hamlet atop a hill, bordering the minuscule former kingdom of Dhadi Rao. In pre-independence times the region was divided into several very small kingdoms that were referred to by the British collectively as the Shimla Hill States. These were princely states ruled by human kings reinstated by the British. They were later consolidated into a district named District Mahasu, an indicator of Mahasu influence over the territory, and became part of Himachal Pradesh after 1971.

Shiraji is located in a region that was witnessing an economic boom at the time of my visit, owing to a sudden spurt in apple cultivation and demand. Some parts of the region had switched from an agro-pastoralist economy to apple horticulture and tracts of high-altitude land, earlier uncultivated for much of the year, were now yielding a remunerative harvest of apples. Even as villages such as Shiraji experienced economic growth, Chalda's realm on the other bank of the Tons in Uttarakhand remained largely peripheral, burdened with a subsistence economy and absence of the cash-crop boom.

Chalda's visit coincided, my host in the village remarked, with an apple orchard owner acquiring a BMW car in an area that would rarely catch a glimpse of any kind of automobile until a few years earlier. It was here that Chalda ordered the construction of the grandest of all Mahasu temples. The construction took five years, and the ongoing work extended Chalda's stay in *pansi* to nineteen years, as against the usual twelve. The delay was so unprecedented that when I commenced fieldwork in 2009 there was talk on both banks of the river about the divine king perhaps turning sedentary, preparing to settle in the grand palace that he had ordered for himself. And now, in the winter of 2012, immediately after the consecration of the temple, the divine king had abruptly announced his plans to leave, to travel and be with his subjects across the river, forcing this tough expedition, as if testing his subjects' fidelity.

During the expedition I admired the determination and stamina of a large number of men – scantily clad and ill equipped for the rain and snow of the upper reaches – who had trekked with us the past weeks to ensure smooth carriage for their king's orders to proceed to the other bank. Carrying the royal palanquin on their shoulders to retain the purity of their divine king's vehicle, they trudged barefoot across the snowy passes, with the divine *sakti* overpowering and driving them day after arduous day. The difficulties of bearing their king being a matter of faith, the tougher the test the more the merit they believed they would derive from it.

Even as the procession made steady progress for over a month, excitement began to mount on the other riverbank. *Sathi*, across the river, were gearing up to welcome the divine king. Meanwhile, the state government's bureaucracy, headed by an Indian Administrative Service officer responsible for the district, the District Magistrate (DM) of Dehra Dun, was also preparing to receive the royal entourage. A delegation comprising the region's elders, the *sayanas*, had met him. The top bureaucrat, the chief secretary of the state, had asked for arrangements to be made for the thousands of people who would congregate to receive and send off the divine king. One miffed delegation member reminisced that this high-ranking official had made caustic remarks about the mass frenzy generated by such rituals. He had, however, taken note of the administrative need for maintaining peace and issued suitable instructions. The DM had visited the region and made arrangements to keep things under control, since public sentiment was on the edge due to delays in the arrival of the king. As the elders recalled, river crossings were usually accompanied by violence.

Engineers of the Public Works Department inspected the flimsy steel-cable suspension bridge across the Tons that separated *pansi* from *sathi*, over which he was to cross with his retinue, and declared it unsafe for large crowds. A police contingent from the headquarters at Dehra Dun was deputed to maintain order and ensure that not more than twenty crossed the bridge at a time. Newspaper and television reporters looked for vantage points to get a clear view of the crossing, even as the council of elders put their heads together and mobilised ranks to make arrangements to feed and accommodate the thousands who would escort their king across the boundary, seeing him off until he was, they hoped, ready to get back after twelve years. The official arrangement, quite similar to those made to receive a political figurehead, was a reflection of Mahasu's political significance.

As I arrived in Bhotanu, and met the *khat sayana* (native head of the council of elders) for this group of villages, he welcomed me warmly and invited me to a hearty meal of goat's meat and rice.

As I sat cross-legged on bare earth in the fields with the Rajput *sayanas* – the lower castes were being served in terraced fields below us – I could sense a deep undercurrent of resentment within the group. Engaging in conversation, I became aware that the bone of contention was a news item published in a newspaper across the river. Having finished the meal, we proceeded to the home of the *khat sayana*, the newspaper report still dominating the conversation. The clipping was circulated amongst the elders, being read and re-read several times. All averred that the reporting was offensive to the *pansi*. The journalist in question, Raghuvir Rawat, a prominent member from the faction across the river, had authored it, describing Chalda's return to *sathi*, with the headline referring to the impending river crossing as a homecoming after nineteen years. Adding insult to injury was the article's announcement of a specific date for the river-crossing ritual.

The *pansi* minister was furious. "This attitude is responsible for the *devta* delaying the crossing for so many years, almost settling down in our region. If *sathi* is Chalda's home, is this the home of his in-laws? He is equally our *devta-raja*. How dare they describe it as a homecoming, as if from exile? And announcing a date, only Mahasu can decide on a date. How dare they announce a date in the newspapers! These blokes need to be taught a lesson!" he fumed. Even as strategies were being formulated on how this "propaganda" would be countered, the *vazir*'s mobile phone rang. It was the Dehra Dun DM, asking for a specific date for the river crossing. Government machinery had been deployed and could not be made to wait indefinitely, at the mercy of a god's whims. The *sathi* were running out of patience and further delays would make the large crowds on the other bank even more restive. In the conversation with the government official the minister was respectful, but evasive, stating quite clearly that it was not within his powers to decide on a date and that only the divine king could tell when he deemed it fit to cross. Despite his nonchalance, it was evident that he would have to facilitate the river crossing soon.

In this manner, modern and secular government practices often come into conflict with the traditional Mahasu polity. The divine kings must exercise their power within the ambit of state structures, and to that extent their freedom to move and act is curtailed. As the British did for Mahasu and his retinue, the state and the divine king pretend to misrecognise each other as long as the one does not begin to undermine the other. Conflicts emerge in instances where the state insists on altering tradition. This intolerance of the modern for the traditional, even though increasing by the day, still leaves some scope for renegotiation and adjustment. Generally, such confrontation forces the state to take cognizance of Mahasu's social and political organisation.

While it appears on the surface that the government is in control, the work of a traditional polity is evident in the divine king's processions. For most Mahasu subjects, daily life revolves around duties to the deity – accompanying him on his tours when the entourage comes visiting their region, or journeying along when a significant tour is under way. This journeying, ritually performed, is generally referred to as *devta ka kaam* (the work of gods). And such work, as one of the deity's ministers put it, is religio-political, for "*devniti* [policy of the gods] and *rajniti* [politics] can never be separated." Sutherland (1998), writing about the region, refers to such ritualised politicking as a theistic sovereignty. The ritualised regime of the deity's processions represents the region as politically sovereign, even though successive state actors – the Nepalese Gurkha, the British, and the Indian state – have attempted to appropriate it to their political boundaries through cartography, revenue regimes, and administration.

In 2010–11, accompanying the palanquin of Pabasik Mahasu from the temple in Thadiyar in its journey to Village Chattra, I experienced how the god seeks to reassert his sovereignty – a sovereignty that is not just theistic. To initiate a procession and for the deity to rise from his current seat and visit a village, several conditions must be met. The village has to unite and extend an invitation. This is easier said than achieved since many villages want to invite the divine kings – in the first place, to bring an end to communal social conflict. The procedure for inviting the divine king involves, as noted, applying to the deity's minister in writing with a small amount of money or silver as tribute. The minister proposes the visit before the god and reserves a date only after the deity's assent has been obtained through his possessed oracle or *mali*. The royal visit is an event of immense significance for the village as it affords the opportunity to display "communitas" (Turner: 1967) by hosting extended families and visitors from all the neighbouring villages. The sheer act of inviting and feeding guests and expending scant resources is the performance of

Photo 3.1: The Mahasu procession crosses the bridge over the Tons.

community sacrifice. The population of the village swells nearly ten times during these tours, and no visitor is allowed to remain unfed or without a warm bed to sleep in.

Four years had elapsed since the village of Chattra had invited the deity and he had agreed to visit. The intervening period had witnessed bitter quarrels over land and property in the village due to fragmentations of land – owing to a growing number of claimants and the specificities of inheritance. The situation had reached a tipping point, so that members of the two principal landowning families now refused to even talk to one another, though they were neighbours. Young boys within these families, cousins, whose homes stood across a small compound, had grown up without exchanging a word – a situation almost unthinkable in a mountain village, where community living is of the essence. The village had grown from being a small hamlet of two households to a settlement of sixteen extended families and as many households. A family in the hills usually consists upwards of twenty people, with cousins, uncles, and aunts all clustered together. The influential among these got together and decided it was about time they extended an invitation to the divine king, to stem the growing discord over land and resources within the village.

On the appointed cold winter morning, Pabasik Mahasu's palanquin began its journey to the village, where every family had dispatched their able-bodied men to fetch the god from the temple at Thadiyar, down below in the valley. Even the estranged cousins had arrived. Low-caste men had arrived to carry the god's baggage, the drummers, and the trumpeters, to ensure the god rose from his seat and took the prescribed shorter route – for a single wrong turn after crossing the bridge on the Tons towards Hanol would mean a long detour and an indefinite stopover, delaying the god's arrival at the village, where malicious spirits were anxiously awaiting exorcism. The men of the Rajput castes would, of course, lend a shoulder to the palanquin in procession.

One could feel the nervous energy at the Thadiyar temple as the entire male population of the village waited in anticipation for the god to rise. The moment arrived when the minister felt that sufficient numbers had gathered for the procession's progress. The box-like palanquin had been readied with the divine king's idol concealed inside, wrapped in red cloth. First to be lifted out of the small shrine outside the temple complex was the *nisan*, symbol of Kailath Bir, the deity of the lower castes who had slain the demon Kirmir and which accompanied Pabasik Mahasu as a bodyguard. The symbol is a long iron tong with pieces of coloured cloth strung to it, accompanied by a bell that can be slung over a shoulder. As the drumming reached a crescendo, the bearer of Kailath's symbol trembling with the effect of possession, all eyes shut in fear and reverence, and low-caste men touched their ears out of obsequiousness; the palanquin, with its poles bearing tiger heads in gilded silver, and draped in spotless white muslin brought in earlier by the host village, emerged from the palace of the raja. Having surveyed the courtyard, going around it a few times, the divine king was in procession, moving down the precipitous path to the Tons River, where it would cross the swinging wire bridge (the one considered too fragile to carry more than twenty at a time). It would then take the winding path leading up to the village, or perhaps take another turn towards Hanol, as the bearers feared.

The drummers led the way, playing vigorously, even as the trumpeters raised the pitch announcing the king's presence. The minister stayed close to the palanquin, ensuring that the deity lodged inside was neither disturbed through contact with the overhanging branches and creepers nor desecrated by the low-caste men carrying the god's tents, cooking pots, and musical instruments.

For most of the time, the palanquin, though carried on the shoulders of high-caste men from the host village, seemed to move of its own volition. As we crossed the creaking steel rope bridge across the Tons and reached a T-point on the pathway, the procession awaited Mahasu's decision on which way to turn. To everyone's relief, the divine king's possessed palanquin bearers decided to turn left. Had the palanquin taken the path to the right, it would have meant that the god wanted to visit his elder sibling at Hanol, and the impatient hosts in Chatra would have had to organise a series of time-consuming and expensive rituals through their representatives in the shrine of the deity's brother before the god could proceed to their village.

We continued to climb, even as the drummers kept up the tempo. At times the palanquin would careen dangerously towards the deep gorges we were leaving behind. At other instances it would surge ahead, as if shifting gear. As we climbed and passed one terraced field after another, more men joined the procession. Trying to stay ahead of the procession on the minister's insistence, and since I had a camera in hand, I almost stepped over a man lying on the gravel across the narrow pathway at the halfway mark where the god's procession was about to arrive. He had torn away his shirt and flagellated himself with stinging nettle (*Urtica dioica*). He trembled in a trance, obstructing the king's path. As the

Photo 3.2: The protestor carries Kailath Bir's *nisan*.

palanquin reached him the local oracle bearing the palanquin also became possessed. A protracted but silent negotiation, only through gestures, followed between the god and the squatter. The one obstructing the path had now begun to stretch his limbs, as if in a fit, refusing to budge and let the procession move forward, reminding one of Gandhi's satyagrahis (protestors), who symbolically obstructed the work of government via civil disobedience in pre-independence India.

Finally, the god's oracle, now in a state of rage, asked for the symbol of Kailath to be brought before him. The enthusiastic fellow carrying the symbol had meanwhile continued his ascent, not stopping for further negotiations. This led to a lot of shouting and name-calling, until the rattled youngster sprinted back down the steep pathway to the god's palanquin. The divine king finally conferred Kailath's symbol upon the protestor, therewith making him a custodian of sorts. This satisfied the possessed protestor and the procession was once again on its way, the weary researcher grateful for the brief respite afforded by this assumption of office, negotiated through protest.

The entourage moved on whilst the shadows between terraced fields had begun to lengthen. And then two young women, who had thrown off their *datoos* (customary scarves that cover the heads of a married woman) and left their hair untied in a display of spirit possession, scrambled down the steep hillside, screaming and writhing in pain. It seemed like we had run into another protest. The divine king's oracle heard out the unintelligible mutterings of the women, constantly comforting them while also gesturing that they let the procession reach the village where the divine king would address their complaints. Meanwhile, the first protestor, who now bore the symbol of Kailath on his shoulders, re-entered his trance, jumping violently, constantly gesturing towards the palanquin as if questioning the god's motive in visiting the village.

After all the protesting spirits had been ritually pacified with the tossing of rice and placing the heads of the human spirit-vehicles

Photo 3.3: Oracle pacifying possessed women, palanquin on the shoulders.

under Mahasu's trumpets, the procession resumed its journey uphill. Finally, arriving at the outskirts of the village under a huge peepal (*Ficus religiosa*) tree, the palanquin danced, as did the possessed spirits opposing his entry to the village. The diminutive shrine to Kailath, the deity of the lower castes, was believed to be here and this warrior of Mahasu had to be propitiated before the village could be accessed.

On reaching the village boundary, the palanquin was received by the village priests holding smoking incense in long ladles. The Mahasu priests always appear before the god with their legs uncovered. So, none of them wore trousers, only a loincloth and shirt. This was followed by as-yet-unmarried young women offering floral or banknote garlands to the palanquin.

The palanquin bearers, weary with all the climbing, seemed in a hurry to carry the palanquin to the designated spot in the village square and place it there, but the divine king would have none of it. His oracle was clearly agitated over something. He declared that the divine king had decided to take a detour on the narrow winding path leading to another point above the village. Up climbed the fatigued palanquin bearers. The palanquin travelled to the edge of a disused rice field up the hill. Here, another tree stood at the edge, its base overgrown with bushes. The palanquin headed straight for the thorny bushes and the bearers were forced to tear into them, which left them bruised and bleeding.

"Here, this is my land! No one dare encroach into it!" shouted the oracle in the shaking, high-pitched voice (*cheriya boli*) of the divine king. Only then did the entourage notice that Mahasu was addressing the residents of a hut just below the edge of the precipice, until now completely concealed from view. The drumming and trumpets began to sound once again, followed by another round of loud cries from the god's warriors accompanying his procession. The deafening noise had the desired impact. Women and men hurriedly emerged in a state of disarray from the cottage. They pleaded before the palanquin, confessing that they were indeed guilty of dumping garbage at the sacred spot, and committing themselves to cleanliness in future. The ruler had just drilled some civic sense into his subjects.

Once again we scrambled downhill with the procession, hoping that the divine king would now assume the designated space and rest for the night. But he had other plans. As the procession was about to enter the courtyard, the palanquin became still and the oracle bearing it stood stiff, as if turned into solid rock. The chief organisers of the procession came forward and pleaded, but to no avail. The god would not budge an inch. After a long hiatus, the agitated oracle indicated that someone had climbed up to the balcony of a house that fell in the immediate path of the procession. The offender had not just dared to climb to a position above the god but been disrespectful enough to keep his shoes on. A gauntlet had been thrown to his supremacy. The boy was pulled down from the balcony amid cursing and name-calling.

Forgiveness was begged for by the organisers and finally the procession moved.

While the procession had entered the village, the minister and a few elders of the village, exhausted from all the climbing, decided to sit on a platform facing the courtyard where the divine king would normally stay the night. They had been sunning themselves and chatting in the evening sun as the palanquin completed its anti-encroachment drives in the village and went into the courtyard. The fact that the village elders had assumed a position thigher than his own designated space infuriated Mahasu. Another round of apologies and remonstrations ensued, but the god was not ready to accept the affront as it involved his own chieftains, whom he thought should have had better sense. The palanquin turned back, to take another round of the village. Every time the palanquin moved, it was accompanied with loud drumming and fanfare. People folded their hands and touched their ears, a gesture indicating the begging of forgiveness. Finally, the officials understood what was offending the god, the platform was cleared of all squatters, and the palanquin entered the courtyard. There it rested for a few moments and then decided to proceed on another round of the village, as if wanting to inspect the space – only to turn back after a few minutes.

This time, too, everyone thought, the god would agree to settle in the village square, the communal space designated for the divine king. As the palanquin arrived, the bearers were jerked up the platform where the minister and the elders had been sitting and had offended their deity. "The *devta* would like to rest on the platform and not the square," announced the oracle. It was clear that the god would not settle for the ground while some of his subjects sat on a higher platform.

What this meant, to the consternation of all, was that Mahasu was now going to stay on the platform, a space that was an individual's property and not common to the village. The owner of the platform was quite rattled at the prospect of having to host the god and his entourage all by himself, and the social backlash this would lead to once the god had left. He had already fought with his kin across the courtyard. The village had invited the divine king to end the discord and this move from him could in fact intensify it. He could not afford more bad blood and stand accused of usurping the god from the village. If matters were not resolved soon, the man would stand completely isolated from the community.

Bystanders averred that the man was in trouble and Mahasu would certainly bring upon him his curse (*dos*), despite claiming his hospitality. No individual familial unit, whatever the resources at their command, could ever satisfy the divine king with their hospitality. And not being able to satisfy the divine king would invite his *dos* and make them the recipients of his curse. There were quite a few long faces in the family. The village too was on edge. They had organised the visit to foster unity, and their divine king seemed inclined to accept the individual most responsible for the discord as his host. As the palanquin was placed on the platform, a fresh round of possessions, arguments, and very serious negotiations ensued. The homeowner's wife was possessed and exorcised of the spirit that was leading to discord. As the sun dipped and dusk set in, it turned out that the deity was not singling out this one individual for his favour but was upset that public land had been encroached upon and his own officials had forgotten the protocol due to a divine king. He was merely claiming the captured public land, the newly built platform for the community, by wanting to settle on it for the night. The palanquin moved once again. The owner of the house with the platform had sworn to demolish the platform within three months, and he was also asked to remove the steps leading to the platform, another act of encroaching on public (or the *devta*'s) land that had led to disputes in the village.

The elders of the village now thought they had convinced Mahasu of their good intentions, and the palanquin moved decisively towards the compound where the divine king's tent is usually

Photo 3.4: Village elders negotiate with the Mahasu oracle on the platform.

pitched. It moved a few steps and then stopped dead in its tracks. The oracle seemed oddly agitated. The village elders had once again to rush to the palanquin to placate him. They touched their ears and bowed, hands folded before the palanquin and gesturing, as if begging forgiveness. However, no-one could figure out what had earned the divine king's ire. Finally, the oracle pointed to a signboard hanging from a balcony. The government's forest department, announcing a project, had fixed the signboard.

Initially, none could comprehend why the deity would take offence at this inconsequential object. At that moment the oracle raised his voice loud enough for all to hear, announcing,

Tum meri praja ho, yeh mera kshetra hai!

(You are my subjects, this is my territory!)

The divine king was clearly indicating that he had sovereign rights over the village and, if the people accepted him as the raja, he

Photo 3.5: Removing the government sign as the Mahasu palanquin waits.

would brook no competition from this trespassing entity called the Government of India. Mahasu, the god who extracted tribute from the Dilli Durbar, the court of the Mughal emperors of India, the god who forced British residents to capitulate and whom the state chief minister begged for grace, would not take this insult. He turned away again, threatening to return to his palace, much to the chagrin of the entire village. The signboard was removed, even as the palanquin toured the village once again. The elders rushed to the divine king with the promise that no government signboards would be permitted in the village henceforth.

The drums and trumpets sounded once again and the palanquin swiftly circled the courtyard twice, as if consecrating sacred space. Mahasu's tent was pitched in the middle of the courtyard, with spires (*kalash*) over it, indicating the sacredness and royalty of the abode. With one final flourish of drums and trumpets, the deity entered his tent to rest for the night. The feasting, praying, and making of offerings began, since everyone in the village had been fasting until then. Mahasu was finally satisfied and in repose, at least for the night, only to move on to another destination the next day.

Processions, like other rituals of the divine kings, help construct worlds of meaning for their subjects. Undoubtedly, they are reminiscent of the ritual of conquering the quarters in India, a ritual employed historically by certain groups of actors to retain hegemonic control over territory – in the recent past for proselytising missions and presently for political mobilisation. Mahasu processions, however, while serving to mark sovereign territory and mobilising subjects, also serve to reinforce a sense of solidarity within the larger realm and underline the specific identity of the local, socio-spatial units, in the overall federal structure of the Mahasu realm. Each place the procession halts in or that is added to the divine king's itinerary becomes a part of the deity's expanding network, where the worship of local gods is discontinued in favour of Mahasu. The logistics of the ritual, when looked at from the mundane aspect – of meeting the expenses for the ritual journeyings, the cost of moving and the customary honorarium to be paid to ritual functionaries – reveal how these networks operate expansively. While, in removing the signboard, Mahasu rejected the territorial sovereignty of the mundane state, claiming the divine king's right, it is in the logistical detail that the community's social involvement becomes evident.

At Hanol, Chalda Mahasu stays for the night as a guest of his brother and the expenses are met from the treasury of his brother, the Bautha Mahasu of Hanol. At other places he is a guest of the villagers, while in human kingdoms that owe allegiance to him – kingdoms like Tharonch and Dhadi Rao – he is a guest of the human kings. In Khashdhar the villagers alternately divide the expenses for Mahasu's one-year stay between themselves and the *dhyantis*, the out-married daughters. Most places visited by the deity are seats of *sadar sayanas* situated at the apex of local hierarchies of power. They control and manage the logistics of Mahasu tours, and through these tours they, as the local elite, reinforce each other's authority. By presiding over these mass festivals and fairs that mark the arrival of the divine king into their territory, and by publicly displaying their proximity to the power centre, they gain significant prestige and political leverage. By sharing expenses in a conventionally prescribed manner, the entire realm participates in this mass sacrifice of displaying allegiance.

For the ordinary Mahasu subject, these celebrations provide a sense of identity and belonging, an existential meaningfulness derived from the tutelary structure of which each individual is a part. The burden of economic support for these tours, both in cash and kind falls over them in the form of ritualised levies, taxes, and fines. The expenses are also met from the payments charged for ritualised service and voluntary offerings made to the deity. The host populations have to feed the large numbers of functionaries and officials accompanying the processions. Hosting the Mahasu procession is, therefore, an act of collective sacrifice.

Collective ritual journeys like the processions of Mahasu create sovereignty within the frame of what Inden (1990) describes as the "complex agency" of the deity and his collective institutions. What this effectively means is that though the divine kings may be non-human agents, they represent the collective will of their subjects. It is this collective will that is manifested in processional rituals. If the collective will were not to be manifested it would become difficult for the grand processions to happen. The Mahasu minister, discussing the subject of the divine kings turning sedentary, suggested that, if the divine kings were to stop touring, the reason for it would probably be the lack of willingness among the *bajgi* (drummers) to walk and play their instruments in the procession, or the Kolta (low-caste) men to act as porters. He was no doubt pointing to the state government's efforts towards empowering these traditionally suppressed castes by giving them benefits of education and job reservations. If government jobs took away the menials and raised their social status, this egalitarianism would lead to the snapping of a significant link in the collective will, weakening the power of the kingdom. Even though continuity in this aspect is based on the hegemony of the higher castes, and is being challenged by successive secular governments, the performance of temple and processional "duties" by all Mahasu subjects translates into the collective agency of the divine king. Society in the Mahasu realm has managed to retain this sense of duty towards the collective will, and this accounts for the extraordinary longevity of divine kingship.

Sax (2010: 90) has pointed out that the collective agency of divine kings is always distributed in "agentive networks". On similar lines, Galey (1991: 133) remarks that "territorial control finds, more often than not, its legitimacy in relation to sanctuaries and to units of the cult that define social space ritually." Mahasu processions ritually connect the central geographical node of this agentive network, the cult capital of Hanol, with the entire realm. Berti (2008) has pointed out that in the Western Himalaya territorial links are given priority over links of lineage, while Sax (2006b) points out that politico-religious relationships are inscribed in the landscape by means of ritual. In his study of Buddhism and polity in Thailand, Tambiah (1977: 112) characterised the field of power in the Indic kingdom as a "centrally oriented" polity rather than a territorially bounded one. Thus, through ritual journeying the deity shows himself to his subjects and renews his connection with soil and territory while stamping his supreme authority. In that sense, processions also become significant, for wherever they are granted hospitality, the regions are interpreted as territory belonging to the divine kings. In the Mahasu worldview there is no need for marking boundaries with fences and checkposts. This different conception of territory – as a centrally bounded but ever-expanding space – has enabled traditional sovereignty to coexist with the modern concept of territory as a space where the external borders must be marked.

The question remains whether, and for how long, modern governments can allow the coexistence of divine kingship with their new systems. The nation-state has made inroads and established a certain degree of political control even as the overarching ritual presence of the divine kings remains the fulcrum of social life. Galey (1989) suggested that in these mountains relationships between king and subject are even today embodied in practice, in every aspect of life. During my fieldwork I realised that despite tremendous change owing to factors such as roads, commercial apple monoculture, education, and tourism, life indeed revolves around a parallel indigenous idiom of rule by the divine kings, and modern governments have no option but to acknowledge them, even if grudgingly.

For long there has been the realisation that socio-political practices in the Mahasu realm are peculiar. The literature describing social life in the past is scant, and when available (Majumdar 1963; Parmar 1975; Munshi 1954 [reprint 1962] *et al.*) has focused on specific practices such as polyandry. To quote Sutherland (1998: xvi), the region is usually represented in "popular North Indian discourse as a remote place with a marginal society of fallen Hindus and promiscuous women, who, in addition to being polyandrous, also poison or bewitch the hearts of unsuspecting travellers." Stereotypes abound. Coupled with colonial narratives of widespread opium cultivation, head-hunting, human sacrifice, rituals of mass possession and procession, bride price, relaxed rules for divorce and widow remarriage, the region has long remained the "other", a subject of sociological curiosity. Seen from the perspective of the plains, the region is certainly peculiar. For instance, there is sufficient historical evidence to believe that the region was once home to communities of head-hunting Hindus who, until recently, were practising human sacrifice (Zoller 1993: 127). Even the landscape has not escaped tags of negativity. For instance, the River Tons, which joins the Yamuna, in complete contravention of the usual Hindu belief of rivers as holy, is commonly alluded to as Tamasa, the dark river, a British report from 1827 referring to it as the "hot-headed one". In Hindu texts *tamasa* is seen as representing inertia, darkness, and decay. At times in Vedic texts and folklore the river also finds mention as Karmanasha, metaphorically "the destroyer of merit".

In this "other" land of the dark river, the term Mahasu represents a geographical area as well as a distinct political formation, a divine kingship. When I commenced fieldwork, I imagined that

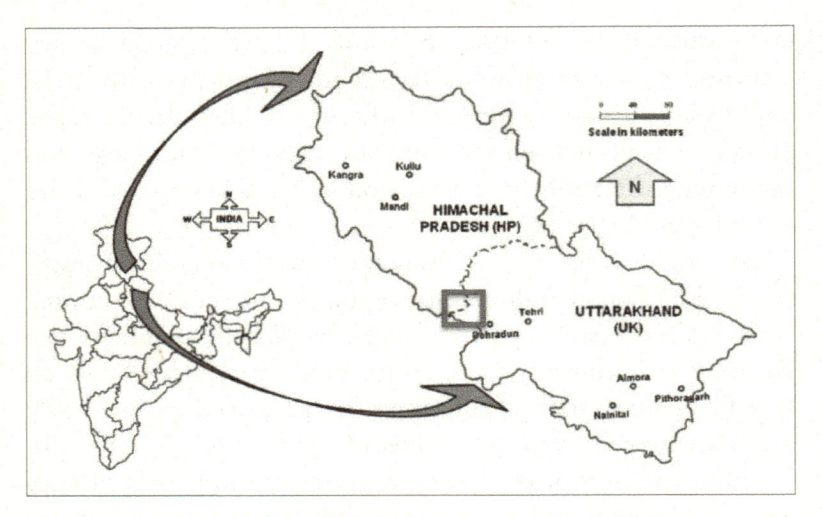

Fig. 3.1: The Mahasu kingdom (in the circle).

it was the Jaunsar-Bawar region that was Mahasu country. But as I delved deeper into Mahasu kingship, I realised that as a geographical entity the Mahasu realm extended well beyond Jaunsar and Bawar in District Dehra Dun to Fateh Parvat and Bangan in District Uttarkashi (both in Uttarakhand) and parts of districts Shimla, Sirmaur, Solan, and Kinnaur – all in Himachal Pradesh. In fact, until well after the end of colonial rule, before the reorganisation of districts in Himachal Pradesh in 1956, parts of these constituted a larger district referred to by the British administration simply as Mahasu (Thompson 1992). Politically, these regions formed the realm of the divine kings, the four Mahasu brothers, of whom Chalda is thought of as the youngest. While the district named Mahasu was partitioned into smaller units post-independence, the resilience of the divine kingship of Mahasu contrasts with most other regions of India, including the hills, where kingship has been subsumed into new political structures and is preserved more as a relic of the past.

The Mahasu realm, though straddling a large area, forms a culturally contiguous region, though some parts such as Dodra-Kwar remained virtually unexplored until recently. The economy here is still largely agro-pastoral. The region has been known for its cultural distinctiveness and independence, never succumbing to efforts by neighbouring kingdoms of Sirmaur, Rampur Bashahar, Jubbal, and Garhwal (all ruled by human kings), to incorporate it. Even the British, after acquiring the region from the Nepal armies, did not establish their normally elaborate machinery for governance here, owing among other reasons to the toughness of the terrain and the volatility of the residents. Until today, barring a few pockets, the region does not have a formal civilian police system.

The cultural and political isolation of the region, however, did not result in the absence of an indigenous political structure. On the contrary, the Mahasu realm and the areas around it are divided into several small territorial units, with local *devtas*, as regional rulers owing allegiance to Mahasu. Their subjects include not only Rajput warrior groups and high-caste priests but also musician-genealogists, called *deval* in Hanol, known in Uttarakhand as *bajgi*, i.e. drummer-bards. A special name is assigned to the musician caste in Hanol because they have the privilege of playing for the divine king at the cult centre. These musicians play the god's *naubat*, a form of honorific drumming, on a regular basis. The god's watchmen and messengers, as also the storekeepers (*bhandaris*) live in the village. The lowest local caste, the *koli* and *kolta*, provide firewood, and undertake other forms of menial labour. All these castes, along with the god's high-caste priests, live in his temple town, giving it a complex local caste organisation.

The practice of ritual, in terms of Mahasu processions and temple congregations, questions distinctions between politics, economics, and ritual. Empirical evidence indicates that Mahasu processions incorporate all these dimensions. In fact, politico-religious relationships are inscribed regularly into the landscape of the Mahasu realm through them. For instance, the several processions crossing the rivers and other geographical, social, and political boundaries in the countryside result in periodic shifts of power from one region to another. When Mahasu is journeying through *pansi*, the collective will of the community on the other bank, the *sathi*, pulls the divine king towards their part of the realm. I have observed delegation after delegation visit Mahasu at the divine king's various halts with requests that since the divine king's tenure in *pansi* was over, the *devta* must return. On the day of the river crossing, when Mahasu finally acceded to the request, the mood on one side of the river was sombre for their divine king was going away for twelve years or longer. Meanwhile the *sathi* were elated as the procession grants proximity to the power centre and proximity to the power centre translates into power. In Mahasu journeys and their attendant rituals the archaic and the contemporary, the political and the religious, the pre-human kingly state and the modern-secular commingle in several ways to create a shifting territoriality which has simultaneously resulted in the survival of a stable sovereignty.

From the general theory of South Asian society advocated by Dumont (1970 [1966]), where political and economic power are separated from the ideological sphere of religion, to the central–peripheral models proposed by the likes of Dirks (2002) and the significance of prestations proposed by Raheja (1988), debates on kingship in India have pointed towards certain characteristics or "essences" of South Asian social organisation. Dirks (1987), for instance, pointed out how comparative sociology has treated the Indian state as epiphenomenal. By pointing out that the political domain in India was not encompassed by a religious domain until the arrival of the British, he has shown that the "crown was not as hollow as it was made out to be" (Ibid.: 3). Stable territorial formations like the Mahasu kingdom represent a regional idiom of kingship that, in the absence of a human entity at the helm, eliminated dependence on successors to maintain continuity and managed to escape the covetousness of successive invaders. The study of such forms of kingship thus throws light on the function of ritual in maintaining political stability, the relation of ruler to the soil, and diverse means of achieving legitimacy.

No doubt, in present times, there is radical change, with democracy at times aligning groups along the lines of political parties rather than clan and lineage groups. People also increasingly seek medical help in hospitals rather than refer illness to their divine king. Courts have overtaken the divine king's juridical authority. With this happening and the secular state empowering lower castes like the Mahasu drummer-bards – ensuring that they break from tradition and no longer remain subordinated to the upper castes for sustenance – one might expect that the ritual polity would disappear. But it does not. One would expect that apple wealth and its consequent materialism would dilute people's loyalties and dissuade them from "outdated" ritual into adopting ways of living that are more secular and mainstream. Yet this too has not happened.

The discourse of globalisation has postulated an emerging world that is borderless, where identity is no longer conceived in terms of outdated models of nation, kinship, or lineage. Even though with the rise in populism and right wing politics the postulation that global flows will subsume such sovereignties may have become outdated, most administrative policy is driven by this very thought process. However, even as new borders emerge in South Asia, people attach even greater significance to historic and ritually demarcated identities. Traditional, centrally oriented territories have not become redundant in the new political dispensations. They may be represented neither in atlases nor in land records or administrative papers, but the territorial demarcations are retained in the minds of the divine king's subjects and are performed and embodied during the ritual journeys of the divine king.

4

Stranger Kings

Social groups often find themselves at the intersections of tradition and modernity. Among traditional societies, change is inherent within continuity and all societies must deal with it. However, when certain ways of living become extinct, a sense of loss is inevitable. As someone who has been visiting Mahasu country for long, I was distressed at times with the attrition of tradition, attributed usually to the inroads of mass media and state intervention in community rituals. During one village festival, I observed the milling crowds from a vantage point and pointed out to a local youngster accompanying me how quickly the headscarves (*datoo*) and the long skirts (*ghaghra*) – apparel commonly worn by the women of Jaunsar until a few years ago – were disappearing as the clothing of not just daily life but also of festive occasions, giving way to the *salwar-kameez*, and to jeans worn increasingly in imitation of screen stars. His response was enlightening: he believed that while educated people from the cities changed their sartorial preferences at the drop of a hat, they wanted to preserve village societies as museum exhibits. While these words point to his discomfort at being observed and written about, they also point to the pervasiveness of change. While social transformation is a continuum, present global flows have quickened its pace. Change being undeniable, it would be incorrect to assume that Jaunsari society remained a relic of the past until the arrival of colonialism. In fact, the danger of projecting the Jaunsari and other indigenous groups as isolated and stagnant before the arrival of the West is all too evident.

Like modern global flows, Mahasu rule perhaps emerged as a result of transformative flows. Like most indigenous social groups, Jaunsari society relied on orality. Textual evidence showing the changes within it is virtually non-existent. Answers therefore have to be searched in folklore. The point at which regional folklore begins to diverge from traditions in the neighbourhood offers some clues on how these transformations worked in the historic and mythic past. Could Mahasu – arriving, according to folklore, from Kullu-Kashmir – also have been an agent of transformation?

The origin myth of the divine kings, narrated to me by the octogenarian drummer-bard of Mahasu Madan Das (who lives near the temple of Maindrath, dedicated to the mother of the Mahasus, Deoladi, as well as the eldest of the divine kings, Bashik Mahasu), clearly projects the divine kings as harbingers of profound social

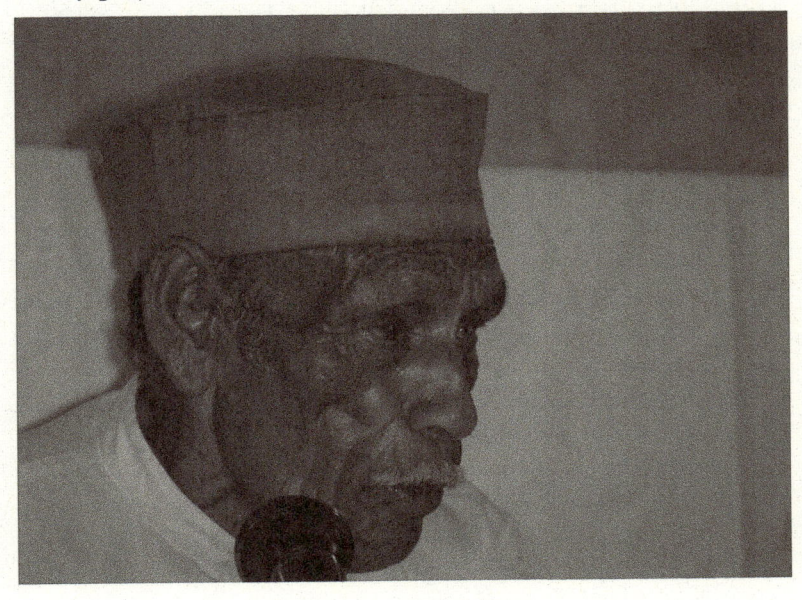

Photo 4.1: Madan Das.

change. The Maindrath temple is located downstream from Hanol, by the Tons, because it was at Maindrath that the Mahasu siblings are said to have first appeared. After narrating the Mahasu lore in 2010, Madan Das was overcome by a debilitating illness that left him demented. His son, however, continues the family tradition and performs ritual duties at the temple of Bashik Mahasu.

This myth, in its own way, drives home the point of how Mahasu's emergence from the soil, through agrarian ritual practice, was a gradual shift from a nomadic pastoralist existence, clearly establishing the divine king's consubstantial ties with the soil of the mountains. The myth also establishes clear links with the gods of the Hindu pantheon, marking a shift from the localised itinerant social structure to assimilation into the larger pan-Indian discourse.

Madan Das' recitation of the origin myth, as imbibed from his father Sant Ram, and passed on through generations as a caste and family legacy, begins by begging forgiveness from the divine king and his audience, for errors that might inadvertently creep into the narration of this unending saga:

Jai Chaar Maasu Devayah Namah!

(Victory to the Four Mahasu Brothers!)

> Doubtless, the *maya* or mysteries of Mahasu cannot be understood by humans, but the perpetual truth stands that even today when in times of trouble, as and when we invite and meditate upon the gods, and beg before them, they pardon our errors, alleviate our fears.

Having left behind Kashmir, they walked, the four brothers Mahasu
Came to the *thaan* in Maindrath,
Blessed is the Huna Brahman who brought you here.
You arrived at the Maindrath *thaan* and killed the demon,
Having slain the demon, you gave us a new lease of life.
Huna Bhaat, priests, *ranas* (warriors), *vazir* (minister), accompanied you,

You, the kings, left Maindrath and came to establish yourselves at Hanol.
With your trickery and wrestling skills, you defeated Vishnu,
You established your throne and kingdom on the banks of the dark river.
Four brothers Mahasu and the *birs*
Divided the kingdom amongst yourselves,
Amongst yourselves you chose rights and authority.
Minister, priest, constable, drummer, all serve you,
Give us prosperity, O! Mahasu *Deva*.
Whoever sings the invocation to the four brothers Mahasu,
Through body and mind, in life finds great happiness forever.
Victory to Mahasu Devta, *swami*, victory be to Mahasu Deva,
With hands folded in respect and a bowed head, we serve thee . . .

The colonial archive took over the Mahasu origin myth in 1815, after the Anglo-Gurkha War. Several British authors have reproduced it in their writings. Rose (1919), Emerson (1911), and Ibbetson (1919) report slight variations on the myth from the version recited by the drummer-bards from Maindrath. Walton's *Gazetteer* (1911) and the *Memoir of Dehra* by G.R.C. Williams (1874), however, record a myth that is very similar to the version presented here. Walton and Williams probably recorded the myth in *sathi* while Emerson, Ibbetson, and Rose recorded it on the other bank in *pansi*. The variations occur owing (among other factors) mainly to the varying locations of the drummer-bards in this vast mountainous landscape, and also to the fact that various narratives focus on different siblings as rulers. While the drummer-bards, in keeping with the oral traditions, add or take away from the myth as times progress, the written word of colonial authors has been frozen in time.

Mahasu lore projects the vast landscape between the two major West Himalayan rivers – the Yamuna and the Sutlej – as well as the waters, gorges, streams, and the snowbound loftiness beyond, as a battleground. Mahasu's arrival, a feat comparable to

Lalitaditya's conquest of the quarters, also encapsulates the fabled land of Kullu-Kashmir, which could either be the geographical area of Kashmir as we know it today or, alternatively, even a mythical representation of the other-world, a heaven where the gardens are tended by the *mali* (lit. gardeners) even as the divine king's oracles are addressed as such.

The origin of the name Maindrath (*main*, lit. spattering; *drath*, lit. blood) infers a bespattering with blood by the demons after the Pandavas departed from the region (in their onward journey towards the heavens, atoning for the sins committed in battle). The Van Parva, i.e. the eleventh chapter of the Mahabharata, refers to Bhima's duel with the demon Kirmir in the forest of Kamyak. Even as the Mahabharata credits Bhima with the dismemberment of Kirmir, Mahasu subjects insist it was their divine king that rid the region of Kirmir's terror. This dismembering, as against killing or death as an end, is a significant part of the Mahasu cosmology, for evil once disjointed displays the ability to regroup and resurface, as with the battle between Kali and Raktabija. To ensure that evil is kept at bay, the divine kings and their deputies, the *birs*, must maintain a vigil, traversing the length and breadth of the kingdom. The Mahasu origin myth takes us back to the period when demons ruled and the Brahman caste invited the divine kings to rid them of their terror.

Oral traditions from Mahasu country tell us that Shiva, while practising penance in the mountains, was constantly harassed by the demon Karmasur, until, one day, much mortified, he decided to self-dismember. He hacked away at his limbs and turned himself into a stone lingam, reasoning that no demon would pester a rock. While Shiva's penance continued, out of the four dismembered limbs of Shiva emerged the four *birs*, the demigods that assist Mahasu. They were Kapla, Kailu, Kailath, and Serhkuriya. All were valiant warriors and, with swords drawn, demanded of Shiva the reasons for their creation. Shiva tasked them to chase the demon Karmasur away from the earth. They chased the demon into the upper reaches. Along the ridge that divides Jaunsar and Bawar, at Bhujkoti (*bhuja*, lit. arms), they chopped off the demon's arms, while he was divested of his head at Mundali (*mund*, lit. head). At Kharamba (*kharaum*, lit. feet), the highest peak in the realm, his feet were chopped off by one of the *birs* during a hot pursuit. Parts of the demon's body, however, escaped to the higher reaches, from where his blood and tears flowed down the mountains into the Karmanasha, the River Tons.

This battle between demon and divine continued unabated. Having vanquished the demon, the *birs* returned to Shiva, seeking further instructions. They were asked to go and rest in the depths of a lake in Kashmir. They turned into snakes and settled in the netherworld. After having meditated in peace, Shiva set out in search of his consort, Parvati. Meanwhile, Parvati had entered a cave to practise penance, and, creating a *bir* (warrior) out of her own divine powers – from her bodily discharge (*mael*, lit. dirt) – had instructed him to guard the entrance against any intruder. Shiva arrived at the cave, looking for his beloved, but was stopped at the mouth by the earnest protector. Furious that the lord of the three worlds was not being permitted to meet his own consort, he decapitated the insolent guard after a protracted battle. Eventually, when Shiva did meet Parvati, she was surprised that Shiva had been allowed access to her chambers despite her instructions. Perhaps the protector had sensed that it was his own father at the entrance. She was, however, inconsolable when she came to know that her protector lay beheaded at the entrance.

Parvati remonstrated with Shiva that he would have to bring their son back to life. Shiva, who had himself caused the trouble, was advised that the only means of rejuvenating the young man was to replace his head with that of a suckling infant found lying beside the mother. Shiva travelled far and finally came across an infant elephant calf suckling its mother. He divested the calf of its head and brought it back to attach it to the *bir*'s lifeless torso. The *bir* was rejuvenated and called out to Shiva, addressing him as father. The anomaly of single birthing had now been corrected with Shiva bringing his own offspring back from the dead. This *bir* was called Ganesha, who was readily accepted as a son by Shiva and Parvati, and, given the ordeal he had undergone, was the most pampered of all their progeny. The case of Ganesha, however, suggested that the sin of causing grief to a mother had been committed. This had to be corrected through sacrifice.

Soon, Parvati wanted Shiva to see how the four *birs* – formed out of his limbs and sent away to the lake in Kashmir – were faring. But before this could happen, a ritual *puja* with the entire family in attendance had to be performed. The Sun God, the Moon God, the tempestuous Kartikeya and the pampered Ganesha, sons of Shiva, were invited to join in. Here, a dispute arose over the right of first worship (*agrim puja*) to be offered to the parents during the ritual. While Ganesha wanted to make the first offering, the Sun, the Moon, and Kartikeya demanded that they were older and hence the right to first worship was theirs. Shiva suggested a contest. "I will go into a meditative trance, meanwhile, all my sons must proceed on pilgrimage to the four *dhams*, the sacred places associated with me. The one who returns first automatically reserves for himself the right to first worship."

The Sun, Moon, and Kartikeya, got on to their swift mounts and were quick off the block. Ganesha, the pot-bellied brat, began to weep bitterly over his inability to keep pace. Moreover, his mount, being a little mouse, was, given Ganesha's bulky frame, no match for Kartikeya's swift peacock. Parvati was moved by Ganesha's plight and suggested that only orphans needed to embark on a pilgrimage. "While your parents are living, your home is the most significant pilgrimage. Circumambulate your parents seven times and that is as good a pilgrimage as any," and, suggesting this, she went on to sit next to Shiva. Ganesha promptly circumambulated them seven times, made the first offerings, and squatted for the rites of worship. Meanwhile, as the elder brothers reached the four pilgrim centres situated in the four corners of the subcontinent, they, in a state of complete exhaustion, were astounded that someone had already anointed Shiva's lingam, the space around bearing rodent footprints.

Upon their return their suspicions were confirmed when they found Ganesha winding up the rites of the first offering. While the others, resigned to their fate, busied themselves in ritual worship, the mercurial Kartikeya demanded an explanation for the foul play that had forced him to forfeit his right as the eldest and fastest. When learning how Ganesha had trumped them, he was overcome with indignation and could not reconcile himself to his mother favouring her elephant-headed son.

Ganesha and Kartikeya are always shown as being at odds with each other. Kartikeya has a "true" birth, he is a warrior, philanthropist, brave and other-oriented, and of course short tempered. On the other hand, Ganesha is born out of Parvati's bodily discharge, usually calm, wise, reflective, and sentient (*chetan purus*) and a little self-centred, also given to gluttony. Ganesha was finally given the responsibility of *ganadhish* (master of Shiva's warriors), another right denied to his eldest brother.

"What good is this mother to me?" Kartikeya demanded of Shiva, in a fit of rage.

"You owe your birth, your limbs and body to her," Shiva replied, acutely aware of the consequences of the statement.

"Then I must get rid of this flesh and these limbs," Kartikeya exclaimed, and proceeded with self-dismemberment. He hacked away at his own flesh and limbs, gathered the pieces into four heaps, and tossed them into the waters at a spot where the four Nagas – the serpents Ullal, Bimal, Basuki, and Bhaduvana – lived in the netherworld. They consumed Kartikeya's flesh and out of their bellies emerged the four battle-ready Naga princes, collectively known as the Chaar Maasu (the four Mahasu) – individually, Bashik, Bautha, Pabasik, and Chalda. From the drops of his blood sprang the subordinate *birs*, the warrior demigods and Mahasu deputies Rangbir, Jangbir, Udaibir, Baitalbir, Angarubir, Chararbir, and Kaluabir. Out of other inferior substances emerged the deities of the lower castes, Kilbalu, Tilbalu, Jwar, and Banar. Other divinities – Narsingh, Bhairon, and Pokhu of Naitwar, Kali, Durga and the four Kalyani Devis, who are subordinate to Mahasu but superior to the deputies – also emerged. On Shiva's orders the entire pantheon went to live with the *birs* who had liquidated Karmasur, now resting in the lake in Kashmir.

Against the backdrop of this narrative emerges the tale of Una Bhaat, a Brahman from Maindrath who travelled to Kashmir to invite the Mahasu siblings, whose arrival in turn inaugurated a new era of political rule through violent acts of intrusion and overthrow. The Mahasus were entreated upon to come and defeat the incumbent demon king, Kirmir Danu. They gained power by consuming his flesh, and therefore, according to the drummer-bard Madan Das, acquired the name Maasu (*maas*, lit. flesh), i.e. those that ingested the flesh of the demon.

Una travelled through eighteen states ruled by the *thakur* Rajputs (*etharah thakurai*) and then the twenty-two estates of the crown princes (*tikke*), with incidents at places named Raithik, Majog, Hatkoti, Kinnaur, Kullu, Nachini Guara (a place where the Brahman women dance), and Kanti Karaunti, before his arrival in Kashmir. Una was given the details of the route by an old sightless Brahman, Burha Pudiyan, who had travelled to the fabled Kashmir once. But why did Una Bhaat want to invite a stranger and make him king?

Una Bhaat headed a large clan. In course of time an ogre named Kirmir Danu (*danav*, lit. demon) appeared at Kalsi, on the banks of the Tons. He terrorised the Bhaat clan, making the hapless villagers a target of his cannibalistic cravings. In due course things came to such a pass that only Una, his wife, three sons, and a daughter survived Kirmir's ravenous appetite. They were forced to take flight into the dense forests upstream of the Tons. It was during his wanderings that Una was filled with an intense desire to seek retribution for the annihilation of his clan and rescue the survivors.

Mahasu appeared in his dreams, expressing satisfaction at Una's resolve to save what was left of his clan. Some accounts (e.g. Ibbetson 1883) also talk of Una's wife Kailavati dreaming of Mahasu and nagging Una into going out in search of the divine king. Una reached the temple at Hatkoti, from where he was directed by Burha Pudiyan to the Mahasu abode in Kashmir, where the divine kings could be requested to come. Burha Pudiyan made it known that no power other than Mahasu had enough divine equipment to overcome the evil strength of Kirmir. Motivated by the prospect of his clan's survival, Una set off northwards for Kashmir and arrived at the portals of Mahasu's royal residence. The gatekeepers of the Mahasu abode were in deep sleep when he arrived. They had kept with them two heavy maces as weapons. Una knew that he would not be able to secure an audience with those he was seeking unless he had the gatekeepers' favour.

He tried to lift one of the maces and the commotion caused by the exertion woke the officials. One gatekeeper demanded to see the audacious one who had dared disturb his repose. "Maternal Uncle [*mama*], I am your nephew," cried Una. The gatekeeper was disarmed by this manner of address – quite common as a term of endearment in Mahasu country for the elderly. "You cannot be my nephew, but since you describe yourself so, tell me what brings you here?" Una narrated his tale of woe, including details of his adventures during his long trip from Jaunsar-Bawar to faraway Kashmir. He spoke of his dream and resultant devotion to Mahasu. The gatekeeper gave a fistful of rice and *masur dal* (red lentils) to Una. He asked him to proceed to the Ghagati Forest. Una was warned that he would encounter a severe storm. Instructions were given that there he should scatter the lentil grains in the wind. This would make the storms abate and get him closer to exacting his revenge.

As Una reached Kanaital, a mythical lake deep in the forests, he plucked out locks of his hair and threw them into the lake. He also spat into it. The locks immediately turned into a snake and the spittle transformed into cowrie (mollusc) shells. Una knew that he was in the strange and magical land of Kashmir. In course of time there emerged from the lake two beacons of magical power, strong and considerate – Mahasu and Kelubil. Observing them from a distance, Una could make out that they had visiting ties and resolved to visit Kelubil's abode. Among the Jaunsari, visiting, and the offering and receiving of hospitality, are of great significance. The ones offered hospitality have a right over those offering it, and it is generally incumbent upon the host to honour the word of the guest.

Una concealed himself in Kelubil's home and awaited the opportune moment. He had heard that the Mahasus visited often, and they indeed arrived in their palanquins late at night. Chalda Mahasu, an exponent of magical esoteric knowledge, kept complaining that he could sense a Brahman's presence. As the *damaru* (two-sided hand-held drum with strings and beads attached; Shiva's drum) beats at dawn announced that the Mahasu brothers were ready to resume their onward journey, Una came out of hiding. Amongst the Mahasu brothers, the first to emerge was Basik, carrying the cloaks of his siblings. Then came Pabasik and Bautha, followed by Chalda. The gods were taken aback at the sight of this strange human. Una took no time narrating his tale of woe. He added that he had followed the instructions of Mahasu's strong gatekeeper to track them down and was now touching their feet, begging their help in rescuing whatever remained of his clan. His perseverance turned the tide in his favour, as the Mahasus, true to their Rajput dharma, could not refuse a Brahman's request.

The Mahasu siblings instructed Una to return to his village, assuring him that they would, at a suitable time, arrive to rid his clan of the evil Kirmir. Chalda Mahasu gave him another fistful of rice, a magical container, and a contingent of soldiers for protection. He advised Una that if ever his clan were starving, one grain of the rice would be enough to satiate the entire earth and the netherworld. The miracle rice would also serve to reassure his clan and forewarn his enemies of Mahasu's imminent arrival. A boon was also granted that if he tossed a few grains of rice as an offering in the Tons from Maindrath village, Kirmir would not be able to harm his clan, while the magical rice would impress upon all that Una and his clan were under the protection of the divine siblings.

Una went on his way at first light of day. He followed the divine instructions. However, to test whether he had indeed been imbued with divine grace, he chose a barren field that had never been ploughed. A prepubescent boy who had never touched a plough was asked to plough the field, and shortly they observed that the wooden plough had turned into gold. Five furrows seemed to have been dug in the earth from where the idols began to emerge. It was evident to the clan that the four idols represented the brothers Mahasu, and that the fifth was an image of Mother Deoladi. There was jubilation all around, and once the excitement subsided they realised that the saviours had arrived a day in advance. The idols had appeared prematurely owing to Una Bhaat's impatience, and because of that each except Chalda appeared to have a defect.

In the Indian context there are few precedents for the worship of idols with imperfections (*khandit murti*). There is also no room for ritual failure in divine matters. Inauspiciousness, and the failure of ritual, can lead to dire consequences, but for the Mahasus the deformities helped define their roles. It is believed that the Mahasu idols, other than those of Chalda Mahasu, are imperfect, even though very few have seen them. In the case of the Mahasu idols, until today no-one is permitted a glimpse and they remain concealed in dark chambers in temples. For subjects, the power of their divine kings is visually represented through palanquins rather than their human images. The deformities in the images were probably associated with magical powers, also defining the hexis of embodiment for the oracles who "become" them in a state of possession. For instance, following Bourdieu (1987), an oracle possessed by Bautha or the seated Mahasu, if lame, would be more authentic and add to the confidence of those seeking divine help. The physical inabilities also helped assign specific roles to the divine kings in a constellation of travelling and established deities. For instance, Bautha, because he was lame, occupied the axis of the cult, perpetually stationed at the cult centre of Hanol, while those less deformed had limited touring areas to attend to. It was left to the physically perfect Chalda Mahasu to tour the entire realm and lead expansionist campaigns.

At Maindrath it was discovered that Basik Mahasu appeared first in one of the furrows. The god's ears were injured, rendering him deaf. Despite this, upon his arrival he was hailed as a king and presented with a parasol (*chatra*). Pabasik, too, was not in perfect health, injured in the eyes; and Bautha was lame. The lame god was consecrated in a shrine on the banks of the Tons; the others were given smaller territories to proceed through, owing to their disabilities. Chalda, the master of the esoteric magical knowledge of exorcism and possession, realised that inauspiciousness had occurred over their arrival and did not stake his claim over any territory, preferring to remain itinerant. Thus, he was given the responsibility of constantly proceeding through the entire realm. The last to appear was the mother to the Mahasus, Deoladi, who was consecrated in the fields of Maindrath, where the gods had appeared. It is interesting to note that in this entire narrative, Mahasu paternity is of no consequence. The issue is perhaps left open ended in order to retain the vital link to Shiva.

Una, the Brahman, now devoted himself completely to Mahasu. The presence of the divine kings had frightened the evil Kirmir. Una knew that the moving Chalda would be the most powerful deity, proceeding at will and conquering new territories, and assigned to his eldest son the responsibility of offering rituals to him. He was given the caste name of *deopujya* (priest). The second born was asked to strike the temple gongs and bells while also looking after the temple affairs, and it was decreed that his clan members would be known as Rajputs. The third-born was encouraged to take up drumming and designated the caste name of *bajgi*. The *bajgis* would be known by the caste name *das*, and though not permitted to cross the temple threshold to enter the sanctum, would perpetuate the god's mythical kingship through recitation of his ballads and ritual drumming. Most castes in the realm, Mahasu subjects (and especially the *bajgis*) believe, have emanated from the same social group. Yet, caste roles leading to occupational difference have acquired rigidity, the severity of the system comparable with, if not stronger than, the caste system in other parts of India.

Tons was designated the middle point in the waters with the ritualistic sprinkling of rice given by Mahasus. A simplified Hindu caste hierarchy, oriented towards serving the deity, was introduced and each god's territorial responsibilities fixed. Chalda Mahasu, the one who walked, would cross the river every twelve years to mark and protect his territories from incursions and make new conquests. An oracular form of polity was established, with processions reproducing remembered landscapes, and power distributed amongst the four divine kings, their *birs*, and subordinate gods.

The Mahasu divinities emerged from the soil with the act of ploughing on virgin land, carried out by a prepubescent boy. They gradually established themselves, driving out not just the demons, but also deities like Vishnu from his temple – when both divinities were locked in a contest to turn all the grains of sand on the banks of the Tons into gold. Vishnu lost, proving incapable of employing his magic to turn sand into gold. Such ritual contests between divinities appear frequently in folklore and help establish the strength of each claimant's consubstantiality with the soil. In this incident too, Mahasu's victory does not simply indicate his relationship with the soil of the realm he covets, but also lends a distinctly agrarian character to the realm. It firmly establishes on the power pinnacle a set of "stranger kings" who follow a Rajput *dharma* and who acquire legitimacy through an invitation from the Brahman and the other caste groups that agree to serve the masters. This firmly entrenched caste hierarchy has contributed considerably to the perpetuation of the Mahasu polity.

Folklore further suggests that, as in neighbouring Garhwal, the Mahabharata tradition may have been the mainstream tradition here as well, until the Mahasu divine kings began to dominate. When and how this happened can only be a matter of conjecture and has been reflected upon extensively by historians through the claims of the Khash people and their kindred *jatis*, who entered northern India along the Hindu Kush around the seventh century BCE and set up interactions with the original inhabitants, the Kiratas. Whatever the migratory patterns, folklore, especially the Mahabharata recited in the temple at Hanol, quite compellingly points towards a Mahasu takeover.

The Mahabharata is rooted in several Indic cultures and the people of Garhwal, living in regions bordering Mahasu country, identify with it strongly. Zoller (1996) has hinted that in the past the Jaunsaris may have shifted from a Pandava-dominated culture to a Mahasu-centric tradition. Despite this change, the epic has not completely disappeared from Jaunsar and lives on in ritual practice and place associations. An analysis of the epic, as internalised by Mahasu subjects, yields an insight into whether there has been a paradigmatic transformation or the change we see is superficial, contained within the matrix of an underlying social continuity.

Over the centuries, the Mahabharata has been retold multiple times in temple courtyards, village fairs, conferences, and texts. The languages used have been multiple, as have been the forms and the interpretations by orators, singers, painters, dancers, wandering minstrels, and scholars. As the epic spread from the north of India to Nepal and then towards Indonesia, old narratives yielded place to new ones and characters were added to the main plot. For instance, Arjuna's son Iravan, also commonly referred to as Aravan, worshipped by the transgender Alis or Aravanis of Tamil Nadu, emerged as one of the characters. Bhima's immortal and valiant grandson Barbareek, worshipped in Rajasthan as Khatu Shyamji, who was tricked by Krishna into surrendering his head (for he had pledged to fight for the losing side in the battlefield of

Kurukshetra), is another representation more popular even than Krishna in these parts. In the Mahabharata of Bengal the story of Draupadi, who led an army of women and routed the Kauravas after Abhimanyu was slain, is one that emerged. The *theyyam* performers of Kerala sing of how the Kauravas compelled a sorcerer to perform occult rites against the Pandavas, and how the sorcerer's wife reversed this. In contemporary times, too, the epic continues to cast its spell with society attempting to look for rational responses to its own moral ambiguities within the epic. The Mahabharata, thus, presents itself as a powerfully diverse narrative employed to comment on myriad local issues, from feminism to caste to war to politics.

Towards the east of the Mahasu realm lies Garhwal, a kingdom that continued to claim territories within Jaunsar and Bangan despite people owing allegiance to their own *devtas*, Mahasu being the most dominant of them. Throughout history, the Garhwal kings coveted the regions of Bangan and Jaunsar. Garhwal is essentially Pandava country in terms of its mythical and folk tradition. Possession rituals are common to both regions. While in Garhwal the spirits of the five Pandava brothers and their wife Draupadi often possess residents, in the Mahasu realm the possessions are often those of Mahasu (in the oracles), the divine king's deputies, evil spirits, and demigods. We have seen earlier how groups in the Mahasu realm differentiate themselves into Mahabharata moieties, the *pansi* and the *sathi*. It is notable that despite this, in the area of Mahasu's influence the Pandavas and the Kauravas are neither worshipped nor appear in possession. However, their association with the landscape is still strong.

According to a folk tale narrated by Mohanlal Semwal (Mahasu priest and secretary of the Hanol temple committee), after the Mahabharata war, when the victorious but dejected Pandavas, having committed the sin of fratricide, were walking towards the heavens via the Swargarohini Peak, they passed through Mahasu country, close to the village of Maindrath, through a place named Ragugad.

A demon who lived there wished to kill and eat them. They negotiated with the demon and it was decided that Bhima would stay either to combat the demon or satiate his appetite while the others continued on their final journey. Bhima asked the family to be patient for a week, saying that by the end of it he would either join them after vanquishing the demon, or they could grieve over his death. The others continued their journey, and, on the bank of the Tons, opposite Shatangdhar, they inscribed a message (which can still be seen as a rock inscription, even though it is not deciphered) for their strong brother, Bhima, whom they had left behind. They walked through Mandagad, and despairing that Bhima had not returned even though eight days had elapsed, they cooked rice as a funerary ritual of remembrance. The place is named after *mand* (rice water), the bank where the river waters begin to acquire a white hue, like starchy rice water. Even as the family were grieving for Bhima, he reappeared, victorious. Having vanquished the demons, the Pandavas could lay claim over the region. How then, did Mahasu rule come about?

Zoller (ibid.) has pointed out that the Mahasu kings, though presenting themselves as successors to the Pandavas, do not tolerate the cult of the Pandavas in their territory. They would rather have their own origin myth, genealogies, and folklore recited within the kingdom, these granting legitimacy to their rule. It is, in fact, these ritual recitations that help engender territory and kingdom, and keep them central.

The most significant among the Mahabharata recitations within the Mahasu realm is an oral epos called the Panduan. It is recited annually in the month of February by the drummer-bards during the Dhaknach festival, on the second of the five festive days. Compared to the narrative Mahabharata of the plains or the version popular in neighbouring Garhwal, the Panduan shows pronounced mythic characteristics and has several points of departure. The prime audience of the recitation are Rajputs. Since the Brahmans, here and in other areas of the Western Himalaya, do not use Sanskrit texts, and merely recite the Puranas, the epic is sparingly used within Brahmanical circles.

The Dhaknach is itself part of a longer cycle of festivals. Over its duration the bards and their womenfolk sing songs for Mahasu, for audiences assembled in the temple courtyard. They also perform dances and short theatrical episodes. All of these are tied together in a manner of depicting "the world" of the Jaunsari in one single recitation. They start on the first day with songs about the creation of the universe and finish on the last day to mock their neighbouring communities. The god-king Narayan, also sometimes referred to as Vishnu, emerges as a crucial and devious character. The creation myth of the god is described in a song sung on the first day of the festival. Even though there are several differences, the connection between the Panduan and the Mahabharata is visible in the intermingling of Mahabharata episodes with the myth of Mahasu, including the killing of other demons by the Pandavas and Kirmir by the Mahasus and their deputies.

This intermixing of two myths helps to show the systematic correlation of different oral traditions that account for change within a continuum. But these "inner" connections do not necessarily have a hierarchical relationship to the mainstream tradition. Instead, they have a synchronic relationship to other regional traditions of the area. Thus, the identity and the significance of one's own oral tradition is inbuilt in relation to other traditions of the region nextdoor and not either in contrast to, or in close association with, the "mainstream tradition". This inclination to connect to regional tradition is characteristic of many *devtas* in the Central and Western Himalayas (Vidal 1988: 51–4). Therefore it is important for the gods to draw clear borders with other gods, not by means of fences or outposts but by means of oral traditions and ritual practice.

The oral traditions of the region, therefore, are not a homogenous cluster of sub-traditions. After the festive times of the Dhaknach, the same bards are found singing songs from the Garhwal or Bangan Mahabharata, where the content is quite distinct from the Panduan, clearly reversing the traits of many of the epic's characters. Since these songs feature characters and episodes that are still found in the mainstream Mahabharata, one can correlate the "little" and the "mainstream" traditions. Since, according to Zoller (ibid.), those who recite and the audience do not consider these contradictions disconcerting, they cannot be seen as an anonymous influence from the "outside", nor can they be seen as attempts at staging disputes among antagonistic positions. In the Panduan, at many places, there is a conscious and ironic effort to relate to the mainstream tradition in the same way as the singing of songs "not fitting" is most of all an expression of loyalty towards one's own tradition. Oral recitations in the Western Himalayas not only complement but also stand in an antagonistic relation with each other. Some recitations seem like an echo of folklore from the neighbouring regions. However, they are neither a summary of those, nor a derivative transformation. This is the case with the following narrative from Jaunsar, which reminds one of the epic, notwithstanding the fact that both just meet on a superficial level – both deal with a conflict between the Pandavas and the Kauravas, and both end with fratricide, the former killing the latter. Thus, both also have shared protagonists whose uniform pattern of behaviour emphasises the impression of similarity. The epic and the Panduan narrative, even though employing similar stylistic means, differ in the local version which is presented with frequent recourse to mythical elements – something usually absent from the mainstream versions.

The story of the Panduan was narrated to Zoller (who translated it into German from Bangani) by an old goatherd who lived in a small village high above Lakhamandal in the valley of the Yamuna. Lakhamandal is, for many in the mountains, the *lakshagriha* – the place where the Kauravas built a lacquer palace for their Pandava brethren with the devious intention of setting it on fire once they had settled in. The Pandavas were forewarned and made good their escape through a cave before the palace was gutted. Thus, for the mountain dwellers, Lakhamandal represents Kurukshetra, the land of the Kauravas. In the north-west of Lakhamandal, in the valley of the Tons, there is Hanol, the Mahasu capital, the middle ground between Pandava and Kaurava territory. Thus, it is also understood locally as the ancient Hastinapura. Hanol is one of the centres where the Panduan is performed during the Dhaknach festival.

The Panduan is enigmatic in nature and usually leaves the listener on the horns of a dilemma. Due to its paradoxical nature, drummer-bards generally refer to the recitation as *bujhana* (the figuring out of a puzzle). The Panduan is neither aesthetic nor naïve nor simple. Its poetic range is beyond question but as Zoller, quoting Appadurai, Korom, and Mills (1991: 4), says, the unravelling of the Panduan requires a willingness to connect with the "otherness" of other worlds of folk knowledge.

The recitation begins with a "prelude in heaven". The gods want to create a perfect dynasty and therefore embark on a pilgrimage to Lake Mansarovar near Mount Kailas. On the way they are disturbed and ritually polluted by a female shoemaker. Hence, with the pure dynasty (the Pandavas) also arises an impure one (the Kauravas). This happens when Kunta (Kunti) worships at the feet of the "lord of the world" for twelve years. The spiritual gift, the seeds of a tree that help to bear offspring, is instead obtained by her sister Gandhari, who gives birth to the Kauravas, out of whom the eldest will be the horned Duryodharan (Duryodhana). Finally, Kunta gets the same gift for herself, giving birth to the Pandavas with the help of the lords' gaze. Another boon granted to her makes her sons immortal. The Pandavas and the Kauravas live together, play ball underneath the tree of the worlds, but finally quarrel with one another as a consequence of Narayan Devta's intrigues. The Pandavas are forced to live in the forest in exile. In the long years of exile they face several poisonous attacks from the Kauravas, while themselves killing a number of demons, liberating Draupadi – who then becomes the wife of Khatirjun (Arjuna) only – while the other Pandava brothers beget offspring from demonesses. Then the battle of Kurukshetra breaks out and the Kauravas are vanquished. As the only one who survived, Duryodharan tries, with the aid of a goddess, to revive his brothers with the waters of the Mansarovar Lake, but fails and is killed. The victorious Pandavas return to the capital.

While the mainstream Mahabharata refers to how the Pandavas lived under lean circumstances in the forest and only started to rule after the defeat and killing of the Kauravas, the Panduan narrative starts by inverting the situation, the Pandavas living incognito after the war, or in some other time separated from the incidents of the war, in relatively better-off circumstances than the Kauravas who continue living in impoverished circumstances. This situation disturbs Narayan (who is called Kapi Narayan here), in the same way as he is disturbed, at the beginning of the epic, over the Pandavas and the Kauravas living together in peace. In the epic he is called Narayan Devta, the god Narayan, but in the Panduan he is a devious and scheming relative. While the Mahabharata is narrative in form, the Panduan is essentially mythical, with very few elements of valour and heroism visible in its characters.

The following translation retains stylistic characteristics of the original Panduan and describes how Narayan emerges as the one who causes discord amongst the cousins.

(1) Well, my loved ones, the Pandavas were doing as follows:
They felt brilliant. When they did that fine, they crafted themselves a pipe of silver and on that they fixed a golden tube for smoking.

(2) And in order that they, the Pandavas, have no-one disturb their repose, they got one after the other their own beds: the mother, Kunti, had her own and the five brothers had set up their own beds (whereas the Jaunsaris, according to past practice, usually slept on the floor, over rugs). And they rested on them.

(3) So the scheming Narayan said to himself (they were his nephews), "So then, I'll go over to my nephews. Gosh! They enjoy their lives to the fullest!!"

(4) He took something to munch along the way and arrived at his nephews'. They lounged on the beds and smoked tobacco while resting. They, thus, smoked tobacco.

(5) His head turns burning hot and in his heart he realises that they enjoy their lives to the fullest and smoke tobacco while resting. They had made a pipe out of silver and fixed a tube made of gold.

(6) They saw him, "Our uncle is here!" They climbed down from their beds.

They climbed down from their beds so that he should not say that they were always lounging on the beds. They sat down, down they sat.

(7) He spoke not a single word. They greet him with "Ram, Ram" and talk to him. He says nothing at all and is set to leave. He stood up and prepared to leave.

(8) It came to his mind. "I'll just go round to the Kauravas and look them up. The Pandavas, they enjoy life to the fullest, for these decadent men, it is passing by quite magnificently."

(9) He came down to the village of the Kauravas. They had just convened a council and sat down. They saw him, he comes in a rush.

(10) "We have seen his face, that's why we have used up all our wealth."

Then he went to the door of Duryodharan, he was the eldest, so he went to his door.

(11) Then he said: "My dear brother, give me tobacco!"

Duryodharan's wife, Bhanomantri, appeared and went in. She crushed peppers and brought a bowl with a pipe in which she had filled the peppers.

She filled the bowl and gave it to her father-in-law.

(12) "What, my dear daughter-in-law, have you brought?"

"My dear father-in-law, we have no tobacco, and this is what we have come to."

"My dear, stuff me this tobacco in the bowl with the pipe!" He gives some tobacco from his own bag.

(13) She takes the tobacco and stuffs it in there, he smokes the tobacco. She took a basket to pick the stinging nettle to cook.

(14) At the very moment he said, "Where are you going, my daughter in law?"

"I am going to pick the nettle, my father-in-law, to eat."

"My dear, don't go, look in my little backpack. I've brought something with me. Cook that! Cook, what's available here, and eat it."

(15) Then she said, "Oh my father-in-law, we have used up everything completely, but for you, I must get something. With them, our cousins, everything is thriving, and we have nothing here."

(16) Then he said: "So dear ones, you have to sicken Duryodharan, and then, my dear ones, we'll see further."

"My dear, then, I must go now!"

(17) Bhanomantri was one who knew how to make mischief without being blamed for it. She made Duryodharan ill; she herself left for her natal home.

(18) Well, her natal home was located in the netherworld, the world of snakes. From there, she brought frog excrement, and in addition to that she got poison.

(19) Then, they let the Pandavas know, "Your brother Duryodharan, tell them, is sick. They should come, tell them, to meet him." But they never appeared.

(20) Then she sent another messenger, and even then they did not come. When she sent the fourth messenger, they came.

(21) "Well, we go there where he is lying in bed, sick." They arrived over there. He was stretched out on the gallery, they sat down close to him.

(22) "My dear, what happened to him?"

"My dear, he is sick. And you, my dear ones, please eat some food!"

She had added poison to the food. They refused the food.

(23) "My dear ones, at least bathe yourself to get refreshed!"

"My dear one, we shall neither eat the food and nor shall bathe in these waters."

They looked so prosperous, it is impossible to describe in words. Then she went out, ran in with the poisoned water, and poured it over them.

(24) As she sprinkled the water on them, they became seeds of the Bekan plant. Now they looked at each other in dismay. Why have we become such a thing, they wondered.

(25) They went inside. "My dear ones eat well!" She served all of them a portion. But whoever out of the five ate a mouthful became a frog and started immediately to prance on the ground.

(26) Now she wakes her husband: "Get up, this is what I have done to the Pandavas, I have turned them, my dear, into frogs!"

(27) "You brazen woman! What have you done? The Pandavas cannot be defeated and cannot be killed. I don't want to know what will happen when they give notice of their plight to their allies."

"My dearest, why worry now, I'll do away with them."

(28) She took them with her to a fortress in the netherworld, left them behind in a well, and on top of that she placed a boulder. On top of that boulder she spread earth and planted a tree. After having disposed of them thus, she returned.

(29) The mother [of the Pandavas] waited for them, waiting they would come either today or tomorrow. But they simply did not return.

(30) "My dear mother-in-law, we grieve so much for them, when they have left us. My dear, take care, do not grieve for your brave sons, for they cannot be defeated and killed."

Then the mother created chickens, but they could not find them.

(31) Then the mother created lightning bugs, but they couldn't find them either.

(32) As they all got tired of searching, they said, "We should mourn them." They mourned. The messenger went everywhere in search of the invincible five, and to inform the family.

(33) They had a sister, Rupla. But nobody goes to see her, because how could one convey such a message (of her brothers' disappearance or death) to her easily?

(34) As nobody wants to go, a drummer spoke, "Then I'll go, what else can we do? The message has to be conveyed to her!" He went there.

(35) Now she said, "For what reason have you come here?"
"My dear, I came just like that."

(36) "My dear, no, please tell!"
"My dear, I just came. But even if something terrible has happened, nobody would jump (inside an abyss)."
(This is a reference to the practice of women jumping off cliffs, of committing suicide upon receiving tragic news from their natal homes. The news is often brought in by drummer-bards and their appearance in the village of the in-laws is dreaded by out-married daughters.)
"My dear, please tell!"
"My dear, what is there to tell? The five brothers that you had, all of them have disappeared or died!"
The moment she heard this, she fainted. She was carried inside.

(37) A few days later she got ready to travel to her natal home. Now, her son Diyasuri spoke to her, "You, my dear mother, do not go now. I'll go. I'll find out where my uncles have disappeared."

(38) Diyasuri got up and went to find them. He went from one forest to another but could get no clue of their whereabouts.

(39) A light appeared somewhere at midnight. It struck him. "There, I want to go," he thought.

(40) He went there. A demon was sleeping inside. A fire was lit and he put a foot in the door. The moment he saw the demon that was sleeping, he fled the spot.

(41) As he bolted a short distance, a thought struck him, "My relative, the scheming Narayan, is known to have killed many notorious demons, while I am running away!"

(42) He turned back to the demon and bound his four limbs. He gagged him and lifted him up.

(43) Screamed the demon, "Why have you captured me? Free me!" [and] "Where are you going?"
(44) "I am on my way to search for my uncles. Do you know where they are?"
(45) "No, I don't know anything about them at all, but the fairies of King Indra come to the Mansuri Lake for a bath. They know everything about this region. Go there, they'll tell you where your uncles are," said the demon.
(46) He got up, went to the lake and waited there. He covered himself with a blanket and fell asleep.
(47) In time they arrived. They were sixteen (fairies) in number. Fifteen of them bathed together in the river, but the youngest, Parbati, did not join them as she always bathed alone.
(48) Fifteen of them came thus, and as they saw him, they said, "My dear, who are you there, beside our water? Who knows, if you are not a servant or a sweeper? Don't pollute our waters! It is we, my dear, who come here for a bath!"
(49) They called him bad names. He said, "Hey, my dear aunts, I am fed up of your insults. It seems you don't know that I am somebody too!"
(50) "My dear, just take care! You call us aunt, but who are you actually?"
   "My dear ones, it is as follows. I am related to the scheming Narayan and my name is Diyasuri."
(51) Then they started a conversation and introduced each other. They finished bathing and wanted to leave quickly.
(52) Now, he said, "My dear ones, give me, oh aunts, a promise!"
   "My dear, just tell, why is it that you want a promise?"
   "You loved ones, please give me a promise first!"
(53) There they gave him a promise, "My dear, ask what you wish?"
   "You dear ones, my uncles have disappeared without a trace. Tell me where they are!"
   "My dear, we don't know where they are. But our sister Parbati, who will arrive shortly, will know where they are."
(54) Then, Parbati came. She insulted him. The fairies had given him a letter of reference. As she set her eyes on the letter, she stopped the insults.

(55) Then she heard him out, they introduced each other and they started talking.
(56) Then she bathed, and he said, "My dear aunt, give me a promise!"
   Then she told him, "Don't you think that I will share wealth with you! Tell me instantly, why do you want a promise?"
(57) "No, as long as you do not promise I shall not tell anything." He demanded the promise, she gave her word. After giving the promise, she said, "Now, tell me what you want?"
(58) The following, "My uncles have disappeared without a trace. Tell me how to find them!"
   "I'll tell you."
(59) She knew absolutely everything. She said, "Go like this and that!" She had written a letter for him. After he had left, she commanded, "Come back, I have to tell you something!"
(60) She fixed a thread of wool onto a calabash and advised him, "Wherever this 'pumpkinman' will burst, you'll find your uncles. That's it. Go there without a detour and hesitation now!"
(61) Since back then, my dear ones, there is this 'pumpkinman' [used by oracles to search for lost kin]. Well, then straight on with the calabash he went!
(62) Then he arrived at a market. There was a demon. He had destroyed almost the entire marketplace. And there was a beautiful lady, the demon's adopted daughter.
(63) From the front she looked like snow and sun, from the back like the moon. [She moved] like waves out of fire, was [slender] like a beam of oil. She was simply ethereal.
(64) The demon doted upon her, yet kept a strict vigil over her, for she would bake bread for him.
(65) Then it struck him, "The girl over there is gorgeous. But, I should not fall for her, otherwise I shall get stuck here, and I am on a mission."
(66) But, as he moved towards her, he lowered his head, and even so, his gaze fell on her. As she smiled, he smiled as well, and they immediately fell for each other.

(67) While they spoke to each other, the calabash broke free, slipped away and disappeared.

(68) He talked and talked and talked until the sun set. Then she looked worried and said, "My father will come soon, it's not that he'll devour you in the end."

(69) She hid him somewhere and sat herself down for baking bread. The demon came and said, "Oh, my daughter, today here it reeks of a human somehow. From where does the odour come?"

(70) "Nonsense, my dear, I myself am human. Eat me then!"

"You said it once, better don't say it again. Stop that rubbish!" He left in a huff.

(71) She retrieved the beloved during the day and hid him in the night.

Now he suggested, "My dear, ask your father to look into the future, and find out the cause of his death."

(72) For three days she did not bake bread. As the demon came, he saw that there was no bread baked for him and no water heated for him to bathe in.

(73) He shouted at his daughter, "Daughter, what's the point?"

She replied, "My dear, I am a bit ill today. Besides, give me a promise!"

(74) He replied, "What for do you want a promise? What are you missing?" But he gave her the promise.

(75) She pressed him, "Tell me, what is going to cause your death and what shall it be like? It should not happen that someone were to kill you in the forest and I left here, all alone."

(76) "My dear daughter, you must be joking! Who would be able to kill me?"

"Still, tell me, how is your death going to happen?"

(77) He replied, "My dear one, first there are the seven seas, then the thorny undergrowth. In the middle of the sea, a huge fig tree is located. On top of that huge fig tree is a cage."

(78) "The case with the cage is as follows: the first layer is made of iron, the next of silver, then of gold. Inside there is a parrot. Inside that parrot is my death. But nobody gets to the bird!"

(79) "First of all nobody can cross the seven seas, then cut through the undergrowth, and then climb the tree. And if he can climb, he cannot break the cage. And if someone should make it this far, I'll be there before him. Nobody will succeed in killing or eating me!"

(80) She got up then and baked bread for him. "My dear, that was just what I wanted to ask." She served him the bread. When he had just left, Diyasuri arrived.

(81) They talked to each other: "My dear, have you asked your father?"

"My dear, I have asked him."

"My dear, what did he say?"

(82) "My dear, my father cannot be killed or eaten up by anybody. First there are the seven seas, then the undergrowth, and then there is a fig tree in the middle of the seven seas. On top of that there is a cage, inside the cage a parrot, inside the parrot there is the death of my father. But nobody can reach the parrot. No one will succeed in killing or eating up my father."

(83) He ate the bread. "My dear, I'll go hunting today, stay at home!"

He took the weapon that was lying around and started on his way to the cage.

(84) He crossed the seven seas and cut the undergrowth, climbed the tree and took the cage. As soon as he hit the cage, he struck the head of the demon.

(85) Then the demon thought, "He'll kill me now. He will be behind the mountain of the seven seas, somewhere."

(86) He emerged there. As he arrived, he shouted from afar, "Just wait for me! I am here! We will fight each other!"

(87) While he came a bit nearer, Diyasuri broke one of the parrot's legs. The leg of the demon broke as well. While he came nearer still, he broke the other leg. He just had his arms then.

(88) He shouted, "My dear, nevertheless, I am able to kill you! I am finally here!"

(89) As he broke the wing of the parrot, the demon's arm broke. As he broke the parrot's second wing, his other arm broke as well.

(90) Meanwhile, he had come even nearer, "My dear, still I am able to kill you! I am here! Even while slipping like that, I shall be able to kill you!"

(91) The moment the demon reached him, he choked the parrot's neck. The demon died, he returned to the demon's home.

(92) The girl was baking bread. "My dear, then go now! My father will arrive soon!"

"My dear, eat well and be good to yourself. I am not going to hide myself any more. I have killed the one who was once your father."

(93) For a few moments, she wept. "My dear, are you really weeping about the one who destroyed the marketplace? Eat well, and take care of yourself!"

(94) Then, all of a sudden, realisation dawned, "I came to search for my uncles! I completely forgot about it!"

(95) Then he told her, "My dear, I came to search for my uncles, and the pumpkinman was fixed on my hand, and I have spent all the time here, talking!"

(96) The girl knew what happened to the Pandavas.

(97) The girl said, "I'll find them out for you, but first a field has to be cleared, millet has to be sown, then we will weed the millet and clean it, and then only the search for your uncles can begin!"

(98) "My dear, alright, let's start!" They left and cleared a field.
"Well, my dear, we want to light it up." And they lit it up.

(99) The other day, he said, "My dear, now we want to sow millet!" They went to sow millet. That night, it was simply pelting.

(100) The next day he said, "My dear, come on, we want to keep it clean!"

"My dear, yesterday only we have sown it, and today we will go and keep it clean?"

"My dear, let's just go!"

(101) Then both of them started. They saw that the millet had grown very high. They worked to keep it clean.

(102) The next day he said, "My dear, come, we want to harvest the millet!"

"My dear, is it true, is it already ripe for cutting?"

They went and harvested it. The next day they brought it in.

(103) Then he said, "Thus, where are my uncles?"
They went there, and she said, "My dear, dig here!"

(104) "My dear, you dig!" He did not believe her. She dug. But they couldn't find the Pandavas.
"My dear, you dig further!"
"My dear, I won't dig." Then she continued digging.

(105) When she hit a rock, she said, "Lift up the rock!" Then he went, lifted up the rock and looked underneath.

(106) "My dear, here are your uncles!"
"It is impossible that these be my uncles! These are frogs! My uncles were very special people!"

(107) "Your uncles have been turned into frogs! Lift them up!" And he lifted them up.

(108) But, after all, he was Diyasuri, with a divine connection. He performed some magic and made them stand up. While they stood up, and returned to their original form, it seemed, my dear ones, as if a light would arise for the world.

(109) Then they introduced each other, and he said, "Come on, my dear uncles, today I'll take you to my home, tomorrow we will return to your own home."

(110) And he took them to his house and the next day they went home, their sister and Diyasuri and the five Pandavas.

(111) On the way, Bhim said, "You go home, I'll go over to the Kaurava place and then come."

(112) "What have the Kauravas done?" they asked. They insulted Draupadi. They forced her to clean the cow dung. They insulted our mother as well, made her grind the flour in the mill.

(113) And for supervision, they brought a monkey, since she was a *dharmic* mother.

(114) Bhim arrived there, in disguise. Then he spoke to her, "My dear, who are you, mother miller? Please give me a little to eat!"

(115) "My dear, what do I have to give to you?" She started crying.
"Well, my dear, my son Bhim was just like you."

(116) "My dear, can others, Oh! Mother, not resemble your Bhim?" He tested her; he had already recognised his mother.

(117) "My dear, they forbid me to give something. As soon as I would give something away, that monkey over there will beat me up."

(118) "My dear, Oh, no!" He strangled the monkey and killed him.

(119) When he sat down to eat, the mother recognised him instantly. Seven spouts of milk sprung from her breasts. He ate what she had given to him along with the milk, and along with the milk, he also ate the earth.

(120) After having walked a little, he hit his mace onto the ground, and the earth . . . shook! The ones who were sitting on it were startled.

(121) "My dear, what is going on here?"

"My dear, the Pandavas have come from somewhere. She, Bhanomantri, has destroyed our lives. They returned from somewhere. They are tough guys."

(122) Then Bhim beat them all to death. He took Draupadi with him, also his mother and Bhanomantri too.

(123) He got the cow dung cleaned by Bhanomantri in his house now, and they enjoy life to the fullest.

In the end, a short ballad is sung in which Duryodharan bemoans his bitter fate after the killing of the Kauravas. This is how the Panduan appears before the audience, on the "little threshing floor" before the temple entrance. The vocals are rendered by the *deval*, the master drummer-bards from Hanol, who stand with their drums slung around their shoulders and accompanied by a chorus of women from their own caste. The other musicians squat on the floor, while the Rajputs sit on chairs and stools and continue to interrupt the one reciting the epic, attempting to correct him, leading to heated arguments about the veracity of the anecdotes presented.

While the Mahabharata deals with "conflicts over land" (Hiltebeitel 1991b: 395) and with "regionally dominant landed caste traditions", at the heart of Panduan is the establishment of a connection with the Mahasu origin myth by referring to the problem of disruption of the natural or preordained flow of ritual, caused by the premature arrival of the divine kings. The Panduan repeatedly highlights the problem of a disturbance in the genealogy, the Kauravas assuming a prime position in the hierarchy, their mother earning it for them through falsehood. According to the Panduan, Gandhari obtained blessings from the sages, blessings that Kunti was entitled to, through deceit, to ensure that her offspring gain the advantage of primogeniture. This sets the stage for familial discord between the Pandavas and Kauravas, both claiming what they believed was their legacy.

The "prophecy of the lord", performed on the first day of the Dhaknach, declares that initially it was the demons who ruled the world. Their reign was to be displaced by a dynasty of the gods. The plan failed since not one but two dynasties arose, in which one was associated with the netherworld and the other with death. The fate of the Kauravas, the group whose origins were mired in falsehood, is blamed on Gandhari's lack of patience. The separation between the Pandavas and the Kauravas, caused through the machinations of Narayan, leads to the Pandavas exerting themselves throughout the narrative, as ascetics or warriors, to bring the first epoch to an end by annihilating themselves with a set of twigs (*siati*). In doing so, they find a "solution" to the dynastic problems caused at their birth.

The following recitation in Village Dagoli in Bangan (Zoller: 1996), also commonly recited in temples in Western Garhwal (Nautiyal 1981: 138f.), goes like this:

> Hey, the three daughters of *Imti Raja* are born,
> hey, Kunta (Kunti), Gandhari and mother Parvati,
> hey, the eldest Parvati married the 'Lord (of the world)',
> hey, the next, Gandhari, married Kauru,
> hey, the youngest, Kunta, married Pandu,
> hey, Kunta wished to bathe in a lake,

hey, Kunta walked a bit,
hey Kunta reached a lake that sprang out of the earth,
"Hey, in that earth-born lake, I won't bathe,
Else the gods should call me the daughter of a potter",
Hey, Kunta went a bit further,
Hey, Kunta reaches an iron-forged lake,
"Hey, in this iron lake I won't bathe,
Else the gods should call me the daughter of a blacksmith",
Hey, Kunta went a bit further,
Hey, Kunta reached a lake that emerged out of copper,
"Hey, in that copper lake, I won't bathe,
Else the gods call me the daughter of a coppersmith",
Hey, Kunta went a bit further,
Hey, Kunta reached a lake fashioned out of gold,
"Hey, in that golden lake, I won't bathe,
Hey, the gods else call me the daughter of a goldsmith",
Hey Kunta went a bit further,
Hey, Kunta reached a lake filled with milk,
"Hey, in that milk lake, I will bathe,
Hey, the gods will then call me the daughter of a goddess",
Hey, Kunta went to Haridwar,
Hey, Kunta went to Badrinath and Kedarnath,
Hey, Kunta returned home,
Hey, the King Sun looked (at her),
Hey, she gave birth to the generous Karna from the King Sun,
Hey, Kunta retraced her steps,
Hey, King Wind looked (at her),
Hey, Kunta returned a bit,
Hey, she gave birth to Bhimsen from the King Wind,
Hey, Kunta returned a bit,
Hey, King Indu (Indra) looked (at her),
Hey, she gave birth to Arjun from King Indra,
Hey, Kunta returned a bit,
Hey, King Dharma had a look (at her),
Hey, she gave birth to Yudhishthir from King Dharma,
Hey, Kunta returned a bit,

Hey, the seven Rishis (saints) had a look (at her),
Hey, she gave birth to Sahadev from the seven Rishis,
Hey, Kunta returned a bit,
Hey, King Pandu had a look (at her),
Hey, she gave birth to Nakul from King Pandu,
Hey, Kunta went to Hastina (Hastinapur),
Hey, in Hastina were living two gents,
Hey, the Kauravas and the Pandavas, the brave brothers,
Hey, a leopard dug (out of the ground) the mango tree [the *ameri buti*, or the tree of immortality]
Hey, under a good omen it comes up [like] sieved milk,
Hey, the tree grows high,
Hey, around this tree the battle took place,
Hey, the Pandavas said, "The tree is ours!"
Hey, the Kauravas said, "The tree is ours!"
Hey, the Pandavas play with Pandava – like dice,
Hey, the Pandavas win the place Hastina,
Hey, the devious Narayan threw an evil obstacle,
Hey, the Kauravas play with Kaurava-like dice,
Hey, the Pandavas lost the place Hastina,
Hey, the Kauravas won the place Hastina.

In the Panduan, therefore, it is not Shakuni, the maternal uncle of the Kauravas, who is derided as a villain for enticing the brothers to play a game of dice, ensuring the Pandavas lose through deceit. Here, Narayan is blamed for the Pandavas losing their kingdom, and for the consequent annihilation caused by the battle with their cousins. It is as if Narayan (Vishnu), according to Mahasu subjects' understanding, was responsible for the destructive Mahabharata battle. Also significant is the attempt to connect with Shiva, since Parvati is considered the eldest of the three sisters.

This deception on the part of one moiety over another prepared the background for the Mahasus to arrive and drive Vishnu away from the seat of power at Hanol. The recitation thus links, in a roundabout way, genealogical disruptions and ritual improprieties, causing faults in the descent of the estranged cousins and the arrival of the Mahasus. Such impatience that leads to disruptions results even now in constant bickering over sharing of offerings and hosting the *devta*, between the *sathi* and the *pansi*.

Panduan employs the dimension of time through the "immortal" tree, situated in the centre of the world. The principal female characters, Kunti and Gandhari, eat the seeds of the *ameri buti*, the plant of immortality, and bear the five Pandavas as well as the sixty Kauravas, respectively. And beneath the *bori ki buti*, the banyan tree in Kurukshetra, the cousins play ball, and beneath this tree their descent is revealed to them. This tree also becomes witness to the gory Mahabharata battle. The two trees represent the beginning and the end, birth and death. The two worlds, the worlds of the beginning and the end, always remain separate, in two geographical halves, with the two capitals Hastinapuri and Jaintpuri finding expression in the geographical concept of the two moieties *sathi* and *pansi*. In the Panduan, the Kauravas are connected again and again with the netherworld. Inhabitants of the central Tons valley often compare the areas of the Kaurava temples, for upstream of Tons there are indeed temples to Duryodhana and Karna, to the underworld. Even though borders and boundaries may separate the little kingdoms of the Western Himalayas, geographical and ontological dichotomies do not separate their inhabitants. For all of them, their own god is always a benevolent divinity, the axis of their world; and the god of the next village or valley is an oppressor.

There was, as the Mahasu origin myth tells us, an additional genealogical step between the Pandava and Mahasu, the reign of the demon Kirmir. The Mahasu myth thus establishes the divine kings as rulers of the third era, situating them at a temporal distance from the Pandavas, while also retaining continuity in terms of outlining the consequences of disregard for ritual propriety on account of lack of patience.

Contrary to the Mahabharata, in the Panduan ethical considerations take a back seat. It simply depicts the conflict between cousins squabbling over universal lordship and succession, where, since the beginning one group stands connected to a transcendent sphere and the other group with the netherworld. The ritual recitations continue to create and re-create the world of the Mahasu subjects, connecting pasts with contemporary realities, ensuring estranged cousins and the divine kings remain a palpable presence.

In the present, one can witness a transition from a divine-king-centred polity to a democratic political system. Yet, the survival of Mahasu political ritual points towards the resilience of traditional practices. It is the rituals of the divine kings, the efforts to perpetuate or negate them, that lend vitality to social life in the Mahasu realm. Ritual, probably a category invented by anthropologists to describe occurrences that are routine and meaningless, emerge as events that engender multiple layers of meaning for all those that perform or experience them. Rituals, essentially, are embodied experiences for the mountain dwellers, and it is precisely this embodiment in practice that accounts for their continuing significance.

Current ritual practice and myths associated with it, preserved in a community's oral tradition, indicate a social dynamic. That the *devtas* can still sway public opinion, at times to the detriment of the government, is a reality. Generally speaking, too, in these hills, the *devtas* continue to be significant political actors. For instance, in 2012, when Alfred Ford, Henry Ford's great-grandson, decided to build his 350 million dollar ski resort on the mountain slopes of Himachal Pradesh, the agentive powers of the divine kings came to the fore. Even though the government of the day had agreed to partner the project, concerns of how the project would impact traditional culture and the environment prompted the locals to consult the *devtas*. The community convened an assembly of the divine kings, accompanied by their oracles. More than three hundred *devtas* were consulted in the assembly to determine their will. The gods did not approve, and, despite government backing and court orders in favour of the project, the gods and their officials managed to ward off what, at the time, was India's largest foreign direct investment project in the tourism sector. And this is not an isolated incident.

In July 2017, Jamlu Devta of Malana in Himachal Pradesh, a region infamous for the production of high-quality *charas* (hashish) known as Malana Cream, "ordered" villagers to shut down all guest houses that attracted tourists. Most villagers shut down their thriving businesses in compliance with the divine decree. Apparently, the divine king was angered because the guest-house business was seen as a threat to local moralities. Anurag Thakur, member of the Indian Parliament from Hamirpur in Himachal Pradesh, also a senior official in the Board of Control of Cricket in India, does not fail to invoke the Indra Nag a day before all Indian Premier League Cricket matches, to ensure that rain does not wash out the matches in the home ground, Dharamshala. After years of delay in the Karchham-Wangtoo Hydroelectric Project, in 2006, when construction finally resumed, people of the affected villages rallied to Wangtoo in Kinnaur District, in keeping with the wishes of their *devta*, to set up a symbolic shrine and vowed not to let the work proceed.

If, in this day and age – when it is assumed that everything can be sacrificed at the altar of economic expediency disguised as development – rituals can cause governments and economic interests to capitulate, it clearly points towards the political vitality of divine kingship, negating the view that generally derides religious ritual as losing its significance in social life. Sax (2009) says that under conditions of modernity in the West, the word "ritual" has become a term of suspicion. The situation is no different in India. Rituals, especially those that entail possession and the making of offerings, are usually considered exploitative and ineffective by the "educated" classes. However, this may really reflect an individual's disposition of disbelief. A public rejection of ritual may just be a display of one's *stated* social position, of projecting oneself as being educated, scientific, and rational.

The arrival of the stranger kings in the Western Himalayas,

therefore, indicates that social transformations have taken place, playing on different registers, from pastoral to agrarian, from the sovereignty of Vishnu to that of Mahasu, from tribal god or a pastoral deity to an agrarian divine king connected to Shiva, mandating the entrenchment of a caste system. Jaunsari society, from the standpoint of the average Mahasu subject, has weathered and transcended these transformations.

5

Being Young

THE ARRIVAL OF THE British in Mahasu country marked the age of meticulous office records and journals. Historical evidence from the time before colonial officialdom made inroads into these mountains is scanty. In pre-colonial times, as we have seen in the previous chapter, narratives from the past were preserved through ballads – the *haruls* and *pamvaras* recited during temple rituals by the divine king's drummer-bards.

During the course of field research I hoped to come across documentary evidence of Mahasu's transactions with neighbouring kings, some of whom, like Jubbal, had quite a reputation for record keeping. The intent was to understand whether kingly protocol was extended to the Mahasu divinities by neighbouring human kings. Meetings with the divine king's ministers on either bank of the Tons yielded little documentary evidence. The minister of *pansi*, the region on the upper bank of the river, shared one document that was in his possession. The king of the neighbouring state of Jubbal had executed it in connection with a dispute relating to two villages, Barash Dhal and Badal, lying partially in Jubbal state, adjacent to Mahasu territory. A dispute had arisen between the two ministers, on opposite banks of the Tons. Both were staking a claim over *kut* (a share of the crops) offered to the divine king's temple. In the document, the Jubbal king had issued a proclamation (year not clear) in favour of the minister from *pansi*. It was unusual for ministers appointed by Mahasu to seek justice from a king other than their own. The *pansi vazir* clarified that since the villages abutted Jubbal, the king of that territory had in this instance been asked to pronounce judgment.

What puzzled me even more was that, given a history of several such disputes even in recent times, why could no evidence of proclamations from Mahasu be found in possession of the ministers? Finally, a village elder explained that Mahasu proclamations, always made during public hearings attended by a large number of community representatives, were never issued in writing. His oracle announced them and the fear of his word was such that none could object to or violate them. In Mahasu country, it was standard practice for treaties and deeds pertaining to the divine kings to be consigned to the flames once they had been executed. This was done in order to prevent future disputes through counter-claims by others on what had been publicly announced by the divine king and accepted by the community. Mahasu, being a divine rather than a human king, had no seal or signature to append, and therefore had no need of paper. In Mahasu country, territorial control was not a matter of scripted treaties and signed documents, as with human kings or the colonials. It was about people's allegiance and the recitations of the drummer-bards. Wherever folklore was accepted as currency, the divine king remained the undisputed ruler. However, with the arrival of the British, and their practice of maintaining land records, the signing of agreements after a resolution of land disputes – referred to as *rajinama* – became common. In fact, it was the British who introduced the first land record, the *wajib-ul-urz*, that is until today the basis for determining land ownership.

The Gurkhas, who ruled over this region after conquering it in 1791, either had no need for maps and deeds or were negligent record keepers themselves. In fact, they acquired a reputation for destroying historical records upon their arrival in the Shimla Hill States. Miedema and Miedema (2014: 22) report that the Government of Nepal's official copy of the Treaty of Sugauli (the treaty through which Nepal acceded Indian territory, including Mahasu country to the British) cannot be found in the Nepal national archives or in the recently taken over Narayanhiti Palace in Kathmandu. None in these parts had foreseen a time when another power would intrude and seek written evidence of claims over territories their divine kings constantly marked through processions. When I questioned a village elder in the little hamlet of Bhattarh, where a new Mahasu temple was being consecrated, about the absence of written records proclaiming Mahasu territory, he described the divine king's territorial integrity through an analogy:

> When one works up an appetite, one cannot satiate hunger with a diet chart (*bana kar*). One can only satisfy oneself by eating. It is the same with Mahasu. When his procession arrives at your village, everyone knows the king is there. When things begin to go wrong in the village, we seek to propitiate the divine king, ask for the solutions he has to offer. We just know that only our divine king (*devta raja*) can solve our problems. Agreements and deeds are for mortals, not for our Mahasu.

The divine king formations in the Western Himalayas relied heavily on orality. In fact, the histories and events of the past were also preserved and transmitted through generations in the form of ballad and song. In order to achieve this continuity, specialist *bajgis* (drummer-bards) were included in the caste hierarchies. The written word had little significance for the kingdoms, and the divine king's word sufficed for his subjects. The Mahasu *vazir* of *sathi*, Diwan Singh of Bastil, recalled that while on tour to a faraway hamlet a few years ago, the divine king's entourage was visited by all the landowning families in the hamlet. They had come to pay their half-yearly tax. When they were told that the government of free India was now collecting the taxes, and that Mahasu had not collected tax in the region since independence in 1947, the families were adamant about paying up their dues, because they had been told by the oracle of their local deity that defaulting on tax would earn Mahasu's wrath. As against the colonial insistence on the written word, the hill man's cosmology was more centred on orality and divine pronouncement.

It was with the advent of the British that gazetteers and office dispatches became standard administrative practice. Dispatches from the first officers to arrive in these remote mountains indicate that, after defeating the Gurkha armies, the British remained reluctant masters. Despite their liking for a landscape that offered a welcome respite from the heat and dust of the Indian plains, they were not enthused by the idea of administering the rugged terrain and its refractory people. However, in order to secure trade routes to Tibet and beyond, as well as the frontiers with China, they were forced into establishing control. The Gurkha had, before them, established a vice-like grip over Mahasu territory, and despite religious commonality there was little social intermixing between them and the natives. Given the despotism of the Gurkhas, colonial subjugation would not have been as traumatic an event for Mahasu subjects as for groups in the plains of India. In fact, the end of the oppressive regime of the Gurkha probably came as a respite.

The British wrested control over the region following a battle where they suffered several reversals in the initial stages. In their first encounter with the British, the Gurkha, though heavily outnumbered, almost turned the tables on the colonial power. Perhaps, for the first time ever, the British were forced to recognise enemy valour by erecting a memorial in Dehra Dun for the Gurkha, after the Battle of Khalanga. They eventually co-opted the Gurkha into their own military, forming the 2nd King Edward VII's Own Gurkha Rifles, or simply the Sirmoor Rifles. To this day, the Gurkhas form a significant part of British and Indian militaries. The Anglo-Nepalese War ended in 1816, and the territory lying between the rivers Satluj and Tons in the Western Himalayas passed into the hands of the British. Though the main reasons for the war, fought between two alien powers, were global – control over international trade and territory being the main objectives – the war had consequences for Himalayan divine kingships. A global trading power had now assumed control over a divine king's territory and two completely divergent cosmologies were now eyeball to eyeball.

Analysis of historical events that followed this unexpected cultural encounter helps us frame divine kingship in a more nuanced manner. It also enables us to put native–modern encounters in perspective, going beyond the binaries of nationalism and colonialism. What were the implications of the Anglo-Gurkha War for social systems in the Western Himalayas?

In the zones of cultural contact where a modern technologically equipped and organised global power assumed control over a marginal people, assimilative pressures on ethnic social groups would have been immense. With the British in a hurry to assume control – they initiated road building and appropriated hill stations like Shimla and Mussoorie – the Mahasu realm had no choice but to face the new dispensation. The question is whether in the process of cultural contact with the global apparently subsuming the local, change was only a one-way process. Could this circumstance also have led to a pragmatic revaluation of cultural categories on the other side? Is it possible that the seemingly inconsequential and peripheral polities in the remote mountains also changed the colonials?

Sahlins (1981: 67) offers a model for understanding outcomes in circumstances that bring two radically different social systems face to face. He underlines the fact that people act in historical circumstances according to their own cultural presuppositions. Describing contacts between two radically different social systems, he argues that both systems are altered in the process, irrespective of scale or size. Sahlins' example – a meeting between the Hawaiians and Captain Cook – shows the encounter between an indigenous culture and foreign traders/settlers, and by analysing structural and historical implications tries to make sense of the actions of societies when they find themselves confronting unfamiliar cosmologies.

Obeysekere (1992) criticised Sahlins, and this led to an extended debate between the two. Obeysekere argued that myth-making isn't the sole preserve of natives. He suggested that the myth of Captain Cook as a "figuration" of the Hawaiian god Lono among the natives was perhaps a figment of the Western imagination. He proposed a universalist model for understanding cultural contact by privileging reason and the possibility of numerous other interpretations among native groups as well. In response to Sahlins' idea that cultures interpret the world in drastically different ways, Obeysekere pitched for a common "mode of thinking" underlying human actions and thoughts, enabling cultures to empathise with each other despite their striking external differences. He argued in favour of a "practical rationality" as a common universal thought process. This contradicted Sahlins' view and its corollary – that anthropologists err when they describe other groups in terms of their own cultural frameworks. Sahlins responded to Obeysekere by arguing that Obeysekere was denying a different rationality to the natives if their cosmology appeared to be at odds with Western rationality. Each accused the other of imposing Western epistemological concepts on other cultures.

Irrespective of whether we subscribe to Sahlins or Obeysekere, it is clear that cultural encounters offer interesting insights into how one group can impact the social life of the other. Whether it was the beaches of Hawaii or the hill fortresses of Khalanga, Jaithak, and Nahan in Mahasu territory, the encounters of British officers with the divine kings perhaps impacted both cultures. The arrival of British officials in Mahasu country was marked by unprecedented change, even though, on the face of it, they merely wanted to drive the Gurkha out and restore status quo in the West Himalayan kingdoms. While the British were securing trade routes to Tibet, ensuring they had enough *bethus* (bonded porters) and free labour for their expeditions and for establishing hill stations, the regions ruled by these divine kings were brought under direct British control.

Now, divine kingship apart, the British encountered unusual practices such as polyandry and head-hunting. While they had a clear strategy in relation to the human kings deposed by the Gurkha – i.e. restoring their territories to them and permitting them to rule under their own watchful eyes – the recognition they granted the divine kings was limited to letting them keep temple privileges and to not interfere in their rituals. They set up their own mechanisms for the collection of revenue and appointed officials with juridical authority. The political clout of the divine kings was curtailed since the British directly controlled a large part of Mahasu territory. To comprehend whether the Mahasu regime impacted the British, we need to look at the arrival of the British from the perspective of these kingdoms.

With the Gurkha driven out and the British having decided to give back the "little kingdoms" of the mountains to kings or their descendants deposed by the Gurkha, they set about finding human claimants to these territories. Regions such as Jaunsar-Bawar and parts of what were known as the Shimla Hill States had on the other hand to be brought under direct British rule. In some regions of indirect rule, however, it was crucial for the British to retain control owing to strategic and economic interests; in others the prospective rulers did not inspire confidence; and in still others the ambiguity of divine kingship, something that did not fit into comprehensible social and political categories, forced them to retain control. As a result, large swathes of Mahasu territory came to be directly administered by the British. The more inaccessible parts of this territory, the middle lands where some clans owed allegiance to divine kings and others to human rajas – such as the region of Rawain – were passed on to the human king, the Raja of Tehri, primarily for revenue collection.

In 1829, Dehra Dun was placed under the charge of Major Young as Superintendent. Young had participated in the Anglo-Gurkha War and later commanded the Sirmaur Battalion of the

Gurkha soldiers he had fought against. It is said (Hadow: 1923) that the Gurkha held him captive for some time. He was a larger-than-life figure and emerged as the leading protagonist in these mountains. He was far from being an aloof political administrator and led an active social life. In some records of the time he is called "King of the Doon", a sobriquet that seems to have fitted him. Young's "reign" lasted from 1815 until 1842. By 1833, he had been officially appointed Political Agent to Dehra Dun for the East India Company. His various responsibilities included being commander of the forces, judge, magistrate, collector, and surveyor involved in land settlements. His official role combining military and civilian responsibilities was highly unusual for British administrators even in those times. And he was only in his thirties!

Records of the period also indicate that the colonial administration under Young engaged in various ways with the Mahasu traditional realm despite the fact that Mahasu subjects and the British subscribed to divergent conceptions of sovereignty. While for the British the chief concerns were protection of trade routes and revenue, territorial integrity in terms of access and cartography, and the establishment of order, Mahasu sovereignty was translated through individual faith and devotion, establishing consubstantiality with the soil, gift-giving and receiving, ritual processions and temple ceremonies, and the offering and accepting of hospitality, all reflecting duty to the divine king.

Among the British – as Sax (1991) has pointed out for the West – the loci of residence (houses, towns, states, nations, etc.) are geographically bounded entities with definite borders. Territory was defined in external terms of location and/or legal definition. The significant aspect of this region was that, having beaten away the Gurkha, the British could now access trade routes with Tibet to further the Pashmina wool trade, and more generally obtain revenue from the region.

Even though the divine king also extracted revenue from his subjects, in the Mahasu realm – as in many parts of South Asia – territory was, and is to an extent even now, understood in terms of biophysical entities. People and places, in relation to where they reside, are engaged in a continuous set of exchanges; they have determinable and mutual effects upon each other because they are a part of a single interactive system. The travelling divine king was in essence the binding force in this vast system of interdependencies. While the Mahasu borders were never definitely bound, the divine king's movements gave rise to exchanges, with the host community coming together and hosting the divine king as if performing a communal sacrificial ritual. Mahasu travels established his consubstantiality with the soil and renewed his relationship to it. Thus, Mahasu territory was an ever-expanding network of groups offering tribute and hospitality to the divine king. Maps and treaties did not bind it. Mahasu's territorial control was steeped in orality, rather than in treaties and land grants. The temple where his origin myth could be recited, areas where his oracle could, in a state of possession, pronounce judgments, and where the community could mobilise enough resources to host him, his subjects intuitively knew, belonged to him. For the Himalayan divine kings, as Sax (2002: 170) has pointed out, control over territory and people was and is still mutually entailed.

The general impression among scholars is that the political implications of divine kingship were incomprehensible to the British. Sutherland (1998), describing colonial attitudes in Western Himalayas, says: "The British could not grasp the political significance of religion to *pahari* or mountain people . . . The positivist thinking of British colonial administrators could not fit religious forms like divine kings into any category they knew of: as neither 'economics', 'politics', 'work' but they misconstrued them as elements of irrational 'belief' and erroneous 'custom' that made the *devta* subjects to them the 'patients' of superstition." British dispatches of the time referred to Mahasu subjects as "detestable, slothful, treacherous or sanguinary." G.R.C. Williams (1874) wrote: "The superstition of these mountaineers is as gross as their filth and immorality. The Mahasoo Devta, a deity whose eccentricities will again demand attention, exercises most pernicious influence over their minds, and he is only one of the many spirits, demons and devils, constituting their religious scarecrow." Most colonial narratives, like many contemporary indigenous ones, described Mahasu as a tyrant. And in the context of British dealings with Mahasu, another notion that persists is that the British considered the divine kings, including Mahasu, quasi-kings so inconsequential that they did not feel the need to engage with their collective agency. This may not hold true in the face of evidence related to initial encounters between the administrators and Mahasu.

While the construction of the Chakrata-Tiuni-Shimla Road was in progress, in 1827, Chalda Mahasu's procession arrived in the region. This distracted the workers so much that they would disappear for days on end to attend to the divine king. Of Chalda Mahasu, Young (Atkinson, 1884) noted:

> The way this Chalda-Mahasu, after every twelve years, rides his palanquin and with a large procession replete with musical instruments, roams the Jubbal-Bushair [Bashahar] and Jaunsar areas with a heavy retinue of sixty-seventy servant-workers, he rests for six months at one place, and even the villagers who protest loudly with the small increase in the annual assessment of land tax, happily pay the religious tax of eight annas, while collecting generous portions of ghi, he-goats and rations.

That was the time when Young called a meeting of the elders in the hamlet of Kalsi, on the outskirts of Dehra Dun. The Gazetteer tells us that: "To check the exactions, Major Young passed a summary order at Kalsi in the presence of the assembled Sayaanas (elders), banishing the Deota Mahasu and his attendants from Jouansar-Babar (Jaunsar-Bawar) and also commanded the Vazir (minister) to abstain from accepting any invitation on the part of Mahasu without the sanction of fort." The Gazetteer, however, also notes that the diktat was probably honoured more in the breach. This vignette informs us that the British administration was aware of Mahasu's parallel regime, at least his claims of *kut* or tax, in cash and kind over his subjects. Though they did banish him from the territory, they did not restrict the collection of revenue for his regime, despite the fact that they were very touchy about even minor diversions of revenue from their coffers. Perhaps Young and his administration chose to misrecognise the collection of taxes by the divine king as an act of gathering temple donations for religious rituals; to have done otherwise would have required extensive actions for which they had no inclination or capacity at the time. Thus, according to Bourdieu's (1977) idea of misrecognition, the colonial attempt of treating Mahasu polity as mere tradition transcended their intent towards a conscious manipulation of Mahasu's court ritual. Records indicate that Young was proactively engaging with Mahasu, at times hostile to the divine king, even banishing him from territories acquired by them. As long as Mahasu sovereignty complemented British expansionist designs, they played along and treated him as a king, even accepting his adjudication in matters they were themselves

Photo 5.1: Young (left) in a post-retirement portrait, and Sudarshan Shah, the Tehri (Garhwal) Raja.

unable to bring to closure. However, despite doublespeak and self-serving agendas, as was common in colonial politics, there were times when the British were forced to strike deals with Mahasu, granting him the status of a sovereign.

Almost immediately after assuming the office of Resident at Dehra Dun, Young was forced to attend to the task of revenue and land settlement, especially in the Rawain, beyond the Tons. The borders in this region had not been clearly demarcated after the Anglo-Nepal War. The British handed Rawain over to the Raja of Tehri for purposes of revenue collection owing to the region's proximity to the kingdom and the fact that they did not recognise divine kings. While the Raja of Tehri claimed revenue from villages in the region, the *vazirs* or the divine king's chief ministers preferred to deposit revenue to the Raja of Sirmaur as partial subjects of the state, and not of Garhwal. The Tehri Raja had gifted the region to the Sirmaur kings following a matrimonial alliance. But the borderlines between territories of human as well as divine kings were constantly shifting according to context. The elders of Rawain resented being subordinated to a human king, especially the tyrannical Tehri Raja, who they said had little claim to valour or power and was in fact completely dependent on the British. Their petitions to Young's court indicated that the Rawain elders preferred to deal directly with the British, rather than with the Raja of Tehri, in negotiating the terms of paying revenue and providing *begar* or (un)free labour.

In the events that followed, Mahasu and the newly appointed Resident of British Garhwal, Young, emerged as the main actors. Mahasu represented the collective will of the various *khumris* (councils) headed by their *sayanas*. Embodying the divine king and giving him a voice was the *mali* or the oracle. The two other significant figures were the reinstated human kings of states adjacent to Mahasu territory, Tehri and Sirmaur. Relations between the elders (who owed allegiance to Mahasu) and the Raja of Tehri were, however, always strained.

Young at Dehra Dun was in a valley quite some distance away from the site of the dispute. On horseback it would have taken a few days through narrow and thickly wooded tracks between Mussoorie and Barkot to reach the divine king's temple at Hanol. Even now, the District Magistrate of Dehra Dun, under whose jurisdiction the region falls, travels into the region only once every six months or so. Even in a remote region such as this, however, the dispute and its ramifications did not limit themselves to Young, the rajas of Tehri and Sirmaur, and the divine kings. The claims and counter-claims of litigants reached the office of the Resident at Delhi and the Governor General at Calcutta, the highest colonial office in the country.

The Tehri king construed the elders' refusal to pay revenue to him as insolence, a direct result of instigation by the British agent. The Resident's presence made it difficult for him to deal with the elders using traditional methods of coercion. In December 1819 the Rawain elders, representing a region sandwiched between Jaunsar-Bawar administered by Young and the kingdom of Tehri, complained to Young of acts of oppression on the part of the Raja of Tehri Garhwal, Sudarshan Shah. Twenty-four complainants from Rawain made several accusations that included the luring and selling by him of daughters of his own subjects, forcing the village elders to pay salaries to soldiers employed by the Tehri raja, and misappropriating money set aside for the divine kings. The complaint clearly indicated discontent over the ways of the Tehri king, which thereby reveals British awareness that, despite their sovereign control over the territories, tributes continued to be paid to the divine kings.

Several witnesses were brought in by the elders to testify that daughters were indeed "carried off and given away". In an interview with Rajmohan Rangarh, the minister of Raja Karna – a divine king from Naitwar in the Rawain – the practice of abduction of women by the raja's representatives during their visits to Rawain was confirmed. The abduction of women by the raja's men was common practice, a means of forging alliances forcibly. In a dispatch, Young himself informed the Governor General of a custom designated *ontalee*, according to which "women were abducted and retained in the King's *zenana* or harem and disposed off to his advantage, by which the ruler of the Province claimed a right over the widows and female children of persons dying without heirs or next of kin." Sheep and women were treated as wealth in these agro-pastoral communities. The elders were, however, aware that the practice would appear offensive to British sensibilities: in an 1833 report, William Fraser, then an Agent to the Governor General, had referred to it as an "obnoxious custom" still prevalent in the region.

On Young's mediation in the matter between the Tehri raja and the elders of Rawain, a *tussuleenama* (agreement) was signed on 16 January 1833. During his adjudication in the dispute, Young made clear his displeasure with the raja, giving credence to the Rawain elders' version of the events. He was aware of the simmering discontent because the British had granted authority over them to a human rather than divine king. He noted, rather presciently, that the dispute would not be resolved easily and that Gobind Singh Bisht, one of the more belligerent elders from Rawain, would persist in opposing the Tehri raja. In a dispatch he noted emphatically that the raja had no power to reduce the *sayanas* of Rawain to obedience and that the elders had, for the time being under his authority, been "goaded into insubordination against his [the Tehri raja's] vicarious authority".

The raja of Tehri, Sudarshan Shah, responded in a letter on 25 January 1833 to the complaints, claiming that Gobind Singh Bisht and Sheodutt Mohurrur (the *sayanas* and main complainants) were his servants, in charge of Rawain. Through this response the raja was not only claiming the territory of Rawain but also defending himself against the charge of abducting women: "my servant has been convicted of embezzlement and to secure impunity has proffered a false complaint against me." In an effort to clear himself of the abduction accusation – a charge quite offensive to the British – the raja played his trump card when claiming that he did not need "to eulogise his family and yet [that he was] reminding [the British] of the veneration of the dynasty [his own] by all tribes of hindoos [Hindus] and rajas of hindoostan [Hindustan] as the denomination of Budreenath." Here, he was alluding to his dynastic title of *bolanda badri* (i.e. the mouthpiece of Badrinath), the earthly incarnation of Vishnu, one of the most sacred deities of the Hindu pantheon. In Garhwal, on the India–Tibet border, stands the shrine of Badrinath, also referred to as Badrinarayan, a depiction of the creator of the universe and the human form. The raja claimed the title since the pilgrimage site of Badrinath is the most venerated of the 108 *divya desams* (divine destinations) of the Vaishnavas. While the Mahasu divine kings articulated their claim over territory through a human oracle and through the vanquishing of the local god Vishnu, the Raja of Tehri claimed, as is usually the case in human kingship, to be the human voice of the pan-Indian Vishnu. The *bolanda badri* title was thus asserted to convey his exalted status and underline the legitimacy of his claim over a larger territory than had been allowed him by the present dispensation. Lord Badrinath is also venerated as the overlord of several Himalayan divine kings.

Unimpressed with the raja's arguments, Young sent his report to Fraser, the Resident at Delhi, who in turn noted in a letter that "the proof of guilt is on the Raja's breast and 'tis natural he should protect himself with recrimination." Fraser wrote to the raja, reacting caustically to his claims over his exalted status by reminding him that he was now "Raja, not of Garhwal, but of Tehri, and a pensioner to the British Government."

In an indirect reference the raja, through his constant complaints to Delhi, insinuated that Young had been partial towards the Rawain elders in giving credence to their complaints. As an ally of the British, the raja expected Young to believe him rather than the elders from this isolated region. Defending himself against the charge, Young claimed he had made the settlement not in his courtroom but after travelling deep into the mountains, assessing the situation on the ground. Young had met the elders in person. He was thus probably displaying an understanding of local custom, suggesting that while he himself was offered hospitality in Mahasu country, the raja of Tehri had no claim over territory since the divine king or his council of elders would not offer any hospitality to the raja. He underlined the fact that he had even invited the raja to join him in his travels, but the king had refused. In this manner, Young displayed a deep understanding of one of the most significant aspects of Himalayan kingship, the ability to travel and seek hospitality from one's human subjects. Control over territory thus emanated not just from control over land but from control over land and people bound together. As Dumont (1962: 73, following Bhandarkar 1929) has pointed out, the term territory "connotes at the same time territory and population". This suggests the close relationship between king and country often seen in South Asia.

By emphasising the raja of Tehri's refusal of the invitation to join his tours, Young is saying that since the raja could not expect hospitality from the population he had no claims over allegiance and therefore territory. On the other hand, it is evident that by travelling through Rawain himself Young had usurped the kingship role, and that the village elders were almost responding on cue. Undoubtedly, the Tehri raja must have resented the fragmentation of a large part of his kingdom by the British; but he had only the colonial regime to thank for his return to some semblance of power. His constant petitioning to the Governor General and the Resident at Delhi points to his acceptance of British suzerainty, despite resentment over the fact that it was Young who controlled the larger part of his kingdom, earlier conquered by the Gurkha. His refusal to join Young on his tours of the mountains indicated that as a king himself he would not visit the territory of another sovereign, Mahasu, at the invitation of a third party.

For the raja, the dilemma was that travelling to the region with Young would have been tantamount to publicly displaying acquiescence to the British. Seeking hospitality from the divine kings' subjects while travelling with the British agent would have been doubly demeaning and seen as a gesture of submission to Mahasu as well as the British. On one occasion the raja, instead of joining the tour, sent his seal through his attorney, Dhurrum Datt, who came with the raja's uncle, Purtum Shah. Young had waited many days for the raja to arrive for the revenue settlement, after sending repeated invitations.

Since the raja was not prepared to visit the region, Young proceeded to Rawain on his own. The elders scrambled to offer him hospitality and Young had no trouble traversing the difficult terrain. A few days later he received a letter from the raja declining to meet him or "entering into any other mode of settlement with Rawain than that which his ancestors had pursued, and which he had himself followed for eighteen years." It was clear that the Raja of Tehri believed that if he visited Rawain now, he would be an unwelcome guest and expose his tenuous link with the territory.

Young's travels into Rawain and meetings with the elders can be seen as an attempt to bring about the revenue settlement in this middle land, between the realms of Tehri and Mahasu, coveted by kings, divine and human, through their elders. Even though Young appears biased in favour of the men from Rawain, his sincerity is evident. The raja, meanwhile, further discredited himself before the British, claiming (in 1833) that the agent's *munshee* (clerk) had been bribed by the elders, and that Young, under the clerk's influence, had been "altogether uncourteous" to the *bolanda badri*.

Fraser, a powerful figure in Delhi who had fought alongside Young in the Anglo-Gurkha War, completely endorsed Young's stand against the raja. Young proceeded to Rawain to meet the elders. In his dispatches he repeatedly stated he was undertaking the Rawain land settlement in the best interests of the supreme government that had vested in him complete authority to adjudicate in the matter, as he deemed fit. The raja, relenting under Young's arguments, further diluted his claims by writing to the Resident at Delhi saying he feared he would be murdered in Rawain and he needed troops to be sent from Dehra Dun for his protection – with them he could embark on the tour of Rawain. Sensing he had the upper hand, since the authorities would never agree to send troops to protect the raja in a territory where the agent felt safe, Young demanded an apology for the raja's insinuations, thereafter promptly providing the troops. He ridiculed the raja by stating that he himself had "nothing to apprehend from people of Rawaeen (Rawain)", even as the man claiming to be king feared his hosts.

On his way to Rawain, Young reached Barkot after five days and, upon arrival, received a message from the raja requesting him to wait another five days until he completed his pilgrimage to Haridwar. The British Agent waited the five days out and received messages that the raja was indeed on his way but would not cross the river to enter Rawain, and would rather camp close by, within Garhwal territory, avoiding the appearance of seeking Rawain's hospitality. Though the raja was petitioning the British Resident's court and had become king through their proclamation, amongst his own subjects he could not be seen as submitting to another, visiting without an honourable invitation, an act that would severely dent what remained of his authority.

Aware that the raja would now have to accept his terms for the land settlement, Young also saw this as an opportunity to get rid of certain customs he felt were untenable within his own administration. He prepared a settlement banning the practice of *ountalee*, by which young women were retained in the raja's harem or disposed of to his advantage; and *chuntroo*, the practice of exacting a heavy tax from a successor inheriting property. The settlement drafted by Young gave the elders rights over villages under direct control of the British, where they could now collect revenue and give it directly to the British. On his way back, he went to meet the Raja of Tehri, in his camp on the border of Rawain.

Over their meeting, the raja finally agreed to all provisions of the settlement drafted by Young, except the clause on forgiving the "upstart" elder, Gobind Bisht from Rawain. The raja considered him "his own servant" who had turned rebellious and therefore worthy of severe punishment. Young was unwilling to concede this and refused to hand over the elder, whom he considered a loyal ally. He was aware that certain death awaited the elder if tried for rebellion. A stalemate was imminent. The issue was negotiated for two days and finally Young managed to convince the raja to agree to all his terms, including pardon to his man. Letters setting a deadline for the implementation of the agreement were exchanged. Young, for his part, endorsed the settlement immediately. He advised the elders to accompany the raja's brother and attorney to visit the raja's camp in order to meet him and express gratitude for agreeing to the settlement. Young's account claims that at the camp there was reconciliation between all parties.

In the above incident, Young may be seen as expanding his own cultural capital through the task of visiting and accepting hospitality, with the elders of Rawain also using the opportunity to express their fealties to the new parallel power centre. Despite the reconciliation mediated by Young, the raja repeatedly objected to revenue settlements in Rawain. In his defence, he lamented the fact that, owing to Young's policies, the region's revenues that went into the British exchequer through him had actually declined from Rs 35,000 to Rs 18,000. The raja utilised every opportunity to oppose the methods adopted for the settlements, stating that rather than the administrative (read, coercive) methods employed by him, Young was employing temple methods – which he considered infelicitous.

According to the practice in the divine kings' temples, settlements on competing claims for land were made through a swearing of the oath in the temple courtyard. The method was referred to as a *lun-lota* (lit. salt and a mug of water) stipulation. The soil of respective lands, or its produce from where the disputants belonged, was brought before the divine king. In the presence of the Mahasu oracle an oath was sworn, with the Mahasu priests slowly dissolving chunks of rock salt in the water, projecting to those swearing the oath that, if the veracity of their claims was not proved, the divine king would dissolve them into thin air in the manner in which water dissolved the salt. Usually, this instilled enough fear in the hearts of those making a false claim to refuse to swear the oath. If both sides stuck to their claims, the oracle would get possessed, and, having examined the soil or its produce, begin questioning the disputants and their witnesses, leading to a pronouncement of the judgment in either party's favour. Young proposed this method as a final resort, taking the Rawain land settlement to Mahasu's court rather than settling it in his own, a method the Tehri raja could not agree with at all.

Despite the fact that Young and the raja were not on very cordial terms, the administrator preferred to take a balanced view, and having met him, appreciated in a letter to Delhi the readiness of the raja to "accept instructions and follow the rules he was furnished with, on re-assuming his rule". As a future course of action, he advocated "preserving the dignity of the ancient house" (of the raja), while opining that the raja should be allowed to rule during his lifetime. Also, he clearly advocated the adoption of a "middle course" with a policy of reverting power to the elders (only) once the raja bloodline had ended.

However, drawing parallels between his own administration and that of the raja's, Young repeatedly invoked his own pastoral power reflected in the satisfaction of the Jaunsaris under him, as compared to the discontent within the people of Rawain under the raja. He conveyed his own thoughts on the raja's intentions to the Governor General's office by saying that he "will not be surprised if the Raja were to send his emissaries to Rawain ostensibly for revenue collection, and they were maltreated and that the Raja would be quite keen to see that some lose their life, giving him enough reason and opportunity to strengthen his case against the complainants." Young was aware of the Tehri king's intention to seek retribution from the Rawain elders at any cost, in an effort to restore his stature as sovereign in the region. Even if this meant sacrificing the lives of his own officials, the raja would resort to it, forcing punitive action against the Rawain elders, either through his own men or through the British.

The British administration, benefactors to the raja, in order to conclude this particular case, debarred the raja from adopting any means for opposing the resistance offered by the Rawain elder, Gobind Bisht. Young also asked the elders to at once deposit the previous year's revenue arrears either to the raja or to the British treasury. The British Agent at Delhi completely agreed with the dispensation as proposed by Young. Letters from Young inform us that by June 1835 the Rawain Settlement appeared to have been sealed in accordance with his recommendations, confirming that: "*Jagheer* [land grant] of Gobind Singh and Sheodutt be continued contrary to the wish of Raja of Garhwal [*sic*.; meaning Tehri] on principles of justice and good policy." For the human rulers, the significance of revenue collection overrode considerations of territory. They had established overall political control over the region and since the little kingdoms had been restored by them, along with their token sovereignties, now it was best left to the kings and the elders to continue bickering over territory and political control.

As for the British Resident, his efforts were deemed satisfactory by his superiors and he was asked to assume charge as an army Brigadier by the 1840s, commanding the 2nd Clap Regiment, and then promoted to Commandant of the Sirmour 2nd Battalion. The dispute over the Rawain settlement, however, did not end there. Young's service record from 1847 onwards shows his services as exemplary. He receives high praise, especially for his role in the Anglo-Gurkha battles in the hills. The only blemish on his otherwise brilliant career is a set of "objections raised by the Raja of Garhwal [*sic*; meaning Tehri], on his role in the Rawain Settlement". The records on his actions of 16 September 1835 point to an "an inquiry to be instituted into the complaint of the Rajah of

Garhwal that a part of his estate, named Mahsoodeotah [Mahasu *devta*] had been unjustly transferred by Young to the Zameendar of a neighbouring estate."

The Raja of Tehri continued to complain about the land dispensations made by Young and tried queering his pitch through a long petition, running into well over a hundred paragraphs, to the British authorities, saying that estates which ought to have been under his control had been unjustly given away by Young to the *vazir* of Bautha Mahasu as *mauff* or *gunth* villages. *Mauff* was revenue-free land granted by pre-colonial rulers, a practice continued by the British, to religious institutions like the *devta* or to the needy. It was commonly understood as a privilege granted by rulers, whereby peasants resident in such villages deposited revenue directly to the temple and not to them. *Mauff* could be withdrawn at any time. It was a privilege granted to Mahasu not as a king but as a religious endowment, the Resident ignoring the fact that *kut* (tax in kind) was also collected by the divine king.

As is common practice in India, deities and temples are treated as "legal persons" and own properties. The five villages close to the Mahasu temple at Hanol – Chattra, Puttarh, Nenus, Baaghi, and Maindrath – had in the past been granted by the Raja of Sirmaur to Mahasu. Gift-giving between kings, like the offering and receiving of hospitality, was an established practice and defined hierarchical relationships amongst sovereigns. In keeping with the prevailing practice, land records for the gifted villages were promptly destroyed, since maintaining a record of gifts given away was tantamount to keeping an option open for future claims. The possibility of such claims, even several generations down the line, was not appreciated by Mahasu, and could invite his wrath. Mahasu's kingship followed traditions of orality, and unlike the meticulous record-keeping and cartography of the British, the divine king paid scant regard to the written word.

The Raja of Tehri, in a desperate bid to consolidate his truncated kingdom, was claiming the villages as part of his territory since his ancestors had given the villages as dowry to the Sirmaur rajas. The

Sirmaur kings had in turn gifted them to Mahasu. To the Rawain elders' way of thinking there could not have been a more unkingly gesture – bringing a claim upon something ancestors had given away as a gift to a daughter – suggesting grave desperation on the part of the Tehri raja to add to his diminished kingdom.

However, with no documentary evidence to back or discredit the raja's claim, Young found it difficult to decide the issue of ownership. Going by local sentiment, he declared the five villages in question as *mauff* or *gunth* villages, despite protests from the raja. On receiving the Raja of Tehri's complaint, the agent at Delhi was called upon to furnish a report. The raja had managed to get the case reopened after his attorney met and pleaded his case before the Governor General. Fraser, the Resident at Delhi, placed the papers before the Governor General with a note on the file saying that one word from the high office would be enough to relieve the people of all miseries under the raja, hinting that the British could easily take away Rawain and even Tehri, dispensing with the ally. Unaware of Fraser's strident opposition to his views, the Tehri raja continued to petition the British against the settlements made by Young.

The latter had already explained in a dispatch to Lord Metcalfe, the Acting Governor of Agra Presidency, that he had ascertained that the Sirmaur raja, under whose territory the villages originally fell, had endowed the temple and lands to Mahasu. The evidence of the minister and the elders was obtained, and everyone confirmed that the revenues of the *gunth* villages went directly to the divine king and not to any human king. Most witnesses also confirmed that the villages had earlier been a part of Sirmaur, whose raja had been sending offerings to Mahasu as a regular practice. This showed that there were gift-giving relations between the human and divine kings. The same could not be said about Mahasu's relationship with the Tehri raja: this explained the Rawain elders' affinity to the rulers of Sirmaur, and their opposition to the Tehri Raja.

The Raja of Tehri, in order to refute the elders' claims, brought in a witness named Bhagchand, the elder of Baukwan from across the river, who claimed that the villages had traditionally been a part of Garhwal. Ojur Singh, minister from Hanol, soon deposed in Young's court that Bhagchand's statement "is false and River Tonse [Tons] is a boundary between Sirmaur and Srinagar [the Tehri capital]. The villages around Hanol have been *mauff* [exempted from revenue]." The Agent at Delhi, after having examined the papers of the settlement, reported that he was satisfied that Young had tried to do everything within his powers to unearth written evidence of ownership. "Having failed, however, in procuring satisfactory evidence by means of regular investigations, he had been forced into taking recourse to a practice prevalent in the Hills, of deciding boundary disputes by the administration of a solemn oath."

It would be pertinent here to quote the proceedings of the case verbatim, as described in the colonial dispatches, with a few explanatory notes and terms added in brackets.

> To this proposal [of invoking Mahasu's oath in his temple to determine true ownership of the villages], the Vukeel [attorney] of the raja of Gurhwal [Garhwal] acceded and it was agreed that if the four headmen of Jounsar [Jaunsar] would take from Zemindars [landowners] of Baukwan, the oath required of them that the Raja should forego the claim. To this the former party readily consented, but on their proceeding to the River to complete the Ceremony in the usual form the people of Baukwan, Garhwal refused to administer the oath and consequently the attempt to decide the question in conformity with the usage of the Country was unsuccessful.
>
> The claim advanced by the Raja has not been supported by concurrent Testimony and may with all fairness be rejected but should the H'ble the Lieut. Governor be disposed to concede the point it would appear from the para of Col. Young's despatch that the concession will be attruded [sic] with an inconsiderable sacrifice on the part of Government.
>
> The document produced by the Raja's Vukeel [attorney] subsequent to the 4th February last together with evidence transmitted by Raja of Nahun [Nahan] and Ranas of Joobul [Jubbal] and Outroonch

[Utroch or Tharonch] having proved unsatisfactory and seeing no hope of coming to an understanding thro' the means of a regular investigation I [Young] determined to proceed to Unoree [Hanol] with the Raja's Vukeel and if no better means offered to adopt the mode Customary in the Hills in Cases of disputed boundaries and to take advantage of the readiness expressed by both parties to decide the point in dispute by a solemn oath taken on the spot.

Young tried for almost four years to resolve the issue under statutory law in his courts at Dehra Dun, but no settlement could be arrived at since none of the parties could either produce a document of ownership or agree to a settlement. Having exhausted all legal options, Young decided to rely on Mahasu's divine justice, informing the Raja of Tehri that the dispute would now be settled employing Mahasu's juridical authority. There seems no doubt that Young did try all the available legal options, including an attempt to obtain testimonies from the rajas of the neighbouring kingdoms. When he got no clear answer, he decided to travel to the Mahasu temple in Hanol for a solution.

Young could have issued a decree in favour of either party or referred the matter to a higher authority within the colonial hierarchy. Instead, he chose to travel into the mountains. By doing this he was probably acutely aware of undermining the Tehri raja's sovereignty. He was invoking the local trope of processional ritual, travelling through territory and seeking hospitality, meeting vassals who would call on him, extending his own influence over the Jaunsaris by resorting to Mahasu's adjudication.

And so Young set off at the head of his own procession. As one who exercised overall control over territory, his journey from the valley into the mountains can be perceived as a dialogue between the colonial power and two indigenous forms of political organisation, the human king of Tehri, claiming a divine connection; and the divine king Mahasu, who spoke through a human oracle. He was addressing these two constituencies and their subjects through the single act of seeking justice – rather than delivering it himself. Young's action can also be considered a representation of the imperial *digvijaya*, a conquering of the quarters. He was clearly out to establish a new order, attacking regressive practices such as *ountalee* and *chuntroo* in the Rawain, established and practised by the raja's predecessors. He was redefining a geographical space through a land settlement agreement even while digging the soil with hooves or feet and establishing his own consubstantiality with it. He was meeting the elders, protecting them from the oppressive raja, even stating that he had nothing to fear from them. This, at a time when the raja, claiming to be king, felt threatened in the territory and sought British protection. In spite of Young's kingly act, it would be difficult to imagine that he, given the significance of the ritual purity of the king's body in Indian culture, could have replaced either of the rulers. He was merely making a display of power, leaving the choice of subjecthood to the subjects.

Young's repeated invitations to the raja, despite past experience suggesting that the raja would not venture into the divine king's territory, were aimed at showing the raja his place in the new order. The very fact that Young was endorsing Mahasu's customary system of justice will have been an affront to the raja. At this point, a clear shift in the cultural categories of the British Resident is evident, even if possibly done to spite another claimant to power. The same official who had come to occupy territory by defeating the Gurkhas was now seeking justice from a divine king he had banished not very long ago. No wonder the Tehri raja complained that Young was "altogether uncourteous" to him, giving precedence to a divine king's juridical authority over the living representative of Badrinath. Probably, the Rawain Settlement was intended to be just that – a public rebuke and an affront.

The Mahasu temple-palace at Hanol is situated, as we saw, on middle ground where the moieties of *sathi* and *pansi* share rights and arrive for mediation. By himself travelling to this seat of mediation and asking for the disputing groups to bring soil from their lands for the *lun-lota* stipulation, Young would establish one faction's control, a judgment pronounced through local cultural categories so greatly at variance with his own. Once a decision was made, a legal document would be executed in favour of the winning party, the divine king's orality flowing into the colonial legal system. More subtly, through his own presence for supervising the settlement, Young was establishing his own networks in the region.

Young himself describes, in his dispatches to his superiors, what happened when he arrived at Hanol:

> With this view I arrived at Unoree (Hanol) in company with the Raja's Vukeel (attorney) and all the parties concerned on the 27th May 1836. Here I proposed to them generally that they should come to some arrangement whereby the question might be decided agreeable to the Custom and Usage of the Country where disputes regarding boundaries are of frequent occurrence and where from want of written Evidence legal proof is often wanting.
>
> After a long consultation in which I did not interfere, the Raja's Vukeel brought me an Ukraarnamah or agreement by which he bound himself on the part of the Raja to give up all claim to the jurisdiction of the four villages in question if the chountroo or four headmen of Jounsar would take from Zemindars of Bankwan [Baukwan] the oath required of them, and if they declined to take oath that the Raja's claim should be considered [void]. Established, this I agreed to but there was a clause added to the Ukraurnamah [agreement] which was declared unusual and which I considered unjust and inadmissible Vizt. That if any member of the Chhountroos/or from the headmen of Jounsar/ died within the space of 12 months from the taking of the oath/ of which the chances were incalculably against the latter party/ the villages should revert to Gurhwal.
>
> After a great deal of angry discussion on the subject the difficulty was apparently overcome and the parties proceeded to the River to complete the ceremony in the usual form when suddenly the people of Baukwan Gurhwal drew back and refused to administer the oath [while formerly] expressing their readiness at the same time to swear should they be called on to do so.

The witnesses appearing on behalf of the Tehri king were ready to swear the oath before the British officer, but not in the Mahasu temple. The swearing of the oath would be a solemn promise of truthfulness of the human king's claim over the disputed land, a binding contract with their own divine king to tell the truth. Even if they considered the Garhwal raja their sovereign, administering the oath of another king would amount to severing a relationship with the soil and accepting a different sovereignty. The men from Garhwal very likely did not expect Young to seek justice from Mahasu through traditional means when they agreed to become witnesses. But when it became clear that they would have to swear Mahasu's oath, they backed out, choosing to give up their claims rather than accept another's sovereignty, giving Young the opportunity to decide against the Tehri king. According to Young:

> The raja's Vukeel then made out an acknowledgment which was presented to me stating that the four Chountroos [elders of Hanol] according to their agreement remained in readiness to take the oath but the people of Bhukwan refused to administer it saying [earlier] we will take the oath. Considering the business settled, I wrote to the Raja immediately acquainting him with the result and after completing my tour thru' the district returned to the Dehra [Dehra Dun] on 6th of June.

At this point, after a brief description of the region, Young, "professing the general opinion of the River Tonse being a boundary," reiterates that the raja's stand was unjustified. "In my opinion the Raja has failed to prove his claims by legal Evidence and he has lost his suit by the reference made to the usage Custom of the Country in deciding similar cases but should a doubt remain on the mind of His Hon. Lt. Gov. of the Western provinces the point in dispute may be conceded to the Raja without any considerable sacrifice on the part of our Govt . . ." Young was aware that he could reverse his decision should the higher authorities so desire. However, the colonial ideal of ease of administration and revenue collection with borderlines demarcated naturally, as in this case by the Tons, made it convenient for him to adopt traditional means of adjudication. Whatever the thought process behind his move to seek divine justice, it is clear that the colonial administration accorded the agentive power of final adjudication to the divine king, with Young camping at Mahasu's temple-palace for ten or more days, a prospect that would appear preposterous and unimaginable to contemporary administrators.

Referring to the clause about the lifespan of the chieftains, inserted at the last moment by the Tehri raja, Young noted that to the clause

> the Mookhteear [headman] of the Raja replied that it was the custom of the Country of Gurhwal and that the Raja would not be satisfied if it was dispensed with. The Chountroo remained on the spot the whole day in readiness to take the required oath but Iry Singh and the people of Baukwan on the part of the Raja refused to administer it to them. In the evening of the same day the Raja's Mookhtaar [chief representative] Ramanand Iocee presented an Ekrarurnamah [document of settlement] stating that Iry Singh and the people of Bhukwan on the part of the Raja refused to administer the oath, saying, "We will take it". The raja's Mookhtear at the same time – stated to the Political Agent that he considered the people of Bhukwan to "be *jhoota*" [liars] and that he gave up all claim on the part of the Raja in consequence.

On 8 August 1835 Metcalfe submitted in reply copies of a letter and its enclosures from Young which clarified that the enquiry into the complaint against Young had been dropped, since the raja or his attorney had failed to appear before the court (of Mahasu!). When the Governor General read this out to the raja's attorney, he responded that the raja's witnesses and papers were ready but were never examined by Young. The Agent at Delhi was informed that the attorney had been instructed to show cause of absence of his raja's witnesses and documents and Metcalfe was directed to call upon the political agent (Young) to enquire into the matter and report the result.

In the intervening correspondence it was noted that the Raja of Tehri was subjecting the chieftains to oppression and preparing to expel them from their own villages. In his own defence, Young stated that he had been unable to procure documentary evidence through which he could verify the claims of the raja.

> The Political Agent of Deyrah Dhoon [Dehra Dun] having failed to procure satisfactory evidence by means of a regular investigation into the claim of the Rajah of Gurhwal to the four villages attached to Mahasoodeota [Mahasu Devta] he was desirous of having recourse to a practice prevailed in the Hills of deciding boundary disputes by the administration of a solemn oath to which both the parties readily consented but eventually the people on the part of the Rajah declined the test and his claim not being supported by concurrent testimony, the local Officers were of the opinion that it might fairly be rejected. Since the Raja did not have the hard evidence to prove his claim and was also unwilling to take recourse to the customary modes of decision making, his claim was considered as rejected and it was deemed that he had lost the case.

The Lieutenant Governor, however, gave the raja the option to prove his claim, if he could clearly do so, at any future period but for the present the case was decided against him and the investigation terminated. In this manner, the highest office in the colonial administration also endorsed the adjuration of Mahasu, keeping aside all norms of civil jurisprudence as established through their own cultural categories.

What we observe here is a new alliance emerging between Young and Mahasu, to the exclusion of the Tehri king. The new constellation resulted from the "structure of the conjuncture", as proposed by Sahlins (ibid.), and explains how each side changed the other. "Structure of the conjuncture" is located between cultural expectations of what an event should look like, what, and how, it should mean, and how individuals exploit it for their historically meaningful purposes. Here, Young is seen as employing a method of justice that would generally be seen by colonial administrators as archaic. But the "conjuncture" here is the space where history is produced. Sahlins' (1985) models show how to study the conjuncture's "structure" by focusing on a particularly notorious arrival – in his case that of Captain Cook at the island of Kauai in 1778, followed by his murder at Hawaiian hands the following year.

According to Sahlins, Cook's fate was the outcome of a singular confluence of perceptions. To the Hawaiians, Cook might have appeared as if he were re-enacting the ritual of the "dying god" Lono, who returns every year only to be killed again in a confrontation with the king. This explained the grand welcome he received on his first visit, while on his return he was "asking" to be sacrificed, as, to the cultural categories of the natives, that is what Lono would do. To his British comrades, on the other hand, it seemed like the Hawaiians murdered Cook because he accidentally offended their feelings of taboo. Each perspective implies its own kind of cultural logic, the former a ritual logic, the latter a causal logic. Both perspectives have to be given weight in historical analysis.

In our case, upon the ascension to power of the British Agent, Young, the Tehri king became a victim of a particular confluence of perceptions, or of a "structure of the conjuncture". Young's perception of agency was influenced by his understanding of kingship in the Indian context and a pragmatic approach to land settlement. This incident resulted in a radical altering of cultural categories on the part of the colonial rulers. For the Tehri king, it was nothing short of a tragic curtailment of authority and status, while for Mahasu subjects it was a reaffirmation of the durability of divine kingship.

Young's engagement with the divine king shows that when two completely divergent thought processes clash, it is not just a simplistic case of the invader attempting to subvert the vanquished. Conquests also entail a coming to terms, with a gradual understanding of the other's modes of living emerging between the contenders. The initial stage of colonialism was a period of conquest and exploration during which individuals like Young encountered divine kingship with fewer preconceived notions than today's "indigenous" and "democratic" governments.

6

Emerson Emerges

BY THE 1850s, THE BRITISH were firmly in control of the Western Himalayas. They had succeeded in curtailing the powers of human kings in the Punjab Hill States, the Mahasu realm, and Tehri. Three major projects – establishment of the summer capital at Shimla, the leasing out of forests, and the land settlements – had been accomplished. The British had stepped in to establish an administrative presence in the mountains because reports had indicated growing Chinese and Russian influence along the borders of the Punjab, as well as immense economic opportunities that the trans-Himalayan trade routes passing through the region offered.

In the previous chapter we saw that, upon arrival, despite the need to establish territorial and administrative control, the officers of the East India Company were respectful and engaged with local custom and open-minded towards the political archetype of divine kingship. We have seen how Young, the newly decorated officer-turned-administrator, acquiesced to Mahasu adjudication. Young's accounts of his encounters with Mahasu indicate a bureaucratic and self-serving yet empathetic approach. In this context, it is significant to trace Young's life, to make sense of the context of his conduct. It is this context that indicates how notions of discovery, valour and fair play influenced the colonials in the early days of Company rule.

Fredrick Young came to India at the age of fourteen to take up a career in the British Army. His first years were spent serving under General Lake, the man who destroyed the Irish rebels at Ballinamuck at the close of the 1798 Rebellion. At the time he was only seventeen. After seeing action in the Second Anglo-Maratha War in 1805, Young rose up the hierarchy to be appointed *aide-de-camp* to the colourful Ulsterman Major-General Sir Rollo Gillespie. Sir Rollo had survived shipwrecks, yellow fever, frauds, court-martial, murder trials, mutinies, allegations of bigamy, and a raid on his home in which he killed six of his eight assailants with a sword. Fredrick Young became his assistant in 1811, learning along the way about India and its people. Over the next three years, Sir Rollo conquered the Dutch Javanese city of Batavia, deposed the Sultan of Sumatra, and killed a tiger in the open on the Bangalore Race Course, with Young by his side. Recognised for his pluck and courage, Young, too, distinguished himself in the Battle of Bharatpur.

In the year 1814 Sir Rollo and Young were sent to Dehra Dun to fight for the British East India Company against the Nepal armies of the Gurkha. A war had become inevitable because the Gurkhas had begun threatening British interests in India and around it. Seeking a quick and decisive campaign, the British eventually committed 22,000 troops to the campaign and the attack on the Gurkha fortress of Khalanga in Nalapani, Dehra Dun, was to be Sir Rollo's last hurrah. As he led his men in a head-on charge to the fort, a Gurkha sniper shot Sir Rollo through the heart. He died in Young's arms, twenty-seven metres from the palisades of the Gurkha fortress, even as five other top officers lost their lives on the first day of the battle.

Over the next six weeks, Young watched with mounting admiration as the 600 Gurkha within the fortress stood their ground and refused to submit. In February 1815 the British forces attacked another prominent fort at Jaithak, also held by the Gurkha. When they learned that a force of Gurkha soldiers was on their way to relieve the besieged fort, Young was dispatched at the head of a column of 2000 native troops to intercept. However, this was the moment when Young's irregulars were surprise-attacked in the Sirmaur Hills by a band of 300 Gurkha and, as one contemporary put it, the British column "incontinently fled", leaving Young to face Gurkha wrath.

"Why don't you run away like your men?" asked the Gurkha.

"I haven't come all the way just to run away," was Young's reply.

This answer pleased them. "We could serve under men like you."

So saying, it is believed, they entertained Young and his officers and began to teach them their language, even as Young petitioned his superiors about the need to incorporate the Gurkha into the British Army. According to his daughter Hadow's (1923) account, when Young was released he was summoned to explain his experiences to his superiors. He described the Gurkhas' immense soldiering qualities and vouched for the men as a hardy, brave, humorous, and likeable people. His opinion, she says, proved instrumental in persuading the British to enlist the demobilised Gurkhas to serve under the Company.

Early histories of the Anglo-Nepalese War refer to the defeat of Young's irregulars at Jaithak but the Nepalese, unlike the British, were not known to take prisoners of war. For them, victory in battle denoted something quite different from what it did to the British. In battle, once the Gurkha run out of ammunition, they are known to have used bayonets or their *khukris* (the Nepalese dagger), with the war cry of "*Jai Mahakali, Ayo Gorkhali!* " (Victory to Kali, here come the Gurkha!) They would not return the dagger to the scabbard until it had tasted blood. In their wars against the Chinese in Tibet and with the Sikhs in the Punjab, their military protocol allowed for no prisoners. All those left on the field were simply massacred after the battle. But fighting against the British was probably different. Not only did the British take prisoners, but also, as the Gurkha had witnessed, they gave medical aid to wounded enemies. This, according to battle accounts, greatly impressed the Gurkha and battle accounts from Nalapani, the scene of the Anglo-Gurkha War in Dehra Dun in the Western Himalayas (Pemble 2009), refer to wounded Gurkha soldiers walking towards British medical teams, receiving treatment, and rejoining battle against the enemy. Incidents such as these point towards the early years of colonialism as belonging to benign invaders who were prepared to accommodate the other.

Even though Allen (2001) says – "At the end of the day history is what survives for the record and, on that basis, the story of Young's capture is only legend" – Young's service record clearly mentions his arrest by the enemy in the Anglo-Nepalese War. Pemble (1971) too states that Jenkins' romantic account of her father's captivity, published in 1923, is probably pure mythology. "But it is no less interesting for that," he reasons. "It demonstrates just how powerfully the Gurkhas appealed to the Western imagination in the 1920s." Even though some may doubt the veracity of Young's capture, it does point towards the ideal of manly valour and virtue that the British upheld at the time. Probably the new masters of the land appealed as much to the local imagination as the Gurkha did to British ideals of chivalry.

The consequences of the war also testify to the open-mindedness of colonial officials in the early years of conquest, as the British not only inducted the Gurkha into their own army but also erected twin obelisks in Dehra Dun, memorialising a battle quite disastrous for them. This was a battle in which they not only heavily outnumbered the enemy but were also much better equipped. As an immediate reaction to their frustration, the British armies, having trounced the fort after days of siege, razed it to the ground in an effort to wipe out all memory of the battle. The twin obelisks still stand at Dehra Dun, one in honour of their own officers and the other for the valorous adversary, even though the Major General and his fallen men are commemorated at the head of the left obelisk, visible as one enters the memorial, while the Gurkha are mentioned, rather sheepishly, on a plaque at the rear of the other.

Young is known to have frequently quoted his opinion of the Gurkha. In 1829 he declared "the superiority of the Gurkha army over any other with which the British power has come into contact." He is also said to have often quoted their credo, "*Kafar hunu bhanda marnu niko!*" (It is better to be dead than alive as a coward). Perhaps Young had spent enough time in the mountains to develop a deeper understanding of local sensibilities. During the later stages of the Anglo-Nepal War, Fraser, Young's fellow officer, proposed that the British East India Company assemble several thousand Gurkha prisoners and deserters into an irregular unit that could serve the company. Most recruited were not 'real' Gurkha as such, but men hardened by the mountains, coming from Garhwal, the Shimla Hill States, and Kumaon – and several Mahasu subjects as well. At this time, the British forces were slowly pushing the Nepal army higher and higher into the mountains. After the defeat of the Nepalese armies, Fraser's irregulars became an official regiment, the Nasiri Paltan. These troops were eventually grouped together under the term "Gurkha" and became the backbone of British Indian forces. In 1816 Young became the first British officer to command a regiment of the Gurkha when he was sent to raise a regiment at Sirmaur in North India, close to Dehra Dun, some 150 miles beyond Nepal's western border. "I came there one man," he later said, "and I came back three thousand." These 3000 soldiers formed the Sirmur Battalion, later to become the 2nd King Edward VII's Own Gurkha Rifles. Young would serve as their commander for the next twenty-eight years.

Lieutenant Young was promoted to Captain in 1816 and Major in 1824. By June 1833 he was a Lieutenant Colonel and serving as Agent in Dehra Dun. He built a shooting lodge nearby and inadvertently founded the hill station of Mussoorie. He also apparently planted the first tea and potato ever grown in the Himalayas. In 1836, in a letter, the bishop of Calcutta described him as "the King in fact of the Dhoon [Dehra Dun]" his "reign" lasting until 1842. During this time he was not only commander or "beloved chief" to his men, but also judge, magistrate, collector, and surveyor involved in land settlements, his official role combining military and civilian responsibilities. This was a dual role highly unusual in Company officialdom, granted him by making an exception to the rulebook. And this was a man only in his thirties, his attitude indicating the benign machismo the colonials of the time stood for.

Miedema and Miedema (2014) inform us that Young subdued insurgents and dacoits in the Dehra Dun valley and the surrounding area. He pushed for and succeeded in establishing Landour, in the hills close to Dehra Dun, as a cantonment and convalescent depot for weary soldiers. He was well known for his hospitality and Young's palatial home was always open to visitors. He was a devoted churchman. He also collected and exported birds and snakes to England in the interest of science. He imported the first pack of English hounds ever brought to India. The large-scale cultivation of potato and tea in the region is a part of his legacy and he is credited with the economic resurgence of the mountain region long ravaged by war. His daughter writes effusively about his efforts: "Under his control . . . the desert blossomed as the rose." Young adopted the daughter of a native chief (unnamed) who had been orphaned in the then ongoing war against the Gurkha. In time, Mary Dhoon, as she was called, was sent to Ireland with an English nurse, her education and upbringing entrusted to Young's relatives. Essentially a self-educated man, Young is said to have remained well read and up-to-date on current affairs.

Young displayed remarkable resilience for a colonial official, spending fifty-two years in India. This can be attributed to his understanding of the people he ruled over, including perhaps the Mahasu agentive networks that he got so entangled with. His enduring rule – comparable to that of other British officials such as John Shore, Henry Ramsay, and G.W. Traill in British Garhwal and Kumaon – point towards the early days of respect and empathy for local customs and traditions.

However, in a matter of decades, as Dirks (2002: 82) points out in his work on the phenomenon of caste, for the British, "concerns of conquest gave way to the preoccupation of colonial rule." Dirks suggests that the mercantile logic of conquest, for political control as well as revenue collection, gradually yielded ground to the bureaucratic imperatives of the imperial state. By 1857 the uprising, a watershed in the history of British India, had also significantly impacted colonial attitudes. As Streets (2001) puts it, "the rebellion was both a military mutiny and a peasant rebellion; it included murders and atrocities on both the British and the Indian sides; and it was significant not just in military terms but in ideological and historiographical terms as well."

What the British referred to as a rebellion, or a mutiny, was a revolt against suppression as seen from the standpoint of the natives. Whatever the nomenclature, the uprising, some historians believe, was the direct result of a lack of comprehension and a growing impatience among colonials with traditions amongst the natives that increasingly seemed to them irrational. Whatever the factors responsible for the uprising, as Dawson (1994: 81) describes it, it left a deep impact on colonial policy and attitudes, dramatically increasing racial antagonisms between the British ruling class and native populations.

Gradually, it also became obvious to the British that despite a robust movement of people and goods across the borders in the Western Himalayas, volumes of trade were not large enough to sustain their interests, limiting economic opportunities in the region. However, as Guha (1989) points out, with the British establishing monopolistic control over the region's resources, the immense forest wealth of the Western Himalayas, in terms of strategic and commercial significance, became the new focus of British policy. By 1870 a forest administration had been put in place and the colonials began to notice the distinctiveness of the ethnographics here. To develop a better understanding of the ethnicities, a census report (Ibbetson and Maclagan 1872) was compiled. Rose (1919) published the findings of this first in-depth survey in the form a Glossary of Castes. Despite the literature being published on the region, it seems that the earlier curiosity and empathy towards local tradition was yielding to a hardening of attitudes that depended more on the book and less on personal knowledge. Caste particularities became the new interest of the gazetteer discourse, a factor that could prove divisive, helping to perpetuate colonial rule.

The events of 1857–8, however, had little impact in the Western Himalayas, for other than a public uprising against land settlements in the kingdom of Bashahar, hill stations like Mussoorie and Nainital remained safe havens for their British populations. Notwithstanding the peace in the hills, the incidents in the plains universally impacted British attitudes towards the natives, leading to growing imperiousness and racist bias.

British respect for and interest in Indian traditions declined after the uprising. Dalrymple (2002: 9) marks this change by asking the question of "how and why the easy relationship of Indian and Briton, so evident in the time of (William) Fraser (and until the early nineteenth century), gave way to the hatreds and racism of the high-nineteenth-century Raj." For him, the "uprising, it is clear was a result of that change, not its cause." Two things, in particular, seem to have put paid to this easy coexistence: one the rapid success of British power which bred "undisguised imperial arrogance", and the other the ascendancy of evangelical Christianity and the activities of missionaries. The British, after having quelled the uprising, responded to native beliefs with an iron conservatism and racial bias, utilising every opportunity to deride alternative cosmologies. By projecting native beliefs as superstition, and themselves as reformists, they were in fact justifying the prolonged occupation of the region, now beginning to be resented by peasant groups.

The British officials of the Raj (Emerson, Atkinson, Williams, *et al.*) increasingly began to project divine kings like Mahasu and their human vassals as tyrants and interlopers. The British were also losing patience with human kings. For instance, the king of Suket was deposed in 1878 for his inability to manage affairs within his kingdom.

Within almost a century since the arrival of the British, the mountains had transformed considerably. Gradually, the Western Himalaya, as described by Alam (2008), changed "from being the bulwark of British rule to becoming its most vulnerable part." The region experienced resistance movements, which, though directed against local rulers, went against land settlements, the very basic tenet of colonial rule forcing the British to intervene as partisan mediators, their intervention generally going against the interests of the peasantry. Gradually, resistance movements acquired the form of mass movements (*dumhs*) in the Punjab Hill States, as much as the unrest in Rawain across the Pabbar acquired the form of *dhandaks* (peasant rebellions) against the Tehri raja. What is noteworthy in these movements is that they were all directed against the powers reinstated by the colonial administration – human kings and their tax collectors – now increasingly seen as imposed upon the people by colonial rule. The British were forced to meddle, to their own detriment.

For instance, the Bashahar rebellion of the mid-nineteenth century saw a massive mass mobilisation of peasants against the first cash-based land revenue settlement implemented in the region. As Alam (ibid.) informs us, this rebellion was pacified through an intervention of the British officer G.C. Barnes, who set up his court in a place called Bagee, where peasant groups and the king assembled to air their grievances. Barnes fragmented the mass of protestors, spending two days in segregating them according to clan and *pargana* (region), asking them to record their grievances, one group at a time. Though the rebellion was successfully and shrewdly pacified by Barnes, it brought out the contradiction between the colonial need for scientific revenue settlements and the demands of the peasantry to resurrect traditional polities, demands that now seemed quite implausible to the British.

As Bijalwan (2003) informs us, after 1824, when the British decided to return the Rawain region to the Tehri king Sudarshan Shah, the principality of Athoor in the Rawain rose up in rebellion against the Tehri raja, protesting what was known as the custom of *tihar*, where land grantees of the British forced peasants to pay arbitrary tax rates. In 1851 the custom was reinstated and the peasants rose up once again, even though, with the Tehri king himself travelling to the site of the protest, the protest lost steam before he could reach the spot. From 1877 to 1925 the region saw at least five major peasant rebellions.

The Suket Rebellion of 1877–8 saw the deposition of the king under popular pressure. The Mandi Rebellions of 1871 to 1909 clearly indicate the shift in British attitudes towards popular mobilisations by the Himalayan peasantry, Alam (ibid.) describing them as transformations "from an indulgent paternalism over 'noble savages' to an increasingly unsympathetic approach to peasant unrest." Here, the British had for the first time to take recourse to military force to crush mass civil protests. More violent protest movements like the Rawain *dhandak*, also known as the Tilari *kand* or the outrage of Tilari of 1929–30, and the Dhami Rebellion of 1939–40, were to follow.

Alam also points towards a gradual shift within the hill states from pastoralism as the most significant economic activity in the past, to agriculture, during the colonial period. Land and forest settlements had been put in place and a money economy been introduced. British hill stations now infused incomes into mountain households since they provided ready markets for agricultural produce and labour. Forest operations also began yielding monetary rewards, reducing the significance of pastoral livelihoods. The turn of events, with the colonial power supervising the transformation of a primarily pastoral people into an agrarian society dependent on a money economy, meant that communities were now economically empowered to raise their voice against decadent state practices of appropriation, such as the imposition of *begar* (bonded labour), the arbitrary confiscation of peasant lands, collection in kind of agricultural or pastoral produce, and the levying of duties and imposts on people considered outsiders or the subjects of other kings. People's anger was generally directed against human kings, widely seen as puppet regimes. It is noteworthy that, amidst this change, divine kings like Mahasu – neither legitimised nor greatly disturbed by colonial rule – continued to appropriate economic surpluses through ritual tours and temple ceremonies – methods that were now somewhat constrained for human kings owing to public unrest.

In the case of the divine kings, it was traditionally the oracular *mali* who imposed levies in the form of *dolacra* and *dand* – tributes paid or fines imposed upon individuals, groups, and clans – on behalf of the divine king. People, in those times as in the present, were socialised into accepting the divine king's diktats, bringing in their surplus produce for community projects like grand processions or the building of new temples that were and are still seen as collective sacrifice. On the other hand, in the hill states, human kings imposed levies at the behest of the colonials. It was British officials who made land settlements, while the function of adjudication was also, to a large extent, appropriated by them. As the hills began to reverberate with calls for freedom, in tandem with those arising from the plains, resentment mounted against human kingships propped up by the colonial regime.

According to Moran (2007: 165), for the kingdom of Bashahar and other hill states of the Western Himalayas, the turn of the twentieth century was a period of intense political turmoil. Having recovered from the jolt of the 1857 uprising for some time now, the British were contending with the task of governance and control. A new crop of officers had emerged with little patience or empathy for custom and ritual. As for divine kings like Mahasu, and his growing aggression towards fellow deities, they observed the phenomenon closely, but since the attacks did not in any way immediately challenge their control over the region, they did not feel threatened enough to act.

However, for British officers encountering Mahasu's particular form of divine kingship, represented by constantly feuding groups, the highlanders — far from being the "noble savages" of the past — had now become a challenge. A new breed of colonial administrators, having firmly established control over the mainland, had begun a process of consolidation in these little Himalayan kingdoms where they had themselves once reinstated human kings. "Modernising" factions within the kingdoms had also begun to align with colonial policy to weed out polities, especially human kings, that were now considered depraved and archaic. According to Moran (ibid.), "these factions were gradually granted ascendancy over traditional rulers, forcing the traditional power centres to seek recourse to ritual" even more aggressively, to retain their toehold over power. For instance, according to Moran, Raja Shamsher Singh of Bashahar, in order to oppose the British-supported factions in his kingdom, resorted to the imposition of special taxes on the population. This was done in order to reaffirm his position as the "religious" head of state. The tax was imposed for a performance of the *udyapan jag* (the great sacrifice) in order to "apply ritual authority over his guests, which was beyond the control of his rivals." Despite the great pomp and ceremony, the divinities from the adjoining regions of Kinnaur stayed away from the sacrifice, reflecting simmering discontent and instability within the kingdom under the raja.

It was during this period of turmoil for indigenous rulers and of aggressive consolidation for the British, that Emerson arrived in the Mahasu realm. His accounts of the encounters with Mahasu point to his efforts to undermine the divine king's authority and disengage the cult, even as the divine king adapted or retaliated, in keeping with the demands of the situation. Emerson remained administrator of the Simla Hill States, Mandi, and Bashahar from 1911 to 1919. He had assumed administrative control over the region in the wake of the August 1909 attack on the otherwise popular forest officer Alexander James Gibson, in the forests of the Pandrabis Range of Rampur, falling within the jurisdiction of

Bashahar state. According to Moran (2007), the attack was a direct result of "jungle politics". The attack also points towards growing political wrangles between communities and colonials over the region's forest wealth, as well as contests over lands lying between Garhwal and Bashahar, largely a part of the Mahasu realm. The attackers, eight of them, were natives, later identified as employees of the forest department. They were arrested and, during interrogations, confessed that Surendra Shah, originally a prince from Garhwal, adopted by the king of Bashahar as his son and heir, had persuaded them to assault the officer in return for exemption from *begar* and taxes. Even though the right to such exemptions rested with British officials, the insinuations against Surendra Shah convinced the British of the involvement of the "Garhwal Party". With the needle of suspicion pointing beyond Mahasu territory towards Garhwal, Surendra Shah was expelled from the state of Bashahar and declared incapable of succeeding to the throne. The state of Bashahar was thus left heirless, paving the way for the British to take charge, another step in the direction of appropriating territory and establishing total administrative control.

British officers were now more racially conscious, with the chasm between religion and politics becoming wider and appearing irreconcilable. Emerson's (1911) interactions with Mahasu, obtained from his work titled "Typescript of Unpublished Anthropological Study of Mandi and Bashahar", indicate his unease at Mahasu's growing political clout and the challenge of dealing with the divine king. There is an attempt to carefully analyse Mahasu divine kingship even as the imperious administrator in him is trying to undermine the god.

It was during the time that Emerson assumed control of the Simla Hills that he encountered Mahasu's strident expansionism. Though the divine king was targeting minor deities in the region, defeating them and expanding influence, the process in itself pointed towards a much deeper undercurrent of social change sweeping the mountains. As both Rose and Emerson have remarked,

Mahasu marked a clear departure from the "theophany" of the Himalayan deities. Theophany, to them, referred to visible manifestations of a deity in the rituals and practices of followers, and the manner in which a deity was revealed to his followers. Mahasu was clearly different from the other pastoral kings of the Western Himalayas. Brought in by the Brahman, a lineage linked to Shiva, and emerging from the soil after the ploughing of the fields, the divinity constantly sought to establish consubstantiality with the soil, showing it as markedly agrarian. Even though the nuances of divine kingship were not clearly grasped by officials, they appeared intrigued and alarmed that a divine king, with a distinct "foreign" origin and ethic, was expanding his influence by trouncing other deities.

Emerson's work records the ascendance of the cult of Mahasu as it overwhelms the pastoral gods Chasralu and Shalu. Mahasu, to establish a new order, took recourse to ritual practices such as raiding pastures and goat sacrifices, both prevalent in the mountains, and his expansionism was part of the social transformation of the ideological world of the Himalayan peasant, taking place because of the growing influence of the mainstream. For Shalu, as for many pastoralist deities of the mountains, shepherds in an alpine pasture discovered a ram from their grazing flock, transfixed to a rock. When they tried to remove the animal, they found it impossible. Considering the ram possessed, it was sacrificed via beheading. Lying below the decapitated animal, they discovered two dazzling images of an unknown deity. One of the images rolled down the precipice into a gorge and was carried away by the torrent. The other was brought back to the village and consecrated in a temple as the god Shalu. Over the years, Shalu became the dominant deity amongst the pastoralists, forming what Emerson described as a "confederacy of villages", with the pastoralists themselves performing the rituals at his temple.

Shalu emerges from pastureland, upon the sacrifice of a goat. Shepherds discover the deity and establish it. In comparison, Mahasu was invited to the land, sought out by a Brahman. The Mahasu myth clearly establishes the divine kings as Rajput, the dominant caste that could not turn down the entreaty of a Brahman. For Shalu, shepherds performed the ritual worship, and it was amongst their communities that the deity remained confined. In the Mahasu cult, caste roles were clearly defined and only Brahman priests could perform the rituals of worship. The emergence of Mahasu from the soil, through the act of ploughing by a pre-pubescent boy, established not only their consubstantiality with the soil but also their caste-based purity. The Mahasu myth links the divine kings to the Shiva pantheon, establishing unambiguous links with Kartikeya as well as the Naga worship tradition. A comparison between the two deities and their conflict, as witnessed by Rose and later Emerson, indicates that Mahasu, a deity connected with mainstream Hindu caste-based agrarian ritual practices, was taking over the religio-political realms from indigenous pastoral gods. Though oral histories and literary accounts (also probably transcribed from recitations by colonial authors) do not ascribe a definite date or time to these events, they point towards a transforming social order. It is quite evident that while Shalu, and others like Chasralu and Vishnu, were indigenous deities, Mahasu arrived as the covetous "stranger king".

Emerson provides an interesting account of the conflict between Mahasu and Shalu. The subjects of both divinities, Mahasu and Shalu, were of course neither exclusively agrarian nor pastoral. They practised agriculture, pastoralism, hunting-gathering, and other professions, much as they do today, but Mahasu's conflict with Shalu and then Chasralu points towards a renegotiation of identities on the part of the communities – under the watchful but uncomprehending eyes of the colonials.

The Mahasu cult was employing familiar ritual strategies – causing epidemics, possessing women, causing water sources to dry up – for forcibly winning allegiances and expanding territorial control. Emerson, observing this phenomenon, was confounded, torn as he was between his own "rational" attitudes and the reality of a non-human agent's appropriation of power. He dealt with people who were convinced that the divine king's essence could permeate inanimate objects. These objects, including weapons, idols, coins, even humans and livestock, once imbued with the divine essence, transported the deity. If ignored or not acquiesced to, misfortune or pestilence in the host community was inevitable. Handa (2006) says that at the Burondo Pass (overlooking the Duling Lake in Andhra Valley of Himachal Pradesh, close to the town of Rohru), past kings of neighbouring states had established checkposts where oracles were stationed to frisk every human and animal crossing over to ensure they were not carrying objects or were themselves imbued with Mahasu's essence. Neighbouring kingdoms were wary that these objects, animals, and people, once inside their kingdom, would disrupt the social order until Mahasu was acceded to. Mahasu was even reputed to attach himself to sheep and livestock in the transhumant flocks travelling up and down the valleys. Therefore, each animal had to pass through the local god's oracle's "scan".

During the course of Emerson's appointment as settlement officer of Bashahar state, he and Mahasu crossed each other's path several times. Mahasu was recognised as a land owner and the ownership was described by Emerson as a "religious endowment". Wherever he had been worshipped for long, people tilled the land owned by the divine king, either paying a levy on the land through produce or by contribution of labour. But, as in Shalu's case and several others, Mahasu was intruding upon the territories of local pastoralist gods; the divine king's actions were bluntly described by Emerson as blackmail: ". . . where they had accepted him without demur, the burden was trifling; but where backed by the ancestral god, they had put up a stiff fight, his terms of peace were severe and involved considerable expense to the peasants." When Mahasu burdened these villages with his levies, they would often petition the British to renegotiate the taxes they paid to the state. According to Emerson, the requests were so numerous that the British had to adopt a general policy of refusal.

> Mahasu, I used to tell the petitioners, was not their family god but an outsider who had forced himself upon them; he was grasping already but, if his exactions were encouraged by the state, there would be no limit to his ambitions, and he would certainly invade the few villages into which he had got no footing. The villagers, recognising this formula as borrowed from their own conception of the god, usually accepted it in good humour and made the best of a bad job.

In the instance of Shalu's village the requests were so persistent that Emerson was forced to hear the petition, asking the villagers how Mahasu had taken control over their territory. The familiar story of how one of the peasants had unwittingly brought in a vessel imbued with Mahasu's essence, leading to a series of misfortunes, was narrated. He was told that upon consulting the local god's oracle, it became known that Mahasu had indeed entered their village. The oracle suggested that the village immediately adopt Mahasu as their new deity. Shalu, through his oracle, refused to accept this proposition, threatening that if his worship were abandoned he would afflict the villagers with even greater troubles. Emerson writes:

> Choosing what seemed the lesser evil, the peasants rejected the advice of the diviner, and for several years their decision was justified by good harvests and general prosperity. But then commenced a further period of misfortune; crops were thin, cattle disease was rife and the peasants grew poor. They knew Mahasu was the author of their afflictions, but the local god was obdurate, and as yet they dare not disobey him openly, although there were rumours for his disregard of their interests.
> It was at this stage that the village was disturbed by a strange incident. One evening, soon after nightfall, the wife of one of the peasants was preparing the evening meal for her husband and herself. The room where she was working was in the upper storey of the house. Immediately below were the sheep and goats and below these again were

the household cattle. An inside ladder, consisting of a log with deep notches in it, connected the three rooms. The woman was bending over her cooking pots when suddenly there was a scurry amongst the animals below, and as she looked around to see the cause, a panther ran up the ladder, and, springing on her, knocked her down. For several seconds it stood over her, but then hearing the neighbours approach, it ran down the ladder and so escaped. Its victim was a little scratched, but the beast had made no attempt to maul her and the next day she was none the worse. The villagers were sorely puzzled by the incident. "It could not have been a panther," argued they, "for had it been, it would have carried off a sheep or goat; nor could it have been a man eater for it would then have killed the woman. It was not an animal at all. It was Mahasu wandering in a leopard's form."

The village was now satisfied that Mahasu had indeed given a signal, and defying the ancestral deity they recognised Mahasu from that day. "A god who could assume a leopard's shape at will was clearly better as a friend than as an enemy," they reasoned.

But Mahasu having been rejected for so long would not make easy terms of peace. The villagers had to build him a proper shrine, arrange for his daily service and provide him with much incense. At the same time they had to maintain the worship of the family god [Shalu], for, although they had ignored his wishes, they were unwilling to cast him aside altogether. Finding this double expense a burden on their slender resources, they begged that the state should bear a portion of it.

Emerson sympathised but refused to help. His refusal, punctuated with his mounting concern for Mahasu exactions, underlines the British policy of not interfering with divine politics as long as revenue kept flowing in. It also tells us that Mahasu was appropriating allegiances as well as wealth that belonged to the local gods, the polity consolidating its position as a response to a growing resentment against the British.

In the realm of Mahasu, deities trounced by the divine king were not banished. They were, like Shalu, allowed to coexist as inferior deities. For instance, in the Mahasu temple at Hanol, close to the entrance, there is a nondescript shrine to a deity generally referred to as Vishnu. We have seen earlier how Narayan (Vishnu) appears as the devious character in the Panduan. There is ambiguity on whether Vishnu was a local deity or the god from the Hindu trinity. Bhatt (2010) has reported that before the Mahasu temple at Hanol was declared a protected monument by the Archaeological Survey of India in 1920, idols of the Hindu deity Vishnu were indeed installed at the diminutive shrine in the courtyard of the Hanol temple. Today, the idol is displayed in a small museum close to the site, even as an old image of the Hindu deity with his consort, Lakshmi, still lies in the sanctum. The Mahasu origin myth, continuing from the slaying of the demon Kirmir, describes how the four brothers challenged Vishnu, the deity occupying the *kot* (fortress) of Hanol, which was at the time occupied by the *barahbishi* (the 240 Rajput families). These men were ambidextrous in the art of fighting with the *khanda* (a long sword) in either hand, and known as much for their valour as for their brusque manner.

As narrated by *bajgi* Madan Das, the Mahasus sent their emissary, Serhkuriya, to tackle Vishnu. He camped on the square opposite the temple, referred to as the Shailpatangan. The Mahasu siblings arrived at the time when the evening worship rituals were in progress. They sent their emissary to ask Vishnu and his consort, Devi Chitrakshin, to vacate the throne. At the time, the *dhaki* (drummer) was playing a beat in praise of Vishnu. They ordered the *dhaki* to play drumbeats in their praise and not Vishnu's. "Why should I play new drum beats when the new deity cannot provide for me?" he retorted. Asked how much he was paid to play the drum, he replied, "A cap full of grain for each child of mine and half of the previously baked stale bread [*pichli raunt*]." He was promised double the reward, and so began to beat the drum in praise of Mahasu.

Hearing drumbeats in praise of another and feeling insulted,

Vishnu rushed out of the temple, when Mahasu's deputy Serhkuriya declared, "Now that you have vacated the throne, we have a challenge for you. Whoever wins will own the palace. On the banks of the Tons, using the royal vessel [*supa*], we will drop gold in a constant tumble. We will do this for nine days and nine nights. Whoever exhausts the stock of gold first, loses."

Vishnu was confident of his immense wealth and accepted the challenge. While on the banks, Serhkuriya used his magical powers to transform sand into gold dust. Vishnu exhausted his stock quickly, while the Mahasus kept pouring sand that appeared to be gold. "How much gold do you own?" questioned Vishnu. "From Dakpathar to Datmir, our gold lies scattered. Then our *devtas* and *birs* have their own wealth . . ." replied Serhkuriya. Vishnu stood vanquished, not because he was poor, but because he did not have the magical power to make dust seem like gold. He begged to be given some space and share of the ritual worship that would henceforth be offered to Mahasu. A little shrine was dedicated to him to the right, in the open courtyard of the Mahasu temple, while his consort, Devi Chitrakshin, bolted into the forests of Chattra, where a little shrine to her houses her idol.

Through this episode, we once again come across the familiar trope of Vishnu retaining control over territory until forced out of the shrine, the seat of power; and Mahasu not forcibly entering the temple but compelling the enemy to venture out by employing insult as a strategy, and then winning over territory through magical ritual. The Mahasus become claimants to kingship once the rituals are appropriated. What we also see here is that the vanquished king is still permitted some space in the power structure, now being treated more as a guest, the privilege of playing host passing on to the newly anointed kings.

Emerson's ethnographic narrative, like that of the other officers of the civil service (Walton 1911; Ibbetson *et al.* 1919), points to a similar conflict involving Mahasu and Chasralu, representing a change in British attitudes from the times of Young. Gone

Photo 6.1: The Mahasu temple at Hanol and, front right, Vishnu's diminutive shrine.

were the days of engagement, of empathy, now yielding to denial, confrontation, and refusal to provide any administrative concession to ritual practice. Colonial narratives were now looking down upon the cult with a disparaging gaze, refusing to acknowledge, even from the standpoint of the natives, Mahasu's role in providing pastoral care, as rainmakers, and as safety valves against social and familial conflict.

According to Emerson, Chasralu, another local divine king, was a rival with whom Mahasu had a bitter feud. One day, Mahasu lured his enemy within reach and smote him with his sword, so that Chasralu fled in terror with a gaping wound. Mahasu with his deputies pursued him into the mountains. The chase was long and arduous, but given Mahasu's warrior instincts, he soon closed in on his enemy. As Mahasu was about to hack his enemy down, Chasralu saw a crack in the mountainside and took refuge in the cavern. True to the kingly codes of giving and receiving hospitality, Mahasu neither entered nor stormed the cave. But the rival could not be permitted to stay in hiding without having accepted defeat. According to Emerson:

> There he lay concealed, gaining new strength and courage, while his ancient enemy held council with his ministers. "Who of all my servants," asked Mahasu, "is bold enough to drive Chasralu from his lurking place?" But no one had the courage to assault the god entrenched within his cave. A minor deity, however, whose name was Jakh, proposed a plan, in an effort to save his ally and his own kingdom. "Let the accursed god," said he, "stay in his gloomy cavern, doomed to eternal darkness. I, with four other of your gods, will stand as sentinels upon the five approaches to this burrow, so that he cannot take his flight by the mountain passes, or by the valley, or by the river. We will be surety of his safekeeping if, in return, you grant us jurisdiction over our respective charges and pledge your word to leave us undisturbed."
>
> Mahasu would have liked to see his ancient enemy hacked to pieces before his eyes, but failing any other way to wreak his vengeance, he approved Jakh's plan, renouncing all control over the actions of his former servants and territories they were to guard. Departing with his brothers and other members of his court, he found a haven, after many wanderings in the village of Hanol, which became the centre of his worship. Jakh and his four companions stayed behind to keep their watch and ward upon all exits of the cave. Jakh, who now lives in Janglik, watches the mountain passes to the North, Beri Nag keeps guard upon the Pabar River, whilst, if the prisoner attempts to issue to the South, he must pass the watchful eyes of Chillam and Narain and Nag of Pekian. Chasralu, cribbed, cabined and confined on every side has had to stay within his dungeon but as the years passed he won his share of glory and renown. His five gaolers formed a confederacy of gods and he himself became associated with their worship. Temples were built to him in several villages, while curious rites were celebrated at his cavern. Lately, however, his reputation has suffered partial eclipse, for Mahasu faithless to his word, has cast a doubt upon his presence in the cave.

Some two decades before Emerson wrote his manuscript, one of the Mahasu priests, a man feared for his knowledge of black magic, came to the group of villages where the five guardians are worshipped, and informed all that his master's ancient enemy [Chasralu], had vanished into space. He did not blame the warders, since the prisoner had not escaped through any lack of vigilance; nor indeed escaped at all; he had melted into nothingness, merely ceased to be; but, he argued with unerring logic, since there was no prisoner to guard, there was no need as well for five deities to hold him fast; Mahasu, his master, would therefore return among them and resume his former rule.

The villagers, however, knowing Mahasu and his ways were by no means anxious for this honour, and very angry at the breach of faith, swore that they would not have the god inside their hamlets. They turned his messenger away, threatening him with diverse pain and penalties if he ventured into those parts again. But, from that day misfortune fell upon the villagers and did not cease until the people gave their grudging homage to the foresworn god, who has now assumed possession of several of Chasralu's temples. But, even now they deny the disappearance of the latter from the cave, although his cult is not so flourishing as formerly.

By the time the Punjab Census of 1883 was compiled, people had stopped visiting Chasralu's cave, fearing Mahasu reprisals. Emerson visited the area in the second decade of the twentieth century, and at the time Chasralu worship had all but disappeared.

It is significant that unlike the local deities such as Shalu and Chasralu, Mahasu borrowed a lot of the ritual and social practices from the plains of North India. Mahasu (when pronounced as *mahashua*), in fact, appears to be an agrarian deity adapted to pastoralist ritual practice, acquiring a name with Shiva connotations, conducive also to the local dialect, sounding similar to the names of local deities. According to Emerson, Mahasu abhorred the sight of blood, animal sacrifice, and meat-eating, practices not common with other native deities. This does not mean that people adopting Mahasu subjecthood turned vegetarian. The subjects of the divine king continued with goat sacrifice, even more so in Mahasu shrines, but out of sight of the deity, with the priests offering worship to the divine king turning vegetarian when on duty.

Mahasu has an extreme dislike of leather, not just shoes; leather belts and wallets are also taboo in his shrines. He does not care for alcohol either, so in the Hanol temple and around other Mahasu shrines there is a taboo against drink – even though drinking the locally brewed *soor* (rice beer) is very much a part of life here. While deities like Shalu and Chasralu did not enforce restrictions on drink, trying to enter a Mahasu shrine in an inebriated state can invite physical chastisement. Another strong taboo relates to menstruating women: they are not permitted to get close to Mahasu shrines or palanquins.

There are several ritual practices in Mahasu shrines that seem to be at odds with those of pastoral gods, the most remarkable being the enforcement of a strict caste. Mahasu maintains ritual distance from those performing menial tasks, while, for gods like Shalu, shepherds perform the rituals; Mahasu can only be ritually worshipped by chosen Brahman priests. The divine king's low-caste subjects cannot even enter his shrine, while those permitted to enter seldom get to see his images.

Another aspect of Mahasu rule was the zealous protection of hierarchical allegiances. Mahasu would not tolerate his subjects giving equal status to rival deities. As mentioned earlier, the deities were incorporated into the Mahasu family of divinities but treated as inferior, their earlier shrines either falling into disrepair or the images placed, as in the case of Vishnu at Hanol, in unpretentious shrines in Mahasu temple courtyards. Mahasu maintained a bevy of officials who, amongst other duties, also kept an eye open for any resumption of worship of the *devtas* Mahasu had subdued.

With the arrival of the British, the establishment of hill stations, and large-scale road building, new economic opportunities were emerging for the peasant communities in the mountains. A new world was intruding upon their traditional pastoral mode of living and Mahasu's growing belligerence probably reflected the change. This transformation, in large measure, was also brought about by a change in attitude of the British towards the traditional system of what Sutherland (1998) describes as "government by deity".

Land settlements, forest leases, the growth of towns like Shimla, Mussoorie, Nainital, Ranikhet, Almora, Chakrata, and Kasauli, and with them growing access to markets, opened new windows of opportunity for Hindu orthodox practice to bring together hitherto fragmented communities under Mahasu divine kingship. While human kings who had fallen to the colonial powers were protested against by their subjects through indigenous idioms such as *dhandaks* and *dumhs*, here was a divine king emerging as a unifying force and a rallying point in an ersatz display of dissent against colonial rulers and their vassals.

In Emerson we again encounter Sahlins' idea of mutual influence when the rationalism and scepticism of officialdom collides with tradition. Emerson is left wondering over whether to perceive Mahasu as a political or as a supernatural phenomenon. Writing almost a century after Young, he says:

> The intensity of the superstitious terrors inspired by Mahasu was first brought home to me during a short march of six to seven miles. At the camping place from which I started, the mention of his name was anathema; for the village was the centre of Shalu's worship, a deity with whom the Kashmir god was then at enmity. In the adjoining hamlet there was also a temple to the local Shalu and the brazen vessels, the horns and rags, nailed to its walls, testified to the veneration paid to the god by former generations. But a temple to Mahasu was near completion, a sign that in future the devotions and offerings of the peasants would be divided between the rival claimants although the family deity was likely, for some time to come, to get the major share.
>
> The manner by which the interloper had gained a following and a shrine was typical. For some years, the curse of barrenness had fallen on the women, crops and herds. Few children had been born within the village, while the sons the wives had given to their husbands before the curse descended had sickened and suddenly died. The seed, sown on the terraced fields, had failed to yield its increase; for if, by chance, the crops were good, some calamity destroyed them before the harvest was gathered in. The sheep had ceased to lamb and the goats to bring forth young, while the herds were decimated

by a strange disease. At nightfall, the owners would shut their beasts in the lower storeys of their houses, but in the morning when they went to tend them, some half a dozen would be either dead or dying, despite the fact that on the previous evening they had all seemed well and healthy. At last a skilled diviner was summoned to expound the meaning of these omens of a demon's wrath.

When he comes to describing the oracle's possession, Emerson turns reflexive: "... with head thrown back, fists tightly clenched, and muscles rigid, he swayed from side to side until successive tremors passing through his frame showed that some god or demon had become incarnate in his person." The text is then deleted by hand – an instance of the educated and secular officer in him coming to the fore – as if he is in doubt over whether an exact description of the oracle's manner would make him appear a believer in the divine king's magical power. He continues:

> Speaking in Mahasu's name, he told his listeners that untold to them, some object sacred to the god had come within the village boundaries, and with it too had come Mahasu, who never quits possession of any article, however trifling, once dedicated to his service. The ruin he had brought upon the hamlet was but a means of signifying his arrival; and until a fitting dwelling place was ready for his spirit, the villagers would fail to prosper. Hence, the half-built shrine above the village site. Strangely enough, the diviner in this instance, as in many others which had come to my notice, was not connected to Mahasu's cult in any way, the terror of the god's name having obsessed the soothsayers as strongly as it had the people. In the adjacent village, distant but a mile or so, the former generation had raised a temple to Mahasu. It stood close to the road and facing it upon a narrow strip of land once cultivated, but long since given over to the service of the god. Within the courtyard were several images, each consisting of a thin block of wood, with the upper portion cut into the uncouth likeness of a face. These represented the five divine wazirs [probably the *birs*, the Mahasu deputies] and a large pile of ashes heaped before the lowest proclaimed this as the figure of Chaharya, the fifth attendant, whose only perquisites are ashes from the altar of the master. Mahasu had remained content with this shrine for many years, pursuing a course

of righteous living; but of late he had grown fretful, manifesting a tendency to vex his worshippers. Crops had been indifferent on the land for several seasons, especially in the early harvest, a fact for which their northern aspect was sufficient explanation. The peasants, of course, assigned the failure to a supernatural cause, and to their cost called in the inevitable diviner.

Mahasu, it seems, was upset that the site chosen for his shrine had been rendered inappropriate by a public road passing close to it. It is not known whether the British constructed the road after the temple had come up, but Emerson says with his characteristic derision:

> His sanctuary lay exposed to the prying eyes of strangers, a drawback any self-respecting deity would resent. A little higher up he had seen a nicely levelled piece of land, offering a worthy situation for his shrine. Yes, he meant the headman's field, the one close to the village site, richly manured twice a year so as to yield two bountiful harvests. If this was given to his service, and a sanctuary built thereon, his present dwelling place could come in handy for his chief *wazir*, less sensitive, as became a servant, to the public gaze. Indeed, in this connection, it was hardly fitting to the dignity of a mighty god that his first minister should be exposed to cold in winter and heat in summer without a covering for his head. So the *lambardar* [the village chief] had lately dedicated to the god one of his most fertile fields, where for the future no furrow would be turned, while the villagers were only waiting for the necessary timber to erect a new and better sanctuary – an act of homage which they vainly hoped would keep Mahasu quiet for some time. They had overlooked the other four *wazirs* for whose comfort fresh demands were certain to arise; and as Mahasu never asks but of the best, I could only hope he would cast his envious glance upon a field, belonging to an owner rich enough to bear the loss.

Emerson is also probably dropping a hint here that the divine king's minister was instrumentalising the oracle's possession, using the god for personal pecuniary benefit.

In the meantime, Mahasu was carrying on his feud which, when I visited the village, was at its height. A warning of his wrath had occurred some six or seven years before. Almost next door to the shrine there had stood a building on the edge of the precipitous slope, and occupied by several cultivators, adherents like the other villages of Shalu, their ancestral god. One night, a few days after the annual festival in honour of Mahasu had been celebrated; the master of the house was ladling barley from the store bin. His wife stood by his side, holding open the bag of goatskin into which the grain was being poured. A second man, a near relation, had just crossed the threshold, when suddenly, without a moment's warning, the building started sliding down the slope, and before the inmates could escape, the roof collapsed pinning them beneath the beams and rafters. For a hundred yards or so, they travelled with the debris, until a clump of pine trees arrested their motion. So noiselessly had this occurred, that their neighbours did not know until the morning what had taken place. Almost without hope, they commenced to clear the ruins, when to their amazement out from the heaps of wood and stones came the men and woman a little bruised but otherwise unhurt. Mahasu, as though to prove his power, over life and death, had killed the goats that were tethered in the lower storey of the building. The present *zaildar*, a descendent of the perjurer who had brought misfortune on the hamlet, told me the story of Mahasu's "playing" as he termed it. When he had finished, I asked whether he was still loyal to the cause of Shalu. He answered that he was, but added as an afterthought that as his house was in a lower portion of the village, the "playing" of the jealous god had so far neither injured him nor his. A survivor of the landslide was present at the time, and I asked him also whether he would like the home of Shalu delivered to his rival, so that the people of the village might live in peace. With sturdy courage, he answered that Shalu was the family deity, not to be renounced without good cause; and if the god himself consented to give up his sanctuary, that was his affair otherwise he, the peasant would remain faithful to his father's god. Believing, as he did, that Mahasu had toppled down his house, brought death or sickness to many of his neighbours and that his anger would continue until the shrine was handed over, he showed a spirit worthy of a better cause.

The latest incident in this battle of the gods has been the building of a smaller shrine a year before to house Mahasu's chief *wazir*, the people trusting that this fresh concession would appease his anger for some little time. The quarrel, however, could have only one issue. Mahasu's victory was assured; and in all likelihood it only needed an unforeseen calamity to befall the *zaildar* and his family to bring about surrender.

This incident points towards Mahasu's strategy for expansion. Disruption of order, and then its restoration once allegiance through ritual is obtained, seemed to be the design of his expansion. The divine king was interested only in abject surrender from subjects and their undivided devotion. The colonials, looking at Mahasu's movements through the prism of their own strategies, sometimes construed the divine king's actions as unbridled territorial expansionism. But, not having to deal with a human, their "rationality" rendered them helpless to check it.

Successively secularising regimes were unable to gauge the political significance of Mahasu rituals, and though wary of the expansion, no longer engaged with the divine king. This provided an opportunity for an undercurrent of political unrest to manifest itself in the form of Mahasu's domination over minor kingdoms and divinities, leaving the divine king and his subjects in a stronger position to negotiate with the colonial power. Government officials in contemporary Uttarakhand, the bureaucracy of independent India modelling itself completely on colonial lines, almost always dismiss the Mahasu polity as blind faith. And yet, as we have seen, officials and political leaders are often seen invoking Mahasu to improve their career prospects through promotions and transfers.

Mahasu's growing clout befuddled Emerson. But he was attempting to comprehend the state of affairs by questioning victims about their preferences in relation to the divine. And yet he seems to derive pleasure in refusing requests for support. While in most cases he refused the requests, there were instances where, quite like the divine kings, he had to bend before the collective will of the community.

> ... in the above case the black-mailing tactics of the god did not succeed, but a few months later, much against my will, I was to assist towards his propitiation. We were then camped in a village where the ancestral god was a Naag deity, connected with the five gods whom Mahasu had originally appointed to keep a watch on Chasralu, his hereditary enemy. For some years previous to our visit, Mahasu had been poaching on the serpent god's preserves and as he had lately secured definite recognition, the usual deputation presented itself a short while after our arrival in the camp. The villagers, they said, had for some years been groaning under a load of misfortunes due to their ill treatment of the god Mahasu. Warned by experience, they had now built him a temple at great expense to themselves, but not so far appointed a regular attendant to perform his daily worship. If they called in a Brahmin from outside, they would have to grant him a plot of land in the village and also pay him in kind for his services, a permanent expense they were unwilling to bear. They, therefore, asked that two of the villagers be exempted from doing a period of their free labour for the State, and should instead give service to the god, being responsible for the temple worship and thus saving the village the cost of an outside attendant. In those days, part of the revenue of the State was realized by means of free labour, and begaris, as they were called, were diverted from state service only in very exceptional cases. As Mahasu was not a worthy subject on whom to bestow favours, the request of the villagers was rejected. A few minutes later, however, my old friend Parma Nand, the zaildar [government official responsible for tax collection] of the tract, came to me in great distress and declared that for his sake, if for no other reason, I must give Mahasu the two begaris he demanded. As he was neither a resident of the village nor a subject of Mahasu, there was evidently something behind the insistence, so I refused to reconsider my order until he gave me the full facts of the case.
>
> He hesitated for some time, but at last, his very keen sense of humour getting the very better of a certain shamefacedness, he told me

how he came to be mixed up in the affair. Some thirty years before, a peasant of this village had married a girl from a valley where Mahasu's cult was already established. The couple lived happily for some time, until the man married another wife contrary to the terms of the marriage contract. His first wife finding herself no longer mistress in her own house, promptly ran away to her parents, where she took an early opportunity of getting even with her faithless spouse. Going to the shrine of Mahasu, she told the story of her wrongs, nailed a votive offering to his door, and invoked the curse upon the husband. The god took up her cause, and soon afterwards the man fell ill, several of his cattle died and after that all his crops were poor. The news of the curse had, in the meantime, reached the village and it was whispered that Mahasu had come to avenge the wrongs of his supplicant. The victim tried to placate the god by adopting his worship, and other families in the village followed his example as a precaution which might do good and at any rate could do no harm. The local deity at first disdained to notice this encroachment on his rights, but when Mahasu's cult spread to many households, he took counsel with his neighbours, the confederacy of the five gods, who were also interested in this trespass of their former master. A council was held attended by these gods, their diviners, attendants and followers, and it was resolved to adopt such measures as would drive Mahasu once and for all away from the neighbourhood.

Mahasu cannot bear the sight of blood, nor should a ewe be ever slaughtered in his name; he abominates the smell of fish and garlic and loathes the taste of liquor. Knowing of his idiosyncrasies, the gods and their followers turned them to their own purpose. Invading the village, they entered every house where Mahasu had received a welcome. His emblems were seized, desecrated and thrown into a torrent. Ewes were sacrificed in large numbers, their blood sprinkled in the houses and their flesh paraded round the village; garlic and rotten fish were rubbed upon the walls, and copious libations of liquor were poured on the floors. Never had the great Mahasu been treated with such indignity. His senses of sight, and taste and smell offended he fled the place in wrath, while the five gods with their followers chuckled over his discomfiture. But their mirth was short-lived. The village did, indeed, prosper for some years, Mahasu's worship was abandoned and the circumstances of his visit were remembered only to exalt the prowess of the local gods. Then, one winter, the population was decimated by an attack of typhus fever; the first time the disease had ever visited the neighbourhood.

As is often the case, it became endemic and fresh outbreaks kept occurring after short periods of immunity. Mahasu had clearly thrown down the gage of battle; but, for the present, the people supported by their gods, held out against his attacks. This only made Mahasu more angry and respites grew less frequent until at last the peasants decided on unconditional surrender. But Mahasu, mindful of the blood and fish and garlic, exacted a penalty such as he had never exacted from any other village. Scorning a formal recognition, he demanded a temple with regular attendants, a litter with images of gold and silver and a band of trumpeters and drummers. Nothing less would he accept, and a public subscription was opened to fulfil his needs. Over a thousand rupees had been collected, out of which Parma Nand, the zaildar had himself given two hundred. At the time of our visit, the temple was near completion, images were being made and the Raja's sanction was shortly to be obtained to the conferment of a litter and trumpets on the god. But Mahasu, dissatisfied with the rate of progress, had given strong hint to the villagers to bestir themselves. During the previous winter typhus had been more virulent than ever and a number of deaths had taken place. It was at this point that Parma Nand had become involved in the affair. Anxious to stay the hand of the avenger, he had sworn an oath to Mahasu that when I visited the village he would persuade me to give two begaris as attendants in the temple. He had, in short, become surety for my compliance with the god's demands, and hence his close concern with my order of refusal.

Emerson had to now contend with a request from an official of his own administration. He was ambivalent about whether to accept his own notions of Mahasu tyranny as superstition – leading to a lack of engagement and allowing the suffering of a close acquaintance – or make a concession and bow to Mahasu sovereignty.

The dénouement was so unexpected and so ludicrous that Parma Nand and I chuckled for some time over the humour of the situation. But it was really no joke for him as he was careful to explain. If Mahasu did not get his two attendants, the zaildar was a perjured wretch, and no argument of mine would convince him to the contrary. Typhus fever might or might not be due to filthy houses, in which the cattle and the flocks shared the scanty accommodation with their owners. He was too polite to contradict my views; but this was long before the days of rural uplift and, for his part, he would rather adopt Mahasu than sanitary living as a remedy. Nor did it console him to be told that he had done his best to perform his portion of the bond. The punishment, he knew, would fall on him and not on me. So, finally, we compromised. The State was to give one begari and the villagers were to provide the second attendant. This apparently satisfied the zaildar who did not again raise the question. But when I next saw him, two months later, he mentioned casually that a new granary, which he had just completed, had been burnt to the ground and the grain inside destroyed. Presumably, if Mahasu had been given no begari at all, Parma Nand would have lost his dwelling place as well.

This minor concession extracted by Mahasu from the colonial official was significant in itself, since the divine kings, in comparison with their human counterparts, now began to appear to their subjects (since the time Young sought Mahasu's adjudication almost a century earlier) to be in a better position to negotiate with the colonial powers, especially in matters of protecting tradition. With Emerson following a conscious policy of refusal of requests to support Mahasu expansionism, this was a minor but definite victory for the divine king. Despite Emerson's "rationality" and scepticism towards Mahasu rituals, the official could not avoid getting directly embroiled in Mahasu ritual politics.

The following description of his personal encounter with the divine king, again dismissive, indicates that the divine king's agency was indeed gaining strength – enough to rattle the topmost official of the administration.

... the following morning we struck camp, our next halting place being a couple of thousand feet higher up the valley. Our second boy, then about nine months old, was carried in a dooly [palanquin] with open sides, but with a railing all around to keep him from falling out, and as he had just reached the venturesome stage, we had tied a stout rope above the railing. An orderly was deputed to walk by his side and keep an eye on him. About half a mile from camp and opposite the village where Mahasu had played his trick on the woman [as the panther], we left the beaten track for a short cut up the hillside. The path was steep and so strewn with boulders that the bearers of the dooly had some trouble keeping it straight, and, while they were struggling along, the baby crawled between the rope and the railing, and over-balancing himself, landed on his head below. Fortunately, the spot where he fell was fairly soft and beyond a shaking and a lump on his head, the size of a walnut, he suffered little from his adventure, the orderly coming worst out of the affair.

Several weeks later, we were again on tour in the same direction, one of our marches being along a road from which we could see our former camping place nestling in the middle of a forest a thousand feet below. When we were directly above it, I was walking close to the dooly, still in charge of the orderly. He and I chanced to glance down at the same time, and the prospect evidently awakened memories in his guilty conscience.

"Sahib," said he, "do you know why the baby sahib fell from his dooly?" I made the obvious reply.

"No Sahib," said he "I was not to blame, for less than a second before he fell, the baby was sitting down playing happily."

"Why then did he fall?" I asked.

"The Sahib may remember," replied he, "that, the day before, the villagers had begged for a grant from the State to buy incense for Mahasu's shrine and their petition was refused. Well, it was close to the shrine that the baba [the baby] fell from his dooly, and beyond a doubt it was Mahasu who upset him. For how could a tender child fall from such a height and not be hurt, or fall by accident on soft ground when stones lay all round? The god did not wish him, but only to show a miracle."

I accepted the explanation, but warned him that it would be he and not the god who would suffer, if Mahasu played any such tricks in future. The man, it may be added, was a native of the village in question and merely voiced the popular view.

Analysis of Emerson's descriptions helps us come to terms with processes of state-making and explains why groups like the mountain communities of the Western Himalayas resist it. Unlike Young, in Emerson's engagement with the divine king, attitudes had transformed and hardened, altering social equations, compelling the divine king to enforce his ritual regime. For both Mahasu and the British, structure had gradually begun to dominate the practice-induced two-way process of contact.

Young had engaged with the divine king in order to conclude the Rawain Settlement in a manner he felt correct, in the process also serving the larger interests of empire. In doing so, he was tacitly accepting and performing Mahasu sovereignty over the Himalayan regions. However, as we travel down the winding lanes of historical contact in Mahasu territory, we come across a marked change in the attitudes and terms of engagement between the colonials and Mahasu. This transformation in attitudes becomes evident in how social groups are looked at, top down, and the manner in which their ritual practices are textualised.

The marked differences in attitudes between Young and Emerson indicate that the opening up of remote locations led to the accumulation of information about the other, greater accessibility, and the introduction of a money economy leading to interdependence – aspects that we generally equate with the modern, the secular, and the developed. But this did not by default lead to a more liberal acceptance of the other. If anything, this may indicate a growing orthodoxy, a narrowing of mindsets.

In response to the British project of state-making in this region, Mahasu was responding with aggression. Not only were the pastoral gods being subjugated, but the neighbouring regions under human kings, whose influence was anyway on the wane, were also being forced into hosting Mahasu on tour. In that sense, Mahasu's growing belligerence can be seen as a response to changing colonial attitudes. Scott (2008) proposed the idea of Zomia, describing such peripheral regions as "non-state space", where the state found it difficult to establish its authority. He refers to such areas as fluid, with people constantly in motion, with no permanent organisation or allegiances, ephemeral leadership, pliable and fugitive subsistence patterns, and shifting linguistic practices and ethnic identity. In such spaces, economic, political, and cultural organisation is a strategic adaptation to avoid incorporation in state structures. Events during Emerson's tenure point towards the regions on the periphery of the realm of Mahasu emerging as Zomia-like non-state spaces where the divine king's belligerence towards the pastoral gods forced them into severing familial and trade ties with Mahasu-ruled territories. Regions like Dodra and Kwar, for fear of Mahasu subverting their local gods, refused to maintain any relations with the realm, forcing themselves to withdraw from the mainstream. On the other hand, the Mahasu kingdom, a conceptual state based on orality and ritual, in its effort to avoid colonial empire-building (attempting to escape instruments of the state such as tax collectors) found itself too in a Zomia-like state.

Mahasu's expansionism emerged as an effective strategy enabling the divine king's subjects to negotiate with the colonial rulers. In 1935 the British gave special status to the area falling under the Mahasu realm. In independent India the Mahasu polity, carrying forward the legacy of collective action, managed to strike a bargain with the state, securing tribal status, and consequently privileges for itself.

7

Duty Bound

In the summer of 2013 a research project named SFB 619 at the University of Heidelberg officially came to a close. Since the project focused on the dynamics of ritual in Asia, the closing ceremony, it was felt by most social scientists involved in the project, had to include a simulation of rituals as practised in Asia. To me, as someone working on rituals and having been part of the project, the ceremony was not only intriguing but also revealed how rituals from South Asia, associated with temple ceremony and court etiquette, were perceived by academia in Europe, and in this case adapted to the closing of a university research programme. After speeches and a song titled "Rituals Change" came the sham violence of saffron-coloured soft cushions hurled at each other in the assembly hall. Outside the magnificent Alte Aula (the university's old hall) stood a palanquin awaiting the chief of the research group, who was to be given a farewell fit for kings. The palanquin had been fashioned out of a patient's chair with handles, probably brought from a hospice. It was decorated with shiny cloth and odd trinkets brought back from fieldwork in India. The participants carried saffron-coloured parasols in a procession on Heidelberg's main street. Professor Axel Michels, crowned and clad in a robe, was seated on the chair-like palanquin. In his hands he held a pumpkin and a gourd – the equivalent of sceptres. For a bunch of tourists from India walking the streets, it was quite amusing to hear a group of Europeans shouting, "*Axel Michels ki jai!*" (Victory to Axel Michels!)

Once the procession wound its way through the Hauptstrasse (the main street) and entered the Uniplatz (the University Square), the professor was asked to smash the pumpkin and the gourd – the equivalent of making a sacrifice – and formally declare the research programme closed. Much merry-making followed. We may well have been in Hanol rather than in Heidelberg.

For the organisers, the ceremony represented their interpretation of an honourable send-off. Perhaps it was also something of a send-up, a lot of the ritualisation having been improvised to fit the celebratory mood of the occasion. Decisions on the chronology of events of the day were arrived at after deliberations amongst scholars who had been studying similar rituals in various parts of the world. It would not be incorrect to suggest that something Bell (1992) referred to as a "ritual sense" was driving people's actions in their curation of an event that had been fulfilling for them as well as for the "king" of their project.

Looking back at the ceremonies in Heidelberg, it is quite evident that the entire event was choreographed to underscore the hierarchy within the project's offices. The speeches, the seating plans, the toasts, and of course the palanquin ride, besides offering the researchers a catharsis after years of work, also drove home points about the project's power structure. Very similar, perhaps, are the palanquin processions of the divine kings one comes across in the Himalaya. These processions, as they approach a village and community, become an expression of the power relationships between the divine king's realm and the host village. They reflect the entire realm's goodwill towards a specific village or homestead, as much as telling us what purchase a community or clan has within the Mahasu polity to pull the divine king towards it.

Referring to deity-ruled diminutive polities of the Western Himalayas, Sutherland (2003: 32) argues that "Evidence . . . vividly demonstrates how processional practices integrated Hindu rural polities in a world-ordering scale of peasant, monarchical, imperial and cosmic formations during the period of indirect British rule

Photo 7.1: The Chalda Mahasu palanquin in procession.

from 1815 until independence – and . . . under previous forms of foreign rule." He argues that the processions of the divine kings help weave together time and space into equations of power and understanding. A political construction of space and time is the key to decoding the historical archive of practice inscribed in the landscape. This space and time, he says, engenders a shared sovereignty, a collaborative rule commonly referred to as *devta ka raj* (lit. rule by deity).

Mahasu palanquins are usually made of gilded silver embellished with images of the Hindu pantheon, with elongated handles in the rear and front. The handles help to mount it on the shoulders of the oracles and upper-caste men from communities hoping to host the divine king. The roof of the palanquin rises up in a low pyramid with miniature *shikharas* (pinnacles), quite like the Mahasu temples, marking the four corners of the palanquin box. The deity is placed inside the box, wrapped in red cloth. When the divine king prepares for procession and is seated inside the palanquin, placed by the priest on duty at the behest of the minister, its lower part is covered in fresh white cotton cloth or muslin brought by the aspiring hosts. At times, to keep the cloth in place while traversing hill slopes, a rope is tied around the palanquin box – in the manner of peasants tying a rope around their waists to keep their buttonless coats firmly wrapped around them. Interestingly, at times, a *dangra* (battle-axe) is inserted in the rope tied around the palanquin, in the manner of humans carrying a *dangra* (hand-axe).

The Mahasu palanquin's arrival at a village is always referred to in terms of the presence of the *devta* – the deity – and not his vehicle. The villagers always talk in terms of *devta ka swagat* (lit. welcome to the god) or *devta ka chal* (lit. movement of the god) rather than making specific references to the palanquin as it arrives or moves. For the Mahasu subject, the palanquin is the divine king himself, not a representation. In contrast, in the contemporary,

Photo 7.2: A battle-axe tucked in a warrior's belt during the archery festival of Bissu.

"rational" political world of bureaucracy and vernacular media, the palanquin is always referred to as *dev doli* (the *devta*'s vehicle). The palanquin also connects the Mahasu realm to mainstream Hindu tradition through the images, even as little gestures like the carrying of the ritual battle-axe on the waist connect Mahasu with the pastoral practice of alpine pastoral communities.

Priests carry whisks and ensure that external objects, even leaves from trees, do not defile the palanquin. The palanquin is never placed on open ground, always resting in a tent, a temple, or a high-caste home of Mahasu's choosing. While upper-caste men and the oracles take turns carrying the palanquin, the women are restricted to making offerings. Some men are drafted to carry the divine king's jewels, images of the *birs*, the ensigns and parasols, his tents, and cooking vessels. The minister carries the Mahasu sword. The procession is led by drummer-bards, the *bajgi*, who through their drumming provide the fanfare and ritual recitation of the genealogies. In some regions the wives of the *bajgis* sing and dance before the palanquin, even as a large number of goats – whose sacrifice was deemed rejected by the divine king – accompany the procession. In the case of Chalda Mahasu, the *chatrai* (the militia of the divine king) walk along.

Mahasu processions are pageants with thousands in attendance. It is incumbent upon host communities to advertise and generate crowds that match the divine king's prestige, as much as it is socially significant to seek the divine king's blessings once the palanquin visits them. But at the heart of the pomp is power politics. The mobility of the palanquin presents the aspect of Mahasu divine kingship where either the subjects travel to seek their divine king's audience or the kingdom itself travels to the subjects. To an extent, the processional ritual undertaken by the king helps unite the realm from within. The processions ensure that power relations are defined in a village setting where proximity to the *devta* defines hierarchical position. Such hierarchical positions are often linked to entrenched caste positions too, and the Mahasu cult appears strongest in pockets where caste-based differentiation remains well defined.

I focus here on the rituals of Mahasu *puja* performed at Mahasu temples, my effort being to illustrate how relations of political power are encoded within them. Through a description of the ritual of Mahasu *puja* I hope to show that ritual control over Mahasu *puja* leads to interactional patterns of political control over the cult of the divine king. Through an elaboration of this ritual and the role of the Mahasu priests, also referred to as *deopujyas*, we understand how even though the Rajputs are able to corner the bulk of economic resources – and are therefore politically strong – their social rank, and that of others, is transitory and dependent on complex processes of ritual control where interdependencies all too often emerge. Thus, even though the Rajputs may be visible as those who dominate the cult, it is ritual practice that ascribes value to other social classes and leads to the distribution of power. Leverage over ritual practice enables the relatively powerless groups, the Bajgi, Kolta, and even the Brahman, to resolve their social positions in their interactions with the dominant Rajputs. The term Rajput itself does not connote a uniform group but encapsulates a complicated set of groupings, each involved in their own negotiations of power with others. In that sense, social rank is intensely negotiated and cannot be bracketed into strict hierarchical boundaries.

In earlier chapters, I focused on the longevity of the Mahasu cult on account of the adaptive capacity of rituals. We saw how the religious cannot be separated from the political, and how Mahasu rituals performed in temples, as well as in the divine king's processions, almost always translate into political effects. We have looked at instances of Mahasu's cultural contact with outside influences and the effects produced. These rituals have withstood the test of time, even as the attitudes of the world outside have been transformed. Now we see how significant to Mahasu kingship and interactions of power in his realm are the establishment, through ritual, of relationships with the soil, gift giving and receiving, the offering and accepting of hospitality, and negotiation of allegiances as markers of political power – in preference to the concept of establishing control over land and resources. All these actions of divine kingship socially inscribe power relations, and the medium of this inscription is the ritual, which is central to social life. In fact, it would not be incorrect to say that, going by the traditional codes, life revolves around *devta ka kaam* (the work of the divine kings). Here I deal also with the innovative potential of ritual, describing how different social groups are engaged in a constant contest for proximity to the divine king through control over ritual practice.

For the priests that perform it, the ritual of Mahasu *puja* begins with the gaining of competence to perform the *puja*. This competence is attained through fasting and ritual bathing in the temple spring as a purifying practice. The priest (*deopujya*) has to go through these rites to get rid of external defilements. With a change into fresh clothes after his icy bath, he is ready to commence worship. As the priest walks up to the temple from the temple spring – a water source close to the temple is always retained and segregated for priests to bathe in – an official walks ahead, flailing his arms in a gesture informing everyone that the pure one is arriving and they may not approach him lest he be defiled. The divine king is invited to assume his seat through an invocation. Mahasu *puja* involves sixteen purifying rites, including cleaning, bathing, fasting, adornment in new clothes, and offering water, clarified butter, or oil. The sprinkling of water and presentation of flowers, incense, sweetmeats or coconuts, and fire or lamp oblations, follow. If necessary, divine kings may be awakened through an invocation and, once the ritual is finished, given a send-off or even sent to bed.

Within this broad framework of rites fall the special offerings, such as the offering of *dhal* (lit. shield) or tribute by visitors to the temple. *Dhal* is an offering in exchange for protection, and may be given by a woman to her husband, by a man to his father or elder brother or elders, and by elders to the divine king. *Dhal* is offered as acceptance of subordination, with the resultant assurance of emotional and political security. One usually approaches the Mahasu sanctum, hands folded over the chest, and then bows before it, placing the nose between the gaps of the fingers and then touching the chin with the fingertips. Low-caste men, however, stand outside the temple, at a considerable distance from the threshold of the outer verandah (*mandapam*), facing the temple, and in a gesture of supplication remove their caps and keep them inverted on the ground, like a bowl. A rubbing of the nose to the ground follows.

According to Bhatt (2010), the ritual of *puja* offered at Mahasu shrines can broadly be categorised into eight occasions – rituals of regular worship to the divine king, rituals of the rites of passage, rituals of social differentiation, rituals of the spread of the cult or diffusion, rituals of sovereignty, rituals of the festive cycle, rituals of distinctive offerings or *yajna*, and rituals to ward off Mahasu's wrath (*dos*) with the ritual of sacrifice (*bali*).

The ritual of worship, performed day in and day out at Mahasu shrines, is connected through the *sandhis* (cycles of time) weaving together dawn, noon, and dusk. At the Mahasu temple at Hanol, depending on the time of the day, each *puja* is referred to as *prabhati*, *namti*, and *sandaul*. The *prabhati* is essentially a ritual of waking up the divine king and his deputies. The ritual is accompanied with beating the kettledrum with prescribed beats of the *naubat* (temple fanfare). Once the priest has purified himself after a bath at the freezing waters of the upper spring called *devta ka paani* (lit. water of the gods), he arrives at the temple. The ritual inside the sanctum sanctorum is secretive and the priest performs it all by himself. The details of the ritual were therefore narrated to me in parts by various priests at Hanol, which I compiled over the years. Once inside the sanctum sanctorum, the priest commences the *patri puja* (the offering of leaves and flowers). The leaves are Chhamra (*Cynodon dactylon*) or Phaja (*Prunus cerasoides*); the flowers offered are usually the Nagras (Daffodil, *Narcissus tazetta*), grown at the rear of the temple in the deity's garden, referred to as Kungvari.

The Chhamra is a grass that gives out a pleasant fragrance upon burning and it is offered during summer. During the winter Nagras, and for the extreme winter months Phaja, are offered. It is obligatory on the priest to collect the offerings keeping his feet unshod, and the collection is usually done when he goes out for the ritual bath. Then he cleans the offerings in the *devta ka pani* and brings them to the temple. As the priest enters the first chamber of the sanctum, known as the Chandi-ki-pol (the silver chamber), his deputy hands him two large bells of bronze and a vessel for offering incense called *dhupauchi*, a small vessel filled with clarified butter called *tambi*, and a silver bowl for rice known as *saar*. At this point the priest enters the inner sanctum alone. He makes the offering to Mahasu and his deputies almost in a state of trance. The beating of the drums and blowing of trumpets adds to the atmosphere. The priest makes the offerings, first to the *lakhau*, a bronze lamp, then to the images of fauna (birds, lions, etc.) kept in the sanctum, and finally to the Mahasu images and those of the deputies, to the accompaniment of the ringing of bells. Once the priest has offered the *dhal*, the bells stop ringing, the drums continue. Followed by this is the *akshat puja*, also locally known as *chawal jhapna* (rice offering). Rice is offered in a gold bowl to the deity while a lamp is lit with the help of an ignited pine twig lit from the lamps that are kept burning constantly, the use of matchsticks being forbidden. The rice is mixed with clarified butter. This mixture is called *akshat* and is offered thrice to each of the objects in the same order – the lamp, animal images, and then Mahasu, followed by the deputies. A grain or two of rice is placed on the Mahasu image. Finally, incense is offered. In offering the incense, the order is reversed, with Kailu, a Mahasu deputy, receiving the offering first, then the lamp, followed by Mahasu, the trumpet of Kalka, and others. The priest then smears vermilion, kept in the inner sanctum, on his forehead, picks up a part of the *patri* leaves offered, and places them over the left earlobe. His legs bare, he emerges from the inner sanctum, carrying the offerings of rice and *patri*.

It is now the turn of the Mahasu subjects waiting outside the shrine to receive the offerings through the *thani* (the temple official), who distributes the rice and the vegetation as *prasad*. But before that he distributes the *patri* leaves/flowers to the divine king's officials. In this he follows the caste hierarchy, distributing in order of Brahman priests first, Rajput *vazir* next, and then the others. Towards the drummer-bards he tosses some rice (not offered to them), while some rice is reverentially placed over their drums and trumpets. The *thani* then walks towards the *rawali-pand*, the building adjacent to the temple that serves as the temple kitchen. Here, he tosses some rice and places some on the hearth. Only then do the subjects, waiting patiently and hands folded, get the *patri* leaves/flowers and rice. The *patri* is promptly placed over the left earlobe and rice pressed to the forehead with the palm of the hand to make them stick there. The remaining raw grains that stick to the palm are chewed upon.

The priest now commences what is known as the *baahar-ki-puja* (the worship outside). He walks around all the little shrines, offers rice and *patri*, and then tosses rice in all the four directions, finally tossing some on his own seat, the hearth that keeps him warm and the cash box where visitors offer money. He tosses some rice in the direction of the nearby Mahasu temples (for instance, Thadiyar and Maindrath in the case of Hanol) and in the directions of Kedarnath and Badrinath. He passes close to the temple kitchen, tossing rice towards it and then enters the temple garden where offerings are made to the images of the Mahasu deputies, finally arriving at the shrine of Kali. The final offerings are made here and the ash from the burning incense is dropped in the *ghatval*, a little pit in the garden. The priest then returns to his chamber and, pouring water over the temple bells, picks them up and begins to ring. The ringing of the bells signals the end of the puja, and the drummers, who have been playing all along, stop.

With the end of the puja, the priest can now enter the temple kitchen and end his fast. He eats the food he has cooked prior to the ritual worship. The afternoon and evening pujas follow a similar pattern, except that during the *sandaul* (evening worship) the offerings of flowers and vegetation made in the morning are removed from the images and the deity requested to retire for the night.

Mahasu puja, like most practice in the Mahasu realm – the rituals of rites of passage, rituals of the *devta* imbuing objects with his essence, rituals expressive of sovereignty, those of festivity or the occasional distinctive puja, rituals to ward off Mahasu's wrath or offence (*dos*), and the rituals of sacrifice (*bali*) – all underscore the differentiation between castes, neatly laying out the hierarchies and declaring the dominance of one group over the other. However, the puja ritual also differentiates between groups internally, by privileging a few and excluding the rest. For instance, it is the upper-caste *nayab vazirs*, the Rajput ministers, who are *jajmans* (patrons) of the puja, and it is at their pleasure that the *deopujyas*, the Brahman priests, perform the ritual. Not all Brahmans, though, can perform the rites of puja. Only the Brahman caste men from specific villages are permitted to perform the priestly function as *deopujyas* (the divine priests), and a detailed division of duties in the temples is stipulated and sanctioned by the clan polity. This power over performance of rituals that results in proximity to divine kings and therefore to political power is closely guarded as family and clan inheritance by a select few. Usually passed on to the eldest male in the family, the institution of *panti* (duty to the divine kings) demands competence that is tested at difficult times (for instance, in case of drought one should be able to coax the *devta* into bringing rain through efficacious practice), and follows a strict code that binds those who accept being duty-bound into an exclusive group.

Duty is usually passed on through the generations within the clan and can be performed only by those who don the sacred thread and go through initiation by another *deopujya*. The initiation involves receiving the secret *sandhya* mantra, which in no case can be shared with another, except during an initiation. The *deopujyas* (henceforth referred to as priests), once initiated, are expected to don the sacred thread slung over the left shoulder on the right of the body across the chest and the back. The thread itself measures eighty-five widths of the human palm (*pichasi angul*) and can only be installed by a priest. While preparing to don the sacred thread the priest has to fast, and donning makes it obligatory on the priest to follow a strict code. While performing the ablutions, the thread must be wound around the right ear to prevent being defiled. If the thread were to snap, the priest would have to interrupt everything and squat at the spot until another priest brought a replacement and replaced the defiled thread. According to Bhatt (2010), the priest would have to forgo his meals for at least four days in such an eventuality. Conversations and touching other humans as well as ritual objects is prohibited until the snapped thread is replaced.

According to Harish Dobhal, a priest at Hanol, restrictions imposed on the *deopujya* priests include those of commensality and social contact – tantamount to seclusion. Priests on duty are permitted to consume only food cooked on their own or by members of the immediate family (including women) when not on duty. They can partake of *kacha* or food cooked with water and not oil as a medium in other high-caste homes. However, while on duty in the temple they need to cook their own food, assisted by the *thani*. Contact with lower castes like the *kolta* is taboo. While not on *panti*, priests can adopt a non-vegetarian diet, provided the flesh is of male goats. The priests, because they are frequently touring with the divine kings, become *svapaki* (those that can consume only self-cooked meals). This, because the palanquin usually travels with a large group and food can easily be defiled, leading to ritual failure during Mahasu puja. While touring with the divine king, they usually eat only once a day, before sundown. The consumption of two substances, water and tobacco, is unrestricted. Tobacco, however, can only be smoked and not chewed.

To perform *panti* or duty, the priest has to travel barefoot to the *devta*'s temple. The donning of *kopin* (the loincloth) is essential. Conversing with low-caste women without donning the loincloth invites the *devta's* wrath. Before the priest can cook his meal, the temple kitchen (*rawli pand*) must be thoroughly washed. The priest is expected to remain undefiled until the *bari puja* (big puja) at sundown. If the priest happens to see a corpse or a dead animal, he must bathe again and forgo a meal. If he happens to touch a low-caste individual – *kolta*, *bajgi*, *chura* (janitors), *musalman* (Muslim), or *dangar* (an animal with all four limbs on the ground), he has to sacrifice a goat and once again forgo a meal. Equally strict purification measures need to be followed if the priest comes into close proximity of women, especially menstruating women, who are viewed as sources of defilement.

While it would be impracticable for Rajput peasants and pastoralists, as well as the lower castes, to honour such ritual restrictions, even from amongst the Brahman only a few can follow the rules of priesthood. The few that do are thought to possess special powers, their self-sacrifice granting them the privilege of close proximity to the divine king. However, on Mahasu tours, when the palanquin needs to be carried long distances through harsh terrain, the Rajputs also get to come close to the seat of power. The political capital of the drummer-bards is also enhanced since without their ritual drumming and recitation the deity would neither wake up nor move or sleep. In that sense, the divine king becomes ambivalent on his tours and the kingdom more inclusive.

When it comes to the making of offerings to the divine king, it is the Rajputs who exclude other groups through monopolistic control over that right. But what makes caste negotiable is ritual control, according to which even the drummer-bards, much lower in the caste pecking order, can, even though rarely and at grave risk, get even with the Brahman and Rajput, asserting their importance by refusing to accompany the procession or to recite before the commencement of a temple puja. The Mahasu origin myth itself recounts that the divine kings, in order to defeat their rival Vishnu, had to bribe his *bajgi*, and they can still be counted as significant by refusing to oblige the Rajput. This change could be ascribed to more employment opportunities arising out of reservation benefits extended by the state to the lower castes as well as tribes. Inclusion in one social group, enhancing their leverage for acceptance in another, the drummer-bards perhaps feel that accompanying the divine king in the processions does not add to their cultural capital as compared to other, more lucrative jobs. Despite this, many still perform their duties to the *devta*.

The most significant periodic celebration at Mahasu temples is the Jagra, or the night vigil of Mahasu, organised on the basis of lunar calculations, on the fourth and fifth of the brightest fortnights of the month of *bhadon* (beginning mid-August). The Jagra rituals are clearly segregated into the rituals of *harare* and *nirore*. Groups of pilgrims keep trickling in before the dates of the *harare* rituals. They set up cooking hearths in the temple compound and around it, with foodgrain and cooking utensils being provided from the temple store. Motley groups – men and women from the

Photo 7.3: *Tandi* or parallel dancing rows with the drummers.

regions of Bawar, Fateh Parvat, Bangan, Chaupal, Rohru, and Jubbal – congregate at Hanol on the preceding night. Increasingly, groups of businessmen from the plains, for instance, the brass-making town of Moradabad and media representatives from Dehra Dun, have also begun to come.

The *harare* rituals commence with sunrise and yield place to the *nirore* rituals close to midnight as the night vigil commences. For participants in the Jagra, it is essential to offer tribute or *dhal*. As night falls, a *chira* or ritual torch is lit atop a branch of the Shirul (*Bombax ceiba*) tree, with the lower part or handle of the torch secured to the ground. Groups of young men and women dance around the flame throughout the night even as the *bajgis* try to keep pace with the movements of the *tandis* (human chains). Two men or women join hands behind the third person's back and make a circular formation. They move sideways to the beat of the drum, the choreography permitting the entire community to join. At times men and women make parallel rows. The drummers conduct the dance by their playing and vary the beat with the mood of the large group swaying to it. The songs sung and danced to usually relate to Mahasu genealogies, praise, and invocation.

Close to midnight, the priests' duty shift changes and new priests assume charge. The rituals of *nirore* commence with the change of duties and reflect the cleansing of the divine king's abode at the end of the monsoon, the ritual bathing of idols and weapons marking the period of separation of the *devta* from the palanquin until the time of Vijayadashami.

Priests other than those performing routine temple rites perform these rituals. They are specialists and come from specific locations. For instance, in the case of Bautha Mahasu at Hanol, it is the priests from Chattra and Nenus villages that come and perform the ritual. In case of Bashik Mahasu, it is the Dobhal priests from Bagi. A number of drummer-bards congregate and at the opportune time a signal is given by the priests, resulting in a fanfare of drums and trumpets in the forenoon. *Nirore* is a secretive ritual and no one is allowed to observe it.

The images of the Mahasus, other than Bautha, are placed in their palanquins while Bautha, the seated one, is placed on a low stool made of silver, within the sanctum. For the annual ritual cleansing, Bautha must be raised from his permanent seat of power, the sanctum of the temple at Hanol. Placing the other Mahasus too in their vehicles during the elaborate rituals of *nirore* seems to be geared towards the task of dislodging the divine kings from positions of power, albeit briefly. This task, even though it may appear as simple as a lifting up of the idol for a cleansing, is of special significance and therefore accompanied with drumming and elaborate ritual. Since the rationale for the divine kings' grip over political power is their consubstantiality with the soil of the land, for a brief recess, before the cleansing can happen, this relationship is severed, and for these critical moments of liminality for the divine king, who is not connected to the soil of the kingdom in the interregnum, elaborate ritual is needed to keep the kingdom safe and ward off evil.

In the case of Bautha Mahasu, once the worship rituals are done and the task of cleansing is at hand, the priest on duty, clad only in a loincloth, enters the dark chamber of the Hanol temple's inner sanctum and places the divine king's idol in a large bowl full of *gaunt* (cow urine mixed with milk). With a dagger held to his own heart, he squats near the altar with the bowl behind his bare back, praying to the divine king to commence his ritual bath. The gesture of holding the dagger is a threat that, should the *devta* not oblige, the priest will take his own life. The divine kings are believed to vacate their seats of power for the ritual cleansing for fear of affliction with the curse of causing a Brahman's death, for the divine king is always represented as the Rajput, who consider themselves protectors of the Brahman. Assured of the accomplishment of the ritual when he can feel the liquid splashing on his back – for in no case can he look at the divine king – he picks up the idol and places it once again on the designated position inside the sanctum. Cajoling via threats is probably a part of the Brahman priests' habitus. They must use all means at their disposal to negotiate their position of ritual superiority in a cult dominated by Rajputs. Threats to cause ritual afflictions are very much a part of this negotiable proximity to the divine king.

Before the cleansing of Mahasu's silver, the sceptres, weapons, plates, and trumpets starts, temple officials carry them outdoors for a public viewing. After a while they are carried to the river and scrubbed clean with sand, lime, and detergent. As Mahasu's *donriyan* (the box-like cylinder of silver, gilded with coins and representing the divine king's suzerainty) is being carried, Rajput men try to seize it from the temple officials in a simulation of the tradition of the looting of this representation of the divine king's power. In earlier times, the *khunds* (the divine king's militia), wearing heavy iron arm-braces as protective gear, would await the arrival of the *donriyan*, concealing themselves behind boulders around the temple. They would then compete for control over it, leading to much violence and bloodshed. Referred to as the ritual

Photo 7.4: Mahasu's silver *donriyan* represents the power of the divine kings.

of the looting of the *donriyan*, now performed only in its mimetic and harmless form (as are several other violent rites), it is followed by the cooking of red rice grown in the divine kings' fields. Cooked in a community cauldron, the meal is shared by the men from *sathi* and *pansi*. This partaking from a common cauldron is a rarity for these constantly skirmishing moieties. Hospitality is what brings the rivals together, albeit briefly. The rituals come to an end with the special drumbeats of the *sandaul* – the invocations are meant to be sung at sundown – indicating that the divine king is resting and may not be disturbed till the next morning.

While the performance of the rituals described above was earlier a matter of privilege, it is increasingly being done out of a sense of duty. The priests who perform the rituals now feel tied down to their positions, the work of the divine kings performed nowadays more out of fear of the divine king's wrath falling upon them and their families, less out of a sense of privilege. This is happening because traditional patterns of dominance are being challenged by government schemes of empowerment. With reservations for lower castes and tribals having assumed a new importance, a new class is emerging whose occupational commitments do not permit fulfilment of the norms of temple duty.

The general refrain among the priests is, "We give up so much to serve the *devta*, we awaken him and perform rituals until he sleeps, we trudge in the snow with his palanquin, and it is the *sayanas*, the Rajput elders, that walk away with all the benefits. We do not even get the traditional rights that we had over temple offerings, since these people control the politics." The politics referred to are not just contemporary electoral politics that lead to control over the executive administrative functions of religion and state; they refer also to control over resources like land – a factor vital to social dominance. The Rajputs' ability to manipulate support from temple officials, especially from priests, has made them dominate the electoral politics of democratic institutions. Very seldom has there been much opportunity for the priests and low-caste *bajgi* to voice their protest. While the state and its officials look down upon the priests as those that exploit religion for personal gain, their policy is focussed on improving the lot of the lower castes, the *bajgi* and the Kolta. Given the demographics, seats in political positions are now reserved for the lower castes. For instance, Kabir Das, a *bajgi* elected on a reserved seat to the district panchayat (the village-level elected assembly in Chakrata), is the custodian of common lands and will make significant administrative decisions. Traditionally a regular fixture in Chalda Mahasu's entourage, he could not, owing to official engagements, make it to the procession recently when the *devta* entered Bawar.

Given the constitutional ideal of egalitarianism, with job reservations for all those falling within the category of "scheduled tribe", which extends job reservations even to Brahman and Rajput in this region, both *deopujya* and *bajgi* often threaten to give up the tough codes that the *devta* system imposes on them, especially when they migrate for employment to urban areas. The Rajputs construe this as the greatest threat to the system of divine kingship, even as they believe the work done by subordinate castes is their bounden duty.

The Mahasu *vazir* told me: "In the near future, the *devta* might turn sedentary. In fact, we shall ask him to stop travelling since we cannot find enough people – priests, drummers and porters – for these arduous journeys. No one wants to perform traditional duties and follow the tough codes any more. They are all used to travelling in Jeeps and eating at restaurants. How can the *devta* continue his tours?" Social change has led to transformations in ritual as well. For instance, Chalda, or the walking Mahasu's twelve-yearly cycle of processions alternating his movement through *sathi* and *pansi*, has been going on unhindered ever since people can remember, but the *chal* or the constant travelling of Chalda Mahasu was in recent times interrupted for almost seven years, with the divine king arriving at the village of Shiraji after altering his usual route, ordering the construction of a new temple, and extending his stay until the community came up with a befitting edifice. The ambitious project of building the temple continued for seven years, fuelling speculation that the *devta* had turned sedentary and would settle in this grand temple. Had modernity altered the traditional codes of caste so radically that the divine kings would not find enough reason and manpower to travel? Are the agentive powers of the institution of *devta* losing their leverage over the community, especially in the face of change that modern living and the state's social engineering brings? Before we reach a conclusion, we must examine the nature of Mahasu's ritual worship and its constituents, and look also at the institution of *panti* (duty to the divine king). These practices, traditionally leading to inclusion of some at the cost of others, indicate ongoing contestations within the cult.

The distribution of ritual duties reflects an arrangement that grants close proximity to certain groups within the Brahman community to the divine king. For instance, Bashik Mahasu, the eldest of the four siblings, who rules over regions in the *sathi*, is worshipped by the Joshi clan of the village Nenus, the Semwals of Maindrath and the Dobhal of Bagi, with the latter claiming the larger share of the offerings brought in by devotees to their divine king, on account of a general recognition for the village of Bagi as the capital of Bashik Mahasu's territory. Pabasik Mahasu's worship rituals are exclusively entrusted to the Nautiyal clan of Dagoli. As far as Bautha Mahasu at Hanol is concerned, even though it is widely accepted that the Dobhals of Puttarh had exclusive rights, it is the Nautiyal clan of Chattra that have appropriated half the right, and the remaining half is shared amongst the Dobhal of Puttarh as well as the Joshi of Nenus. Chalda Mahasu, the constantly travelling divine king, is accorded ritual worship by the Nautiyal of Chattra, the Dobhal of Puttarh, the Joshi of Nenus, and the Semwal of Maindrath, each receiving a year's *panti* or rights over priestly duties, in rotation, with a renegotiation of duties every three years, and the transfer of duty taking place during the night vigil festival of Jagra. Similar clan-based distribution of duties is also stipulated for other officials like the *thanis* and the *bajgi*.

Recent events related to tales of accommodation and distribution of duties among different clans reveal considerable detail on how claims and counterclaims over worshipping rights have turned contentious. For instance, during Chalda Mahasu's tour of the upstream narrow valleys of Duni-Bhitri in the *pansi*, the priest from the Dobhal clan of Puttarh died. Concerned at the disruption of daily rituals in the absence of the priest, the oracle of Chalda Mahasu was approached. Chalda assured his hosts that the issue would soon resolve itself. He instructed them to place a dry twig in the soil, and if it turned green it was prophesied there would be no disruption. Before the time of the afternoon rituals, a man in a state of complete disarray and absolute possession arrived with the ladle traditionally used to place the incense, and commenced the performance of the ritual of puja. Coming from the Nautiyal clan of Chattra, he was accorded the status of a *deopujya* for his extraordinary feat of traversing the long distance from the Valley of Ramaserai to the region of Duni-Bhitri, the northernmost ridge of the Fateh Parvat mountains, almost on the snow-line. This long distance across a treacherous terrain had been covered on foot to ensure the continuity of the ritual. To reward him for his extraordinary exertions, besides a share in Chalda's worship rights, his clan was also granted a share of Bautha Mahasu's worship.

The Joshis of Nenus acquired worshipping rights at Hanol differently. As narrated by Madan Das, the drummer-bard of Maindrath, several centuries ago the idol of Deoladi, mother to the Mahasu siblings at the temple of Maindrath, was vandalised with a mysterious chopping off of a breast, and her ritual worship fell into disarray. The Joshi clan, who were performing temple duties, was forced to migrate to a village called Gadara, under the patronage of the Rajputs of Village Bastil. The clan finally settled in Nenus, was referred to as the Bhojan clan, and commenced the

Table 7.1: Mahasu *deopujyas* (priests) and distribution of *panti*

Brahman Group and Village Divine King	Moiety of sathi				Moiety of pansi	
	Nautiyal of Chattra	Dobhal of Puttarh	Joshi of Nenus	Semwal and Sharma of Mainadrath	Dobhal of Bagi	Nautiyal of Dangoli
Bashik Mahasu	–	–	Two months (Chaitra and Asauj)	Two months (Mangshir and Magh)	Eight months (Baishakh, Jyeshth, Asarh, Shravan, Bhado, Kartik, Paus, Falgun)	–
Pabasik Mahasu	–	–	–	–	–	Twelve months (Equal division between the two Nautiyal clans for the period)
Bautha Mahasu	Six months (Chaitra, Shravan, Jyesth, Asauj, Mangshir, Magh)	Two months and five days (Asharh, Paush, Kartik – Fifteen days, Baishakh—Ten days)	Three months and five days (Bhadon, Falgun, Kartik – Fifteen Days, Baishakh - Twenty days)	–	–	–
Chalda Mahasu*	One year	One year	One year	One year	–	–

*In the case of Chalda Mahasu, usually on tour, the above four clans worship him by taking turns every three years, the change taking place during the night vigil festival of Jagra.

worship of the divine king Mahasu. The raja of Garhwal, who considered the region his own territory, did not take kindly to the priests of another king living in his territory, especially with the divine king extracting tribute from the villagers the raja considered his own subjects. The Mahasu idol was confiscated and the divine king's officials imprisoned in the Garhwal capital. While the officials were confined to a dungeon, the idol was given away for smelting to add to the kingdom's treasures. The head of the Bhojan clan took a grave risk, and, disguised as an ascetic, entered the capital of Garhwal. Here he learnt that every time the smiths attempted to smelt the idol of a strange god, it would fly off the smithy, singe and scald them, causing much consternation in the Garhwal capital.

The ascetic of Bhojan then visited the Garhwal king in an effort to negotiate the release of the idol, a foolhardy gambit that could, given the ruthlessness of the Garhwal rajas, have cost him his life. Already rattled by the fracas caused by the idol, the raja acceded to his request and let him take the idol. The disguised ascetic then dreamt of the imprisoned Mahasu officials, and demolishing the wall of the dungeons freed them to enable an escape to Hanol. As a reward for the risk undertaken in order to retrieve the *devta* and his officials, the divine king, through his oracle, decided to grant four days' share of the worship to the Bhojan clan, the Joshi of Nenus. While the priests of Chattra reluctantly agreed to part with their share, those of Puttarh, initially at the behest of the Mahasu minister, refused to accept the new arrangement. The Bhojan clan of Nenus, since then, vowed not to maintain any commensality with the Bastil *vazir*'s clan.

Mahasu's wrath was bound to manifest itself in the form of mishaps in the minister's clan as he had colluded in the disobedience to him. When the minister's family began to experience inexplicable illness and misfortune, the oracle was consulted; he pointed out that the minister was being punished for defying the divine king. The minister had to capitulate, agreeing to intercede with the Puttarh priests and convince them to part with four days' share of the offerings. The Puttarh priests had by now made up their minds to defy all authority – that of the fellow priestly clans, the divine king's oracle, and now even the minister. Rattled by this defiance, the minister called a meeting of the chiefs to deal with the Brahman clan's insolence.

The confabulation resulted in the hatching of a devious plan. Since the minister, himself a Rajput, could not have chastised the Brahman (as he could the *kolta* or the *bajgi*!), he decided to do it by inciting an altercation. When the priest from Puttarh was arriving at the temple to offer ritual worship, the priest from Nenus was asked to also proceed for the ritual bath – in preparation of a parallel ritual worship. The moment the Puttarh priest arrived at the temple entrance, having finished with the ritual cleansing, a *bajgi* was deputed to touch and defile him. The moment this was done, there ensued an argument between the Joshi of Nenus and the Dobhal of Puttarh, followed by a scuffle.

The Puttarh priest, having been defiled, could not perform the ritual puja and the priests from Nenus quickly replaced him. The Puttarh priests wanted to resume their duties but now the Nenus Brahmans, with support from the powerful Rajputs, including the minister, would not let them into the temple. Even after several violent incidents, with no resolution in sight, the dispute was finally taken to the Sub-Divisional Magistrate's Court in Chakrata. The community, at the minister's behest, testified against the Puttarh clan, and the courts granted worshipping rights to the Joshi. The Puttarh clan, adamant as ever, refused to accept the court orders too, until finally Mahasu's divine justice came into play. Several men from the clan began to die of mysterious unnatural causes. Worried over their sudden decline in fortunes, they consulted the Mahasu oracle and were advised to compromise and surrender a part of their share of the offerings. After several rounds of negotiations, the Puttarh clan, under protest, agreed to concede two months of Asarh (June) and Paus (December) and a half-month of Kartik (October), the lean periods of ritual worship at Mahasu shrines. Later, to further cement affinal relations, the Puttarh clan agreed to surrender another four days in the month of Baisakh (April). Thus, the Puttarh clan was left with worship rights amounting to two months and nineteen days in a year, accepting the new arrangement under protest.

In 1993, as the Nenus priest arrived at the temple of Hanol to resume his "duty", the Puttarh priest refused once again to part with his *panti*, claiming rights over the entire month. This led to heated arguments and both priests decided to perform the ritual cleansing and afternoon rituals simultaneously. The conflict soon escalated into another violent altercation, with both clans coming to blows in the temple courtyard. It was finally decided to settle the dispute through community deliberations, inviting the entire clan with Mahasu, acting through his oracle, as final arbiter.

A community court was set up with the Mahasu oracle occupying centre stage. It was decided that the services of priests from both clans would remain suspended until a final decision was arrived at. After protracted arguments and negotiations, Puttarh's share was increased by six days during the ritually active month of Baisakh, their annual share now being a period of two months and twenty-five days. The Nenus clan was finally granted three months and five days towards their share.

Conflicts over duty rights reveal that *panti* is treated as inherited family property, a customary privilege. With civil courts intervening in the assignation of temple duties, *panti* acquires the status of a legal object of distinct value, the ownership of which can be enforced through the process of law.

In the Mahasu realm ritual duty translates into political power and quite often political clout is needed to secure rights to worship. The human royals of neighbouring kingdoms have often intervened to ensure that particular Brahman clans acquire rights over *panti*. While in the regions of Duni-Bhitri and Ramaserai, and owing to the influence of the Garhwal kings hailing from the

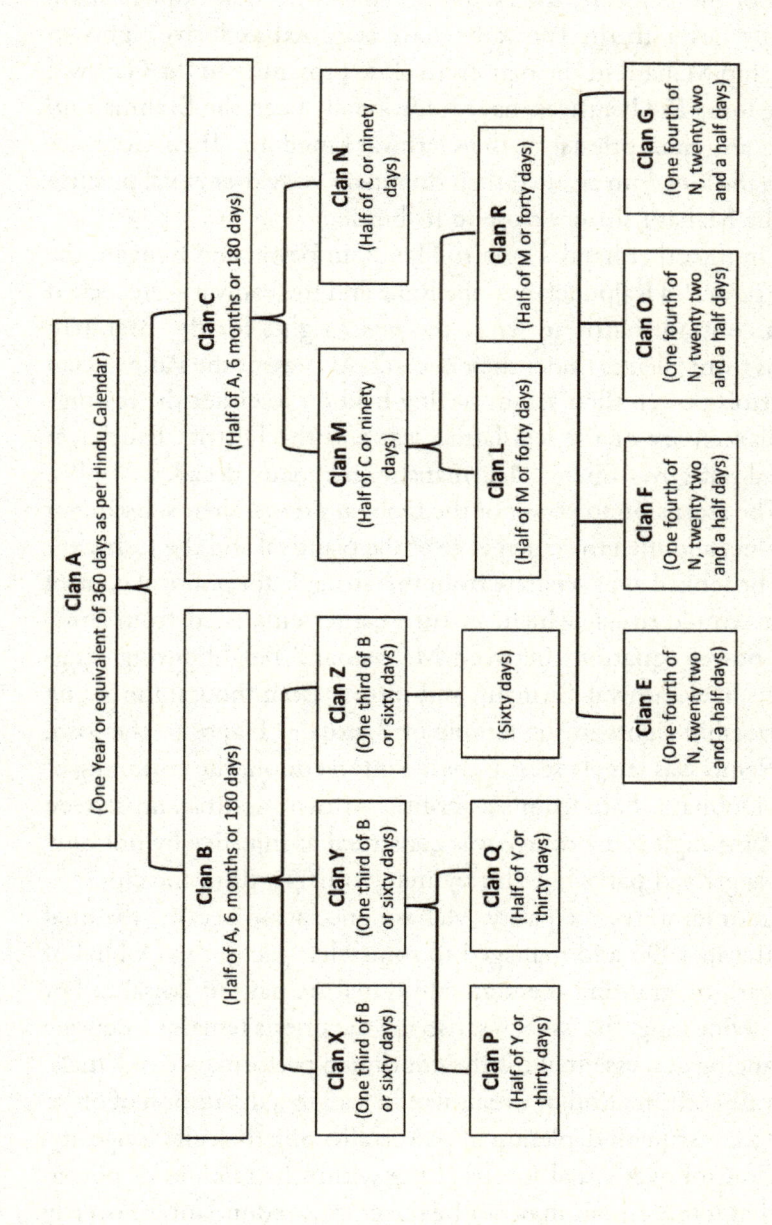

Fig. 7.1: Inheritance of worshipping rights for Brahman clans in the Mahasu temples.

clan of the Panwars, the Nautiyal clan – who traditionally share family ties with the Panwars – have acquired exclusive rights to worship Mahasu in the regions in close proximity to the Garhwal kingdom. The Nautiyals have traditionally been the Brahman *raj purohits* (chief priests) of the Garhwal kingdom. Their close ties with the kingdom ensured their dominant sway over ritual practice in the Mahasu shrines close to its borders.

On the other hand, closer to Hanol, in Bawar and Bangan, the two powerful Rajput clans – the Rana and the Panwar – are locked in a constant battle to wrest the *panti* rights for the Brahman clans from villages under their control. At present the Panwar clan controls power, their scions having held on to either the region's parliamentary or the legislature seat and the District Panchayat (local self-government) chairmanship for many decades.

The ascension to power of the Dobhal priests, their subsequent decline, and then the emergence of the Nautiyal and the Joshi cannot be looked at as separate from this struggle for political control over temple ritual, which, in turn earlier emanated from shifting power equations between Mahasu and neighbouring kingdoms like Garhwal, Sirmaur, and Jubbal. Even though the giving of worship rights in the temple of Bautha at Hanol to the Joshi of Nenus was largely seen as divine intervention, the curtailing of the Dobhal's share from six months to two months and sixteen days through court decree was construed as injustice by not only the aggrieved party but also by many others within the cult.

In order to restore parity, Mahasu once again became the final arbiter in 1993 and managed to somewhat pacify the Dobhal of Puttarh by granting them an additional six days in Baisakh. For the divine king, the issue of satisfying the priests remains a delicate balancing act, essential for the continued performance of rituals. Any discontinuation of rituals would lead to a disruption of order and a consequent depletion of power, affecting the cult's longevity.

Control over ritual means rising within hierarchies of power. In that sense, rituals may not be the empty, redundant, or overtly religious acts that do not lend themselves easily to political description, as is sometimes made out. With ritual emerging as a means to secure power, their performance and control is continually contested and leads to conflict and negotiation within broad categories generally thought of as caste. Caste, therefore, also emerges as a fluid social state. Undoubtedly, one is born into a particular caste, but it is control over ritual practice and the resultant proximity that it offers to the axis of power that determines rank and dominance. Folklore provides insights into how processes of inclusion and exclusion within a specific caste group alter equations of power.

The Ranas of Bakaan from Village Bastil have traditionally been the ministers to Bautha Mahasu at Hanol. Bija, from this clan, was one such influential minister and most regional chiefs were under his tutelage. Almost eleven *pattis* (lit. strips of land) or regions were under his political control and so were the powerful Rajput clans, the Chauhans and the Tomars. Since the Ranas were the most powerful of the Rajputs, they would give away their daughters in marriage only to the ministers of Bangan who served Pabasik Mahasu across the Tons. In the region of Nimga, in the village of Kot, lived the Nimga Rajputs, who also controlled eleven *pattis*. Being very influential within their domain, they would marry their daughters only within the Rawat clan, and considered the Ranas of Bakaan, despite their immense influence, somewhat inferior to their own stature. Matrimony, a political move amongst the powerful, is carefully planned to enhance social status.

Bija sent a marriage proposal to the Kot Rawats asking for their daughter's hand, through a messenger named Saeriyaa. The Rawat refused the proposal, leading to bloodshed. Bija ordered the torching of the fortresses of the Nimga Rawats of Kot. The destruction of the fortresses through magical spells cast by the Nartaik priests of Chilharh Village is described in a *harul* (battle song), popularly known as the *harul* of *sathi-pansi* chronicled by Lakshmikant Joshi (2007: 126):

Maulae Maulaiyae Rae Kaeri Maulae,
Charae Gainae Mahasu Rae Chari au Bhai.

Let us form a chain with arms around each other and sing praises to the four Mahasu siblings.

Hatae Gainou Kotiaa Duroa Mai,
Aeti Aago Gaine, Aunaouli Ri Dhai.

Let us sing praises to the mother goddess at Hatkoti. Let us sing praises to the Bijat deity residing in Choorii.

Thnae Gaini Maindrath Deladi Mai,
Aeti Aago Gaine, Aunaoli Ri Dhai.

Let us remember Maindrath where Deoladi Mother (mother to Mahasu) resides. Let us recite the name of Hanol before telling this tale.

Bholau Daeni Bisarae Pauindau Lai,
Shathi Ri Panshi Ri Harolou Gai.

Through an oversight we have scattered the mud. Now comes the Harul of *sathi* and *pansi*.

Kali Dhaenaliae Rae Dhaoulaou Dodhau Rae,
Kautho Ra Jhaugada Haula Man Chae Ra Yudhaou.

The blackest of cows yields the whitest of milk.
Why this feud, why this war?

Kali Dhaenaliae Rae Dhaoulaou Doodhau Rae,
Vila Ra Jhaugda Haula Man Chae Raa Yudhaou.

The blackest of cows yields the whitest of milk.
It is a regional feud, for humans it is war.

Maulae Maulaiyae Rae Kaeri Maulae,
"Saeriyaa" Bhakana Paudaou Thaulanae Jae.

Let us form a chain with arms around each other and sing. A man of the Bakaan clan, called Saeriyaa, visits Thaulnaa.

Ago Baushae Agani Pacho Ghaurou Rae Bheti Rae,
Thaulanae Tini Raoutae Hainshae Dethi.

He sits in the courtyard, with the wall behind him.
He salutes the Rawat [Rajput from Kot Nimga] to signal his arrival.

Ago Di Thi Haishae Pacho Sadnau Liye,
Marae Vila Saeriya Kaeni Khe Aaye.

The Rawat responds to Saeriyaa's salute.
"What brings you here?" he demands.

Aunaou Dahunaou Saradaou Goaou Manicahe Thodou,
Taere Aao Yajnae Manchae Lorho.

In spring season, grains and wealth, everything goes/grows.
I have come to your region looking for a bride.

Kori Kaporia Bhooji Li Bhangau Rae,
Raoutae Ri Baetki Bija Bhakaan Mangaou.

The intoxicating drink is always fermented in a vessel of fresh mud.
Bija of Bakaan asks a Rawat's daughter for a bride!

Katii Bakurichae Rae Gadi Li Loi Rae,
Bija Sitae Baetaki Koi Marae Authi Na Koi.

Only a goat may be skinned for leather, there is no suitable girl for Bija in our village.

Gheae Ghee Aaliyae Bhaouti Lo Ghee Aou Rae,
Ghaourae Shoni Rawata Mui Jajanu Ri Dheou.

Only in a vessel meant for heating clarified butter can this be done.
O Rawat, I have heard that you have Jaajnaou's daughter at home.

Obaou Bolae Kotou Oondae Taousau Rou Pani,
Dahounae Deoulae Dhaouni Taerae Thaoulanae Ani.

Above is your palace [Kot or fortress of the Nimga Rajput] and below flows the Tons.

O Rawat, I shall send to you a basket full of wealth [in return for the daughter's hand].

Hai Hani Saeriyaa To Aero Na Boulae,
Daounae Setae Raouta Kaundi Na Toulae.

Hey Saeriyaa, do not utter such words.
Do not try to buy out a Rawat with your wealth.

Bhatae Choudi Chawadi Haouri Jugae Na Laundau,
Khaousahe Setaey Mitri Jugae Na Launadau.

I shall not give up good food for green, raw rice.
I shall never become a kinsman to a Khash.

Saurali Shikhoriae Saouraou Lou Gaendaou,
Khaushae Setey Baetaki Kaoudi Na Daendau.

On a pine tree the flowers bloom only at the top.
I shall never marry my daughter to a Khash.

Kotaey Ri Namti Bajae Bastilaou Kangaou,
Jaena Daela Baetaki Kotay Roujaoulaou Bhagou.

When the *naubat* (fanfare) sounds in Kot, one can hear the drumbeats in Bastil.

If you do not give your daughter's hand in marriage, I shall raze the fortress to the ground and ensure that Kot remains fit only for poppy cultivation.

Bidri Gauinae Chtkiiae Lou Pani,
Bhaji Jayaa Saeriyaa Tu Pansi Ri Dhani.

Can it rain when the skies are clear?
O Saeriyaa, come out of this desire for a foothold in the *pansi*.

Bhaji Jaya Panshiya Tu Sathi Ri Dhani,
Kotayae Rae Pathrou Naoui Tousaou Khae Lani.

O Rawat! Even you should not get into a spat with *sathi*.
We shall ensure that the stones of Kot fortress are thrown in the Tons River.

Bhaji Jaya Rawata Vija Ri Dhani,
Kotou Ri Deolou Jolou Khae Lani.

O Rawat! Do not clash with Bija.
Now I shall ensure that your doorframe is used as a levelling tool and I shall plough the land on which your house stands.

The seeds of this conflict between the Rana of Bastil and the Nimga Rawats of Kot were sown much earlier at the time of the arrival of the Khash. The Khash are believed to have been later settlers into the region and there are several theories pertaining to their coming. For instance, Sankrityayan (1991) believes that it was the *kirata* who were the original inhabitants of Jaunsar-Bawar, and the Khash migrated from the plains much later. The generally accepted view is that the Khash were displaced from Central Asia and entered the Himalayas along the Hindu Kush, spreading across the cis-Himalaya from Kashmir to Nepal, adapting themselves to native traditions.

Nimga Rawats come from the Daragad Valley and ruled over *tikoj* (the throne of Kot). Their fortress was strong and situated on a vantage point from where one could maintain a vigil over the entire valley up to the Tons. The access to the fortress was narrow, chiselled out of rock, and the fortress had its own water source, a freshwater pond, fed by an underground canal. In the Dargad Valley, traces of the fortress, once believed to be impregnable, can still be seen. To add to its defence, the well-known *tantrik* Nartaik priests of Village Bijauli, close to Chilharh, were given charge of protecting the fortress through their magic spells. The Nimga Rawats consider themselves the only *suryavanshi* (descendants from the Sun dynasty) Rajput clan in the region, superior to the Khash Rajputs, like the Rana ministers of Bastil, seen by them as upstart usurpers of power.

The clan named Mangteoun that today lives in the village named Penuwa were the Khash ministers to the Rawats, while Mangareu from the region of Banadhar were the Khash Rajput warriors that formed the militia (*khund*) that protected the fortress. According to Rana (2004: 210), the Rawat siblings squabbled over succession to the throne. Thirteen militia chiefs were called upon to settle the dispute but a resolution could not be found. Finally, the minister and priests declared Vir Singh Pithu the successor. The other siblings left the fortress, considerably depleting its defences.

While the dispute was leading to cracks in the fortress' defence, the marriage proposal from Bija, the Khash of Bakaan, arrived. When the Nimga Rawat refused to give their daughter's hand in marriage, Bija entrapped the *tantrik* Nartaik priests of Village Bijauli, responsible for protecting the fort, into colluding to raze to the ground the fortress of Kot. Having once employed their knowledge for an unjust cause, and having offered it to the Hanol minister, the *tantrik* knowledge of the Nartaik, according to local beliefs, is still trapped within the confines of the Mahasu temple at Hanol.

Thus, even amongst groups like the Rajput, believed to exercise hegemonic control over the cult, especially with reference to lower castes, there are conflicts within. Within groups from the same caste, contestations to ascend the hierarchical ladder are a constant occurrence. These contestations revolve around ritual control, as in the case of the priests forced to lower their ritual guard over the fortress of Kot – thus allowing the dominant group to arrest their ritual powers within the confines of their own seat of power. Ritual emerges as the means through which groups like the Brahman, Rajput, and even suppressed castes like the Kolta, can collaborate against other powerful coalitions and edge closer to the power centres.

The conflict between the Nimga Rawats and the Ranas of Bastil is still quite evident in the tug of war for control over the temple that traditional Mahasu officialdom and the government-appointed temple management committee is constantly engaged in. While the Mahasu minister traditionally enjoys rights and privileges over temple ritual and offerings, some activists, with active support from groups on the opposite bank of *pansi*, have successfully campaigned with government to give the Hanol Mahasu temple finances to a committee. While the Mahasu minister refused to join the statutory committee formed by the government (even though invited), a descendant of the Nimga Rawat clan – the influential vernacular journalist Raghubir Singh Rawat – was at the helm of the group that campaigned for its setting up. The temple committee has, since its inception, collected more than two crore rupees as offerings and is engaged in an effort to improve visitor facilities at the temple. With offerings received at the Mahasu temple at Hanol going into a government-controlled bank account, another situation of conflict is emerging. While earlier there was no accountability for money and gold received at the temple, the present transparent system is severely testing the moral and political authority of the Rana minister from Bastil and the different groups of priests governing the cult.

There are several ways in which ritual has been interpreted. It is sometimes seen as maintaining the way things are, at others subverting the status quo. Ritual has been seen as a performance, as a re-enactment of myths, as therapeutic, formal, changing, given, constructed, about words, about experience, empty, enriching, sacred, secular, for individuals, for groups, for societies, a key to interpreting culture, the way a culture passes on its values, rigid, flexible, a universal phenomenon, about particular rites, and about a particular way of performing. Many of these usages, of course, represent contrasting views. Once considered traditional and unchanging, with routine as its defining characteristic, ritual, while it can still be these things, also has the capacity for being experimental, subversive, and counter-cultural.

Religion, society, and culture are mutually influential and ritual has a role in the transformation of society and individuals. Earlier theories posited a simple mirroring of society and culture, but it is now recognised that ritual is also generative of society and culture. In fact, as Grimes (2011: 12) points out, ritual is endowed with the quality of "bending" time and space. Rituals often happen at special times in set-aside places. Grimes underlines the fact that sometimes rituals derive their force not from repetition but from their singularity, their rarity; so the idea of ritual should not be defined in a way that precludes either singularity, rarity, or invention and improvisation. Breaking the monotony of ritual activity, springing a surprise by threatening to obstruct ritual activity at a particular and crucial time, and going against the norms of society in the act of restricting the performance of the ritual itself, can lead to far-reaching social transformations, in the process shaking up established hierarchies and social structures. However, for groups that rely on them, even subversions must occur within the overarching ritual framework.

This fact was brought home to me during the river-crossing ritual of Chalda Mahasu (see chapter 3) from the *pansi* into *sathi*, after a nineteen-year (against the usual twelve) sojourn in the now apple-rich region of Himachal Pradesh. As mentioned earlier, the delay had become a bone of contention between the moieties. Walking for more than a month, the Chalda entourage arrived at the village of Thadiyar overlooking Hanol, the temple being the first stop before the ceremonial crossing of the river over the suspension wire-bridge. The palanquin had just arrived and entered the kitchen of a Rajput chieftain for a night's rest. The next morning it would tour the village riding the shoulders of the divine king's oracle, chasing away all evil spirits before crossing the river. While the Chalda palanquin is known to spend more time in the temple in this village, it would now probably stay only one night, given that the crossing had become imperative owing to the growing impatience on the other bank.

Upon entering the Mahasu chamber in the temple in the village of Bhotanu in the *pansi*, we sat on the floor with the weary priests. The palanquin was placed in the same chamber. People had blisters on their feet, their faces sunburnt after days of walking in the mountains. A trickle of devotees had begun to come in with offerings, which were gladly collected by the priests. Because I was accompanying a young Brahman *deopujya* from across the river, the priests accompanying the Mahasu palanquin greeted us warmly. Each priest was introduced to me with their names, their clan names, and the village they came from – not on account of my research interests but following the usual practice of an individual identifying at all times with the soil of the native village. For the Mahasu priests, it is essential to not just retain consubstantiality with the soil of Mahasu's *gunth* villages, the villages even the British would not tax, since revenue from them accrued to Mahasu; but also to flaunt their exalted status. Village and clan are of immense significance, a kind of differentiating factor between the common Brahman and the exalted *deopujya*.

When I inquired about the crossing time, no definite answers were forthcoming. At length, one of the priests agreed to discuss the issue, reluctantly stating that the crossing into *sathi* might take several days, even months, because they had plans of delaying it until justice was delivered to them. He repeated the lament that I had heard several times, that it was them, the *deopujya*, who rang the bell to awaken the divine kings, carried the palanquins across rocks and ridges, followed strict codes, and worked tirelessly during their *panti* or duty, and yet the Rajput *sayanas* had begun to claim a percentage from their collections. So their share of the offerings, granted by the divine kings, had progressively shrunk. Across the river, in *sathi*, so complete was Rajput dominance that their demands were summarily rejected and dismissed as sheer greed. The only hope for them was to ensure that their demand of a fair share was met, in writing, before they let the divine king cross the river. Ironically, priests who always swore by Mahasu's quick justice now demanded an agreement in writing on government-stamped bond paper, registered as legal tender in a court of law.

Equally interesting was that only at this point, when the priests chose to complain about their earnings, was the usual discourse of the palanquin moving of its own volition inverted. At all other times, when I questioned the priests about the ardour of these ritual journeys, they would say that the *devta* drove the palanquins and walking those long distances was no exertion at all.

The priest accompanying me (probably because he came from *sathi*) confided, once we had left the chamber, that he thought this talk of delay was sheer brinkmanship on the part of the priests, considering that large crowds had begun to gather on the opposite bank. With the government apparatus preparing for the event, the *pansi* would not be able to hold on to the divine king much longer. These priests he said had no inkling of the belligerence and political clout of the *sathi sayanas*, the Rajput elders from the opposite bank, who had already run out of patience.

It was clear now that the ritual of river crossing, historically marked by conflict and violence, was once again becoming contentious in multiple ways. Within the *sathi*, the group expecting to receive and host for the next *barabasha* (twelve-yearly touring tenure), a conflict over succession to the position of *vazir* was brewing between siblings. The two brothers, claimants to the position of minister in this vast region, were both born to the now-deceased minister, out of polyandrous wedlock. While one claimed the right to succession on account of being the firstborn (probably not to the minister but to another brother), the other claimed rights on being born of the minister himself. Kartar Singh, minister at the time, had introduced Jaipal Singh (born to his wife through his brother) as his successor to all the clan chiefs, who had accepted his choice without demur. He had been gifted the white turban, a headdress anointing him as the future minister. But over a period of time the minister had begun to have second thoughts, and favoured Diwan Singh, his own offspring. As Diwan Singh grew older, even though the minister preferred him as a successor, Jaipal Singh had consolidated his position amongst the clan chiefs and the political factions within the region's powerful and ruling political party, the Congress. Over a period of time, the conflict having gone through several confrontations and lawsuits, a compromise had been worked out. Jaipal, who was advancing in age, would remain minister during his lifetime and be succeeded by Diwan Singh.

During the time of the river crossing, Jaipal had taken ill and his son, Jagmohan, contrary to the deal struck earlier with Diwan Singh, was attempting to step into his shoes. On the other hand, Diwan Singh had also begun to assert himself, claiming succession according to the arrangement. With the entire moiety vertically split over the issue, and each clan expressing solidarity with the man they thought would best serve their interests, confrontation was imminent. Closely linked to this succession dispute was the issue of the traditional clan-based control over Mahasu temples, slipping away from the hands of the Rajput chiefs with the recent constitution of the government-appointed temple committee. This public trust, referred to as a "society" (*samiti*) by Indian law, was now claiming rights over the offerings received at the temple, with the money going to a bank account, audited and held accountable to the public.

For the Rajput clans it was important to be seen as exercising their traditional rights by playing host to Chalda Mahasu's entourage. But the temple committee controlled the purse strings and was in no mood to let go of their new-found control over temple resources by themselves organising the divine king's ceremonial welcome. Whoever was seen as hosting the divine king as well as the men from the opposing moiety of *pansi*, would be perceived as close to the power centre on the significant day of Chalda Mahasu's arrival in *sathi*. Once again, receiving and offering hospitality was emerging as the benchmark for social rank and political status.

In the context of these succession disputes, the *vazir* from the opposite bank had a crucial role to play, in handing over charge – the palanquin, regalia, and treasures – for safekeeping.

For the coming twelve years, these had to be given to the person he recognised as the minister on the other bank. This entrusting of the Mahasu palanquin and wealth for the next decade and two years, a ritual performed in full public view before the elders and men from *sathi* who had gathered to welcome their divine king, would amount to an anointing, making a statement on whom the other bank recognised as rightful successor to the position of minister. There was a fair amount of speculation about how the *pansi* minister disliked Diwan Singh, the man who was otherwise gaining popularity on the other bank as the incumbent *vazir*.

Against the backdrop of this turmoil, the constant feud between the *sathi* and *pansi* was also playing itself out. Groups on the opposite banks, as mentioned earlier, have always been inimical, and the issue of hosting the divine king had the potential of escalating the conflict. The frequent delays in the crossing, which the *sathi* construed as a dilatory tactic of the *pansi* minister and oracle, coupled with internal conflicts amongst the *sathi*, had ensured that the entire community was kept guessing whether the ritual river crossing would indeed take place. Only Chalda Mahasu, upon arrival, could resolve these conflicts. The *sathi* had waited too long for their divine king to return. One of the visible ramifications of this delay was that several families who performed the ritual of tonsuring their infant's head only when Chalda toured their villages had not been able to do so for close to two decades. Infants had grown into twenty-year-olds with dreadlocks, without ever having had a haircut. They were understandably anxious about Chalda Mahasu's arrival!

Meanwhile, the priests had threatened that unless their share was guaranteed in writing, they would not perform the rituals – ringing the bell to awaken Chalda Mahasu, reciting the invocations for his vehicle to cross the river. The usually dominant Rajputs were indignant and at their wits' end at such a demand that threatened to create a deadlock. They could not surrender their share of the offerings so easily, and yet their *devta* had to be brought home without the risk of ritual failure.

By evening, thousands had gathered on both banks, some to give a tearful farewell to their divine king, others to accord him a rousing reception. After a tour of the village the oracle approached the temple and, before entering it for the night's rest, announced that the *pansi* minister was now free to attend to his household chores. In a statement loaded with significance, the Mahasu oracle declared, "Now, it is up to my *deopujyas*, the priests, who have accompanied me for the last nineteen years, stood by me, walked with me, and ensured that I was worshipped continuously, to carry me across the river into *sathi*! The *pansi vazir* is now relieved of his duties until my next tour."

The priests were jubilant at what they thought was a vindication of their contention, the divine king himself granting them ritual control over his mobility. The declaration now afforded them control to press forward with their demands even more effectively, even as the friend from across who had accompanied me muttered under his breath that this river crossing would also be marred by violence, since the priests were now in control of the *devta* and appeared in no mood to relent.

On the other bank the elders were equally adamant, interpreting the oracle's pronouncement as a signal that the divine king was now prepared to cross. According to them, the work of the priests entailed nothing more than a performance of ordained duty, for which they were amply compensated through the existing arrangements of *panti*. They were getting the privilege of remaining close to their divine king, getting food from the temple and adequate offerings. Was that not reward enough for these rapacious priests? The situation appeared to be worsening, when in a scathing comment on the elders from across, the divine king declared through his oracle, "In the *sathi*, my regime has been compromised, handed over to the government. My *niyam* [rules] are not followed anymore. Why should the *devta* cross?"

Even though the reference was probably to the ban on goat sacrifice in the Hanol temple courtyard, imposed by the government in collusion with the temple committee under pressure from animal rights activists, the priests believed the divine king was referring to their own plight. However, when I discussed the import of the statement with some of the elders across the river, they claimed that the divine king was not critical of them, or for that matter sympathetic with priests. He was referring to the constitution of the temple committee by the government, a body that was usurping their rights over the temple. The divine king was acting through his oracle as an agent commenting upon the state of affairs, but not pointing fingers, allowing the community to go through its own churning to determine its will, even as all the aggrieved felt the divine king spoke on their behalf. The oracular statement was thus open to multiple interpretations, each side understanding the word of the god to serve their own interests.

Having articulated the community's will, the palanquin turned abruptly, through a mere gesture that changed moods quickly, and gave the most emphatic of all messages. Rather than entering the temple, it moved to the minister's home. If the palanquin had entered the temple, it would indicate that the divine king was preparing for a long haul, at least a few weeks' stay. By entering the minister's home, the message was sent out loud that, despite the priests' resentment, Chalda Mahasu preferred to cross over quickly, perhaps as early as the next morning. The tide had once again turned, and those wanting to negotiate their positions would have to work overtime to settle their grievances. The priests were somewhat subdued and everyone looked glum, even as the usually mild priest from the other bank fumed, "They are trying our patience! Wait till the *khunds* (militia) from across enter the village and take the *devta* forcibly! Our people, awaiting his arrival, have not congregated for a picnic. They have come for a resolution of pressing problems, and quick justice, and that can only happen once Chalda Mahasu arrives. These people must let the crossing happen or prepare for trouble."

The next day one could see hectic activity and a sense of urgency on both banks of the river. By entering the minister's home, Chalda

Mahasu had indicated that he would cross soon into *sathi*. The time, though, had not been indicated and people would have to wait for the final signal. By afternoon the eldest Mahasu Bashik's palanquin arrived at the temple of Hanol, from the *devta*'s seat at Maindrath, in order to receive the royal visitor, his younger sibling Chalda. The huge procession had walked from Maindrath, some sixty kilometres, and this heightened expectations that Chalda would now announce his intentions to rise. Men who accompanied the palanquin told me that they had never experienced the Bashik palanquin maintain such a scorching pace. They had had to sprint through the entire stretch to reach. Bashik's sense of urgency was an indicator that the crossing was now imminent.

The priests, meanwhile, crossed the river to arrive at the temple of Hanol, to participate in the negotiations that were reaching a feverish pitch. Neither the priests nor the Rajput elders were prepared to relent. The priests wanted a written undertaking that they would not be forced to share the offerings received by them during Chalda Mahasu's tour of *sathi* with the Rana elders of Bastil. The Bastil elders, however, were bent upon enhancing their share. The priests were smug in the knowledge that ritual control, for the moment, rested with them. Unless they rang the ceremonial bells with their invocations, Chalda Mahasu would not rise to cross. This was the only opportunity for them to negotiate, knowing that once the divine king was across without a written agreement in place, they would be at the mercy of the Rajput. Post-lunch, they crossed the bridge in what was to be their site of duty for the next twelve or more years. In the evening, before sundown, they crossed for supper, and once again expectations of a breakthrough rose but abated when the priests returned without even a verbal assurance.

By night, tempers had flared up. Bashik Mahasu's oracle pronounced that the *devta* felt slighted at having been kept waiting to receive his brother and conveyed his feelings to the *pansi* minister, as well as his militia, through a messenger. As night fell, conjecture gave way to dejection and indignation. For the thousands gathered in the winter cold around the temple in *pansi*, there was no food or shelter. While *sathi* had prepared for a feast, they could not feed anyone since their *devta* had not yet arrived. The ability to offer hospitality being at the core of representations of power, the feast would play a major role in further negotiations. However, the *pansi* were now in a quandary since they would have to host the hundreds of people who had arrived for the send-off.

As far as the politics was concerned, for the *pansi* this was now an internal squabble of the *sathi*. The divine king had declared his intention to cross and the *pansi* minister had even been relieved of his charge. The *sathi* had been unable to break the several deadlocks, those over succession, between committee and elders and the one among the priests and the elders of Bastil. For the *pansi*, it had been close to two decades of constant service to their divine king, a *tapasya* (penance) as the minister described it, which was heading towards an acrimonious anticlimax. According to the *pansi* minister: "When Chalda Mahasu decided to move from Shiraji, it was evident that he would cross. He has been travelling for thirty days. Why couldn't they settle their differences in this period? It has always been like this for *sathi*, rather than looking for solutions, they prefer confrontation."

As dusk fell over the mountains, little bonfires were lit and were visible in the temple courtyard on both banks; people and Chalda Mahasu's goats huddled together around them in an effort to keep warm. Shortly, a long row of lights was seen, moving in the pitch dark, across the fields on the other bank. "Look! They are coming to take the *devta*," said the friend accompanying me. And everyone's worst fears seemed to be coming true as the row of torchlights was soon seen moving over the bridge on the Tons. As the group came closer, one could see that both claimants to the position of minister of *sathi*, Diwan Singh and Jagmohan, were accompanied by several of the divine king's militia, some of them with rifles slung on their backs. It was evident that they were none too pleased with the delay in the crossing. The men from *sathi* arrived in the temple courtyard and confronted the priests squatting in the temple verandah. Heated arguments between the priests and the men from *sathi* ensued, and threatened to escalate into physical violence, until the *pansi* minister suggested that rather than fight it would be more useful to consult the divine king himself. They squatted in the temple courtyard and the loud argument now centred on which oracle should have the final word on the crossing – the oracle from *pansi*, the host territory where they squatted at the moment, or the *sathi* oracle, to where the divine king was destined. Since the divine king had already asked the *pansi* minister to relinquish charge, and handed it over to the priests, he was reluctant to participate in the debate. Because the arguments were taking place in his territory, he was forced to sit through them, acting as an arbitrator. The *sathi* insisted that since the *pansi* minister and his officials had been relieved by the *devta*, it was their own oracle that would be consulted on the issue. The priests, however, insisted that since the *devta* was still in *pansi*, it was the *pansi* oracle that ought to have the final word. The men from *sathi* did not trust the *pansi* oracle since they had all along suspected and now blamed him squarely for the delay in the crossing. More heated arguments followed, where incidents from the past, when each group had insulted the other, were raked up. Amidst all the name-calling, one of the priests stood up to announce: "It is soon going to be midnight! If this argument continues, and the midnight hour strikes, we will not perform the last ritual for nightfall. The *sandaul* will be missed."

This break in the ritual would anger the divine king no end. The sudden interruption also made everyone realise that no-one had had supper. If the ritual was skipped, thousands of people waiting on both banks of the river would have to go hungry, a situation that went against the principle of *sadavart* (feeding every pilgrim) enshrined as one of the cult's basic tenets. Both sides relented and agreed that oracles from either bank should sit together and, as mouthpieces of the same divine king, try and reach an amicable solution.

The two oracles were now possessed, and once again there was little agreement. While the *sathi* oracle's view was that the Chalda palanquin must rise immediately and perform the long-overdue crossing, the *pansi* oracle averred that the crossing should not be attempted unless the priests were satisfied. With no settlement in sight, someone suggested that since the two oracles could not agree, a third be consulted. The oracle of Pabasik Mahasu was sought out. He worked up a possession and, being himself from the *pansi*, could only be consulted by the reluctant minister from this bank. The question posed by him to the divine king's oracle, however, did not pertain to the scheduled time of the river crossing. Instead, the *pansi* minister began questioning the oracle on whether the grievance of the priests was justified and needed redress!

This was the final straw for the men from *sathi*. They rose from their positions and began to climb the stairs to the minister's chamber, resolutely and menacingly, where the palanquins of the divine kings – Chalda as well as Pabasik – rested. They looked like a determined lot, prepared to go to any length to take away their divine king. This is when the *pansi* minister emerged on the staircase. In an assertive but placatory tone, judging the mood of the men from *sathi*, he said: "Do you think you can take the *devta* away like this? We understand the crossing is overdue, but we cannot let the *devta* go in the dead of the night. Come and take your divine king tomorrow morning, if you will, even if the priests do not relent."

The men from *sathi*, despite this assurance, were in no mood to compromise now. They had had enough of assurances. They climbed up the stairs, even as the *pansi* chief minister and his men looked on warily, as if anticipating their next move of picking up the palanquin, a move that could spark off violence. The *sathi* minister commanded the priests to prepare the *devta* to move. Two of them came forward out of fear, while the others sulked, for they still had not been given their assurance. The *sathi* knew they could take away the divine king even with a couple of priests performing the ritual of awakening the *devta* and raising the palanquin, and they had been successful through the protracted negotiations in driving a wedge between them. As the men reached the chamber where the two palanquins rested, they realised to their chagrin that it was Pabasik Mahasu's palanquin, the divine king of their enemy's territory, that blocked the narrow doorway. The palanquin of Chalda Mahasu, the touring divine king they had come to fetch, stood at the far end of the chamber. To reach the Chalda palanquin they would have to move the Pabasik palanquin first, something repugnant to their own belief. If they chose to as much as touch the Pabasik palanquin, it would amount to defiling it, and the militia from *pansi* would not desist from violence at this act.

I had been travelling with the Chalda palanquin for the past month and recalled that at every night halt during our journey it was Chalda Mahasu that everyone came to seek blessings from. Pabasik was always the gracious host in the background, letting the visitor bask in the limelight. The palanquins would usually be placed in keeping with this etiquette, with Chalda directly in line of sight of the visitor, the Pabasik palanquin always at the far end. Here, the order had been reversed, no-one could tell why. Difficult to say whether the palanquins were placed thus by design, in anticipation of a raid from the *sathi*, but the placement of the palanquins did manage to stop the men from *sathi* lifting the Chalda palanquin and taking it away.

The priest deputed to perform midnight worship, meanwhile, stood at the doorway, waiting to recite the evening invocations for the divine kings to sleep. They were running out of time, for if the invocations started, the question of moving the palanquin would not arise. Thousands would have to go without food, bringing *sathi* hospitality into disrepute. The ability to offer hospitality, being at the core of the representation of power, made it imperative to act one way or the other. Adding to the misery of the *sathi* was the fact that they would be left shamefaced before their brethren across the river if they returned without their divine king. After several minutes of a tense stand-off with the deputed priest and the minister claimants staring at each other, the men from *sathi* relented. They had received an assurance for the river crossing tomorrow. All pilgrims had to be fed. They retreated.

They prostrated themselves before the palanquins, laid their offerings, and returned, descending the staircase, fuming. They would, they declared, come for their divine king tomorrow morning. They had had to fast at their hosts'. Situations such as this reflect very poorly on Rajput hosts, the inability to offer hospitality, especially to an enemy, is sure to leave one accursed. As the torches made their way back over the bridge and into the fields, the *pansi* heaved a sigh of relief, but with the guilt of having been hosts who had failed to offer hospitality to the moiety whose hospitality they themselves would soon be seeking, when the palanquin crossed over. Both sides felt slighted in this battle of nerves. While the *pansi* considered the arrival of the ministers and the *sathi's* militia an affront, the men from *sathi* left without breaking bread, feeling shortchanged, for no resolution could be found on the issue of the divine king's arrival into their territory.

Finally, the worship ritual, usually performed at sunset, was performed just a couple of minutes before midnight. Even before the *sathi* group could return to the temple at Hanol, the *sandaul* or the evening invocation began to play from this end, louder than ever, indicating that Chalda was still in *pansi*, and the chiefs of *sathi* were returning empty-handed.

There would be no feast in the *sathi* tonight. But there were thousands of pilgrims on either bank, under the open skies, awaiting the crossing. Men were rushed to nearby markets. People were awakened and shops opened in the dead of night. A hurriedly prepared frugal meal of lentil and rice was served on both banks. People slept in the cold. Many went hungry, disappointed that the divine king had not crossed. The priests huddled together in animated conversation. They knew that the river crossing was imminent, with both ministers agreeing to it. Confabulations continued throughout the night until it was finally decided that the priests would carry the palanquin, in fulfilment of their ritual duties. However, they also decided that if the fair share of the offerings was not assured, they would abandon the palanquin once they crossed and return to their villages. This would render the divine king's arrival insignificant, since the *devta* had to be carried to the Hanol temple and ritually established to confirm his arrival into *sathi*. In the ritual's absence the elders' control and rights over the realm would also lose some legitimacy.

The next morning I crossed into *sathi* to gauge the other bank's reaction to the previous night's events. In the chamber next to the Hanol temple I met the minister designate, Diwan Singh. Despite the presence of several elders and political figures, he openly admitted that the priests, in collusion with the *pansi*, had outfoxed them. He attributed this to the absence of consensus amongst the community in *sathi* as to who the next minister would be. "Had we been united, as in earlier times, when everyone listened to the *vazir*, they would not have dared to keep the *devta* for so long," he thundered. However, the opinions of most elders pertaining to the priests' greed in demanding a fixed percentage of the *devta*'s offerings had now mellowed. It became evident that even though the ruptures caused after the nocturnal visit of the men from *sathi* would take time to repair, for now it was time for the *sathi* to unite and bring back their divine king. As soon as the priests arrived for the morning meal, they were assured their fair share. Even though they had not managed to extract a written contract, the victory was theirs to savour. The Rajputs had retracted from their earlier intransigent position. Chalda Mahasu would soon cross, and people began crowding around the bridge in anticipation.

Bell (1992) suggests that there is an underlying logic of sorts to most theoretical discourse on ritual and this discourse is fundamentally organised around an opposition between thought and action in a variety of ways, which, she suggests may be problematic:

"In the final analysis the results of such a differentiation between thought and action cannot be presumed to provide an adequate position vis-à-vis human activity. Naturally, as many others have argued before, the differentiation tends to distort not only the nature of so-called physical activities but the nature of mental ones as well." In its place she proposes an alternative way of thinking about ritual activity that stresses the primacy of the act itself and how its strategies are lodged in the very doing of the act itself. "Ritualisation" is the term she employs to describe ritual as a strategic way of acting in specific social situations. Rather than focus on ritual as a distinct, autonomous, and universally recognisable set of activities or as an aspect of all human activity, she draws attention to the ways in which ritual actions distinguish themselves in relation to other actions.

She draws from practice theory, in particular Bourdieu (1987), who uses the term habitus to refer to "the unconscious dispositions, the classificatory systems and taken for granted preferences" which an individual has, that operate at the level of everyday knowledge and are inscribed onto the individual's body, that is, they become a part of who they are as persons. The insight this gives is "to confront the act itself" by addressing the "socially informed body" with all its senses. The body is the factor that unifies all practice. Bourdieu says this includes "the traditional five senses . . . but also the sense of necessity, and the sense of duty, the sense of direction and the sense of reality, the sense of balance and the sense of beauty, common sense and the sense of the sacred, tactical sense and the sense of responsibility, business sense and the sense of propriety, the sense of humour and the sense of absurdity, moral sense and the sense of practicality, and so on." Bell suggests that a "sense of ritual" would be a vital addition to the list.

Practice, then, is a theoretical notion. Bell highlights four features of practice that are used as a basis to discuss ritual activity. Practice is situational, strategic, embedded in a misrecognition of what it is in fact doing, and able to reconfigure a vision of the order of power in the world – referring to this attribute as "redemptive hegemony". Therefore, ritual leaps from being repetitive to something that is capable of being innovative, capable of "reconfiguring" the world. In the case of the priests, the subtle change in ritual design – placing one palanquin before the other – probably an act performed without even realising that they were altering the ritual, in combination with the other set of rules laid down over the years of historic time, made the difference. The priests and their threats of disrupting the ritual in various ways – like playing the evening invocation even as the negotiations went on, bringing the palanquin into *sathi* and leaving – were changes in the historically prescribed tradition that forced the dominant group to reconsider their entrenched positions.

Turner's (1969) notion of ritual as both structure and anti-structure emphasised the need to go beyond looking at ritual as maintaining social control. Turner introduced the notion that ritual as anti-structure could be subversive of structure and the status quo. Using Van Gennep's (1960) three phases of rites of passage as separation, margin (or limen), and aggregation, Turner particularly drew attention to the second, "liminal" or threshold period. In this liminal phase of ritual, people slip through the network of classifications that normally locate positions in cultural space, they are "betwixt and between". It is particularly in this state that people are enabled to experience themselves and their world from a hitherto unperceived point of view. For instance, a phase was arrived at when the divine king was under the charge of neither minister. While one had been relieved, the other could not assume responsibility unless the divine king crossed over. On the other bank too, the two claimants, each trying to cement their position, created a threshold point of ambiguity from where the usually subdued Brahman were able to negotiate their position with the domineering Rajput.

According to Bell, to claim that human activity is situational is to recognise that what is important to it cannot be grasped outside of its immediate context. To say that it is strategic is to suggest that it employs schemes and tactics to improvise and negotiate through everyday situations. By saying that it is involved in misrecognition of what it is in fact doing, Bell means that a practice does not see itself do what it does. Ritual is apt to misrecognise the relationship between its ends and its means in ways that could promote its efficacy. In the Mahasu realm, political ends are met through ritual means. Day-to-day practices – sending out matrimonial proposals, Brahman ensuring others maintain a ritual distance from the divine king, or the Rajput displaying belligerence by threatening to forcibly take away the palanquin and then bowing before the sanctity of the other's palanquin – are strategic acts even though their outcomes can only be speculated upon. According to Bell, "it [ritual] tends to see itself as the natural or appropriate thing to do in the circumstances. Ritualisation does not see how it actively creates place, force, event, and tradition, how it redefines or generates the circumstances to which it is responding." Therefore, when the palanquin was placed in a particular manner, the act, even though a disruptive innovation (being a break from the pattern followed during the entire route), had the consequence of its subtlety going unnoticed within the community. The change in design, in effect, was accepted as Mahasu's *lila* (the will of the divine king).

Bourdieu (1977), who influenced Bell's notion of practice, articulates this knowledge impairment: ". . . it is because subjects do not know, strictly speaking, what they are doing, that what they do has more meaning than they realise." This notion of practice seems to be a bit condescending towards practitioners. For the processional rituals of Mahasu, there seems to be self-awareness about their own role in constructing a ritual space and experience, and its impact on participants, all effectively employed as part of a strategy to actualise change or maintain the status quo, according to the needs of the community. Rather than being about misrecognition for oracles and priests, officials and pilgrims, the sub-events that change the course of the main ritual without disrupting it completely appear as a part of intensely negotiated and thought outcomes. These strategies may not necessarily be "knowledgeable yet unknown" and are in fact the expected outcomes of community mobilisations like the river crossing. Saying that practice is able to reconfigure a vision of the order of power within the world is to recognise that practice negotiates the existing power relations so as to empower individuals within it, without them either having to leave, disrupt, or destroy the whole. This is how communities create situations where the sum of the parts becomes larger than the whole, just like the demon's pieces.

The relationship of the ritual of Mahasu worship to hierarchies of power, and the manner in which groups manage to carve out spaces to empower them and maintain resistant and subversive identities whilst still remaining within the system, is an aspect inbuilt within the processional ritual of Mahasu. The goal of ritualisation, according to Bell (ibid.), is "the creation of a ritualised agent, an actor with a form of ritual mastery, who embodies flexible sets of cultural schemes and can deploy them effectively in multiple situations so as to restructure those situations in practical ways." This is how ritual acts in negotiations of power.

Bell accepts that ritual transforms persons and ascribes this transforming effect to the process of ritualisation itself. In present times, in Mahasu country, the accusation could be made, and is usually made by administrators and observers external to the cult, that those constructing ritual are manipulative. For this to be true, we would have to assume that those who end up on the losing side, for instance in this case the elders of Bastil or the Rajput of *sathi*, can be hoodwinked by the strategies employed. My fieldwork suggests that this is far from the truth. Every single shift in power, however minor, is intensely contested and negotiated.

Meaning resides as much, if not more, with audiences rather than performers. It is the Mahasu subject that lives his life, while the distant observer gropes for meaning and motives. The ones losing their share of the offerings resist change until breaking point, thereafter making a partial and tactical retreat in keeping with the will of the community. During the times when the divine king's oracle from the *pansi* articulated the strategy of the group he belonged to, different groups were able to create various levels of meaning relating to their own situations. Ritualised practices are thus flexible and complex. Their meanings are indeed varied for different groups within a social group. When groups reach a stalemate, it is ritual that forces each one to contest or concede, this becoming the essence of continuity.

8

Tribal Caste

CASTE, USUALLY CONSTRUED as based on linear social hierarchies, is often placed under the umbrella of untouchability and pollution. Caste, though usually exclusivist, can also at times be enacted through forced inclusion. In earlier chapters we have seen instances of how a stringent caste system has remained a source of authority for some in Jaunsari society. Colonial officialdom, while doing little for the oppressed, recognised the need to accord some privilege to the region as a whole owing to its social particularity. Democratic India has meanwhile continued its efforts in caste engineering through affirmative action – assimilating historically suppressed castes into the mainstream. At times these attempts at egalitarianism end up reaffirming the very system they are expected to break.

The cult of Mahasu has traditionally been volatile, intransigent, and monopolised by high-caste Rajputs. Of the social boundaries prescribed by Mahasu rituals, caste restrictions on the lowest Kolta caste are perhaps the most unassailable. Nowadays, caste authority and rank contend with democratic privilege constitutionally granted to the historically dispossessed. A legal system that attempts to empower suppressed castes like the Kolta often clashes with the divine kings' ritual dispensations. As the Mahasu realm becomes more accessible to media and mainstream political flows, the cult of the divine kings is rendered increasingly self-reflexive, largely through the agency of individuals or groups that lead movements for transformation.

Dirks (2002) argued that caste is neither an unchanged survivor from ancient India nor a single system that reflects India's core culture. Rather than being an expression of historic tradition, it is a relatively modern phenomenon, a product of the encounter between India and British rule. He believes that caste has always been a contingent social phenomenon, naturalised by the colonial archive that found it useful for understanding social relations. Before the British arrived, Indian society was fragmented into communal groupings that served as centres for social identity. Despite this, the interrelationships amongst caste groups, and their ritualised relations to power centres such as the divine kings, ensured that this fragmentation, even though exploitative for some groups, never became a bone of contention.

Although there may locally have been ambivalence about caste in the past, it has now become a significant factor in India's competitive politics. Upper castes, for instance, are usually agitated over the affirmative action policies that they believe give unfair advantage to "untouchables". Dalits, on the other hand, say that the benefit of reservations granted them now offers very little in terms of compensation for centuries of suppression.

In the Mahasu realm, too, groups within the upper-caste Brahman and Rajput are engaged in a constant struggle for power, depending on each faction's proximity to Mahasu at any given time. For caste groups like the Kolta, the ritual distance from the axis of power has in the past been so insuperable that the question of bridging it never arose. The Kolta maintained ritual distance from the divine king, performing menial "polluting" tasks like picking up waste and cleaning or skinning dead livestock and providing free labour. Despite caste boundaries not being watertight, the immense distancing ensured that the Kolta were never close to the centres of power. Now, though the state is attempting to empower the lower castes, and even though the lowest of castes are displaying some upward mobility, these caste boundaries do not seem to be blurring. At this point, the reservation of seats in local bodies and increased employment opportunities in locally influential positions (e.g. of schoolteachers and keepers of land records, positions traditionally held by the upper castes) have helped engender aspiration amongst the lower castes. Of the several projects through which the state is attacking caste differentiation, elections is one. While universal franchise forces upper-caste candidates to seek votes from all, certain seats are reserved for lower-caste candidates.

In the Mahasu realm, political relations being based on ritual distance from and service rendered to the divine king, caste exists not as an autonomous "religious" phenomenon – as Raheja (1988: 515, citing Dirks) described it – but as a complex system of social and political relations articulated and ordered by a "divine office". During fieldwork, I had the opportunity of observing the working of a social structure evolved over centuries where religion, rather than sanctioning political power, enacted through the limits imposed by caste, was politics itself. From Weber to Dumont, the ideological models of caste have elaborated religious values of purity and pollution, and on the other hand practical models from Hocart to Dirks to Inden have insisted on the primacy of political power. The West Himalayan system emerges as one where *dharma* and *artha*, purity and power, complement each other in the ritual space of the kingdom and determine each other to such an extent that one cannot be distinguished from the other. This agglomeration has been further complicated with the emergence of the modern state's egalitarian policies of social engineering, making it imperative for the actors to constantly negotiate the boundaries imposed by an age-old social structure.

It would be productive to look at the controversies that radically altered the religio-political landscape of caste within the Mahasu realm in recent times. The case studies taken up here indicate that caste identity is more fluid than usually thought of. They serve to show that though the obsequiousness displayed by menials towards upper castes may point towards the deep-rooted dominance of groups like the Rajput Ranas of Bastil – currently the ministers to the divine king – their control over the cult needs to be constantly renewed and asserted within and without the caste group. The processes of enforcing dominance involve a range of actors and interested parties, all connected to webs of power.

History tends to overlook losers in negotiations of power in much the same way as it shuns counterfactuals. We would diminish our understanding if, while dismissing Rajput dominance as hegemonic, we overlooked the contemporary processes that threaten to dislodge the dominant group from their positions of power.

On 9 November 2000, the West Himalayan hill state of Uttarakhand came into existence, carved out of Uttar Pradesh. Statehood came nearly six years after the two principal regions of the state, Garhwal and Kumaon, launched agitations to obtain it. Political activists and scholars present the popular movement for the creation of Uttarakhand as a reaction to political domination by the plains, coupled with economic exploitation of the hill people in the parent state of Uttar Pradesh. This may not explain the state of affairs in their entirety because the mountain regions, officially designated as "tribal" post-independence, did not share the enthusiasm for the new state. Unlike Garhwal and Kumaon, the "tribal" regions, such as the Mahasu realm in Jaunsar-Bawar, neither witnessed major protests nor were violent conflicts recorded here. Differing perceptions about statehood among regional groups grappling with similar social and economic problems question the very basis of the hill versus plains debate, as much as they call for an exploration of the politics of "tribal" recognition.

In Jaunsar-Bawar the one factor that contributed to widespread disinterest in severance from the parent state was the earlier conferral of the coveted "scheduled tribe" status on them. This classification, bestowed on all residents of Jaunsar-Bawar in 1967, ensured job reservation benefits and preferential treatment in the allocation of development funds for Jaunsaris – as the "tribe" was officially designated. In general, a tribe as officially recognised by the Indian state is a social group with cultural practices distinct from those of the mainstream Hindu communities. The people of Jaunsar-Bawar entitled to the tribal classification are, however, caste Hindus and the privilege granted to them is based on their geographic isolation and practices like polyandry. Having acquired the tag of a tribe, even the affluent and dominant castes, the Brahman and the Rajput, began to benefit from schemes meant usually for the oppressed. How much, and in what ways, this "affirmative action" contributed to benefiting the socially depressed Jaunsaris is open to debate, but there is little doubt that the average Jaunsari considers the attainment of tribal status a major privilege. This is also borne out by the deep resentment at being left out and the constant efforts by culturally similar groups in what is now Uttarakhand and neighbouring Himachal Pradesh, for instance among the people in the regions of Dodra-Kwar and Jaunpur, to acquire tribal status.

While it is not my intent to examine the history of state-making in the Western Himalaya, it would be worthwhile to delve briefly into events that unfolded before tribal status was granted to Jaunsar-Bawar in order to comprehend the current social reality of the region and its neighbouring areas. The region, despite its geo-political similarities, was divided into several political and administrative units before the advent of the colonial powers.

Jaunsar-Bawar is a typical Hindu caste society, even though a little differentiated by its practices, usually thought of by people from the plains and valleys as isolated. Jaunsaris are quite similar to Hindu social groups spread across the South Asian mountain chains and foothills. The process of this group acquiring "tribal" status gives an interesting insight into how states initiate affirmative action for groups they perceive as the backward other. The gradual move towards "tribalisation" began as early as 1816, at the conclusion of the Anglo-Nepalese War. Once the British, after initially suffering huge losses, had successfully driven back the Nepalese armies from the region, they were confronted with the task of administering vast tracts of difficult yet strategically significant terrain that showed little promise of yielding revenue. Aitchison (1892) informs us that they decided to restore the small kingdoms in the region to the kings the Nepal armies had deposed during their campaigns. Even as the British were enchanted by the landscapes and salubrious surroundings, they were alive to the need to retain control over certain areas that allowed access to potentially profitable trade routes with Tibet and China. In Jaunsar-Bawar, particularly, they were impressed with the manner in which people had stood up against the Nepalese forces, once they had begun their assault on the Gurkha strongholds (Fraser 1820). The colonials deemed the regions of eastern Garhwal, along with the hill station of Mussoorie and the valley of Dehra Dun, including the adjoining Jaunsar-Bawar, as British Garhwal.

The drawing of the *Dastur-ul-Amal* (the customary code of conduct) by the British endowed the people of Jaunsar-Bawar with a special status. The region was later classified as a "partially excluded area" by the Government of India Act of 1935. This special status differentiated between the people of Jaunsar and others in the province while ensuring that there was no formal police force in the region, and that revenue officials performed most administrative and judicial duties. Post-Independence, though, an order of the President of India signed in 1950 refused to recognise any social group in the state of Uttar Pradesh as a tribe. With the enactment of the Panchayati Raj Act of 1951, a new law that sought to bring self-governance to villages in the country ended all special rights of the traditional councils of elders dominated by the Rajput castes – the *sayanas*, *sadar sayanas*, and *chauntroos*. In 1952 the administrative unit of Chakrata (administrative centre for Jaunsar-Bawar) was divided into two development blocks, and village-level committees as well as panchayats (village-level local self-government bodies) were constituted. Like the rest of India, judicial powers were devolved to these village committees. By the end of 1962 came the abolition of the *zamindari* system, the system of feudal lords and landholdings.

Through a notification of the Extraordinary Gazette of the Government of India, keeping in view the earlier colonial classification (Notification No. 107, 24 June 1967) for the Jaunsar-Bawar region as backward, and owing to the prevalence of unconventional cultural practices such as polyandry, black magic, and bride price, as well as owing to poor economic development indices, the inhabitants of the region were classified as a tribe. This meant the granting to them of privileges such as job reservations, restrictions on land acquisition in the region by outsiders, and the protection of certain traditional practices. This then led to acrimony, followed by representations to the government from within the community and from those groups that were kept out of the tribal fold. The opponents to the tribal appellation of the Jaunsaris reasoned that in a Hindu caste society where the prosperous Rajput and Brahman dominated, only the traditionally suppressed castes such as the Kolta, Bajgi, Dom, Chamar, Nath, etc., deserved privileges. Consequently, in 1969, another amendment was introduced to the laws that would exclude the *khasas* – the Rajput and the Brahman, from the tribal appellation, leading to protests now from the excluded privileged castes. A joint committee of the Indian Parliament was dispatched to the mountains to ascertain whether the Rajput and Brahman castes amongst the Jaunsaris qualified for the privileges of a tribe. On the basis of testimonies placed before the committee, the amendment would be considered.

The elected member of the Legislative Assembly of Uttar Pradesh from the region, Gulab Singh, himself a Rajput with a large support base within this group, testified before the Joint Parliamentary Committee (Bhoria 1975) that in the region, "it was the Rajput and Brahman that borrowed money from the Kolta." A fallacious statement was thus made, not only ensuring that his own community and constituency retained privilege, but also emphasising the otherness of the Jaunsaris to groups in the neighbourhood.

Through his statements he also ensured the grant of a very special favour to his own Rajput caste, claiming this privileged group was even worse off than the Kolta, the group they had suppressed for ages. The Member of Parliament from the Tehri Garhwal constituency, Manavendra Shah – public representative from the area and scion of the Tehri royal family – joined hands with Gulab Singh and deposed before the committee (ibid.) to the effect that "since Hinduism was not the dominant faith in Jaunsar-Bawar, untouchability was not practised here." In effect he denied the existence of the caste system, stating that such practices were associated with Hinduism and did not exist in Jaunsar-Bawar. These two crucial testimonies, going even by the standards of present-day mendacity and political expediency, did not present an accurate picture of Jaunsari society and were largely responsible for the blanket approval of tribal status granted to all Jaunsaris.

Social groups such as the Jaunsaris, once they have tasted the fruits of what Young (1989: 258) describes as "differentiated citizenship", would not easily let go of their tribal identity. As Shah and Schneiderman (2013) have shown in their study on Nepal, shifting the terms of positive discrimination inevitably unsettles a host of vested interests. This is what happened in the region. Vested interests came together to ensure that the Indian state's "positive discrimination" towards the group as a whole continued. The result was that upper-caste Jaunsaris gained access to better education and government contracts, deriving the greatest benefit from the tribal status granted to the region as a whole, even as the Kolta had little opportunity to improve their lot. The region remained "tribal" despite recommendations to the contrary by the Kolta Inquiry Committee of 1960, constituted to look into the anomaly of a small pocket of high-caste Hindus enjoying tribal status. All caste groups within the region, including the Brahman and the Rajput, were blended into the Jaunsari Tribe under the notification of the 1967 Extraordinary Gazette of the Government of India (Bhoria 1975). The amendment has not come up for discussion since, political compulsions having ensured its abandonment.

Tribal categorisation in India, as we can see in the official criteria established by the Lokur Committee in 1965, is quite pliable. The conditions laid down for considering a group a tribe include (Government of India 2005):

(a) Indication of primitive traits
(b) Distinctive culture
(c) Geographical isolation
(d) Shyness of contact with the community at large, and
(e) Backwardness

Measured thus, the Jaunsari qualified for the "tribal" tag, but their claim was by no means greater than that of other neighbouring groups excluded from the category.

Shah and Schneiderman (2013: 4) suggest that the implementation of affirmative action often triggers nuanced and sometimes counterintuitive transformations in social relations, and that although affirmative action policies always transform society, these transformations are not always along expected lines. Inequalities persist or are refigured. In Mahasu country, the introduction of the tribal tag for a caste-based society served only to entrench the hegemony of the already dominant Rajput. This became a tribal analogue of what in India's caste politics has been described by Béteille (1983) as the "creamy layer". This refers to a small group of people, recognised as historically underprivileged through legislation, deriving benefits – such as reservations in certain professions and employment preferences in the government – generation after generation, because, once empowered they manage to establish the right connections for upward social mobility. In fact Béteille (1991, 1992) has questioned whether reservations do not in fact give caste a new lease of life, benefiting only the better-off among the communities they are set aside for. This is quite the scenario in Jaunsar-Bawar, where, in order to retain their dominance, it became imperative for the Rajput to keep the region marginalised. One clan has dominated the region's politics for nearly five decades, creating conditions whereby the Kolta remain subjugated and distant from educational and job reservations. For as long as the region has no access to development projects – roads, schools, and tourism income – the elites preserve their constituency by selectively doling out government largesse to supporters.

The achievement of getting upper castes included in the tribal category so endeared Gulab Singh to the people of his constituency that he created history by getting elected unopposed in the next election. His family still sweep elections in the region because clan-based councils headed by the Rajputs control most votes in the region. It is the clan chiefs, under the directive of the Mahasu *vazir*, that support the family politically and ensure all caste groups cast votes in their favour in exchange for patronage in the form of government contracts and employment. The Kolta have been pushed even further to the social periphery. This runs contrary to the origin myth which maintains that it was from within the bloodline of the *bhaat* Brahmans that the Rajput, the Bajgi, and the Kolta emerged. Even today, many drummers insist through their ballads that the Brahman and the drummer are in fact progeny of the same mother. In a village, a folk song tells us, lived two Brahman brothers, Hauru and Chauru, the former taking the role of *deopujya*, the latter the role of the *bajanewala*. But whereas the lower castes attempt to establish social affinity with the influential castes, the upper castes draw lines of hierarchical distinction between castes, based on purity and social roles. For the drummer-bard Madan Das, the *pamvaras* – ballads extolling the basic characteristics of the dominant caste – are *zamindaru geet*, i.e. songs of the landlords, meaning that menials sing in praise of their powerful masters.

The songs apart, even deities' palanquins show caste preferences. We have seen that the Mahasu *doli* can only be carried by either Brahman priests or Rajput hosts, the Bajgi and Kolta keeping their distance while walking with it and performing ritual duties. While Mahasu is the deity of the hegemonic castes, the lower castes have their own deities. *Bijat* is one of them. According to Sutherland (1998: 99):

Just as the class status of individuals is signified by cars in Los Angeles, where people say, "You are what you drive", so in Rohru-Bashahar the caste status of whole communities is denoted by the ritual vehicle of their tutelary god. Formal differences of vehicle designs are encoded with the triple symbolism of mythic, social and spatial convention that signify: 1. divine "species" (*jati*) and "brotherhoods" (*biradari*); 2. different human "castes" (also *jati*); and 3. the *ghori*, village hamlet spaces where communities of different castes reside.

The Koltas, who have traditionally provided agricultural labour, now have ownership rights over lands as a part of the government's land reforms, though landless agricultural labour has always been (Alam 2008: 202) an integral part of the rural economy in the Western Himalaya. Described in the Gazettes as non-family labour, the Koltas (also known as Kolis, Doms, Dagis, and by several other occupation-specific names) were meant to provide, according to Alam (ibid.), "ritually subordinate agricultural labor". Emerson (1911) describes the deep entrenchment of caste distinctions thus:

> The menial tribes have always been the servants of the Kanets [the Rajput], and in portions of the hills their status is still little higher than that of slaves. In Bushahr, they are not allowed to wear ornaments of gold or a certain form of dress, or to build curved roofs on their houses. If a Koli has illicit relations with a Kanet woman, the punishment, up to comparatively recent times, was death. In Mandi, they were similarly forbidden to wear gold, fine clothes and even the hill jonquils in their caps. There are several trusts in Mandi in which Kolis, etc., are not only excluded from the houses of Kanets, but are not permitted to come within a certain distance of them. Each house has an imaginary boundary-line around it, well known to the low-caste people of the neighbourhood, and for a menial to step across it brings defilement. If a cow dies inside the compound, the Kanet himself removes the carcass. He strips naked and after the body has been removed performs ceremonial ablutions. More than this, if a Koli even throws a stone from outside from the boundary-line so that it falls within it, the Kanet will throw away his metal cooking vessels. The touch of a low caste man carries defilement and the clothes have to be washed at once. An intrigue with a woman

involves exclusion from the brotherhood, and this is the rule, so far as I know, throughout the hills, although in some parts secret intrigues of this kind occasionally occur.

Fieldwork also shows caste distinctions in practice. They indicate interplay of hierarchies, and the resultant homologues of power and purity, heredity and function, as indicated by Dumont (1970). They also show that caste lends to the society a distinctive structure, with the boundaries of caste, though quite rigid, undergoing a process of intense negotiation with the emergence of democratic powers that run parallel to feudal power structures that functioned on the basis of these distinctions. Sutherland (1998: 30) feels that the system of divine kingship in the mountains offers a non-brahmanic model of hierarchy where a complex construction reconciles interest in power, territory, and wealth (*artha*) with a caste order (*dharma*) and a political economy of cosmic power. Instances of public discrimination against lower castes help us understand how caste distinctions actually operate.

During festivals such as the *jagra*, Mahasu's night-long vigil at his palace or temple, there is considerable cordiality on display between Rajputs, Brahmans, and lower castes. While it is the Brahmans that ride the animal tableaux that dance around the temple courtyards, it is the lower castes that carry them on their shoulders. The *bajgi* continue their drumming duties and in moments of drunkenness late in the night the distance between caste groups seems to dissolve. But the backslapping soon dissipates into strict hierarchical difference once the festivities are over. The *sayanas* from Rajput family lineages appoint the elder who walks ahead of the group in a procession. He is offered the first puff of the *hookah* (hubble-bubble) and the first glass of *sur* (home brewed rice liquor) at any drinking party. If a goat is sacrificed at the temple, the Rajput headman is offered the heart and the liver while the Kolta make do with the hoofs (*khur*).

Mahasu temples can only be built in villages where Rajputs reside. Only Rajputs have the right to function as *vazirs* (ministers)

Photo 8.1: The *bajgi* play the drums at the entrance of the Hanol temple.

and *sayanas*. They also function as *thani* (assistants to the priests in ritual performance) and *bhandari* (inventory keepers of the temples). As a priest, the Brahman is subordinated to the Rajput *vazir* and the headman, who usually commissions the temple rituals, performing the role of *jajman* by proxy for Mahasu. However, while assisting the priest as the *thani*, the Rajput subordinates himself to the Brahman – even in this role, the Rajputs ensure their complete control over resources. These officials man the god's palace or temple and have unhindered access to all areas of the temple, except the inner sanctum.

The other major caste, significant in the god's bureaucracy, the *bajgi*, is the divine king's herald and the custodian of Mahasu lore. He is the *bhat* (genealogist), the *charan* (herald), *magadh*, *bandi*, and *sut* (performer of all menial roles), and yet he is not permitted access beyond the *dhakeur*, the first chamber's threshold at the periphery of the temple verandah.

The ones on the absolute periphery, the outcasts and the untouchables, the Kolta, can enter the temple courtyard but for them Mahasu's *bhandar* (store), lying adjacent to his palace or the divine

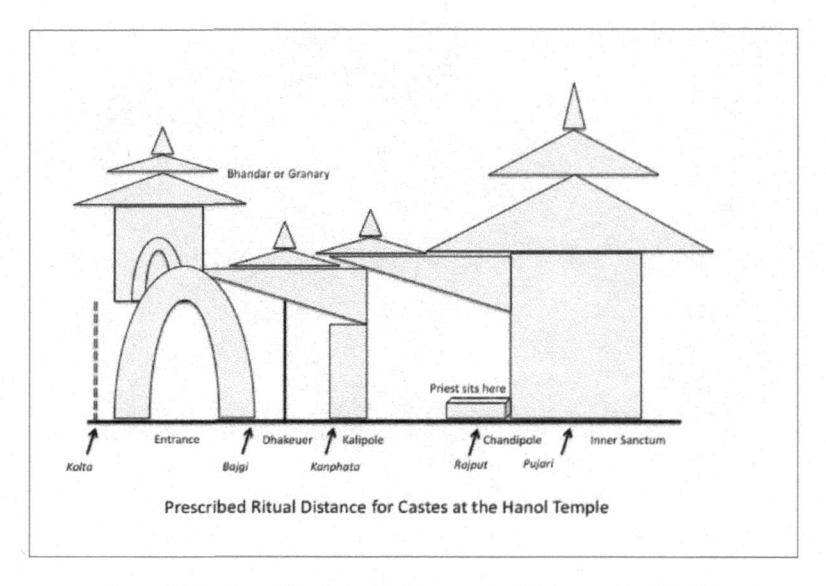

Figure 8.1: Prescribed ritual distance in Mahasu temples for various caste groups.

king's temple threshold, is the untransgressable boundary. While performing the roles of ploughmen, curriers, tanners, woodcutters, and porters, their ritual distance from the god ensures they have no role in the cult's governance. The only ritually significant task assigned to them is that of messengers. They are particularly the bearers of news of death of parents and siblings, news that they are entrusted to carry over long distances, to *dhiyans* (out-married daughters). Folklore is replete with instances of the out-married daughter overcome with ominous foreboding upon the arrival of a Kolta from the *mayat* (mother's village). In the temple, while every visitor is entitled to a meal through Mahasu's round-the-clock kitchen, a practice described as *sadavart*, the Kolta are not entitled to cooked food. They receive only grain in return for services rendered.

The Kolta are thus the perpetual victims of a caste-based social structure. While overtaking a higher-caste person on a narrow mountain trail, a Kolta is expected to saunter downhill. He has to move barefoot while moving in upper-caste quarters. Each community earmarks a separate downstream patch of spring waters for the Kolta, usually referred to as *harijan paani* (water for the polluted). They are expected to maintain a safe distance from high-caste homes and are not permitted to ascend the stairs of a high-caste home. For receiving the daily wage from Rajput employers, usually given away in kind, the Kolta have to squat beside, not at, the front door. Prohibited from pronouncing the customary salutation of "Ram, Ram", they are expected to greet the upper castes with "Maharaj! Maharaj!" (Lord, Master), hands respectfully folded. They sing and dance with the upper castes in temple courtyards but are not permitted to touch the temple walls, let alone enter, or have access to the backyard. The Kolta remove their caps before the temple doorway and keep it inverted in a gesture reminiscent of begging. During a community feast they are expected to bring their own utensils (Bhoria 1975: 776).

I was once invited by the government administrator, the SDM (sub-divisional magistrate) to breakfast in Hanol. Arriving, I was led to a low-caste home where in a little lawn the official's entourage and other locals welcomed me. After discussions on how to improve facilities in the temple, in which the Rajput men participated enthusiastically, they prepared to leave without the customary rounds of tea – since we were in the home of a lower-caste person who had climbed the social ladder by becoming a journalist reporting for an influential local newspaper, and was now able to invite the administrator. While tea and food were offered to the administrator and me as people from the "city" whose caste backgrounds seemed ambiguous, the hosts dared not offer it to the Rajput men. And when it was time for the meals, the entire high-caste group walked out, saying they had already eaten.

The Burhi (or old) Diwali is commonly celebrated in Jaunsar a month after the rest of the country celebrates Diwali. The delayed celebration is usually blamed on remoteness, the news of Rama's glorious return to Ayodhya reaching Jaunsar a month later than the rest of the country. During the festival, the Kolta collect dry grass from the forest and bring it to Rajput homes. The drummers then collect it and a bonfire is lit in the temple courtyard. While the Rajputs act like guests of honour, the Kolta amuse them with song and dance (Singh 1975: 894). Close to midnight, the Kolta visit temples of their own minor deities while the Rajputs squat outside the main shrine. At dawn the Kolta queue up before the Rajputs, who are seated on chairs, and sing:

"*Teri darki Raja Saheba hamari budhiyat aayi*"

(O King! we are here to welcome you, you have brought this festive spirit to our land).

Once the Rajputs are satisfied with the singsong greeting, the Kolta are served *sattu* and *sur* (local brews), by Bajgi women, who have received this material as a donation from Rajput women. In these celebrations it is mandatory for the Kolta to visit Rajput homes and offer twenty-five walnuts in the chief's name and twenty-five in the name of the divine king. These walnuts are later distributed to the entire village.

The Kolta's subordinate status is accentuated during the ritualised dancing in the temple courtyards. In the sheep-and-goat dance they cover their heads with the skins of these animals. Yoked to a plough, steered by the Rajput, the Kolta prance about, mimicking the movements of cattle. Similarly, in the cow-and-dog dance they dress as cows and dogs. As drudges in an archaic social system, they become the vehicles of Rajput and Brahman performers, enacting the roles of bulls in the bullock-cart dance. In the elephant dance, the last ceremonial performance of the Burhi Diwali festivities, an elephant is fabricated on a wood frame and covered with a cloth, replete with trunk and tusks. The *sayana* or his representative rides the elephant, flailing unsheathed swords like a king in battle. The Kolta take turns to carry the contraption. It is required of each adult male Kolta that he lend his shoulder to the contraption lest the Rajputs take offence. During other performances, the Kolta often find themselves at the receiving end of obscene gestures during particular dance sequences when the Rajput displays a mock phallus (fashioned out of cloth tied round the waist) chasing low-caste minions posing as cattle, in an apparent effort to force intercourse – much to the amusement of women and children assembled in the temple courtyard.

As night falls, all the distancing and humiliation dissipates as the need for libidinal gratification takes over. The Natiya Banbhan is an amorous song recounting the encounter between Natiya Brahman and Dumri, a low-caste *dom* woman from Poensha. In it a Brahman asks the woman out to the fields to drive away invading monkeys (Bhatt 2010: 272), and the song goes:

> Dumri: O! Son of a Brahman, look, your *dhoti* has fallen to the ground.
> Brahman: Why don't you pick it up for me, Dumri?
> Dumri: Son of a Brahman, I wouldn't touch you, nor would you touch me!
> Brahman: O! Dumri, your *ghangri* [skirt] is now falling to the ground.
> Dumri: You pick it up, O! Natiya Brahman, but my touch will defile your sacred thread.
> Brahman: I will do away with the sacred thread; I shall place it on a rock and then invite you to intercourse, for I cannot hold myself any longer.
> Dumri: O Brahman's son! Do not touch me, for it will spoil your *jati* [caste].
> Brahman: [How does it matter?] While returning home, I shall sacrifice a goat and be purified!

The song is sung during nocturnal recreations, with much mirth and laughter amongst men, women, and children.

Among the lowest castes, endogamous and commensal boundaries are sharply drawn depending upon the category of unskilled labour practised. On the basis of variations in the social and economic roles, the Kolta are differentiated into four categories

(Sankrityayan 1961; Saksena 1962), *khandit-mundit*, *mat*, *sanjayat*, and *neti dauli*. Of these, the *khandit-mundit* project serfdom at its nadir, since those in this group have no rights over land they cultivate. On the death of their master they are obliged to tonsure their heads as a mark of mourning. Williams (1874) describes the wages they get as "board wages" (*roti-kapra*, unleavened bread, and used clothes) or some rent-free land to live on. While the *mat* Kolta are "owned" by their masters – because of loans raised by their ancestors on exorbitant interest rates and their inability to repay – the *sanjayat* take turns in the service of their Rajput masters, also reporting births and deaths in the village. In a sense, they are record keepers for the village, maintaining an oral register of births and deaths. The *neti dauli* are the most emancipated among this lot.

When the government of Uttarakhand decided to constitute a statutory committee to look after the financial affairs of the Mahasu Devta temple at Hanol, the committee consisted entirely of Rajput and Brahman members. When a low-caste individual was appointed SDM and consequently also became chairman of the temple committee, there was resistance in permitting him to enter the temple. It was only later, when a woman from a low-caste background succeeded to the post of SDM that, upon her insistence, low-caste men were inducted into the committee. Such members and women were still not permitted into the temple.

In the context of social roles assigned to various castes, the narrative of Nand Lal Bharti, a Kolta by birth and subjected to social bracketing on account of his caste, brings to light the transformation, or lack of it, that can be affected by the presence of an actor that contests convention. For the Kolta, tradition has it that offerings from them to their divine kings are accepted outside the temple. They face abject humiliation at community functions should they dare to defy caste norms, or even extreme violence if they falter in what the Rajputs perceive as their duty to maintain their distance. Bharti, influenced by the national discourse of egalitarianism, challenged the village caste regime by giving up his caste name and adopted "Bharti" (literally meaning, Indian) as his new family name. He challenged norms by refusing to wear the traditional cap worn by his community, exchanging it with a straw hat or a baseball cap. He even attempted to cross the most inalienable of boundaries for his caste, the temple threshold.

Having earned fame as a dance troupe leader, representing the folk culture of his community, he travelled widely as a representative of the music and dance traditions of the West Himalaya at national festivals. At the Khurasao (ritual of the sacrifice of a hundred hooves, or twenty-five goats) in the Shaant festival, organised in 2006 at the Mahasu temple at Hanol after its renovation, Bharti was called upon to hold the microphone as master of ceremonies. He felt empowered – it appeared a huge reformatory leap on the part of the dominant Rajputs to invite a Kolta to conduct the divine king's ceremonies where he would publicly welcome over a hundred processions of the deities coming to offer tributes to Mahasu. However, the irony was not lost on him that the sacrifice at the temple was being organised as a purificatory rite after a tree collapsed over the temple roof, and low-caste carpenters climbing over the sanctum to repair it were thought to have defiled the shrine. The Mahasu shrine at Hanol is a site protected by the Archaeological Survey of India. As a monument protected under the country's heritage laws, no alterations can be made to the temple complex. When, on a particularly stormy night, a huge peepal (*Ficus religiosa*) tree, right next to the temple, damaged a part of the roof, repairs became a difficult task for the country's heritage protection agency. The most experienced carpenter, Ganga Ram, also known as Jhuinya Baba for his almost superhuman attainments in the field of wood and stone architecture unique to the region (also known as the *kath-khunni* or Koti-Banal style), was called in and worked under the close supervision of Archaeological Survey of India superintendents.

He and his son had to climb over the temple roof, and because

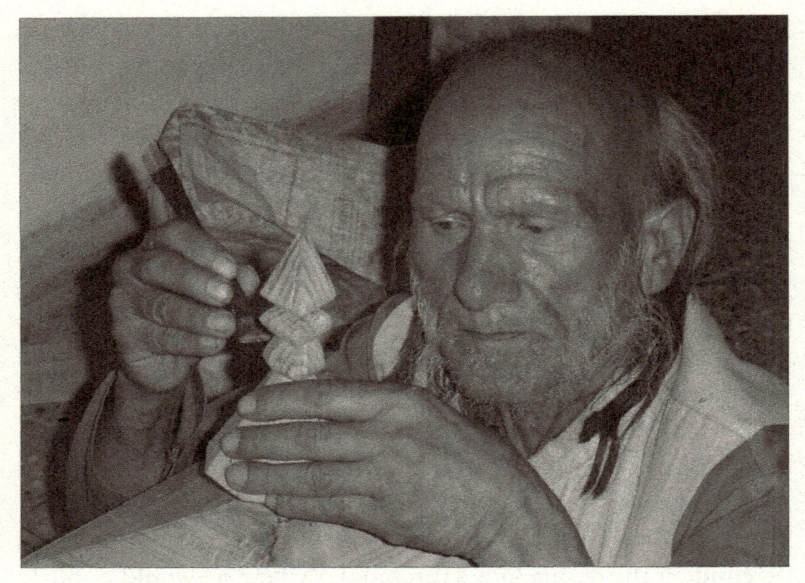

Photo 8.2: Ganga Ram at work.

carpenters come from the lower castes, they were thought to have rendered the roof over the deity impure. Thus, purification with a large-scale sacrificial ritual was called for.

Once the festival was under way, reformist fervour took over the assembly, including the deities who spoke through their oracles in one voice (with the exception of the powerful Chalda Mahasu, who insisted on retaining the cult's traditional "knowledge of caste segregation") that henceforth all caste groups and women could enter the temple. Laws in democratic India stipulate that no individual can be barred from entering a shrine of worship on the basis of religion, caste, or gender. They have been backed by a vigorous temple-entry movement, with reformists leading groups of low-caste men and women of all castes into shrines, at great peril to life and limb. While several shrines in India have reformed, some, like the Jagannath Temple in Puri, not long ago, denied entry to Prime Minister Indira Gandhi on the grounds that she had married a non-Hindu. In 2005, the queen of Thailand,

Mahachakri Siridharan, was not allowed inside the temple as she was a follower of Buddhism and not the Hindu faith.

At Hanol and other Mahasu shrines the practice of restricting the entry of the Kolta, Bajgi, and women of all castes has come under intense scrutiny. As recently as early 2016, Member of Parliament from Dehra Dun, Tarun Vijay, was assaulted after attempting to lead a group of low-caste men and women into the Shilgur Devta shrine at Pokhri. Many politicians like him are eyeing the temple entry movement as a prospect for expanding their dalit vote banks.

In 2006, when the Shaant festival was under way, the reform agenda was revived. Reformists attempted change on the two most contentious issues: temple entry to lower castes as well as women, and the abolition of animal sacrifice. In spite of a complete lack of consensus, it was announced that the Hanol temple had now decided to reform and would discontinue these practices after the festival. However, once the media spotlight shifted, the temple returned to its old ways, the priests refusing to permit entry to lower castes and women.

With the reform announcements, which Nand Lal Bharti and others like him took on face value, it seemed that the old order within the cult was yielding to pressure from the state. After his moments under the spotlight at the Hanol shrine, a couple of years later Bharti and his troupe were invited to perform at the Republic Day celebrations in New Delhi. He decided to seek the deity's grace by visiting the temple at Hanol. As he was entering the *dhakeur* (ante-room), he was accosted by a group of priests who questioned his audacity. He tried to protest, citing his stature as an artist and the earlier pronouncements ending discrimination on temple entry. In his indignation, he even pointed out that his troupe members, all low caste like him, had already entered the ante-room and made their offerings on account of their anonymity. He even reasoned he was being stopped only because he was a celebrated and recognisable figure, and the priests had something personal against him. Else how would priests know who entered with the crowds. When the priests remained unconvinced, he apologised by touching their feet. This was construed by the priests as another attempt at defiling them and proved the last straw. Even as the priest whose feet had been touched ran to get a purificatory bath, the other priests asked the entire group to pay a fine of two goats per person along with five hundred rupees. Each person also had to offer trinkets of gold and silver. Failing to do so right away would invite the deity's wrath. Bharti calculated that considering the size of his troupe, he would have to bring forty-four sacrificial goats.

Initially, he attempted to strike a bargain allowing him retreat with a token fine, but when the priests refused to budge he resolved to confront them and demanded his constitutional right to enter. The Temple Entry Bill granting non-caste Hindus the right to enter and offer worship in Hindu temples was implemented as early as 1939, so Bharti sought shelter in the constitution and confronted Mahasu's priests. In recent times, the rigid rules on temple matters have given way to the rule of law in other Mahasu shrines, like the one at Thadiyar, where all caste groups enter and the deity has gone vegetarian owing to a ban on animal sacrifice under pressure from animal rights groups.

Generally, Mahasu subjects have not questioned the divine king's order. With the emergence of constitutional authority and democratic institutions, there is a shift from temple custom to constitution. The hitherto suppressed who, in earlier times, could either petition the divine king or seek refuge in their own deities, can now afford to challenge norms when the cult seems incapable of reform. Even now, the initial instinct is to approach the *devta*.

Bharti decided to launch his protest in the courtyard of the Mahasu temple at Hanol, sitting in with this troupe, right in front of the divine king, until justice was delivered. He shot off angry letters to the National Human Rights Commission and the SDM.

The Commission directed the SDM to ensure that national laws were honoured. After almost a month of sustained protest, with his troupe performing their repertoire dedicated to Mahasu at the temple gates to make their protest visible, the SDM proclaimed that Bharti and his entire troupe of dancers would have to be permitted to enter the temple. In what would now become a much-publicised media event, Bharti accepted the offer to enter the temple and make his offerings, ending his protest with gratitude. He knew there was no love lost between him and influential members of the cult whom he had rubbed the wrong way. Leaders of all political denominations were asking him, albeit privately, to withdraw his agitation since they found themselves on the horns of a dilemma. To risk their popularity within the caste hierarchy if they supported Bharti's defiance would be as bad as media censure and loss of favour for not upholding the constitution to which they had vowed allegiance.

Bharti's dance troupe, now enthused at the prospect of breaking new ground by entering the temple with government support, arrived at the temple at dusk and immediately on arrival were made to realise that they were unwelcome. Homes around the temple usually offer hospitality to their caste brethren. Jaunsaris are known for their warmth and even a stranger can find a warm hearth and a spare blanket in these mountain homes, quite a few built to accommodate upwards of a hundred people. All doors in Kolta homes were, however, shut against Bharti and his troupe. It was drizzling, and they had been forced to huddle in a corner of the street through the night. The temple shed was still not open to them. The next morning, the SDM arrived with a posse of policemen specially brought in from Dehra Dun. The troupe was led into the temple as they sang and danced in praise of Mahasu. The news media were present in full force, perhaps the first time such a huge contingent had descended upon the temple.

According to Bharti, as the troupe crossed the first threshold, they were greeted by a group of priests in a state of heightened possession, shaking violently and flagellating themselves with stinging nettle. Bharti observed that even the *nath yogi*, the *kanphata* or the *rajguru*, who had been a co-performer with him in his troupe – a man he considered a key sympathiser and who was himself not permitted to enter the temple beyond the first inner chamber – had joined the ranks of the priests. Just then, one of the oracles uttered a loud shriek, and the other priests who were in a trance nodded their heads. The priest entered the sanctum of the temple and emerged with an unsheathed sword. He came out brandishing it, as if ready to claim Bharti's head. All this was happening in full view of the administrative officer and the media cameras trained on the action.

People sympathetic to his cause, aware that he might face violence, had tutored Bharti to stand his ground. He continued to sit inside the shrine, head bowed, coconut offering firmly in hand. The officials attempted to negotiate on behalf of the troupe that had now stopped singing and dancing. They wanted the priests to accept their offerings and provide a glimpse of the elusive deity, as they did for upper-caste clients. The priests were in no mood to relent and the stalemate continued. After waiting for almost an hour in the charged atmosphere, with more than half a dozen possessed priests and oracles venting their anger at them, Bharti and his troupe decided to walk out. He declared to the media corps that he did not desire Mahasu's *darshan* or audience any more. Though Bharti escaped physical injury despite a very real threat, he was neither granted an audience with the divine king nor were his offerings accepted. He had managed to cross a critical threshold, transcending the boundary of the temple, but his recourse to secular government had rendered the entire exercise futile.

The media castigated the administrative officers for not enforcing the law. The SDM declared he had fulfilled the law by ensuring entry to the temple. He could not have forced open the inner sanctum or ordered the priests to accept Bharti's offerings against their wishes, without hurting religious sentiment or causing a riot.

His argument was based on the penal code, which put the onus on temple authorities to permit entry. However, participation in the rituals, ensuring that the priests accepted the ritual gifts to the divine king on his behalf, blessings showered on the gift-givers, were beyond his jurisdiction, and beyond all human office. After all, even *devtas* and their priests had rights!

On the other hand, Bharti's public statements, reminiscent of peasant rebellion discourse that "the king can do no wrong", in fact, invoked Mahasu. He blamed government officials, upper-caste priests, and temple officials for the fiasco while expressing his faith in the divine king. Crossing the temple threshold made little sense unless their tributes to the divine king were accepted. The whole episode makes it quite evident that modern governments, having taken away most powers from the divine kings, have not been able to replace the ritual relations that subjects have forged with divine kings. Despite all social change and a strong resolve to reform, divine kingship has retained its religious relevance.

Bharti declared that he would now lead a delegation to Dehra Dun, the state capital, to meet the Chief Minister and the District Magistrate. A large group of reform supporters agreed to come with him. As news of the foiled bid to worship the deity by a low-caste social reformist spread, mobile phones began to ring with hectic communication between Dehra Dun and Hanol. Top politicians got involved, some for political gain, others worried about the repercussions within the community and outside it. The flows of modernity – content-hungry media, mobile phones, confused political voices – all actors in this quickly expanding web of social connections – were vertically splitting opinion within the community, even as Bharti continued his protest in the temple courtyard.

A few days later at the protest site, a local journalist who also officiated as an oracle to Bijat Devta, the deity of the low castes, entered a state of possession and began to shake violently. He declared that Mahasu did not reside in the temple any more since injustice was being perpetrated in his name. This utterance was tolerated since it was coming from a deity; from a human it would have amounted to the worst kind of sacrilege, leading to violent reprisals. Mahasu's senior *mali* also became possessed at this juncture and both gods began to argue. There were claims and counterclaims, and the entire scene resembled a courtroom, with oracles negotiating their briefs, the entire community becoming the jury. While the former maintained that a true god would never turn away the devout, the latter stuck to the line that certain castes would have to maintain ritual distance as prescribed by tradition. A large crowd gathered and it was quite evident that the final arbiter would be the community itself, caught between the desire for continuity among the haves and the push for change among the have-nots.

It is at junctures such as these that one witnesses contestations between the word of the divine king – his *niyam* (rules) – and the will of the community. The result is often an ambiguous resolution with the divine king finally leaving it to the community to resolve its conflict. The agency therefore rests with the community, even though the resolution is always recognised as having come from the divine king. The government machinery in such cases is a bystander, a mute witness.

The oracles, supported by their diverse opinion groups, were arguing their cases with the media and administrative officers as witnesses. The role of adjudication, it seemed, was now with the community with the divine king as defendant. In earlier times the word of Mahasu's oracle would have been accepted unconditionally, but today was a different day. Now the choice between change and continuity would have to be argued out and intensely negotiated.

Finally, as if gauging the mood of the moment, the Mahasu oracle deviated from his line of argument and began to question the temple priests on why his *bhaktas* (disciples) were being barred from entering his temple. At this, the oracle of Bijat responded by announcing that the temple was under the hegemonic control of a few. After a rather protracted interrogation of Bharti, Mahasu's *mali* asked for different piles of rice to be placed while the possessed oracle was not looking, so that by choosing the correct pile he could pronounce judgment on whether he and his troupe had made the right move by insisting on entering his shrine. This, everyone hoped, would end the stalemate. To decide if the *harijan* could be allowed in, a pile of rice placed on the left would be picked, if not, the one on the right. If women were to be permitted inside, the oracle would place his hand on this pile, and if not, on another; if goats were to be sacrificed, then a particular pile, if not, another. In this manner, nine piles would be placed for final decisions. The oracle then left the scene, to attend to his daily chores, declaring he would soon return to make his choice. Bharti and his troupe, the administrators and the media, were left waiting for the oracle to return. By retreating from the scene for a while, the Mahasu oracle was probably buying time, hoping that the excitement of the moment would die down. By disappearing from the scene he would also cause the Bijat possession to recede, while he himself could confabulate and strategise with the Mahasu minister and other community leaders. It was at this crucial point that the word of the divine king seemed more like the collective will of the community, showing how constitutional authority was tilting the balance in favour of the dispossessed.

The oracle returned in a few hours and, violently possessed, squatted before the piles of rice. Without a moment's hesitation, he picked the pile that indicated that the lower castes could indeed be permitted entry to his temple. There was rejoicing; the goddess Kali possessed her oracle, the *birs* to the *devta* also possessed their oracles. Right then, Bharti and group, accompanied by the SDM and over a dozen possessed oracles, walked into the temple and were granted a viewing of the god's sanctum. Bharti later recounted how he felt at the time:

> When the *devtas* got together to ensure that we get inside, things began to fall in place. People, who had been so agitated and hostile, suddenly their demeanour was transformed. The gods were with us, police and administration stood up to their duty, we queued up,

dancing and singing, each one of us entered and were in the presence of our *devta*, Mahasu. The possessions continued. We were elated that our divine king had finally accepted us!

It is significant that Bharti stressed acceptance. His protests never targeted the divine king, not even the community, but only a section within it seen as the oppressor. It was acceptance that he sought from the divine kings; *they* were the emancipators, agents of positive change, not the state administration or the media.

As the group was emerging from the temple, Bharti was asked to step aside and the Rajput officials of the divine king whispered in his ear that since he had now been allowed to enter, he should not follow up on his case with the National Human Rights Commission. He was further instructed not to push for the arrest of the priests who had earlier manhandled him and blocked his entry into the temple. Having achieved his objective, Bharti readily agreed to this, despite cues from some friends in the media that he must not.

Once the media glare and state attention shifted from the temple site, the temple priests soon returned to the old position of not permitting lower castes and women to enter beyond the threshold. As with most other decisions within the Mahasu cult, the community's first response had been to retain the status quo. Once change was forced upon them, they accepted it, albeit momentarily. The divine king, his minister and priests, had only been forced to make a temporary tactical retreat. To many observers of the cult, such short-lived concessions were also unheard of. It was the TV crews, newspaper reporters, the mobile phones, the deity's juridical authority competing with the national legal system that had made the cult bend. But for Bharti it was the divine kings themselves who made the monumental shift.

Significant in these stand-offs between tradition and reformist agendas is their ambiguous resolution. The divine king adopts an intransigent position until the pressure becomes irresistible. Once the fatigue point of resistance is reached, the divine king makes a tactical retreat, only to revert to the older system at the earliest opportunity. All the same, the temporary change brought about by these acts of defiance forces a rethink within Jaunsari society.

Dirks (1987: 25) argues that caste may not exist as an "autonomous" religious phenomenon but as a system of social relations articulated, ordered, and sustained by the king. "The prevalent ideology," he says, "had not to do, at least primarily, with purity and pollution, but rather with royal authority and power, dominance and order." Though he refers to dominance and order as the primary driving forces in the context of the royal model – the government having taken over many of those functions – it is quite true that dominance and order supersedes concerns over purity and pollution in the Mahasu realm. It is also clear that ritual relations with the divine kings remain largely undisturbed despite the government's appropriation of power.

The quest for dominance and struggle for power also leads to ironical situations. Nand Lal Bharti, proclaiming himself a victim of caste discrimination in his attempts to enter the Mahasu temple at Hanol, has over the years transformed himself into a part-time crusader for his own caste group, struggling for recognition of the Kolta as a backward group so that benefits accruing to scheduled castes, in addition to those granted to scheduled tribes, are given to them. The Indian constitution lays down separate reservation benefits for low castes and tribal people. For instance, in government-funded higher-education institutions, of the 22.5 per cent positions available to various courses, 15 per cent are reserved for scheduled castes and 7.5 per cent for scheduled tribes. To claim the double benefit of caste *and* tribe, Bharti and his group, while fighting for equality, have developed a vested interest in claiming lack of economic and material progress in order to derive benefits from the government's affirmative action policy.

Toffin (2000: 61) describes the dilemma of upper-caste priests who perform ritual rites for the Newari community in a mountain region of Nepal. Members of this social group can retain their superior status in the "full sense of the word only if they distinguish themselves . . ." from their clients, the Newar. For the Rajopadhyaya, who project themselves as the embodiment of the transcendental values of religious life associated with separateness and independence, an opposition to autochthonous values is needed to enable them to stand apart as a superior priestly class. However, ties based on territory and locality push the Rajopadhyaya to incorporate and identify with the *parbatiya* (mountain community) that dominate Nepalese society politically and ethnically. While identifying with the dominant class, their claim to priesthood and social superiority is affected, and while remaining exclusive they risk isolation and the loss of demographic strength offered by numbers in a democracy.

A similar dilemma exists for Bharti and the Kolta at large. If they project themselves as separate from the Jaunsaris, as the most downtrodden amongst the tribe, they risk losing tribal privilege. If, on the other hand, they identify with the tribe in general, most administrators will not grant them the benefits of caste even as they continue to face oppression from the upper castes. The Kolta, despite aspiring to egalitarianism, have been conditioned for centuries into a habitus of subjugation. Even though they want to break the caste mould, they find it extremely difficult to forgo the "privileges" of low caste and tribe, such as the double reservation from the state, especially when survival in a society completely dominated by upper castes is tough.

Bharti, despite his moments of victory in the struggle towards equality, not only earned the ire of the Rajput and the Brahman, but also faced flak within his own community for alienating them from the politically powerful groups and risking the tribe appellation. In fact, several members of his own caste group have not taken kindly to his rebellion, labelling it a "publicity stunt". In order to claim benefits due to them as members of the scheduled tribe, and extract concessions from the politically dominant Rajput, they believe it was necessary to retain the status quo. In order to receive benefits due to the scheduled castes, it was imperative to leverage their untouchability.

By his own admission, Bharti's relationship to the community was comparable to two people going through a painfully contested divorce. There was longing for the past as well as an urgent need to break away from it. On a subsequent visit to the temple, as I broached the topic of Bharti's protest with one of the Mahasu priests, he claimed that ever since Bharti had dared oppose Mahasu's writ the man had been cursed and his personal life was a shambles. His wife had lost her mental balance and medical treatment was proving ineffective. Bharti himself, though conceding that all was not well on the home front, did not attribute his troubles to Mahasu's wrath. In fact he reaffirmed his faith in Mahasu while adopting a rational approach to his wife's illness, explaining it in bio-medical terminology, as against the views expressed by most upper-caste members of the community. Despite his personal troubles, individuals within his own caste group have begun to look up to him as a leader, especially since he has become a popular figure in the local media and an icon for national dalit rights groups.

Life seemed to have come full circle when Bharti, after facing two years of ostracism, returned to the limelight, this time to lead another protest for the issuing of caste certificates to the Kolta. After several decades of extending the dual benefits of caste and tribe to the Kolta, the government realised their folly – doling out double benefits was constitutionally untenable. Soon, it declared a policy of extending only tribal status to all Jaunsaris, withdrawing the caste benefits being extended to the Kolta within the community. Bharti, owing to his new-found status as a community leader, decided to thwart this move by launching a protest movement, ironically now protesting against the emancipation of the Kolta caste, insisting that the status quo be maintained. By doing this he was negating his earlier stand on egalitarianism. After a prolonged and much publicised hunger strike outside the local administrator's office, it was decided that the scheduled caste status for the Kolta would, for the time being, be continued, until a reference on the issue was received from the Indian government. Here, the activist from the Kolta caste forced the government machinery, quite like he did with Mahasu, into a tactical retreat. Bharti and his supporters squarely blamed government officials for succumbing to anti-dalit lobbies.

This brings home the point that democratic government may have usurped many of the divine king's functions, but the mutual relationship of the people with government is not quite the same as with Mahasu. The kernel of longevity of the Mahasu realm, as against human kingships and the democratic government, perhaps lies in the ritualised relations the community shares with their divine king. These relationships offer emotional as well as community security. The same cannot be said for relationships with government, based on laws, grants, and constitutional provisions. Ritual relationships with divine kings may be under strain, more than ever before, but they endure because of the human reliance on embodied ritual, performed in a community setting.

Though Bharti's detractors see victories like his entry into the temple or his winning dual benefits for his caste group as pyrrhic, for the activist himself they have been his life's work and for several in his community they are nothing less than unprecedented paradigm shifts. The change brought about by Bharti indicates a continued churning, a balancing of social forces within the Mahasu realm. The realm is described by Sutherland (1998: 292) as "A ritual choreography of roles defining the triple space of *dharmically* ordered *sakti*: *Brahmans* and their gods at the centre (order), *Kolis* (or the Kolta) and their gods at the periphery (disorder), *Khas-Rajputs* and their gods mediating the extremes in the intervening field where *sakti* is deployed in political relations." In this constellation, the low castes are at the periphery and represent disorder. However, their role is of extreme significance in order to counterbalance the forces of order.

Ancient Hindu mythology also gives us a clue to the significance of the periphery. Shiva represents it and Daksha's annihilation is a representation of what happens when the centre and the mediators ignore the periphery. Even though the lower castes have been dominated for centuries, and divine kingship in certain ways owes its longevity to this suppression, several instances point towards their significance to the realm. For instance, the curse of the *beda* woman is an incident often mentioned by village elders, and, recorded in history, bears testimony to such a fine balance between the periphery and the centre.

According to the *Gazetteer of Sirmur State* (1934: 9), in *samvat* 1139 Madan Singh, the Suryavanshi Rajput ruler of the Western Himalayan kingdom of Sirmaur, agreed to part with half his kingdom and gift it to a woman from the *beda* – a low-caste group of necromancers and dancer-musicians – if she crossed the Giri River between the Toka and Poka ranges by negotiating a suspended rope. When she had successfully crossed the swelling river, balancing precariously on the suspended rope, the raja, in a last-ditch effort to save half his kingdom, pledged the other half as well if she managed to return by the same rope. When she was halfway through her acrobatic feat and it was evident that the raja would certainly lose his kingdom to a low-caste woman, his officials treacherously cut the rope. The woman fell to her death, but her curse ensured that furious floods, swelling up the Sirmauri Tal on the banks of the Giri, swamped the capital of the kingdom of Sirmaur, washing away the raja and his clan, not even leaving an heir apparent (Lal 1993: 51). It was much later that Nahan town was rebuilt by the Bhati Dynasty on the hilltop, away from the furies of a wronged low-caste woman and the floodwaters. While remembrance of episodes like these seeks to empower peripheral caste groups through folklore, the government, for its own empowerment agendas, depends on constitutional provisions and laws. Both approaches may work towards a renegotiation of social positions.

The social position afforded by caste, unlike class, is a negotiable instrument and one cannot take one's dominance for granted. As the modern state's projects of social engineering reach Mahasu's realm, dominance could drown – like the once-impregnable fortress of Sirmaur. While the focus of current social movements is to petition the government and seek greater opportunities for immediate kinship groups among the suppressed castes, the divine king retains his relevance for them since activists like Bharti swear by Mahasu's divine jurisdiction. Such protestors have always insisted that a considerate *devta* like Mahasu can never discriminate amongst his subjects, and that their ostracism is a creation of the priests. On the other hand, the priests have always represented Bharti's protest as a rebellious move against the social norms established by divine kings. Thus, for both groups the divine king is the relevant focal point. In Bharti's case the vernacular media, even while opposing the restriction on temple entry tooth and nail and rooting for reform, credited the deity's "progressive" priests and oracles for finally permitting Bharti and his troupe to enter. They were, however, critical of the government machinery, accusing them of ineptitude in their inability to get Bharti's offerings accepted by the *devta*. This is again an indication of the hold divine kings continue to exercise.

It is also evident that the Jaunsaris are moving towards empowerment by leveraging signs of backwardness, superstition, heterodoxy, decadence, and all the stereotypes of polyandry, easy divorce, widow remarriage, bride price, belief in *devtas* and their oracles, blood sacrifice, illiteracy and drunkenness – using all these to get reservation benefits. This goes hand in hand with an insatiable appetite for state resources gobbled up by adopting the alternative strategy of local cultural resistance to egalitarianism. Caste, meanwhile, emerges as a tool, a transactional strategy to negotiate proximity to power.

9

Rites and Rights

THE UBIQUITY OF RITUALS, religious and political, within social groups like the cult of Mahasu, is quite evident. If agentive power is understood as the ability of an action to bring about transformation in a social group's ways of living, then rituals possess it in ample measure. When a state seeks to extend its influence over an isolated and peripheral region by altering political-religious ritual processes, the act has strong political overtones. Rituals define social realities; when the state intervenes and reorganises them, the effects are far-reaching.

Religious rituals are usually seen to foster unity or engender community feeling. They represent cultural norms and values connected to identity. They bring the past into a living present, enabling participants to share commonalities of mythical times and places, coalescing them with an experience of the present. Ritual performances are in a sense pasts experienced as the present. Quoting Myerhoff (1977), Kertzer (1988) says that by stating and enduring underlying patterns, ritual connects past, present, and future, abrogating history and time. Bringing Durkheimian (1912) analysis into the study of ritual in politics, he further describes ritual as symbolic activity through which constituents in a society sacralise their mutual interdependencies.

Rituals themselves get transformed, much the same as ways of living change. In turn, they reflect the changing identity of social groups in the wider contexts of polities such as the nation-states that encompass them. What happens when a particular ritual, intrinsic to a belief system, is suddenly denied to a social group and attempts are made to replace it by another "less harmful" ritual? The situation is complicated when certain voices within the community also join the clamour for "reform". This situation, while forcing the pro- and anti-reform groups to confront each other's viewpoint, kick-starts self-reflexive processes that begin to look at identity anew. Owing to the polarisation that reform causes, social groups are forced to think afresh about acts hitherto considered routine and natural. In the process ritual, though it may hold its own and survive in spite of confrontations and controversies, is altered in practice and perception.

This chapter looks at the instance of the ritual of goat sacrifice being denied to the Jaunsaris when the media and civil society activists raised the issue of "barbaric practices in the name of religion". As long as forces the community construed as external to it enunciated "reform" – for instance, if it came from the state or its various assimilative arms such as government officials, activists, or media – the community and the divine kings first rebelliously opted for persistence. When continually prodded to change, they adapted by making a temporary tactical retreat. In such cases, for some time, the ritual may be abandoned or altered. When the censure persists, they are forced into a defensive posture, denying the existence of the ritual and even discontinuing its practice for a while, the ritual only returning into visible practice once the external gaze is averted. But when voices from within the community seek a break from the past – protesting against a ritual they see as regressive, the churning is much more nuanced. External voices join the opposition within, especially if the ritual is at odds with mainstream ideologies, and calls for change force community leaders to announce its discontinuation. The act of abandoning the ritual leaves a void and requires an alternative. In case the alternative does not emerge, in course of time the earlier ritual returns with a vengeance, even if altered in practice and perception.

Within India's Hindu caste societies many heterodox systems exist simultaneously, belying the notion of coherence. Uttarakhand exemplifies the political volatility of sub-regional identities and beliefs. Here, cultural differences between the various sub-regions and groups, upland and lowland, rural and urban, tribal and non-tribal, remain unresolved. The fact of statehood has only served to exacerbate these differences, with each group attempting to affirm them even more emphatically.

The Jaunsar-Bawar region had much going for it in colonial times. In 1883, two documents compiled by a British collector, A. Ross, listed the rights and customs in the Jaunsar-Bawar in an effort to comprehend the complex and particularised social system. Titled the *Wajib-ul-Arz* and the *Dastur-al-Amal*, these documents were accepted as standard references for local customary codes. Using them as a basis, the region was accorded special status under the Government of India Act, 1935, even as the "little kingdoms" in the neighbourhood, with similar caste and cultural compositions, were kept out.

Post-Independence, especially in the 1960s, the region fell under the gaze of government planners owing to reports describing the region as one with perhaps the lowest per-capita income and a parallel economy owing to rampant poppy cultivation. The Extraordinary Gazette of the Government of India (No. 107, 24 June 1967), taking into account precedents of British policy, and as a result of intense lobbying by local political pressure groups, included all caste groups within the region into the broad classification of "Jaunsari Tribe", recognised as predominantly agropastoral in occupation, with the sacrifice of goats seen as a mark of their tribalism. Their social order followed calendrical cycles and in fact all festivities and ritual gatherings involved large-scale animal sacrifice. Meat-eating was noted as a part and parcel of local identities, and festivities were marked by boisterous and violent celebrations followed by what Sutherland (1998: xxii) describes as "the serious political work of drinking".

That flesh-eating is integral to the Mahasu subject's concept of ritual was revealed to me by the divine king's own musician. According to *bajgi* Madan Das, the name Mahasu is derived from *Maamsu* (*Maams+su*: deities that consume flesh), rather than the connotations of Mahashiva proffered by some scholars (Jain 1995). They arrived to consume the flesh of the demon they defeated, Kirmir, and, as we saw, distribution of the flesh was a signifier of the regions where the Mahasu kingdom was inaugurated.

The origin myth also explicates the initiation of *bali*, the ritual offering of goats at Mahasu temples. As the Mahasus arrived with their deputies from the fabled lands of Kullu-Kashmir, they proceeded to a lake, Punnath Tal, where the demon lived. While one of the Mahasu deputies agreed to guard the terrestrial world, the other was deputed to reconnoitre the netherworld where the demon lived. Once the deputies had completed their investigation, they procrastinated with regard to confronting and battling the demon. The Mahasus finally asked their deputies, the *birs*, to force demons out of hiding and fight for them. They had to bribe them (*risvat dena*) with the promise that goats would be sacrificed for their consumption during the night vigil, the Jagra, and other festivals like Basant Pancami (locally, *dhaknach*), on the fifth day of the arrival of *magh* (the season marking the arrival of spring). Ever since, the ritual offering of goats to the divine king's deputies became a prescribed ritual.

If, as a subject of Mahasu, you feel that something you deserve is not coming your way, or if your life is full of inexplicable trouble, you can make a vow to visit the deity and offer a goat once the problems are resolved. Or else you could visit the Mahasu temple, consult his oracle, and ask for a remedy, which, once granted, will culminate in the offering of a goat. This is what thousands of people across Mahasu territory do every day. The practice of *bali* or *balidana* is a pan-Indian tradition, with goats in the pastoral regions, in particular, denoting wealth and well-being. From replenishing fertility of the soil – farmers pay shepherds handsomely to halt with them after the winter grazing in fields being prepared for sowing – to their urine providing solvents that soften and bleach bamboo fibres woven into mats and baskets, goats and their functional utility is immense. In most alpine homes the ground floor is reserved for livestock. People inhabit the floors above, the body heat generated by livestock helping to keep them warm. Sacrificing a goat is therefore to give up something quite vital to everyday existence.

Early in 2015, on a freezing winter evening as I approached the little hamlet of Bhotanu on a snowbound ridge in the mountains of Bangan in the district of Uttarkashi, I was warmly welcomed by the *sayana* of the village, an old acquaintance. I had long been trekking with the palanquin of Chalda Mahasu. The host village had been made ready to welcome the large numbers travelling with the procession. The moment I arrived, the *sayana* insisted I squat with other Rajput elders in the terraced fields for a meal of mutton and rice. A reluctant meat-eater, I was confronted with the sight of goats being butchered and skinned right there. Their flesh went straight into the cauldrons, and their skins were stretched out to dry for the drummer-bards to use for their drums. Refusing a meal from an elder is not an option one can consider on these mountain slopes, and as I dug into the goat on my plate I felt, in a sense, the full import of its weight in the lives of the Jaunsaris. The goats we were gorging on had been contributed by every hamlet and village to feed pilgrims who had been walking with the Mahasu procession for close to a month. The animals were ritual offerings, nutrition, even ritual music with their skins stretched and mounted on the drums.

Never before have the dietary habits of the divine kings and their deputies become as big a bone of contention (the metaphor is ironically appropriate) as now. During one of my earlier visits to Hanol, in 1995, goats were being sacrificed at a spot very close to the entrance of the Mahasu temple. In my conversations about ritual practices, *bali* was mentioned casually – there was no specific comment on Mahasu's food habits. The cooking of meat was done right next door, in the *rawli pand*, Mahasu's perpetual kitchen. During that visit, I met a man and his wife who had walked from afar to the temple with a goat. While sipping tea at the only teashop close to the temple, I saw the woman shivering. The symptoms appeared to be of a high fever that had induced mild delirium. I offered some tablets of Paracetamol that I happened to be carrying. The medicine was politely refused with the explanation that it was the *devta*'s *dos* that was causing mischief: the divine king would not exorcise the spirits plaguing the woman unless he was propitiated with a goat. In their understanding killing the goat in the temple was an offering specifically for the divine king. The couple had walked four days through the mountains to arrive at the temple to get rid of the affliction.

Purity and pollution have always been significant to Mahasu, and there has been, as noted earlier, a complete restriction on carrying leather, even in the form of waist belts, wallets, and wristwatch straps, inside the shrines. Wearing leather is associated with impurity, and therefore most Mahasu devotees wear cloth waist belts. However, *bali* was never even remotely considered a defiling act. On the contrary, as Sutherland (1998: 320) puts it when referring specifically to Mahasu shrines, "everyone who eats the cooked flesh of the sacrificial victim, when distributed in its transvalued form as *prasad*, is biologically incorporated in a community as shared 'coded substance' as Chicago ethnosociologists might have called it." It is an act that thwarts Mahasu's anger at non-fulfilment of ritual duty, or causes a reversal of the consequences of what is usually referred to as his *dos*. So it is pertinent here to explicate the processes of attribution of *dos* and its removal through *bali*. It will enable an understanding of how the net of mutual obligations is endangered if the ritual were to be denied to the community.

The divine king's *dos* is closely linked to Mahasu's juridical authority, as also to the notion of propitiation through sacrifice.

Dos usually refers to an offence taken by the divine king due to unintentional immoral conduct, or the violation of social norms, leading to social imbalance. The divine king makes a subtle difference between two kinds of human foibles, *paap* and *dos*. While *paap* may be broadly equated with sin – generally relating to bad intentions but also possibly the result of unintentional action – *dos* is god's punishment. Sax (1991: 92) says *dos* is as much object or substance as action. While the term may relate to damage, harm, consequence, or detrimental effect, several other meanings of the term exist that could connote fault, flaw, guilt, defect, demerit, blame, or disorder. *Dos* may occur when a ritual mistake or omission occurs, or a promise made to the deity is left unfulfilled.

While *paap karma* invites irreversible consequences and falls within the purview of ethics, *dos* could be explained in terms of faults, character blemishes, errors of judgement, or pernicious behaviour, all within the ambit of actions and their reactions, cause and effect. *Dos* and *paap* not only pertain to intentions and actions in the present physical world but also past lives. While the divine king can inflict *dos* upon his subjects, he can also reverse it. *Dos* is causative and the divine king, while possessing the oracle, seeks to diagnose the intentions of members within the clan through an interrogation, a kind of a public hearing leading up to a very public confession of the guilt of having acted against the established order. Thus, *dos* is a curse that is reversible if one comes to Mahasu seeking pardon, offering sacrifice.

While individuals afflicted by *dos* and seeking to recover from its ill effects are usually accompanied by members of the immediate clan, they also bring with them rice or soil from the hearth of the family home. These two elements – the presence of clan members and rice or soil from either the hearth or the family fields – are essential to the diagnosis of *dos*. Clan members are brought in because it is usually a wronged individual from within the clan whose presence is required; the soil and rice are for the divine king's power to establish a consubstantiality with the soil of the home and hearth where the spirit to be exorcised resides. *Dos* is usually diagnosed publicly, in the temple courtyard, and cured with the performance of *bali* and other ritual acts.

Families usually arrive with afflicted relatives and wait for their trusted oracle to finish other consultations. They are then seated in a group, with the individual afflicted by the *dos* directly facing the oracle. A bank note, pledged in Mahasu's name, is kept alongside a little pile of rice from the afflicted family's granary. The oracle picks up a few grains and gradually works up a possession, his body shaking violently, voice raised to a high pitch (*cheriya boli*), the demeanour quite distinct from his usual disposition. He then tosses the grains at the afflicted individual, intermittently observing the grains in his hand very carefully. Then the public interrogation commences and the afflicted individual as well as clan members respond to the divine king's questions. Oracles are usually Rajput or Brahman and are permitted to hold consultations only after they can demonstrate the authenticity of their possession through a test before senior oracles in a temple ceremony.

A few years ago I interviewed Kamlesh Nautiyal, an oracle to Mahasu Devta, in the temple courtyard at Hanol. He explained that he quit his job in the Indian Navy and returned to the village

Photo 9.1: Oracular consultation in progress.

to take up the work of an oracle because the divine king and his deputies appeared persistently in his dreams and even in a waking state threatened him with *dos* affliction if he did not dedicate himself to Mahasu's service. During our conversation, members of an extended family entered the temple courtyard, the parents with great effort trying to subdue a twenty-year-old girl who was very strongly possessed, to the point of appearing violently hysterical. A few men in the family were also possessed, but not aggressive like the young girl. One of the temple officials, the *thani*, accidentally hit her across the face in an effort to protect himself.

At that moment, Mahasu possessed another oracle squatting near the temple entrance. Shaking violently, he announced: "My official has hit another *devta* unduly, I shall compensate him for this indiscretion. I shall pay a *dand* [compensation] to this *devta* right now, from my treasury! I shall meet the family in the evening." The temple official who had hit the girl, upon hearing the oracle's pronouncement, rushed inside and from the sanctum of the temple brought a handful of rice and a hundred-rupee note as compensation for the *faux pas*. In this fashion the oracle, the embodied form of Mahasu as king, compensated the spirit embodied in the girl. In doing so he does not recognise the woman, he recognises the divinity that possesses her. As a divine king playing host to visitors who are carriers of spirits awaiting exorcism and adjudication, he or his officials are not supposed to act violently, however extreme the provocation. Therefore, of his own accord, he agrees to compensate the possessing spirit for his official's fault. The *devtas* are in conversation with one another at the temple, and even Mahasu is susceptible to *dos* and *dand*, curse and punitive action, if officials commit an indiscretion. In that sense, a visit by a human possessed by another divinity is also a political visit with divinities recognising each other, leaving the more mundane aspect to humans.

As the family huddled in a corner to await their turn in the evening, the violent behaviour of the girl made a bystander quip to the oracle: "Pandit, this girl is going to give you a tough time, she just might devour you!" The individual, a casual visitor – though a Mahasu devotee well acquainted with the functioning of the cult – construed this as an interaction between girl and oracle, a human encounter. But as the exorcism progressed over the evening, the visit was again transformed for the actors and their observers into divine interplay.

The girl's father, himself an oracle of another minor deity further upland, Narsingh, had been unable to help her overcome the spirit possessing her and had therefore sought Mahasu's help. As a worried father, he was perturbed by his daughter's inappropriate behaviour and was making every effort to subdue her. The girl was violent and delirious but unable to speak. This, according to my informant's diagnosis (himself a renowned Mahasu oracle, not presently involved in the consultation), was an indication that Lata Bir, a deaf and dumb demigod, possessed her. Meanwhile, I was hoping that the sheer physical exertion of the possessed state would soon sap the girl of all her energy and calm her down. But till the time the oracle returned in the evening for consultation and exorcism, she retained the same level of uncontrollable energetic violence.

The rice was placed on a wooden plank where the family huddled with the oracle; the family squatted, surrounding the girl facing the oracle. As the oracle entered a trance and began to speak in the *cheriya boli* (the shaking voice), the girl only communicated with the embodied Mahasu oracle through gestures. The consultation had begun. After a few tense moments, with the oracle shaking almost as violently as his patient, the girl jumped up in a silent but energetic manoeuvre, even as the oracle signalled to her to squat on the floor.

> Oracle: Why have you dared to possess this woman, Lata Bir? Do you think you can trouble her when she is under my tutelage?
>
> (The girl leapt violently, lunging forward as if she would punch the oracle in the face. The family held her down.)

Oracle: Oh, you think you can eat her bones. If you think you have the power, try it now, I dare you to do it now, in my presence.

(The woman jumped and shrieked violently but did not utter a single intelligible word. The oracle again signalled to her to sit. At this point, the girl's father also began to work up a possession. He was himself an oracle and was, therefore, possessed by Narsingh. Now the Mahasu oracle addressed him directly.)

Oracle: Did you, did you plant an apple orchard last year?

Father (as Narsingh, now himself possessed): Yes, I did.

Oracle: And did you extend your orchard into your brother's land as well, encroached upon it?

(The father fell silent. His brother and his family were sitting beside him. A respected public figure, the local deity's oracle stood accused before a large number of onlookers who knew the family intimately.)

Oracle: There is no justice, you are an oracle! Your brother's wife was anguished over your encroachment. She consulted [*vicar kiya*] a pandit who has put your daughter in the snare [*ghat*] of Lata Bir.

(The girl again gesticulated violently towards the Mahasu oracle. The brother's wife appeared embarrassed at this accusation but did not refute it.)

Oracle (addressing the father): Do you understand what Lata says? There is no justice. You are eating the gold and the goats that are offered to Narsingh, and then you are also occupying lands wrongfully.

Father (hands folded in a gesture of supplication): Please ask him to release my girl.

Oracle: Then you must return your brother's land. There has to be justice. I will take care of Lata Bir. Come together and sacrifice a goat once you are satisfied.

Father (with a gesture of supplication): I return the land. I have given up the claim right now.

(Now the oracle asked the girl's aunt, who had consulted a shaman to put the girl in a snare, to get up and pat her on the back [*peeth jhaadh de*], and as she did that the girl relaxed, as if knots within her had been unravelled. In a short while she returned to being a demure village girl.)

Within a few moments everything got back to normal, the brothers reconciled and chatted with each other while the aunt, the afflicted girl's mother, and the girl herself sipped tea at the stall close by.

My informant, the oracle observing the proceedings, interpreting the adjudication for me, declared that without seeking permission from the higher *devtas*, the demigods would not possess anyone. Mahasu himself must have suggested that Lata Bir should do this so that Narsingh's oracle would have to seek Mahasu's help. The communication is between deities, the humans merely conduits, irrespective of whether one is an oracle or a possessed victim, and Mahasu being the king of divinities (*devon ka raja*) has the final word. Significantly, as peace returns to the family, the final act expected of the family to complete the propitiation of the god is a goat sacrifice, the incident showing that goats are perceived as offered to divine kings with other forms of wealth as a kind of return gift for the well-being they offer to their subjects. Every oracle and priest in the Mahasu realm claims that goats are being sacrificed for the *birs*, not the divine kings. On the other hand the afflicting demigod is seen to be living "off the bones", a kind of parasite within the victim, while the deity himself (Narsingh, in this case) is seen as consuming the goats offered at the temple.

What we see here is that *dos* is afflictive and reversible. *Dos* may arise and afflict due to unintended disrespect caused to the *devta*, or by committing a violation of the *niyam* (ethical code). It arises mainly out of neglect of promises made to the divine king, or misdemeanours such as the neglect of caste norms and the violation of ideal familial norms. A condition like leprosy is a consequence of *paap* and not *dos*. *Dos* can be remedied through atonement, purification, and sacrifice. Removal of *dos* usually culminates in *bali*. In case of a *paap* being diagnosed, the deities are known to say that the victim cannot be helped, or increasingly in present times they suggest that the client visit a hospital or report matters to law-enforcement agencies. If the divine king asks for a sacrifice, those consulting the oracle feel grateful.

Animal sacrifice is also intimately connected with notions of territory, power, and authority. Those performing the sacrifice, usually Rajput, flaunt their ability to use their wealth before the community, declaring through the act their propensity to give up so much to save the community from Mahasu's ire. Goats may also be sacrificed as a purifying ritual if the temple has been defiled by the entry of low-caste individuals or women.

In the present context, *bali*, the priests report, is increasingly offered in new ways. As opposed to the offering made to the divine king in the form of goats, gold, silver (or the pod of the musk deer in earlier times), it is now increasingly made in cash. Goats were earlier offered as a *dhal* (tribute) or an expression of gratitude to the divine king, but now take the form of an offering with an end in mind – a gift seeking a favour in return. The intention of the sacrifice, as quite a few testify, is transforming from oblation or propitiation to requests for the fulfilment of a wish. During fieldwork, as I sat in the temple courtyard talking to people who had brought in goats as sacrifice, I realised that most of them were bringing the animals as gifts; their hope was that Mahasu would fulfil a wish.

Whatever the purpose, most individuals making the sacrifice say that *bali* gave them a sense of fulfilment and calm. Earlier, the best goats were picked from personal livestock, but now that people from urban areas are bringing the sacrificial animal, or those who have taken up apple horticulture after abandoning the traditional pastoral ways, the goats are often purchased. The procedure of sacrificing a goat is well established. For an intended sacrifice, the deity is consulted through his oracles. The deity may demand a sacrifice or forbid it when offered. Once the *bali* is demanded or recommended, a goat is brought into the middle chamber of the temple. As the person making the sacrifice and the goat enter and face the divine king's inner chamber, the door of the inner sanctum is opened for a few seconds. The priest, standing inside this pitch-dark chamber, briefly lights a pine twig, which, for an instant, illuminates the sanctum. He waves it around the several idols inside, with an invocation. Once the invocation is done, the goat must undergo the embodying ritual of *paani puwai* (lit. sprinkling of the water). The priest sprinkles water in the left ear of the goat with an invocation. As the goat quivers and shakes its head and specific muscles on its back move, the animal is deemed to have been embodied by the divine and the sacrifice is considered accepted. According to Fuller (1992), the animal has to be purified, promised, and worshipped before the sword, which has also been worshipped before it descends on the victim's neck. Even though the trembling of the animal indicates that the sacrifice has been accepted, the full preparatory ritual indicates that the deity only takes a victim that has participated in its divinity, the ritual of sacrifice merging the victim with the deity, a process completed by the immolation: . . . the victim is both an intermediary between the deity and the human sacrificer (the donor), and a substitute for the latter. The perfect sacrificial victim, as many myths demonstrate, is the human sacrificer himself. Animal sacrifice approximates that ideal by merging the sacrificer with the deity . . . but also cuts the two parties apart when the victim dies, so that only the animal's life passes to the deity. The human sacrificer remains alive, able to reap the benefits of pleasing the deity by making a sacrifice.

Once the goat is deemed accepted, the door to the inner sanctum is hurriedly shut, and at this point the priest congratulates the sacrificer. The *jeunda* (the sacrificial goat) is hurriedly dragged away from Mahasu's line of sight, from a side door out in the open to the left, out of the temple, for the sacrifice to be performed.

If the goat does not quiver after the first sprinkling of water, the procedure is repeated a few times. If the animal refuses to quiver even after several attempts, it is declared *ghantua* (with connotations that it now lacks virility). The left ear is pierced and the animal is let off, leaving the one offering the sacrifice very disappointed. It is construed that the deity has still not relieved the one bringing the sacrifice of his *dos* and further consultations with Mahasu oracles are needed. But the sacrificer never takes back a goat brought in the name of Mahasu, even if not accepted. The immolation of goats at Mahasu temples thus follows the classical format of sacrifice as practised in many temples across India. This makes the sacrificer a *yajamana* and the sacrifier, the one presiding over the ritual, a *purohita*.

Calls for reform from lawmakers and animal rights groups have led to a decrease in the number of animals sacrificed. A trend that is also visible within the practice is that, increasingly now, the animals are let off as *ghantuas* out of the sacrificer's own aversion to a violent killing. An increasing number of such animals in Mahasu shrines indicate that this practice, of bringing the goats and leaving them to pasture around the shrine rather than immolating them, is on the ascendant, even though the priests believe that a temple ritual is incomplete without the immolation of the offered animal. Not that the *ghantua* is not Mahasu property. The goats left to roam free in the temple quadrangle are also known to be under Mahasu's protection and the slaughtering of such animals would invite the divine king's wrath.

When performing the sacrifice, the *bajgi* behead the animal in one clean stroke with a sharp machete. While the head lies toward one side, the gush of blood from the neck is collected in a bowl, the beheaded animal held upside down. The task of skinning and dressing the animal is also performed by a *bajgi*. The formula for distribution of the share of the meat is predetermined. After the rite, the slaughtered animal is treated as *prasad*, the sacrificer's share of the offering with the divine king's grace in it, to be partially returned to the individual bringing the offering. The rest of it is distributed among the temple officials. The *kolta*, the lowest-caste workers at the temple, get the hooves. The *bajgi* gets the blood, the head (*siri*), and the intestines with a little flesh. The thighs go to the Brahman priest. The *thanis, bhandaris*, officiating *vazir*, and other high-caste officials share the remaining meaty parts. Groups of temple officials can often be seen arguing over their fair share of the meat. Though often meat-eaters, the priests, while officiating in the temple, turn vegetarian. Their share of the meat is sent out to their families. As a norm, other officials in the temple can cook their share of the meat in the kitchen only after the priest has cooked his evening vegetarian meal.

What does it mean to a Mahasu subject to offer a goat for *bali*? Is it just a practice incorporating the functional value of feeding the deity's bureaucracy and giving thanks? If that were the case, alternatives would seem acceptable when constitutional or official norms forbid such practices. The truth is that the connection with the practice seems to go much deeper. The utter dejection and fear observable among people whose goats are not accepted for sacrifice point to a strong emotional connection with the ritual. Sacrifice points also towards a denial of the transience of life despite the ending of a life. One aspect of the ritual is to invoke the sense of identity between sacrificer and victim. I have observed in temples like the Sem-Mukhem in the Garhwal Himalaya that the priest makes an invocation, whispered in the ear of the goat, where the goat is named and assigned the same *gotra* (clan or lineage name assigned at the time of birth, usually different from personal names) as the sacrificer before being beheaded. An attempt is made to establish with the victim an attachment to its "vital aspect".

With the creation of Uttarakhand and increased activism over animal rights, the sacrifice of goats at Mahasu shrines has come under greater public scrutiny and censure. It was around this time that Mahasu's vegetarianism began to be talked about in the media. This led to the community's claim that Mahasu had turned vegetarian – or at least there was a very public denial of *bali* through the circulation of this claim. That Mahasu was himself a vegetarian deity, as the community believes, was not a part of the public discourse even though ritual practice always indicated ambiguity over the recipient of the sacrifice. Historically, sacrifice has been a part of festivities in the Mahasu realm. Emerson (1911: 42) describes Mahasu's annual festival on the fourth day of the light half of the moon in the month of August:

> During the day little happens, but at sunset a ram and a goat are sacrificed, the first being dispatched while the ram is dragged inside the shrine. But the victim is not slaughtered before the altar, for the family of the Mahasu (perhaps its memory of the ploughshare) dislike the sight of blood, and after the god has signified acceptance of the offering through the trembling of the goat it is brought outside again and slain in the courtyard.

Emerson specifically refers to Mahasu's abhorrence of sacrifice, and the ritual practice in the Mahasu shrines broadly corroborates his observations. While all sacrifice is made in the name of Mahasu deputies, the fact also remains that the ritual embodying the victim, marking the acceptance of sacrifice, is performed before the divine king. In these shrines there is no sharing or partaking of food, from a common receptacle, between deity and human. This is different from *bhog* in Hindu temples, where the one making the offering "feeds" the icon (Davis 1999: 1), believing that divinely animated images consume the "subtle portion" of the offered food. At Mahasu shrines, the person making an offering receives his share as a subject, not as a companion in communion. The disclaimer of the sacrifice being made to Mahasu's deputies is now enunciated before the performance of every ritual sacrifice, whereas earlier the recipient of the sacrifice was not considered significant. Many in the deity's officialdom accept, though tacitly, that this stance has been adopted in fairly recent times and is not an ancient tradition. To use Hebdige's (1988: 35) expression, it could be described as a kind of "hiding in the light", an arrangement whereby sacrifice can continue, officials are well fed, sacrificers gratified, while the "reformists", specially those within the cult, are silenced after having been handed over a minor victory suggesting the divine king has accepted their urgings and turned vegetarian.

No doubt this conflict between tradition and conformity to the laws of the state seems paradoxical since the priests emphasise Mahasu's vegetarianism even as goats continue to be slaughtered for his deputies. In the current pan-Hindu discourse, decadent modernity is reflected in meat-eating, and Mahasu, the divine king, is being forced by representatives of this discourse to turn vegetarian. But if Mahasu were a deity that abhorred *bali*, why would goats continue to be consecrated in the sanctum before the deity? If *bali* were *aprahast* (impure ritual) – lacking in propriety and merit since the priest on duty at the shrine has to turn vegetarian and his share of the meat is passed on to his family – the cooking of meat in the *rawali pand* would cast doubt on the divine king's ritual practice of meat-eating.

In a smaller state, the Mahasu region has come into greater political prominence since its residents send two members to the Indian Parliament and at least five legislators to the 70-member Uttarakhand legislative assembly. The economic influence of a secular state over every region is bringing into sharp focus rituals like *bali*. So are the construction of roads, the increasing accessibility of Mahasu shrines, modern education, tourism and the townward mobility of many people from the region. It may not be a coincidence that calls to uphold animal rights came at a time of growing public outcry over the mismanagement of temple funds by the traditional temple councils headed by the divine king's chief minister. Today, the finances of the Mahasu temple at Hanol are controlled by administrators like the SDM, by inexperienced junior bureaucrats appointed for short tenures to the secluded region on what is widely referred to as "punishment postings". They have little understanding of the cult. Temple affairs are quite low on their list of priorities. The rituals appear to them as exploitation via superstition rather than serious political and religious work.

Their decisions on religious controversies are influenced either by the plains' discourse of mainstream *sanatana dharma*, or the "secular" ideals of *ahimsa* enshrined in the constitution, or most commonly now by their personal religious beliefs.

The constitution of India, despite enunciating non-violence against animals in its Directive Principles of State Policy, has left a window open for sacrifice within religious practice through a section in the Prevention of Cruelty to Animals Act, 1960. This makes an exception to the protection of animal rights: "Nothing contained in this Act shall render it an offence to kill any animal in a manner required by the religion of any community." Given the diversity of religious practices in the country, the central government has left the legislation on animal rights to the state governments, and Uttarakhand has enacted no law banning animal sacrifice. In the absence of such a law, anti-*bali* activists call for action against pollution, the creation of public nuisance, and regulations on slaughter. Where does this leave the divine king and his subjects, even as the cult of Mahasu is pulled in different directions by the rationalist discourse and its own ritual compulsions? Of the four Mahasu siblings, it is the ever-itinerant Chalda Mahasu who usually adopts an intransigent position on ritual reform and has a very strong voice in this moment of churning.

In 2000, when a peepal (*Ficus religiosa*) tree fell over the temple roof at Hanol and low-caste carpenters climbed on to the roof, a new *pratistha* (consecration) was required once the repairs had been done. No purificatory consecration is normally possible without *bali* being offered in all four directions on the temple roofs. A grand consecration with more than a hundred subordinate deities was planned to be performed as a grand assembly of the Mahasu divine kings and their subordinate ruling deities, each arriving in their palanquins, heralded by a group of musicians, accompanied by hundreds of officials and devotees, congregating at Mahasu's temple in a grand three-day event. Influential community leaders who had been advocating ritual reform saw this as their opportunity to end *bali*, especially at this crucial moment in the cult's history when all the energies of the realm had been mobilised and were congregating at one point.

By this time, Pabasik Mahasu's followers were quite united in their opposition to *bali*. They had already declared an end to animal sacrifice in his shrines, so that when a new temple to him was consecrated in 1998, across the river from Hanol at Thadiyar, goat sacrifices were not offered. In Hanol, all the same, this notion was significant since most priests would normally say the impurity of low-caste carpenters can only be removed via animal sacrifice. But, given public sentiment, the unthinkable came about. The goats were eventually butchered with a ritual recitation some distance away and only for the feasting. The non-vegetarian gods, those that still demanded sacrifice and were visiting the consecration, had to camp at the far end to avoid polluting the temple with all the bloodletting and flesh-eating!

Bashik, on the other bank of the river, had professed that he would go by what his brothers decided on the issue. At this time, Bautha of Hanol declared it was not yet time for him to decide on the issue of *bali*. He would keep his options open and give his verdict when the time was ripe. He left the question of stopping the ritual open-ended. The fact remained that within *sathi*, where the Hanol temple stands and to which Bashik constantly tours, the cult was vertically split over the issue of goat sacrifices.

Before the consecration ritual, the demands for "reform" became even more vociferous. A decision would have to be arrived at before the grand assembly. A meeting of the four divine kings was called at Hanol prior to the main ritual. The three Mahasus arrived at Hanol in their palanquins, with their chief ministers, elders, officials, and drummers. As the meeting of the four deities was in progress, amid heated debates between possessed oracles and the elders on how the grand assembly would be staged, and whether it would involve *bali* or not, Chalda Mahasu's oracle declared that he would stick to his stance against "reform". He would not side with the reformists, he wanted the consecration done the traditional way, with *bali*. With Bautha Mahasu, the most powerful voice among the deities, adopting an ambiguous stance, the one decisive deity armed with the power to cast the veto was Chalda, the walking Mahasu.

Tum apna puran karo, mein apna khuran karoonga!

"Do whatever you want inside the temple (referring to a vegetarian *purana* recitation by the priests), but there will be sacrifice on the temple roof," was his unambiguous response, conveyed to the entire realm through his oracle.

Sax (personal communication), who was present during the meeting, says that, leaning forward, voice rising to a powerful high pitch, Chalda's oracle declared that his traditional ritual knowledge (*kashmiri vidya,* the knowledge from Kashmir) would not be, indeed must not be, forgotten or diluted; that his followers were free to sponsor a vegetarian ritual involving scriptural recitation, a "*puran*", but that he, Chalda, would have his *khuran*, his *khurasao* (hundred hooves; a sacrifice of twenty-five goats). Thus, with one sweeping statement, Chalda Mahasu decimated the entire campaign against *bali*.

The "reformers" had to now take recourse to petitioning the government. Political lobbies in Dehra Dun were mobilised and the District Magistrate was handed over several petitions asking for a ban on animal sacrifice. The administration announced that they would do whatever was possible to restrict *bali*. But the deity had already spoken and there was no way his loyal subjects would go against their divine king's diktat.

In 2004, during the grand assembly of deities at Hanol, known as the *shaant* and the *khurasao*, the goat sacrifice issue again came to a head. At the grand assembly, held soon after Chalda Mahasu's outright rejection of "reform", an activist raised his voice against goat sacrifices, telling community leaders it was incumbent upon them to change with the times, and that it was not the deity but ministers and priests who had a vested interest in continuing *bali*. He stressed that the divine king, in fact, was a protector and by that definition he would always be compassionate to these voiceless creatures – the goats. In this sense he was merely recalling the narrative of royal patronage, pointed out by Sutherland (1998: 336) – and that Stein (1994) and Dirks (1987) have argued – was constitutive of medieval South Indian "sacred kingship".

This activist, Surendra Singh Suraha, commenced his campaign against goat sacrifice by questioning the elders who effectively controlled the village councils, local decision-making bodies now congregating at Hanol for the big event.

> If the deity really wanted the sacrifice, he would suck the life out of the goat the moment you sprinkle water in its ears. You [temple officials and elders] are addicted to meat and blood [referring to the *tamasic gunas* or facets of food that induce inertia and delusion] and therefore you want the practice to continue. How can a deity who cannot even tolerate the sight of leather and the smell of garlic claim the lives of innocent animals?

He was staking everything – his reputation as a community leader as well as his personal safety – in this last-ditch effort. Opposing the deity in such a charged atmosphere could have sparked off physical violence. By articulating publicly that the ritual was meaningless and served no purpose, he was ascribing new meanings to the ritual itself. He was altering it, even if his attempts were to have minimal impact on the practice of *bali*. Despite his audacious protest, he was ignored and the sacrifice of the hundred hooves was duly performed.

Suraha, himself an avowed devotee of Mahasu and a dedicated reformist – one of the first "sons of the soil" to have come out of the region and be appointed to the position of *tehsildar*, sub-magistrate, and tax collector – had campaigned all his life against animal sacrifice and alcohol abuse. He believed these were the main reasons for the region's isolation and backwardness. He was castigated by the community not only for adopting a stridently anti-sacrifice stance but also for acts which, going by the plains' discourse of *bhakti* motivating him, might be acts of devotion but were nonetheless anathema to Mahasu subjects. These acts included naming his grandson Maasu (after the divine king), something no-one had ever tried for fear of disrespect to the god's name and consequent *dos*. Secondly, he had composed a hymn or *aarti* in praise of the divine king. He had added the word "Suraha" (lit. the right path) to his name in order to indicate his strident opposition to what he considered malpractices in social life in the region.

Despite the grave threat from priests and peers, Suraha stood up at this charged moment before the entire community, asking for a complete ban on animal sacrifice. Perhaps he was spared a violent reprisal for daring to oppose Chalda Mahasu on account of his advancing years, education, and years of service in the government. The presence of administrators and the media from Dehra Dun protected him from harm. When the ritual got under way, the torture of witnessing the beheading of twenty-five goats on the temple roofs in all four directions caused him to faint and collapse. Those present were convinced that he had been afflicted by Mahasu's *dos*, the divine king's retribution for daring to oppose the deity's verdict. Later, Suraha himself tried to explain away his ill health, claiming it was the stress of the protest, the sight of needless bloodletting, his advanced age, and his chronic blood pressure problems that had brought on his collapse. The fact remains that none within the milling crowds dared help him get medical attention. Individuals, among whom I was one – their presence being for academic reasons – helped Suraha reach a hospital, where he was revived.

A few years later, Suraha's ancestral home in Bangan was gutted in a fire and razed to the ground. His young brother, who had long been devoted to Mahasu and the deity's ritual regime and had no record or symptoms of ill health, died all of a sudden. Suraha's own son took ill. Family and friends, convinced of the deity's *dos*, urged him to consult Mahasu's oracle to fathom the reasons for this downturn in fortune. After much coaxing, Suraha consulted Pabasik Mahasu's oracle and was told that he had indeed been afflicted by Chalda's *dos* since he had dared raise his voice against the deity's verdict on sacrifice. The deity's indignation was evident in his instructions that Suraha should not approach him any more; the deity might visit him at some opportune moment.

So, Suraha waited patiently for the deity's next move, and indeed in a couple of years Chalda's parasol (*chatra*) passed through his village. Suraha's family, considering this the opportune moment for him to make his peace with the deity, urged him to go and bow before the parasol. But the deity was in no mood for reconciliation. Suraha later recalled that each time he tried approaching the deity's parasol on the street, it turned away from him. He was beginning to lose all hope when the deity's oracle finally summoned him to the parasol.

Tumne meri bhul bisar kar di . . .

"You forgot all about me and my commands" was the reprimand. "Now go forth to my temple at Shiraji with a *nisan* [symbol] of gold and a sacrificial goat if you want to receive my grace." A man who had campaigned all his life against the goat sacrifice was being asked to carry a goat all the way to Shiraji in Himachal Pradesh, a distance of a couple of hundred kilometres. Suraha was instinctively disinclined to comply, but peers in the village and his family were insistent. It was not just a question of his own well-being, his family's survival required that he keep the deity in good humour. After much cajoling, Suraha agreed to embark on the pilgrimage, goat in tow. In his effort to stick to his non-violent convictions, he did not himself touch the goat. The defeated activist travelled with a heavy heart, the goat was carried by a young companion. Even as he arrived at the temple, he begged the deity not to insist on the sacrifice from him, a devotee who had dedicated his life to the cause of eradicating the practice. He begged permission to donate the goat, leave it in the temple as a living *ghantua* offering. The divine king's oracle was unrelenting: the goat would have to be sacrificed or the deity would not be propitiated. All of Suraha's exertions would have been in vain, with serious consequences for his family if he did not perform the sacrifice. His requests that his young companion hold the goat during the ritual beheading fell on deaf ears: he would have to participate in the sacrifice if he wanted to be free of the *dos*. The ultimate humiliation was meted out: Suraha held the quivering goat as it was beheaded. Informants report a cathartic calm descending upon them once they have performed the sacrifice, but Suraha returned home in a state of complete dejection and agitation. The divine king had erased his life's work.

Some days later, Suraha was visited by a group of influential people within the Mahasu cult. They consisted of community elders, retired bureaucrats, and army men – Mahasu subjects who were sympathetic to the "secular" world. They accused him of disappointing them by abandoning his cause. A visibly broken Suraha revealed what they said to him: "You have done something much worse than what Nathuram Godse did to Mahatma Gandhi! The entire community was looking up to you to take a firm stand, for you had started a movement for change. We would have soon stood up in support. Instead, you gave up the cause out of fear, and backtracked."

Soon after the big sacrifice, the government's administrative machinery began all the same to enforce restrictions on animal sacrifice at Hanol. Having observed the cult over several years, one can say that, time and again, when attempts are made to "reform" the ritual and traditional offerings are denied the *devta*, the complex agency of the community ensures that the ritual is restored. In this particular effort by the government, several subjects other than the divine king's *kardars* (officials) admitted that violent rituals show the cult in a poor light to people from the plains, and therefore *bali* must be done away with. As we have seen, in most disputes where the community opinion is divided, Mahasu ratifies the decision that has already been made collectively by the majority. He imparts the stamp of religious authority to the existing community consensus: the Nand Lal Bharti example made this clear in the previous chapter. In the earlier narrated case of the river crossing, too, the Mahasu oracle, gauging the mood of the community, realised that the time had come for the crossing to happen despite his initial reluctance.

Notwithstanding these instances, a tightrope walk is necessary for the deity between the demands for change and the desire for continuity. The deity's officials – prime beneficiaries of the sacrificial ritual – have to be kept in good humour and fed the meat they think of as their due. On the other side, pressure from the state, the censure from powerful social groups, and the demands of activists like Suraha cannot be entirely ignored. The call to reform makes the cult renegotiate how it operates. For the moment *bali* continues, even if in the grand assembly at Hanol, when several goats were sacrificed, it was declared that this was the last of the sacrificial rituals at the temple. Conversing with a group of *sayanas* later, it became clear to me that the announcement about discontinuing the ritual had only been a ploy to buy time. Reform after excess, everyone knew, was not going to work. The Mahasu *vazir* explained that the community could not simply discontinue an old practice. Had the government and reformists tried to evolve a consensus to end goat sacrifice, he said, things may have been different:

> How can you announce an end to goat sacrifice, and not institute anything else in its place? What else, other than goats, do our poor people possess that they can offer to the deity? To make a new beginning, the ritual will have to be completely transformed. For instance, you would have to introduce the recitation of Shiva-Puran, and then tell the people that we worship Shiva, and not Mahasu. Then, ask them to offer *shriphal* [dried coconut] instead of goats. But as long as we worship Mahasu, we have to go by his decree. If one ritual

form of offering is denied all of a sudden, there cannot be a void, a vacuum [*khalipan*]. You have to replace it with another ritual form. If not goats, what else is there with us to offer to the divine king?

In 2011, the SDM who heads the newly constituted temple committee at Hanol announced a ban on animal sacrifice at the shrine of Mahasu, invoking decisions made at the grand assembly of divine kings. This happened after the media and animal rights groups ran shrill campaigns against *bali* in Dehra Dun. A vernacular television news channel had earlier sensationalised the issue by telecasting a story recreating the *bedavart*, the rope sliding ritual, from a remote location in Himachal Pradesh. This telecast of *bedavart* – a ritual of human sacrifice that disappeared a century ago – showed the *beda* (sacrificial victim) sliding down a rope from a rooftop as *nar-bali* (human sacrifice), despite the

Photo 9.2: Two banners, one welcoming visitors to the temple consecration at Shiraji in Himachal Pradesh, displayed above the administration's banner announcing a ban on animal sacrifice in Hanol, Jaunsar, Uttarakhand.

fact that the ritual is now only ever performed as a harmless acrobatic act. Excitement was drummed up via blurbs broadcast every hour saying the telecast would be of the ritual of human sacrifice from a remote corner in the mountains. This rope-sliding ritual (Berreman 1961), now performed very rarely even in its truncated form at temples, is believed to be a symbolic representation of the ritual of human sacrifice at the altar of the deity Mahasu. The telecast misrepresentation provided even more grist to the "reformist" mill. "Ritual Murder" cried an English daily published in Dehra Dun. It claimed that every winter more than ten thousand goats were daily sacrificed during the month-long festival of Maroz in the temples of Mahasu and his subordinate deities in the Jaunsar-Bawar region. By this exaggerated count, if one were to include Mahasu territories in Uttarkashi and Himachal, the figure for goats sacrificed might run into millions. Gauri Maulekhi, an animal rights activist, in her blog titled "Ritual Slaughter in Devil's Own Country", gave graphic details of the sacrificial ritual, her own attempts to stop it, and police inaction. She was obviously referring, rather sardonically, to Uttarakhand's tourism slogan "*dev-bhoomi*" (land of the gods), contradicting the slogan by suggesting people in the hills acted like devils.

Reformists, in general, contend that a people's sense of community is not fundamentally threatened if it abandons a "regressive" ritual; that history is testimony to the human ability to adapt to different ways of being. Therefore, to them it makes sense to reject traditions that promote violence and cruelty. In their opinion, it is only correct to reject traditions that compromise animal rights and brutalise individuals by making them witness to scenes of slaughter. A large network of animal rights groups and NGOs has emerged post-statehood in Uttarakhand, pointing to the helplessness of animals. This seems the shortest route to media attention, as well as to grants that are now available for protecting animal rights with the Hindu Right resurgent in India now, advocating vegetarianism. The issue of animal slaughter, especially cow slaughter, is prominent on the social agenda. Though animal sacrifice is quite common in some forms of Hindu ritual practice, cow slaughter is anathema to most Hindus. In today's India the conflict on the one hand between Enlightenment-based values of non-violence and Gandhian values of non-violence, and on the other traditional animal sacrifice, has acquired immense significance, even as the idea of separating religion and politics has disappeared. While Enlightenment-based ideals treat animals as sentient beings, traditional animal sacrifice sees the sacrifice as ensuring the well-being of a territory – a replication of the forces of order destroying those of chaos – like Mahasu arriving from Kullu–Kashmir to destroy Kirmir.

When India gained independence in 1947, a debate on banning cow slaughter was in full flow, just as it is today. While India is one of the largest exporters of beef, has the largest population of cattle, the Hindu Right wants a complete ban on cow slaughter. This question was debated when the Indian constitution was being framed and a consensus emerged at the time that no national law should ban the consumption of beef. The goal was instead included in the non-binding Directive Principles of State Policy. Gandhi, who received several representations to support the ban, urged Hindus through a letter (1947) to also respect alternative beliefs, sharing with them his personal dilemma: his non-violence was at odds with his respect for India's plural traditions. In the case of the cult of Mahasu, too, the personal beliefs of individuals, influenced by mainstream Hindu and animal rights discourses, are in conflict with those of temple officials for whom meat offerings are essential daily wages and the equivalent of nutrition for their families. Yet when I shared my fieldwork videos with some friends from the city, they shut their eyes in horror and disgust at the goat beheadings. "But you eat meat all the time!" I said. Their response was: "Yes, we know what we eat comes from animals, but since we do not see the animal being butchered, and since it is already dead when we eat it, we do not feel any aversion."

Very often during my travels with the Mahasu palanquin I encountered individuals who had ventured out of the mountains, got themselves an education, taken up opportunities owing to their special status, and were now individually sceptical of possession rituals and practices such as *bali*. Yet these same people are often forced to return to their native villages when the Mahasu palanquin arrives – family pressure and the fear of Mahasu's *dos* compel them. A former colonel from the Indian army who had come to receive Mahasu's palanquin in the village of Bhotanu, confided in me: "Personally, I am very scared of all this possession stuff and do not approve of the killing of innocent animals. I don't understand much of this because I left the village as a child. But, I am also frightened for my family and do not want to upset the *devta*. Our ancestors believed in these practices, and so we continue to follow their path."

In brief, animal sacrifice and the opposition to it have several layers of denial attached to both positions. City-dwellers opposed to *bali* do not comprehend the nuances of animal immolation, they do not accept that the intention of such killing may be diverse and deeply meaningful to those involved in the sacrifice. To them, all immolation is violence, whereas this is not typically so for the native Jaunsari. City dwellers are not able to make a distinction between the mass sacrifice of goats at festivals like Maroz, and the offering of goats in temples. In fact, both forms of animal slaughter serve ritual functions: while killing goats during festivals is for hospitality and feasting and supplies the need for food, the offering of goats at temples is a ritual function that supplies a religious need even as, in terms of pure functionality, it also supplies the nutritional needs of people who work in the temples. This does not wash within the mainstream discourses of the plains, where "tribal" practices like *bali* are seen as exploitative of innocent hill folk who have "blind faith" in deities and oracles. According to them, groups like the Jaunsaris, officially a tribe, must shed their particularities and assimilate. State development projects are aimed at achieving the twin objectives of egalitarianism and assimilation, and implicitly the obliteration of diversity and pluralism.

If the mainstream discourse had its way, the Mahasu ritual would assimilate and transform by accepting offerings of *sriphal* (dried coconuts) covered with a red cloth – a widespread religious practice in temples across India. Some Mahasu devotees agree this position is reasonable and that tradition must transform in keeping with the times. A former government official, Mahendra Chauhan, a pro-reform activist, gave me an elaborately allegorical description of the *sriphal bali*:

> What is *bali*, after all? Through this ritual, we approach our deity and offer to sacrifice and surrender our ego before the supreme force, Mahasu. *Sriphal* is the most appropriate symbol of sacrificing the ego since the thick fibrous layer on the outside indicates the several strands and layers of egotism. After we have removed our ego, the fibre, underneath is the soft fruit, symbolic of the self and only when that is also given up do we come to the purifying experience, like the sweet water inside the core.

To this the proponents of *bali* pose questions of practice and functionality:

> With coconuts, how can you adjudge acceptance of the sacrifice? A dead *bali* sacrifice is as good as not making an offering. If you end the practice, what will the drummers, who awaken the *devta* and walk with the divine king, eat? How will Mahasu's perpetual kitchens run? Soon the pastures will be overgrazed by all the worthless male goats . . . and then what nutrition will be left for productive livestock?

So, where is the conflict between community ritual and the modernising influence of a secular state headed? Will the forces of secular change transform Mahasu ritual? The declaration of the divine king turning vegetarian, or concealing the sacrifice, has not silenced vociferous animal rights activists. What has further complicated the issue is the voice of change within the community.

In 2012, when it was time for Chalda Mahasu to cross the river and begin his tour of *sathi*, the divine king delayed the crossing, even as the palanquin arrived tantalisingly close at Thadiyar, across the river. As the minister and oracle from the *sathi* visited Chalda Mahasu to persuade him to cross over, the Chalda oracle of *pansi* inquired if the deity's *niyam* – his rules pertaining to *bali* – would be adhered to on the other side. Mahasu was in no mood to relent on the issue of claiming sacrifice and made it a precondition of his return. The minister had to give him assurances that they would disregard the government's statute banning animal sacrifice. He said they would argue with the government that all *balidana* during the Muslim festival of Eid be banned before they were asked to end *bali*. All eateries in the state would have to turn vegetarian if their *devtas* were to be forced into vegetarianism.

The moment Chalda Mahasu stepped into *sathi*, crossing the river with his retinue, the divine king reinstituted the ritual of *bali* at the temple of Hanol. For the moment, *bali* is being offered, albeit discreetly, in a secluded spot, away from public view at the temple. This is how bans and coercive action transform a ritual. When change is forced, the ritual is modified, only to return with a vengeance – as in the *khurasao*, the sacrifice of a hundred hooves. What emerges from this is that absolute ritual transformation may not work unless a credible substitute is offered to the community and they adopt it voluntarily. At best, a ritual can be transformed during the period that modernity seeks to render the older rituals inoperable. Ritual transformation entails conflict and resistance. A social group cannot just abandon a ritual. Rituals are intrinsic to ways of living and follow their own dynamic, encompassing all individual beliefs within the group. The performative aspects of the ritual may undergo gradual change insofar as they are consistent with ideas of adaptation, but sudden cessation is unsustainable in the long run. Ritual practices respond to changing conditions, but stable ritual forms tend to be retained, even as their content changes on account of new pressures to employ and understand them differently.

Conclusion: Change and Continuity

IN 2011, I HAPPENED to be at Shiraji, a nondescript village in what was then Uttar Pradesh. After statehood came to Uttarakhand, the village had become a part of the prosperous apple belt of Himachal Pradesh. The occasion was the consecration of Chalda Mahasu's magnificent new temple.

Chalda Mahasu's arrival at Shiraji had occurred after a dramatic change of plans. Until Chalda Mahasu's arrival, this was a little-known hamlet attached to the palace of the rulers of Dhadi Rao, a small principality in the Western Himalayas. The younger sons of the Rajput ruler, who had all acquired the appellation of Mian, lived in the village. Interestingly, while their own version on acquiring this title with Islamic connotations relates to their men being ferocious fighters, much like the invaders from Central Asia, others held the view that this appellation was acquired since the progeny were inbred on account of the isolation of this little principality. Whatever the reason, family lore informed them that, half a century ago, most of their clan had been wiped out in an epidemic. They had adopted Mahasu worship and established a chamber in the upper floor of the palace for Bashik Mahasu to rest when his procession passed by on its tours. Chalda Mahasu had promised the Rajputs of Shiraji that when the time was ripe the divine kings would visit them. They had since flourished, with apple wealth adding to the family fortunes.

In 2003, close to the time of the river crossing, Chalda Mahasu set a scorching pace. Departing from the village of Kashdhar, he began asking the hosts to establish temples at each place the procession visited. Within a period of two years there were new temples at Thadiyar, Khashdhar, and Bharar. This task done, Chalda changed the usual route plan, and instead of journeying to Bholarh he decided to proceed to Shiraji. His unscheduled arrival now made Shiraji the focus of the entire Mahasu realm. Here, Chalda Mahasu commissioned another edifice, with everyone wondering whether the *devta* was, after all, planning to slip into sedentary retirement. Finally, the day of the consecration arrived.

As more than hundred palanquins bearing the divine kings and lesser deities arrived with their retinues at Shiraji, their bearers busied themselves setting up camps in a large field cleared for the festival. Close to the temple was a sacrificial fire where a *havan* ritual was performed in the Hindu *puranic* tradition. While the oracle of each *devta* was in a state of heightened possession, rarely seen rituals like Himalayan rope-sliding were being performed. Several men who accompanied the vehicles of the divinities carried weapons such as pick-axes, machetes, and swords. They also carried firearms – rifles were slung on their shoulders. While the entire scene appeared far removed from present-day reality, several elements in the event reminded one of its extraordinary contemporaneity. A police contingent was deployed at the site to manage the milling crowds. Technology played an integral part. Land had been cleared by mechanised earth-movers, wood for the temple structure prepared by electronic lathe machines, and subsequently carved intricately by hand. Television cameras were beaming the celebrations live with the help of broadcast vans, while the progress of each palanquin, journeying in from remote valleys, was closely monitored on mobile phones.

The moment the ceremonies got under way, each palanquin began circumambulating the temple, borne by a large group of men raising their weapons and raising loud war cries. Soon, the Indian government's minister (later chief minister of Himachal Pradesh),

Virbhadra Singh, arrived, accompanied by a large retinue, to follow a routine similar to the *devta* palanquins. The hierarchies were clearly defined and translated into precedence on who stood where and which *devta* was higher. For instance, Virbhadra was promptly taken to a vantage point and repeatedly offered a seat, though in deference to so many divinities, he, like the rest of the crowd, preferred not to sit. The palanquins of the more powerful *devtas* occupied positions right next to Chalda's palanquin and parasol, while those considered less powerful maintained an appropriate distance. As the ceremonies came to a close, Chalda announced that the time had come to move on.

The temple consecration was organised as a spectacle in which ritual, politics, tradition, and technology mingled to show the dominance of the Rajput castes. It is this hegemonic presence of the Rajput, in the economic and social spheres, that accounts for the longevity of the Mahasu realm and regime. While such dominance may be exploitative in relation to the lower castes, and may seem to show the Rajputs making Mahasu an instrument of their hegemony, for the Jaunsari the kernel of Mahasu longevity lies in the codes of *sayanacari*, the council of influential Rajput elders. In the Western Himalayas, any time the dominance of the Rajput is challenged by the state or internal forces, it seems that the divine kings are losing their grip over the polity. However, in places like Hanol and other parts of Jaunsar, where Rajput dominance has translated into absolute political control, efforts from other caste groups to break the shackles of this traditional system have come a cropper. In this region the blanket tribal status for the community undergirds Rajput hegemony. Holding the rituals on a grand scale, therefore, is an occasion for the Rajputs to reiterate their dominance. For the Brahman and drummer-bards, owing to their indispensability to the ritual, it offers the opportunity to contest and negotiate a better social deal from their *jajmans*, the Rajput sponsors of the sacrifice. However, the desire for dominance may not by itself be a sufficient explanation for the persistence of the ritual.

An unarticulated aspect that accounts for the survival of these grand ceremonies is the continuous search for legitimacy.

In these Himalayan communities the legitimacy of the upper castes, despite their control over most resources, is not established simply by birth. Legitimacy essentially emerges by establishing and renewing connections with the soil. In cities like Dehra Dun, many claim a *pahadi* (highlander) descent simply because they were born into families that once lived in the mountains. But when it comes to institutions like marriage, a clear distinction is made between those that were merely born into families that once lived in the mountains and those for whom connections with the soil and village have constantly been renewed through visiting, gift giving and receiving, speaking the local dialect, and more significantly, performing rituals that signify belonging to the village community. Amongst the people of Garhwal a clear distinction is made on the one hand between being Garhwali – meaning a naturalised highlander who performs rituals and rites of passage as prescribed in the native village – and being Kathmali, i.e. those that claim to be from the mountains because of their family name but who lack knowledge of the local language and do not practise local rituals. As such, within the traditional system of arranged marriages, a city-bred Kathmali would find it almost impossible to get a spouse from a Garhwali family, even if both bride and groom claimed birth and family origins from the same caste and village.

We have earlier noted that the dominant Rajput in Jaunsari society are widely believed to be from the stock of the Khash people and their kindred *jatis* which entered North India along the Hindu Kush around the seventh century BC, and who interacted with the original inhabitants, the Kiratas. Therefore, it becomes obligatory for the Khash Rajput – largely seen as outsiders by those that consider themselves Rajputs of native stock – to emphasise their legitimacy by sponsoring ritual performances displaying their power. As we have seen, the Panduan harps on the theme of complications caused by upsetting of the bloodline on account of the impatience and foul play of the Mahabharata queens, and by the premature arrival of the Mahasus on account of the overzealousness of Huna Bhaat. The rituals appear as *yajnas* (collective sacrifices) to remove inauspiciousness, correct bloodlines, and legitimise descent. The coming together of village communities to contribute cash, farm produce, and manpower for the divine kings points in this direction. In fact, elected representatives contribute generously from development funds provided by government to elected representatives, in order to – as Bourdieu would describe it – enhance their symbolic capital and convert it into political and social capital.

By refusing to perform their caste roles during these rituals, suppressed groups like the *bajgis* register their protest, negotiating their social positions for status or pecuniary gain. Though voicing dissent may have become more frequent in recent times, protest and negotitation – as evident in the case of the *bajgi* initially refusing to drum for Mahasu and agreeing to do so only after getting a better deal than he got from Vishnu – seems to have been prevalent since early times. This leverage of the ritualistic roles enjoyed by different castes shows caste to be not as watertight as many believe, and points to the possibilities of social mobility. But despite their primacy, rituals, as the first and fundamental factor of control, are counterbalanced by Rajput dominance and control over resources and manpower, leading to a unique stability amongst the Jaunsaris. The increased questioning of this dominance by subalterns, however, has hastened the onset of change. Moreover, caste – earlier a system that divided people and groups on the basis of qualitative hierarchies – is now gradually transforming the same groups into interest groups, each seeking their pound of flesh by leveraging either historical suppression or geographical remoteness. The ritualistic cult and the dominant groups therefore alternate between controlling and being controlled by each other. The space where contestation and collaboration between the dominant and subaltern social groups occurs emerges as the middle ground where one can look for clues to the cult's extraordinary adaptability.

In contemporary India, Mahasu and the system of divine kingship remains vital to social life, but so do democratic institutions. Empowered by the transformative agendas of modern governments, historically suppressed subalterns have begun to question those entrenched in power. In this scenario, divine kings as well as the modern state emerge as performers competing for ideological allegiance, deploying the paradigm of ritual control through their different lenses. But what then lies ahead for Mahasu divine kingship? Is there a clear and present danger of the divine kings becoming mere religious figureheads, with their political functions being usurped by the state?

Throughout this book we have come across examples of how divine kingship has retained agentive power through adaptation. We have seen how decisions that are likely to deeply impact the community – such as the future of the *kolta* as the pariahs of Jaunsari society, or the continuation of *bali* – are intensely contested and negotiated, with the divine kings finally ratifying the collective will of the community. During these times various opposing viewpoints are publicly aired, opinions are allowed to fester, and the consensus is finally articulated through the *mali*. This argue-till-you-drop model of community conflict resolution is ingrained in the social life of the region, and, as long as the system retains its capacity to iron out vexing issues, the divine kings seem set to retain their power and status.

We have also seen that even when disputes are of a deeply personal nature and pertain to issues normally kept under wraps, a public hearing in the presence of the entire clan – with the disputants open to public interrogation and the questions raised being considered a manifestation of divine power – leads to resolutions far quicker than anything reached in a civil court. This is efficacious in the eyes of Mahasu subjects and lends vitality to Jaunsari society. Of course, the likelihood is that as the Jaunsaris move from community life to individualism, nuclear families will replace clans entirely and fewer people are likely then to seek the divine king's intervention.

All the same, it may be wise not to project the inevitable disintegration of divine kingship by modernity. Jaunsari society has shown that its traditions can adapt to modernity brought in by roads, education, forest protection, democratic institutions, job reservations, tourism, and horticulture. Jaunsari modernity has become more differentiated and plural as compared to Western or even Indian modernity.

Perhaps the best indicators of this modernity are the *malis*. More than once, during oracular consultations, when the *malis* have been in a state of heightenend possession, I have heard the ringing of their mobile phones. When the person calling has seemed important enough, the *mali* has halted the consultation and responded to the call. Perhaps it was Mahasu, not the *mali*, taking these phone calls. Once the call was over, bringing the consultation back on track, the *mali* got back to examining the rice, his puzzled clients accepting his verdict, hands folded in devotion. And such *malis* today have clients not just within the Mahasu realm but across the country, perhaps even abroad, all seeking solutions to life's vexing problems. Some *malis* have set up offices in cities like Dehra Dun and Moradabad – clients often find the Mahasu temple at Hanol difficult to travel to.

In response to Sahlins' (1981) phrase "indigenization of modernity", which denotes the resourcefulness and agency of kinship-based societies in adapting to new demands and inputs, Bergmann (2016: 83–4) has pointed to groups that uphold identities that challenge modernist agendas by harnessing modern technologies to seemingly palaeolithic purposes. In his view, peripheral groups like Mahasu subjects are "tactically selective about modernity". They adapt to new careers, education, means of transport and communication, and forms of government, but do so within the ambit of Mahasu polity – not rejecting it but adapting new modes of living to it. This may not be the modernisation envisaged by Marx and Weber. Instead, this modernity has evolved – to use Sax's (2009: 236) application of Sudipta Kaviraj's term – "a logic of self-differentiation" (2005: 497). Crisis and contestations within the cult, in historical times and in the present, reflect the "alternative modernities" that operate within the Mahasu realm. People continue to subscribe to the divine kings' rituals because it fulfils certain needs that modern governments and their agents are incapable of providing. Mahasu rituals knit communities together and restore social relations. One of the Mahasu oracles remarked: "Mahasu is the god of quick justice [*tvarit nyaya*]. Why should people not ask his help when the king himself visits them and they can seek his help instantly?"

In sum, these divine kings retain their vitality for social life in the Western Himalayas, forming a religio-political sheet-anchor. The cult of Mahasu, like the metaphor of the rhizome enunciated by Deleuze and Guattari (1987), continues to sprout roots and shoots from new nodes even as the state seeks to split it up. However one may choose to describe Mahasu – deity, god, non-human agent, fetish or idol – he is a glue that holds together Jaunsaris and various other social groups that the divine king chooses to visit. If observers of the cult – people like me – go about looking for theoretical meaning and signs of decline, that is our problem, a problem of the modern world, and not a problem for these social groups in the mountains, to whom, literally and figuratively, in processions and possessions, the kingdom still comes.

Bibliography

Aitchison, C.U. 1931. *A Collection of Treaties, Engagements and Sanads Relating to India and the Neighbouring Countries.* Vol. I. Calcutta (Kolkata).

Alam, Aniket. 1996. "Unfree Labour under Colonial Impact: 'Beth' in the Simla Hills", *Social Action*, Vol. 46, No. 4, Oct.-Dec. 1996.

———. 2008. *Becoming India: Western Himalayas under British Rule.* New Delhi: Foundation Books/Cambridge University Press India Pvt. Ltd.

Allen, Charles. 2001. *Soldier Sahibs: The Men Who Made the North-West Frontier.* London: Abacus.

Anderson, Benedict. 1983. *Imagined Communities: Reflections on the Origin and Spread of Nationalism.* London: Verso.

Appadurai, Arjun, Frank J. Korom, Margaret A. Mills (eds). 1991. *Gender, Genre and Power in South Asian Expressive Traditions.* Pennsylvania: Penn Press.

Atkinson, Edwin T. 1884 (Reprint 1996). *The Himalayan Gazetteer.* Dehradun: Nataraj.

Barth, Fredrik. 1969. "Introduction" and "Pathan Identity and Its Maintenance", in Fredrik Barth, ed., *Ethnic Groups and Boundaries: The Social Organisation of Culture Difference.* Bergen: Universitetsforlaget; London: Allen & Unwin.

———. 1993. *Baseline Worlds.* Chicago: University of Chicago Press.

Bell, Catherine. 1992. *Ritual Theory, Ritual Practice.* New York: Oxford University Press.

Bergmann, Christoph. 2016. "Confluent Territories and Overlapping Sovereignties: Britain's Nineteenth-Century Indian Empire in the Kumaon Himalaya", *Journal of Historical Geography*.

Berti, Daniella. 2006. "Ritual Kingship, Divine Bureaucracy, and Electoral Politics in Kullu", *European Bulletin of Himalayan Research*, 29-30, Summer 2006; rpnt in William S. Sax, *Divine Kingship in the Western Himalaya*.

———. 2008. "Divine Jurisdictions and Forms of Government in Himachal Pradesh", in D. Berti and G. Tarabout, eds, *Territory, Soil and Society in South Asia*. Delhi: Manohar.

Berglund, Henrik. 2013. "The Global Constitution of Religious Nationalism", in *Religion, Politics and Globalization*, ed. Galina Lindquist and Don Handelman. USA: Berghahn Books.

Berreman, Gerald. D. 1961. "Himalayan Rope Sliding and Village Hinduism: An Analysis", *Southwestern Journal of Anthropology*, Vol. 17, No. 4 (Winter 1961), pp. 326-42, University of New Mexico.

———. 1997. *Hindus of the Himalayas*. New Delhi: Oxford University Press.

Béteille, André. 1969. *Social Inequality*. Harmondsworth: Penguin.

———. 1983. "The Backward Classes and the New Social Order", in idem, ed., *The Idea of Natural Inequality and Other Essays*, pp. 83–120. Delhi: Oxford University Press.

———. 1991. "Distributive Justice and Institutional Well-Being", *Economic and Political Weekly* 26: 591–600.

———. 1992. "The Future of the Backward Classes: The Competing Demands of Status and Power", in idem, ed., *Society and Politics in India: Essays in a Comparative Perspective*, pp. 151–91. London Atlantic Highlands; New York: Athlone Press.

Bhandarkar, D.R. 1929. *Some Aspects of Ancient Hindu Polity*. Varanasi: Benares Hindu University.

Bhatt, G.S. 2010. *Cult, Religion and Society*. New Delhi: Rawat Publications.

Bhoria, K.S. 1975. "The Case of Jaunsaris as a Scheduled Tribe", *Journal of Lal Bahadur Shastri National Academy of Administration*, Mussoorie, XX/2.

Bijalwan, Dr Radheshyam. 2003. *Madhya Himalaya Riyasat mem Gramin Janasangharsom ka Itihas (Riyasat Tehri Garhwal – Dhara and Dandak) (1815–1949)* (History of Village Warfare in a Central Himalayan Princely State – Rustling and Ceremonial Protest in the Princely State of Tehri Garhwal, 1815–1949). Purola, Uttarkashi: Bijalwan Prakashan.

Bijalwan, J.P. 2007. *Tehri evam Uttarakashi Ka Rajnaitik evam Samskritik Itihas* (Political and Cultural History of Tehri and Uttarkashi). Uttarkashi: Jananand Prakashan.

Brass, Paul R. 1990. *The Politics of India since Independence*. Cambridge: Cambridge University Press.

Brughart, R. 1987. "Gifts to the Gods: Power, Property and Ceremonial", in D. Cannadine and S. Price, eds, *Nepal in Rituals of Royalty in Power and Ceremonial in Traditional Societies*, pp. 237–70. Cambridge: Cambridge University Press.

Bourdieu, P. 1977. *An Outline of a Theory of Practice*. Vol. 16 of Cambridge Studies in Social and Cultural Anthropology. Cambridge: Cambridge University Press.

———. 1987. "What Makes a Social Class? On the Theoretical and Practical Existence of Groups", *Berkeley Journal of Sociology* 32, pp. 1-17.

———. 1993. *The Field of Cultural Production*. New York: Columbia University Press.

Callon, Michelle. 1986. "Some Elements of a Sociology of Translation: Domestication of the Scallops and the Fishermen at St. Brieuc Bay", in J. Law, ed., *Power, Action and Belief: A New Sociology of Knowledge*, pp. 196-223. London: Routledge.

Dalrymple, William. 2002. *White Mughals: Love and Betrayal in Eighteenth Century India*. New Delhi: Penguin.

Davis, Richard H. 1984. *Images, Miracles, and Authority in Asian Religious Traditions*. Boulder: Westview Press.

———. 1999. *Lives of Indian Images*. Princeton: Princeton University Press.

Dawson, Graham. 1994. *Soldier Heroes: British Adventure, Empire, and the Imagining of Masculinities*. London, New York: Routledge.

Dirks, Nicholas B. 1987. *The Hollow Crown: Ethnohistory of an Indian Kingdom*. Cambridge and New York: Cambridge University Press.

———. 2002. *Castes of Mind: Colonialism and the Making of Modern India*. Princeton: Princeton University Press.

Douglas, Mary. 1966. *Purity and Danger*. London: Ark Paperbacks.

Dumont, Louis. 1962. "On Putative Hierarchy and Some Allergies to It", *Contributions to Indian Sociology: New Series*. Ch. 10, p. 58. Paris: Ecole Pratique des Hautes Etudes.

———. 1970 [1966]. *Homo Hierarchicus. The Caste System and Its Implications*. Chicago: University of Chicago Press.

——— and D.F. Pocock. 1957. "For a Sociology of India", *Contributions to Indian Sociology* 1: 7–22, 1960.

Durkheim, Emile. 1912 [2001]. *The Elementary Forms of Religious Life*. New York: Oxford University Press.

Emerson, H.W. 1911. Typescript of Unpublished Anthropological Study of Mandi and Bashahr. Personal Papers. London, UK: Oriental and India Office Collections, British Library.

———. 1914. Assessment Report of the Rohru Tehsil 1914. Unpublished Manuscript in the Himachal Pradesh State Secretariat Library, Shimla, H.P.

———. 1920. *Mandi State Gazetteer*. Manuscript, London: India Office Library (MSS.EUR.E. 321); Lahore: Government Printing Press.

Epstein, M., ed. 1936. *The Statesman's Year-Book: Statistical and Historical Annual of the States of the World for 1936*. London: Macmillan.

Firth, Raymond. 1967. "The Work of Gods in Tikopia", *London School of Economics Monographs on Social Anthropology Nos. 1 and 2*. New York: The Athlone Press.

Fraser, James Baillie. 1820. *Journal of a Tour through Part of the Snowy Range of the Himala Mountains and to the Sources of the Rivers Jumna and Ganges*. London: Rodwell and Martin.

Fuller, C.J. 1992. *The Camphor Flame: Popular Hinduism and Society in India*. New Delhi: Viking.

Gaonkar, Dilip Parameshwar, ed. 2001. *Alternative Modernities*. Durham: Duke University Press.

Galey, Jean-Claude. 1989. "Reconsidering Kingship in India: An Ethnological Perspective", *History and Anthropology*, 4, pp. 123–87.

———. 1991. "Hindu Kingship and its Ritual Realm: The Garhwali Configuration", in Allen Fanger, Maheshvar P. Joshi, and Charles W. Brown, eds, *Himalaya: Past and Present*, pp. 173–237. Almora: Shree Almora Book Depot.

Gandhi, M.K. 1947. "Prarthana Pravachan – I" (Prayer Discourse-1), pp. 277–80: Gandhi's Prayer Discourse of 25 July 1947, in *Collected Works of Mahatma Gandhi*, Vol. 88.

Gazetteer of Sirmur State. 1934. (Reprint 1996). New Delhi: Indus.

Geertz, Clifford. 1973. "Thick Description: Towards an Interpretive Theory of Culture", in idem, *The Interpretation of Cultures: Selected Essays*, pp. 3-30, New York: Basic Books.

———. 1977. "Centres, Kings and Charisma: Reflections on the Symbolics of Power", in Joseph Ben-David and Terry Nichols Clark, eds, *Culture and Its Creators: Essays in Honor of Edward Shils*. Chicago: University of Chicago Press.

———. 1980. *Negara: The Theatre State of Nineteenth Century Bali*. Princeton: Princeton University Press.

Ghosh, Partha S. 1999. *BJP and the Evolution of Hindu Nationalism*. New Delhi: Manohar.

Deleuze, Gilles, and Felix Guattari. 1987. *A Thousand Plateaus: Capitalism and Schizophrenia*. Minneapolis: University of Minnesota Press.

Grimes, Ronald R. 2008. "Ritual Media and Conflict: An Introduction in Ritual", in Ronald R. Grimes, Ute Hüsken, Udo Simon, Eric Venbrux, eds, *Media and Conflict*. New York: Oxford University Press.

Guha, Ramachandra. 1989. *The Unquiet Woods: Ecological Change and Peasant Resistance in the Himalayas*. New Delhi: Oxford University Press.

Gupta, Dipankar. 1985. "The Communalising of Punjab", *Economic and Political Weekly*, 13 July: 1185-91.

Handa, O.C. 2002. *History of Uttaranchal*. New Delhi: Indus.

———. 2006. *Western Himalayan Folk Arts*. New Delhi: Indus Publishing Company.

———. 2008. *Panorama of Himalayan Architecture, Vol. 1: Temples*. New Delhi: Indus.

Hebdige, D. 1988. *Hiding in the Light: On Images and Things*. London: Routledge.

Hiltebeitel, Alf. 1991. *The Cult of Draupadi: On Hindu Ritual and the Goddess*. Chicago: University of Chicago Press.

Hocart, A.M. 1927. *Kingship*. London: Oxford University Press.

Holston, James. 1999. "Alternative Modernities: Statecraft and Religious Imagination in the Valley of the Dawn", *American Ethnologist*, Vol. 26, No. 3 (August), pp. 605–31. New Jersey: Wiley.

Hughes, Thomas Parke. 1983. *Networks of Power: Electrification in Western Society 1880–1930*. Michigan: Johns Hopkins University Press.

Ibbetson, Denzil. 1872 [1919]. *Census Report of the Punjab*. Punjab: Superintendent, Government Printing Press.

——— and Edward Maclagan. (1883) 1892. *Census Report for the Punjab*. (Reprinted 1990). Census Report for the Punjab. Lahore: Asian Educational Services.

———. 1919. "The Cult of Mahasu in the Simla Hills", in D. Ibbetson and E. Maclagan, eds, *A Glossary of the Tribes and Castes of the Punjab and Northwest Frontier Province, vol. 15*. India: Superintendent of Government Printing.

Inden, Ron. 1990. *Imagining India*. Cambridge, MA: Blackwell.

Jaffrelot, Christophe. 1996. *The Hindu Nationalist Movement and Indian Politics, 1925 to the 1990s*. London: Hurst.

Jain, Madhu. 1995. *The Abode of Mahashiva, Cults and Symbology in Jaunsar–Bawar in the Mid-Himalayas*. New Delhi: Indus.

Jaunsari, Ratan Singh. 2006. *Jaunsar Bawar: Ek Samskritik, Aarthik evam Samajik Adhyayan* (Jaunsar Bawar: A Cultural, Economic and Social Study). Dehradun: Geetanjali Prakashan.

Jenkins, Louisa Hadow. 1923. *General Fredrick Young, First Commandant of Sirmur Battalion (2nd Gurkha Rifles)*. London: George Routledge and Sons, Ltd.

Joshi, Lakshmikant. Undated. *Haarul: Jaunsar Bawar ke Pauranik Lokgeet* (Haarul: Ancient Folk Songs of Jaunsar Bawar). Dehradun: Winsar Publishing.

Kamboj, Richa. 2010. *Wooden Temples of Uttarakhand, A Study of Art and Architecture*. New Delhi: Indus.

Kaviraj, Sudipta. 2005. "An Outline of a Revisionist Theory of Modernity", *European Journal of Sociology*, 46, pp 497-526, doi: 10.1017/S0003975605000196.

Kautilya. 2006. "Arthashastra", in Steven Rosen, *Essential Hinduism*. New York: Praeger.

Kertzer, David. 1988. *Ritual, Politics, and Power*. New Haven and London: Yale University Press.

Kielhorn, F. 1896. "Pandukeshvar Plate of Lalitasuradeva", *Indian Antiquary* 25: 177-84.

Kohli, Atul. 1992. *Democracy and Discontent*. Cambridge: Cambridge University Press.

Kumar, Anup. 2011. *The Making of a Small State: New Perspectives in South Asian History*. New Delhi: Orient Blackswan.

Latour, Bruno. 1987. *Science in Action. How to Follow Scientists and Engineers through Society*. Cambridge, Mass.: Harvard University Press.

———. 1988. *The Pasteurization of France*. Cambridge, Mass.: Harvard University Press.

———. 1991. *We Have Never Been Modern*, trans. Catherine Porter. Cambridge, Mass.: Harvard University Press.

———. 2001. "Whose Cosmos, Which Cosmopolitics? Comments on the Peace Terms of Ulrich Beck", *Common Knowledge*, Vol. 10, Issue 3, Fall 2004, pp. 450–62. Durham: Duke University Press.

———. 2005. *Reassembling the Social: An Introduction to Actor-Network-Theory*. New York: Oxford University Press.

———. *On the Modern Cult of Factish Gods*. Durham: Duke University Press.

———. 2010. "Networks, Societies, Spheres: Reflections of an Actor-Network Theorist", *Keynote Speech for the International Seminar on Network Theory: Network Multidimensionality in the Digital Age*, Los Angeles: Annenberg School for Communication and Journalism.

———. 2011. "The Only Shibboleth the West has is Science", France's Institut d'Etudes Politiques de Paris (Sciences Po) in New Delhi, in an interview with Deep K. Datta-Ray, *Times of India*, New Delhi.

Law, John. 2007. *Actor Network Theory and Material Semiotics*. Lancaster: Centre for Science Studies and Department of Sociology, Lancaster University.

Lerner, Daniel. 1964. *The Passing of Traditional Society: Modernizing the Middle East*. New York: Free Press.

Lerner, Max. 1957. *America as a Civilization. Vol. II: Culture and Personality*. New York: Simon and Schuster.

Luchesi, Brigitte. 2006. "Fighting Enemies and Protecting Territory: Deities as Local Rulers in Kullu, Himachal Pradesh", *European Bulletin for Himalayan Research* 29–30, Summer 2006.

Luckmann, Thomas. 1967. *The Invisible Religion: The Problem of Religion in Modern Society*. New York: Macmillan.

Lukes, Steven. 1985. *Emile Durkheim: His Life and Work, A Critical Study*. Stanford: Stanford University Press.

Madan, T.N. 1997. *Modern Myths, Locked Minds: Secularism and Fundamentalism in India*. Delhi: Oxford University Press.

Majumdar, D.N. 1963. *Himalayan Polyandry – Structure, Functioning and Culture Change, A Field Study of Jaunsar-Bawar*. Bombay: Asia Publishing House.

Malik, Yogendra K., and V.B. Singh. 1995. *Hindu Nationalists in India: The Rise of the Bharatiya Janata Party*. New Delhi: Vistaar.

Mann, Kamlesh. 1996. *Tribal Women – On the Threshold of 21st Century*. New Delhi: MD Publications Pvt. Ltd.

Marriott, McKim. 1976. "Hindu Transactions: Diversity without Dualism", in Bruce Kapferer, ed., *Transaction and Meaning: Directions in the Anthropology of Exchange and Symbolic Behavior*, pp. 109–42. Philadelphia: Institute for the Study of Human Issues.

———, ed. 1990. *India through Hindu Categories*. New Delhi/Newbury Park/London: Sage.

——— and Ronald Inden. 1977. "Toward an Ethnosociology of South Asian Caste Systems", in Kenneth A. David, ed., *The New Wind: Changing Identities in South Asia*, pp. 227–38. The Hague, Paris: Mouton; Chicago: Aldine.

McLagan, Edward. 1892. *Census Report of the Punjab*. Punjab: Superintendent, Government Printing Press.

Miedema, Virgil, and Stephanie Spaid Miedema. 2014. *Mussoorie and Landour: Footprints of the Past*. New Delhi: Rupa.

Moran, Arik. 2007. "From Mountain Trade to Jungle Politics: The Transformation of Kingship in Bashahr in 1815–1914", *The Indian Economic & Social History Review*.

Munshi, K.M. 1954 (reprint 1962). *Introduction to Social Economy of a Polyandrous People*. Bombay: Asia Publishing House.

Myerhoff, Barbara G., and Sally Falk Moore, eds. 1977. "We Don't Wrap Herring in a Printed Page: Fusion, Fictions and Continuity in Secular Ritual", in idem, *Secular Ritual*. Assen: Van Gorcum.

Naithani, Dr Shiv Prasad. 2006. *Uttarakhand Ke Tirth Evam Mandir* (Pilgrimage Sites and Temples of Uttarakhand). Srinagar, Uttarakhand: Pavetri Prakashan.

———. 2010. *Uttarakhand Gathaon Ke Rahasya* (Mysteries of Uttarakhand Folklore). Srinagar, Uttarakhand: Pavetri Prakashan.

Nautiyal, S. 1981. *Garhwal ke Lok Nritya-Geet* (Folk Dance-Songs of Garhwal). Allahabad: Hindi Sahitya Sammelan.

Nayar, Baldev Raj. 2001. *Globalization and Nationalism: The Changing Balance in India's Economic Policy, 1950–2000*. New Delhi, Thousand Oaks, London: Sage.

Obeyesekere, Gananath. 1992. *The Apotheosis of Captain Cook: European Mythmaking in the Pacific.* Princeton: Princeton University Press.

Pant, Rekha, and P.K. Samal. Undated. *Role of Culture in Sustainable Living and Factors for its Disintegration.* Kosi-Katarmal, Almora: G.B. Pant Institute of Himalayan Environment and Development.

Parmar, Y.S. 1975. *Polyandry in the Himalayas.* New Delhi: Vikas.

Pemble, John. 1971. *The Invasion of Nepal: John Company at War.* Oxford: Clarendon Press.

———. 2009. *Britain's Gurkha War: The Invasion of Nepal, 1814–16.* London: Frontline Books.

Quack, Johannes. 2014. "Porous Dividuals? Complying to a Healing Temple (Balaji) and a Psychiatric Out-Patient Department (OPD)", in Harish Naraindas, Johannes Quack, and William S. Sax, eds, *Asymmetrical Conversations: Contestations, Circumventions, and the Blurring of Therapeutic Boundaries.* New York, Oxford: Berghahn Books.

Raheja, Gloria G. 1988. *The Poison in the Gift: Ritual, Prestation and the Dominant Caste in a North Indian Village.* Chicago: University of Chicago Press.

Rana, Maj. J.P. Singh. 2004. *Jaunsar Bawar Darshan* (Viewing Jaunsar Bawar). Dehradun: Saraswati Press.

———, and Ranvir Singh Tomar. 2008–9. *Jaunsar Bawar Parichay* (Introduction to Jaunsar Bawar). Dehradun: Saraswati Press.

Rose, H.A. 1919. *A Glossary of the Tribes and Castes of the Punjab and North-West Frontier Province.* Vols 1 and 2. Delhi: Low Price Publications.

Rumford, Chris. 2006. "Theorizing Borders", *European Journal of Social Theory.*

Saberwal, Vasant K. 1999. *Pastoral Politics: Shepherds, Bureaucrats and Conservation in the Western Himalaya.* Delhi: Oxford University Press.

Sahlins, Marshall. 1981. *Historical Metaphors and Mythical Realities: Structure in the Early History of the Sandwich Islands Kingdom.*

ASAO Special Publications No. 1. Ann Arbor: University of Michigan Press.

———. 1985. *Islands of History*. Chicago: University of Chicago Press.

———. 2008. "The Stranger King", *Indonesia and the Malay World*, Vol. 36, Issue 105.

Saksena, R.N. 1962. *Social Economy of a Polyandrous People*. Mumbai: Asia Publishing House.

Sankrityayan, Rahul. 1961. *Jaunsar Dehradun*. Allahabad: Vidyarthi Granthagar.

Sax, William S. 1990. "Village Daughter, Village Goddess: Residence, Gender, and Politics in a Himalayan Pilgrimage", *American Ethnologist* 17 (3): 491-512.

———. 1991. *Mountain Goddess: Gender and Politics in a Central Himalayan Pilgrimage*. New York: Oxford University Press.

———. 1994. "Gender and Politics in Garhwal", in Nita Kumar, ed., *Women as Subjects: South Asian Histories*, pp. 172–210. Calcutta: Stree.

———. 1995. "Who's Who in Pandav Lila?", in William S. Sax, ed., *The Gods at Play: Lila in South Asia*. New York: Oxford University Press.

———. 2000a. "In Karna's Realm: An Ontology of Action", *Journal of Indian Philosophy*, 28 (3): 295-324.

———. 2000b. "Conquering the Quarters: Religion and Politics in Hinduism", *International Journal of Hindu Studies*. New York: World Heritage Press.

———. 2002. *Dancing the Self: Personhood and Performance in the Pandav Lila of Garhwal*. New York: Oxford University Press.

———. 2003. "Divine Kingdoms in the Central Himalayas" in *Sacred Landscape of the Himalaya, Proceedings of an International Conference at Heidelberg*, 25–27 May 1998, ed. Niels Gutschow et al., 177–94. Vienna: Austrian Academy of Sciences Press.

———. 2006a. "Agency", in Jens Kreinath, Jan Snoek and Michael Stausberg, eds, *Theorizing Rituals: Vol. I: Issues, Topics, Approaches, Concepts*. Leiden: Brill.

———. 2006b. "Rituals of the Warrior Khund", in William S. Sax, ed., *European Bulletin of Himalayan Research*. France: CNRS UPR 299, and Nepal: Social Science Baha.

———. 2009. *God of Justice: Ritual Healing and Social Justice in the Central Himalayas*. New York: Oxford University Press.

———. 2010a. "The Royal Pilgrimage of the Goddess Nanda", in *Pilgrimages Today*, Scripta Instituti Donneriani Aboensis. ISSN 0582-Vol. 22: 3226.

———. 2010b. "Ritual and the Problem of Efficacy", in William S. Sax, Johannes Quack, and Jan Weinhold, eds, *The Problem of Ritual Efficacy*. New York: Oxford University Press.

———, and Hari Kumar Bhaskaran Nair. 2014. "A Healing Practice in Kerala", in Harish Naraindas, Johannes Quack, and William S. Sax, ed., *Asymmetrical Conversations: Contestations, Circumventions, and the Blurring of Therapeutic Boundaries*. New York, Oxford: Berghahn Books.

Scott, James C. 1990. *Domination and the Arts of Resistance: Hidden Transcripts*. New Haven: Yale University Press.

———. 2008. "Stilled to Silence at 500 Metres: Making Sense of Historical Change in Southeast Asia", *IIAS Newsletter*, No. 49, Autumned Lee Gillette.

———. 2009. *The Art of Not Being Governed: An Anarchist History of Upland Southeast Asia*. New Haven and London: Yale University Press.

Scott, W.L.L. 1852. *Views in the Himalayas, Drawn on the Spot*. London: Henry Graves and Co.

Shah, Alpa, and Sara Schneiderman. 2013. "The Practices, Policies, and Politics of Transforming Inequality in South Asia: Ethnographies of Affirmative Action", *Focaal—Journal of Global and Historical Anthropology* 65 (2013): 3–12.

Shamasastry, R. 1960. *Kautilya's Arthashastra*. Mysore: Mysore Printing and Publishing.

Sharma, B.R. 2007. *Gods of Himachal Pradesh*. Shimla: Indus Publishing Company in association with Institute of Integrated Himalayan Studies, H.P. University.

Singh, Chetan. 2006. "Polyandry and Customary Rights of Landownership in the Western Himalaya", in *XIV International Economic History Congress*, Helsinki.

Singh, Padam. 1975. "Socio-Religious Practices in Kalsi Block", *The Journal of Lal Bahadur Shastri National Academy of Administration*, Mussoorie, XX/2.

Sircar, D.C. 1956. "Three Plates from Pandukeshvar", *Epigraphia Indica* 31: 277–98.

Sneath, David. 2007. *The Headless State: Aristocratic Orders, Kinship Society and Misrepresentation of Nomadic Inner Asia*. New York: Columbia University Press.

Staal, Fritz. 1979. "The Meaninglessness of Ritual", *Numen*, Vol. 26, pp. 2–22.

Stein, Burton. 1994. "Mahanavami: Medieval and Modern Kingly Ritual in South Indian History", in Bradwell Smith, ed., *Essays on Gupta Culture*, pp. 3–51. Durham: Duke University Press.

Streets, Heather. 2001. "The Rebellion of 1857: Origins, Consequences, and Themes", in *Teaching South Asia, An Internet Journal of Pedagogy*, Vol. 1, No. 1, Winter.

———. 2004. *Martial Races, Race and Masculinity in British Imperial Culture, 1857–1914*. Manchester: Manchester University Press.

Sukthankar, V.S. 1977. *The Mahabharata for the First Time Critically Edited: Vol. 1, Part 1: Adiparvan*. Pune: Bhandarkar Oriental Research Institute.

Sutherland, Peter. 1998. "Travelling Gods and Government by Deity: An Ethnohistory of Power, Representation and Agency in West Himalayan Polity", PhD dissertation, Oxford University.

———. 2003. "Very Little Kingdoms: The Calendrical Order of West Himalayan Hindu Polity", in Georg Berkemer and Margret Frenz, eds, *Sharing Sovereignty – Royalty on a Small Scale. The Little Kingdom in South Asia*. Berlin: Klaus Schwartz Verlag.

———. 2003–4. "Local Representations of History and the History of Local Representation: Timescapes in Theistic Agency in Western Himalayas", *European Bulletin of Himalayan Research*, 25/26 (Special Volume on Local Histories).

———. 2006. "T(r)opologies of Rule (Raj): Ritual Sovereignty and Theistic Subjection", *European Bulletin of Himalayan Research* 29–30, Special Issue on Divine Kingship in the Western Himalayas, ed. William S. Sax: 82–119.

Tambiah, Stanley J. 1977. "The Galactic Polity: The Structure of Traditional Kingdoms", *South East Asia in Annals of the New York Academy of Sciences*, 293, 1: 69–97.

———. 1979. "A Performative Approach to Ritual", *Proceedings of the British Academy* 65: 113–69.

———. 1985. *Culture, Thought and Social Action: An Anthropological Perspective*. Cambridge MA: Harvard University Press.

———. 1989. "Ethnic Conflict in the World Today", *American Ethnologist*, Vol. 16, No. 2, May: 335–49.

Taylor, Charles. 1995. "Two Theories of Modernity", *The Hastings Center Report* 25 (2): 24–33.

———. 1992. *Sources of the Self: Making of the Modern Identity*. Cambridge: Cambridge University Press.

———. 2001. "Foreword", in M. Catchet, ed., *The Disenchantment of the World: A Political History of Religion*. Princeton: Princeton University Press, 1997.

———. 2007. *A Secular Age*. Cambridge, M.A.: The Belknap Press of Harvard University Press.

———. 2008. *Buffered and Porous Selves: The Immanent Frame*. http://blogs.ssrc.org/tif/2008/09/02/buffered-and-porous-selves. Accessed March 2012.

Thompson, Kenneth, ed. 1985. *Readings from Emile Durkheim*. New York and London: Routledge, Taylor and Francis Group.

Thomson, R.G. 1992. First Edition (G24). *Gazetteer of the Simla District: 1888–89*. New Delhi: Hillman Publishing House.

Toffin, Gerrard. 2000. "Rajopadhyay Brahmins of Kathmandu Valley", *Himalaya: Past and Present*, ed. Maheshwar P. Joshi, Allen C. Fanger, Charles W. Brown, Vol. IV, 1993–4. Almora: Shree Almora Book Depot.

Trautmann, Thomas, R. 1971. *Kautilya and the Arthashastra: A*

Statistical Investigation of Authorship and Evolution of the Text. Leiden: Brill.

Turner, Victor W. 1967. *The Forest of Symbols: Aspect of Ndembu Ritual.* Cornell: Cornell University Press.

———. 1968. *The Drums of Affliction: A Study of Religious Processes among the Ndembu of Zambia.* Cornell and London: Cornell University Press.

———. 1969 (reprint 2008). "The Ritual Process: Structure and Anti-Structure", in idem, ed., *Foundations of Human Behavior.* Hawthorne, New York: Transaction Publishers.

———. 1987. *The Anthropology of Performance.* New York: PAJ Publications.

Van Gennep, Arnold. 1960. *The Rites of Passage.* Upper Saddle River, New York: Pearson Education.

Vidal, Denis. 1988. *Le culte des divinités locales dans une région de l'Himachal Pradesh.* Paris: Editions de l'Orstom.

———. 2006. "The Test of Traditions: An History of Feuds in Himachal Pradesh", *European Bulletin of Himalayan Research,* 29–30, Summer 2006.

Walton, H.G. 1911. *The Gazetteer of Dehra Dun* (Department Gazetteer of the United Province of Agra and Oudh: Vol. 1). Allahabad: Government Press.

Weber, Max. 2002. *The Protestant Ethic and the Spirit of Capitalism.* New York: Penguin Classics.

Williams, G.R.C. 1874 (reprint 1985). *Historical and Statistical Memoir of Dehra Doon.* Dehradun: Nataraj.

Young, Fredrick. 1836. F/4/1640, 65600 Papers regarding Rawain Pargana – Objection of the Raja of Tehri (Garhwal) Soodurshun Shah to the revenue settlement of Rawain carried out by Lt. Col. F. Young – Complaints against Soodurshun Shah by Chiefs of Rawain. Oriental and India Office Collections. British Library, London.

Young, Iris Marion. 1989. "Polity and Group Difference: A Critique of the Ideal of Universal Citizenship", *Ethics* 99: 250–74.

Zoller, Claus Peter. 1985. "Mandan in Delhi", *Mundus* 24: 150–73.
———. 1993. "On Himalayan Ball Games, Head-hunting and Related Matters", in Heidrum Bruckner, Lothar Lutze, and Aditya Malik, eds, *Flags of Fame: Studies in South Asian Folk Culture*. Delhi: Manohar.
———. 1996. "Eine Mahabharata-Erzählung aus Jaunsar im indischen Himalaya", in Dieter B. Kapp (Hrsg.), *Nanavidhaikata. Festschrift für Hermann Berger*. Wiesbaden: Harrassowitz Verlag.

ARCHIVAL SOURCES

India Office Records, British Library, London, F/4/570, 13990, Extract: Political Letter from Bengal, 11th December 1816.
India Office Records, British Library, London, F/4/571,13998, Para 2 in Statistical and Geographical Memoirs.
India Office Records, British Library, London, F/4/572,13999, G. Birch, Assistant Agent to the Governor General of India.
India Office Records, British Library, London, F/4/572,13999, Page 112 – H. Walker, Lieutenant and Commander, Kotegurh.
India Office Records, British Library, London, F/4/1483, 58486, Complaints of Zemindars of Rawain of Revenue Settlement by Young, Superintendent of Dehradun (May 1832 to July 1834).
India Office Records, British Library, London, F/4/1483, 58486, Complaint of the Zamindars of Rawain of Acts of Oppression on part of the Raja (of Tehri, Garhwal, Soodurshan Shah), May 1832 to July 1834.
India Office Records, British Library, London, Report by W. Fraser, Agent of Governor General, 29 May 1833.
India Office Records, British Library, London, extract from the minutes of Fort William, Calcutta, termed as "Political Consultations of 6 June, 1833".
India Office Records, British Library, London, F/4/571, 13997, Settlement of the State of Sirmur – Retransfer of Part of Pargana of Jaunsar to Sirmur (May 1815 to December 1816).

India Office Records, British Library, London, F/4/571, 13998(1), The Parganas of Jaunsar and Bawar are detached from Sirmur and annexed to British India together with the Kiarda Dun (January 1815 to December 1816).

India Office Records, British Library, London, F/4/856, 22676, Construction of wooden Bridge across river Pabar at Rawain, January 1823 to September 1824.

India Office Records, British Library, London, F/4/1640, 65600, Papers regarding Rawain Pargana – Objections of the Raja of Tehri (Garhwal) (SS) to the Revenue Settlement of Rawain carried out by Lt. Col. Fredrick Young.

India Office Records, British Library, London, F/4/455, 11109, Military Operations against Nepalese, Khalanga, Second Assault.

India Office Records, British Library, London, F/4/456, 11112, Seizure of Nepalese of some villages in Simla Hills belonging to Raja Ram Singh, a Sikh Chieftain.

India Office Records, British Library, London, F/4/570, 13990, Papers regarding the disposal and settlement of territories taken from Gurkhas in Nepal War including Bilaspur, Keonthal, Baghat and the other Simla Hill States, August 1814 to December 1816.

India Office Records, British Library, London, F/4/572, 13999, question as to what type of Judicial Administration should be used in the British possessions in the Simla Hills – cases of murders committed in Jaunsar and Keonthal, November 1815 to May 1818.

WEB SOURCES

http://www.garhwalpost.com/leftnewsdetail.aspx?id=796;&nt=Feature (accessed on 01.06.13)

http://pfauttarakhand.org/2010/12/pashubali-at-devils-own-country-uttarakhand (accessed on 01.06.13)

Index

The letter "f" after a page number indicates a figure.

---

aarti (invocation), 343
Abhimanyu (son of Arjuna), 143
acephalous organisation, 86
adjudication, adjudicator, 49, 177, 195
agency, 63, 68, 93
agent, agentive force, agentive power, 7, 24, 31, 129, 195
agentive network(s), 203
Agra Presidency, 189
agrim puja (right to first offering in a ritual), 134
agro-pastoralism, 23
ahimsa (non-violence), 339
Aitchison, C.U., 292
Akbar, 51–2
Alam, Aniket, 206, 207, 297
allegory, allegorical virtue, 101–2
Allen, Charles, 201
Almora, 34
alternative modernities, 28, 29, 360
Ambedkar, Bhim Rao, 9
ameri buti (mango tree of immortality), 161, 163
Anderson, Benedict, 37
Andhra Valley (in Himachal Pradesh), 213
Anglo-Gurkha War or Anglo-Nepalese War, 33, 88, 131, 170–1, 173, 178, 183, 187, 200–2, 291
Anglo-Maratha War (Second), 199, 201
aprahast (impure ritual), 338
Aravan, Iravan (Arjuna's son), 142
Archaeological Survey of India, 216, 305
Arjuna, 142
artha (related to political economy), 289, 298
Arthashastra, 57, 58
asarh (roughly, June in the Hindu calendar), 257
Athoor, 207
Atkinson, Edwin. T., 34, 176, 205
Axis Mundi, 58
Ayutthaya, 58

baahar-ki-puja (outside worship), 242
Badal (village), 167
Badrinath, 55, 89, 181
Bagan, 58
Baghi, Bagee, 73, 188, 206, 255f
Bagi, 67, 73, 76f, 253
Bahuguna, Hemvati Nandan, 53
baisakh (roughly, the month of April), 258, 260

bajgi(s), bajanewala (drummer-bard), 50, 64, 82, 121, 125, 140–1, 169, 216, 238–9, 246, 251–2, 254, 257, 296, 300f, 307, 324–5, 335–6, 338, 357–8
Bakaan, 261, 266
bali, balidana (animal/human sacrifice), 19, 240, 244, 324, 326, 328, 333–4, 336, 339, 340–2, 345–7, 350–1, 359
ballad, 29
Ballinamuck, 199
bandh kholna (ritual), 48
Bangalore (now Bengaluru), 199
Bangan 65, 124, 143, 146, 248, 260–1, 325, 343
barabasha (twelve-yearly cycle of touring), 67, 270
barah-beesi khund (the 240 militia of Mahasu), 77, 216
Barash Dhal, 167
Barbareek (Bhima's son) 142
Barkot, 179, 184
Barnes, G.C., 206
Barth, Fredrik, 87, 91
Basant Panchami (spring festival), 324
Bashahar, 60, 176, 205–6, 208–10
Bashik, Bashik Mahasu, 5, 13, 14f, 18, 64–7, 69, 76f, 78, 85, 94, 130, 138, 253, 255f, 275, 340, 353
Bastil, 169, 254, 261, 264–5, 275, 290
Basuki, 135
Batavia, 199
Battle of Khalanga, 170
Baukwan, 190, 193–4

Bautha Mahasu (the seated Mahasu), 4, 5, 13, 19, 56, 64–5, 69, 76f, 92, 94, 98, 101, 248–9, 254, 255f, 260, 341
Bawar, 65, 73, 76f, 248, 260
beda, bedavart (itinerant performers), 319, 347
begar (unpaid bonded labour), 178, 208
Bell, Catherine, 235, 281, 283, 284
Bengal, 143
Berglund, Henrik, 10
Bergmann, Christoph, 58, 99, 359
Berreman, Charles D., 348
Berti, Daniella, 26, 68, 122
Betéille, Andre, 295
bethu (bonded porters), 172
bhadon (beginning and mid-August), 247
Bhaduvana (Naga deity), 135
Bhagchand, 190
Bhairon, 136
bhaktas (devotees), 312
bhakti (devotion), 343
bhandari (inventory keepers), 125, 299, 336
Bhanomantari, 149, 150, 159
Bharar, 354
Bharatiya Janata Party (BJP), 10, 11, 41, 43
Bharatpur (kingdom in Rajasthan), 199
Bharti, Nandlal, 304, 307–10, 312, 314–18, 320, 346
bhat (genealogist), 299
Bhati (the Nahan dynasty), 319
Bhatt, 303
Bhattarh, 169

Bhima, *Bhimsen*, 132, 142, 144, 158, 161
bhog (feeding the worshipped icon), 337
Bhojan (a clan), 254, 256
Bholarh, 354
Bhoria, 293–4
Bhotanu, 103, 268, 325, 350
Bhujkoti, 133
bhupati, 94
Bija, 263, 264, 265, 266
Bijalwan, 207
Bijat (lower castes' deity), 36, 262, 296, 311, 312, 313
Bijauli, 265
Bimal, 135
Binnar, 73, 76f
biophysical entities, 175
bir(s), also Rangbir, Jangbir, Udaibir, Baitalbir, Angarubir, Chararbir, and Kaluabir (deputies to the divine kings), 38, 63, 100, 131–3, 135–6, 141, 217, 223, 238, 313, 324, 332
Bisht, Gobind Singh, 180, 185–7
blood sacrifices, 20
Board of Control of Cricket in India (B.C.C.I.), 165
bolanda badri (mouthpiece of Badrinath), 181, 183
bonded labour, 3
borders, 30, 38
bori ki buti (banyan tree in Kurukshetra), 163
Bourdieu, Pierre, 89, 139, 177, 282, 284, 357
Brahman(s), 37, 42, 67, 73, 80–2, 88, 94, 136, 138, 140–1, 144, 211, 221, 239, 246, 249, 250, 257, 259f, 266, 283–4, 293, 296, 304, 316, 328, 336
bride price, 2
British Garhwal, 292
British India, 44, 203
British, British administrators, resident, 7, 29–30, 32, 36, 38, 46, 49, 62, 88, 93, 96, 108, 118, 123, 125–6, 167–70, 172–3, 175–6, 180–5, 192, 197–9, 201, 203, 205–8, 213–14, 221, 224, 233, 288, 291
Brughart, R., 79
Buddhism, 307
bujhana (solving a puzzle), 147
Buli Das, 18
Burha Pudiyan, 137
Burhi Diwali (old Diwali), 301–2
Burondo Pass, 213

cadastral surveys, 94
Calcutta (Kolkata), 179, 202
capitalism, 7
Captain Cook, 171–2, 197
caste, caste system, caste segregation, 1, 9, 20, 80–1, 83–5, 205, 261, 287–8, 315, 320
Central Asia, 265
centre–periphery model, 81–2, 85
Chakrata, 1, 44, 175, 222, 257, 292
Chalda Mahasu, 5, 13, 14f, 16–20, 56, 64–5, 69–70, 75, 76f, 77–9, 83–4, 95, 98–101, 103–5, 120, 138–40, 176, 238, 252–4, 255f,

268, 272, 274–9, 281, 306, 340–1, 343–4, 351, 353–5
Champa, 58
Char Dham, 2, 134
charan (herald), 299
charas (hashish), 165
charkha, 36
Chasralu, 67, 211–12, 217–20, 226
chatra, chatrai, 77, 139, 238, 344
Chattra, 73, 76f, 109–10, 112, 188, 217, 248, 255f, 256
Chauhan Rajput(s), 75, 261
chauntru (council of elders), 67, 79, 193–5, 292
Chausal, 73, 76f
chawal jhapna/akshat puja (rice offering), 242
cheriya boli (of a possessed oracle), 54, 115, 328, 330
chetan purus (sentient being), 135
chief minister, 21, 54, 55, 311
Chillam Nag, 219
China, Chinese, 57, 170, 198, 200, 292
Chitrakshin, 217
chuntroo (heavy taxation), 184, 192
climatic divide, 24
collective agency, 95, 122
colonial, colonialism, 50, 53, 70, 88–9, 95–6, 129, 175, 218, 222
communitas, 109
complex agency, 64, 121
Congress (Indian National Congress), 8, 10, 41–4, 53, 271
conquering the quarters, 120, 131
consubstantial, consubstantiality, 85, 130, 175
cosmology, 31, 132, 171–2

creamy layer (of caste reservations), 295
cultural capital, 82, 185

Dagoli, 160, 255f
Dak Pathar, 217
Daksha, 31
dalit, 9, 288, 317
Dalrymple, William, 205
damru (Shiva's drum), 138
dand (penalty), 208, 329
dangra, 4
Daragad, 265
darshan (divine audience), 310
das (caste category), 140
Dastur-al-Amal (customary code), 292, 323
Datmir, 217
datoo (scarves), 113, 128
deban-ro-raja (king of gods), 78
Dehra Dun, 1–6, 17, 23, 26, 106–7, 124, 170, 173–4, 177–9, 191, 196, 199, 201–2, 292, 309, 311, 347, 359
Delhi, Dilli Durbar, New Delhi, 98, 118, 179, 182, 184, 189, 190, 307
Delimitation Commission, 43
Delueze, Gilles, 360
democracy, democratic, democratisation, 7, 27, 30, 40, 50, 63, 93, 127, 197, 287, 306
Deoghar, 65, 76f
Deoladi, 74, 129, 139, 140, 262
deopujya, 73, 140, 240, 244–5, 252, 254, 269, 296
dev bhoomi (abode of the gods), 348

dev, devta(s), devta raja, 53, 56, 59, 63, 102, 116, 126, 143, 145, 147, 163, 164, 175, 217, 221, 236–8, 244–7, 250–3, 256, 270, 272–3, 275–6, 278–80, 308, 311, 313–14, 320, 329, 332, 345, 350–1, 354–5
deval, 125, 159
devniti, 108
devta ka pani (water for temple), 240, 242
devta raja ka kaam, dev-karya (work of divine kings), 22, 87, 108, 239
Dhadi-Rao, Dhadi, 53, 78–9, 104, 120
dhakeur (temple anteroom), 81, 299, 307
dhaki (drummer), 216
Dhaknach (folk performance), 144–5, 147, 160, 324
dhal (tribute), 240, 333
Dhami Rebellion, 207
dhandaks (rebellions), 206–7, 222
dhanti marriage, 2
dharma, dharmic, 141, 159, 289, 298
dhiyan, dhanti (out-married daughter), 34, 120, 300
dhol (drum), 103
Dhurrum Datt, 183
digvijaya, 66, 93, 192
Directive Principles of State Policy, 339, 349
Dirks, Nicholas B., 37, 81, 86, 126, 204, 288, 315, 342
District Magistrate (D.M.), 106–7, 179, 311, 341

divine kingship, divine king (-s/-dom), 7, 11–13, 20, 23–5, 28, 38, 48, 50, 54, 58, 64, 70–1, 80, 82, 84, 88, 93, 101, 113, 117–18, 123, 126, 140, 163, 171, 175, 185, 211, 220, 237, 256, 274, 276, 280, 287, 314, 324–6, 329, 334, 338, 357, 359
divya desams (divine destinations), 181
Diwan Singh, 75, 169
Diyasuri, 152, 153, 156, 158
Dobhal, 248, 253, 254, 257, 260
Dodra-Kwar, 124, 233, 291
dolacra (tribute), 208
dom (caste), 293, 297, 303
donriyan (silver box), 250–1
dos/prakop (wrath of the divine king), 48, 117, 240, 244, 326–9, 332, 333, 335, 343–5, 350
Draupadi, 143, 148, 158–9
dual sovereignty, 83
Duling Lake, 213
dumhs (mass movements), 206, 222
Dumont, Louis, 37, 80, 81, 126, 182, 298
Duni-Bhitri, 13, 19, 76f, 254, 258
Durkheim, Emile, 321
Duryodharan (Duryodhana), 147–50, 159, 163

East India Company, 174, 198–9, 202
egalitarianism, 305, 317
Election Commission of India, 42
Emergency, the, 10

Emerson, H.W., 50, 89, 98, 131, 205, 209–10, 213–15, 218–19, 222–4, 226, 229–30, 232, 297, 337
enlightenment, 7
epidemics, 49
epistemology, 172
ethnicity, 10, 11
European, 57
exemplary centre, 58, 92, 101, 102

Fateh Parvat, 65, 76f, 124, 248, 254
feuding, 95
Ford, Alfred, 164
Forest Department, 17
Fraser, James Baillie, 180, 202, 205, 292
Fuller. C.J., 334

Gadara, 254
gaddi (seat of power), 79
Galactic Polity, 57, 92
Galey, Jean-Claude, 89, 93–4, 122
ganadhish (master of Shiva's warriors), 135
Gandhari, 147, 160
Gandhi, Indira, 10, 53, 306
Gandhi, Mahatma, 35, 113, 345, 349
Ganesha, 134–5
Gangotri, 55
Gaonkar, Dilip Parmeshwar, 28
Garhwal(i), 1, 33–4, 99, 125, 142–3, 145, 184, 187–9, 193–4, 202, 210, 256, 258, 260, 290, 336, 356
gaunt (cow urine), 249

Gazetteer, 97, 131, 169, 176, 205, 297, 319
Geertz, Clifford, 27, 57, 82, 90, 91, 92, 101
genealogy, genealogical literature, genealogists, 50, 94, 248
George V (king), 98
Ghagati, 137
ghaghra (skirt), 128
ghantua (goat), 335, 345
ghat, ghat lagana (ensnare), 331
ghatval (small pit), 242
Gibson, Alexander James, 209
Gillespie, Maj. Gen. Sir Robert Rollo, 199
Giri, 319
globalisation, global flows, 10, 11, 127
Glossary of Castes, 205
Godse, Nathuram, 345
Golden Belt, 40
gotra (clan or lineage), 336
government by deity, 13, 20, 96, 221
Government of India Act, 292, 323
Governor General, 179, 180, 185, 189, 195
Grimes, Ronald. R., 268
Guattari, Felix, 360
Guha, Ramachandra, 204
gunth (revenue-free villages), 188–9, 269
Gurkha, 45, 108, 168–9, 172–4, 182, 199–203

Hadow, Jenkins, 174, 200–1
Hamirpur, 165
Handa, Om Chandra, 213

Hanol, Hanol Mahasu Temple, 3, 5, 14f, 15–18, 44, 54, 65, 67, 69, 74, 77, 79, 92, 93–5, 97, 110, 112, 120, 125, 142, 159, 161, 188, 191, 193, 215, 219, 235, 248, 249, 258, 260, 266–8, 273, 275, 300f, 301, 305, 307, 308, 311, 315, 325, 328–9, 339–40, 345–6, 355, 359
harare (rituals), 247–8
Haridwar, Hardwar, 1
harijan, 313
harijan pani (water of lower castes), 301
harul (ballads), 167, 261–2
Hastinapura, Hastina, 147, 161
Hatkoti, 136–7, 262
havan (sacrificial offerings), 354
Hawaiian, 171–2, 197
head-hunting, 2, 20
Hebdige, D., 337
Heidelberg, 234, 235
Hiltebeitel, Alf, 159
Himachal Pradesh, 6, 14, 16, 30, 39, 40–1, 43, 53, 79, 102–3, 105, 124f, 164, 268, 291, 344, 348, 353–4
Himalayas, 93, 256
Hindu Kush, 142, 265
Hindu, -ism, Hindu identity, 1, 9–10, 130, 181, 294, 307, 323, 349, 355
hindutva, 10
Hocart, A.M., 36–7
human sacrifice, 2
Huna Bhat, 94, 130, 357

Ibbetson, Denzil, 131, 205, 217
identity, 9, 10, 323
Inden, Ron, 64, 121
India(n), 49, 62, 78, 93, 108, 118, 142, 170, 288, 323, 354, 358
Indian Administrative Service (I.A.S.), 106
Indian Navy, 328
Indian Premier League (I.P.L.), 165
Indic kingship, 92
Indo-China Conflict (1962), 15
Indonesia, 142
Indra, Indu (god of weather), 152, 161
Ireland, 203
Islam, 9

Jaajnaou, 263
Jagannath Temple, 306
jagheer (land grant), 187
Jagmohan, 276
Jagra (festival), 247–8, 254, 255f, 298
Jai Mahakali, Ayo Gorkhali! (Gurkha war cry), 200
Jain, Madhu, 324
Jaithak (fort), 172, 199, 200
jajmana, yajamana (patrons), 244, 299, 325, 355
Jakh of Janglik, 219
jal, jungal aur zameen (water, forest and land), 33
Jamlu Devta, 165
jatis (castes), 142, 356
Jaunsar Bawar, Jaunsar(i) 1–2, 11, 24, 34, 36, 39, 45, 65, 76f, 89, 95, 124, 128, 137, 142–3, 145–6, 148, 166, 173, 176, 179, 191, 287, 290–5, 309,

315–16, 320, 322–3, 350, 355, 358–9
Jaunsari tribe, 323
jero-jeba, 91
jeth (roughly, June), 67
jethang (primogeniture), 75
jeunda (goat), 334
Joshi, 253–4, 257
Joshi, Lakshmikant, 261
journeying, 88, 90
Jubbal, 36, 53, 73, 76f, 125, 167, 176, 190, 260

Kailas, 147
Kailath, 111, 113–14, 132
Kailavati, 137
Kailu, 100, 132, 242
Kali, 132
Kalsi, 176
Kanaital, 137
Kanet, 297
kanphata jogis (followers of Guru Gorakhnath), 81, 300f, 310
Kapla, 132
Karccham-Wangtoo Hydroelectric Project, 165
kardar (official), 345
Karmanasha, 123, 133
Karmasur, 132
Karna, 67, 161, 163
kartik (roughly, October), 258
Kartikeya, 134–5, 212
Kasauli, 222
Kashdhar, 14, 40, 42, 60–1, 76f, 120, 354
Kashmir, 54, 64, 66, 94, 129, 132–3, 136–8, 222, 265, 324, 341, 349
Katanya and Dum, 51–2

kath-kunni style (alpine architecture), 76, 305
Kathmali, 355
Kathmandu, 169
Katyuri, 34
Kauai (in Hawaii), 197
Kaul-Kedari, 18
Kauravas, 13, 18, 93, 104, 143, 145–9, 159–61, 163
Kautilya, 58–9, 76, 79
Kaviraj, Sudipta, 359
Kedarnath, 55
Kelubil, 138
Kerala, 143
Kertzer, David, 26–7, 86, 87, 321
Khalanga, 172, 199
khanda (a long sword), 216
khandit murti (image or idol), 139
khandit-mundit (lowest caste order), 304
Khanduri, Bhuvan Chandra, 53
Kharamba, 133
khash (people), 142, 264–6, 293, 318, 356
khat (land administration unit), 97, 107
Khatirjun, 148
Khatu Shyamji, 142
khukri (Nepalese dagger), 200
khumris (councils of elders), 178
khund, 78, 95, 250, 266, 274
Khurasao (sacrifice), 305, 341, 351
Kilbalu (also Tilbalu, Jwar, and Banar), 136
King Edward's Own Gurkha Rifles (IInd), 170, 202
King of Doon (Major Young), 174, 203

kingship, South Asian kingship, 37–8, 50, 83, 90
Kinnaur, 16, 124, 136, 165, 209
Kinnu, 41
Kiratas, 142, 265, 356
Kirmir, 37, 65, 74, 94–5, 100, 111, 132, 136, 138, 163, 349
koli, 125, 297, 318
Kolta, 96, 121, 125, 239, 245–6, 252, 257, 287–8, 293–7, 300f, 301, 303–4, 307, 315–18, 336, 358
kopin (loincloth), 245
kot, 22, 67, 76–7, 216, 261, 264–6
Koti, 73, 76f
Koti-Banal (alpine architecture), 76, 77, 305
Krishna, 142–3
Kuddu, 100
kul-devta, 78
Kullu, 26, 41, 94, 101, 129, 132, 136, 324, 349
Kumaon, 1, 13, 33–4, 202, 204, 290
Kumbha Mela, 101
Kuna, 46, 48, 67, 73, 76f
Kunta (Kunti), 147–8, 160–1
Kurukshetra, 30, 143, 147–8, 163
kut (temple's share), 167, 177, 188

Lakhamandal, 146–7
Lakhwar, 75, 76f
lakshagriha, 146
Lalitaditya, 132
lambardar (village chief), 223
Landour, 203
Lata bir (a demi-god), 330–2
Latour, Bruno, 22
leprosy, 332

liberal pluralism, 9
lila (play of the divinities), 284
little kingdoms, 173, 323
Lokur Committee, 295
longevity, 50, 82
Lono (Hawaiian god), 172, 197
Luchesi, Brigitte, 68
lun-lota (temple stipulation), 185, 192

MacLagan, Edward, 131, 205, 217
Madan Das, 64, 129–30, 136, 216, 296, 324
magh (arrival of spring), 324
Mahabharata, 13, 30, 93, 104, 132, 142–3, 145–6, 148, 163, 357
Mahasu, Mahasu kingdom, Mahasu Devta, 4, 6–7, 11, 13, 14f, 15, 17–19, 21–4, 26, 28, 30–1, 33–8, 40, 42–3, 48–54, 59, 61, 63–7, 71, 73–6, 76f, 77–9, 82–4, 86–9, 92–4, 97–102, 104–8, 114–21, 123, 124f, 125, 128–32, 138–47, 161, 164, 166–70, 173, 175–7, 182–5, 188–91, 194–6, 198, 203, 208–33, 236–42, 246, 249, 250–2, 255f, 256–7, 259f, 262, 266–9, 272, 274–6, 284–5, 289, 295–6, 298–9, 304–5, 307–9, 311–15, 317–21, 324–6, 328–31, 333–41, 343–51, 357–60
Maindrath, 14f, 64, 73, 94, 129–31, 139, 140, 143, 188, 253, 255f, 262
Majapahit, 58
Majog, 136

INDEX

Malana Cream, 165
mali (Mahasu oracle), 17, 53, 59, 63, 71, 83–4, 104, 109, 132, 178, 208, 312–13, 358–9
mand (rice water), 144
mandaan, 53
Mandagad, 144
Mandala, 56–7, 92
mandapam, 240
Mandi, 36, 41, 209–10
Mangteoun, 266
Mansarovar, 147–8
Mansuri, 152
Maroz, 348, 350
Marriott, McKim, 21
Marx, Karl, 7, 22, 359
mat (middle-caste order), 302
mauff (revenue-free land grant), 188–90
Maulekhi, Gauri, 348
maunds (unit of weight), 51
maya, 130
mayat (maternal home), 300
Mehta, Bhagmal, 60, 61
Metcalfe, 189, 195
mian (heirs of Dhadi Rao), 353
Miedema, Virgil and Stephanie Spaid, 168, 203
misrecognise, misrecognition, 89, 176–7
mobility, 101–2
modern state(s), 35
modernisation (theory), modernity 7, 8, 11, 21, 22, 25, 28, 87, 128, 209, 359
modernity, deficient, 29, 35, 87
Modi, Narendra, 11
moieties, 30, 85

Mookhtear, Mookhtar, 195
Moradabad, 359
Moran, Erik, 208–10
Morocco, Moroccan, 92
Mount Meru, 56, 58
Mughal(s), 29, 49, 51–2
mulq (allegiance-based territory), 58
Mundali (between Jaunsar and Bawar), 133
munshee (clerk), 183
Muslim, 10
Mussoorie, 1, 44, 171, 179, 202, 205, 222
Myerhoff, Barbara G., 321

Nachini Guara, 136
Naga, 135, 212, 226
Nahan, 172, 190
Nainital, 205, 222
Naitwar, 179
Nalapani, 199
namti (afternoon invocations), 240
Nanda Devi Raj Yatra, 34, 101
Nanda Devi, 33–5
Narayan/Kapi Narayan (form of Vishnu), 145, 148–9, 152–3, 160–1, 215
Narayanhiti Palace, 169
Narsingh, 136, 330–1
Nartaik, 265–6
Nasiri Paltan, 202
Nath, *nath-panthi*, 81, 293, 310
National Human Rights Commission, 308–9, 314
Natiya Banban (amorous song), 303
naubat (fanfare), 240, 264

Nauti, 34
Nautiyal (clan of Brahman priests), 160, 253, 260
Nautiyal, Harish, 328
Negara, 27, 90
Nehru, Jawaharlal, 8, 9, 10, 32
Nenus, 73, 76f, 188, 248, 253–4, 256–8
Nepal, Nepalese, 32, 45–6, 86, 108, 125, 142, 168–9, 199, 202, 265, 292, 294, 315
neti-dauli (emancipated group), 304
Newari, 315–16
Nimga Rawat, 261, 264–6
nirore (rituals), 247–9
nisan (symbol), 54, 62, 102, 111, 343
niyam (ethical code), 273, 312, 332, 351
nomads, 130
non-human agent, non-human agency, 21, 30, 64

Obeyesekere, Gananath, 172
Ojur Singh, 190
ontalee, ountalee, 180, 184, 192
ontological, ontological break, ontological fact, 8, 22, 58
oracular possession, 11
orality, oral tradition, 129, 145, 175, 193

paani puwai (sprinkling), 334
paap (sin), 327, 332–3
Pabasik, Pabasik Mahasu, 4–5, 13, 14f, 17–19, 64, 69, 74, 76f, 85, 94, 109, 110–11, 139, 253, 255f, 261, 278–9, 340

Pabbar, 40, 44, 100, 219
pahari (of the mountains), 175, 356
palanquin, *palqi, doli,* 7, 11, 12, 17, 19, 96, 103, 106, 109, 111, 113, 115, 116, 118, 237, 238, 268, 269, 271, 272, 284, 296, 350, 355
pamvara (ballad of Mahasu conquests), 167, 296
panchayat (local self-government), 260
Panchayati Raj Act, 292
Panchpura, 76
pancva dham, 54
Pandava(s), 13, 18, 93, 104, 142–9, 151, 157–8, 160–1
Pandrabis Range, 209
Pandu, 161
Panduan, 144–6, 148, 159–61, 163, 216, 356
pansi, pansibil, 13, 14f, 15–18, 30, 59, 65, 68, 70, 74–5, 76f, 93, 104–7, 126, 131, 143, 163, 167–8, 192, 251, 261–2, 266, 268, 271–2, 280–1, 286, 351
panti, 45, 245, 253, 258, 260, 269, 273, 275–6, 277–8
Panwar, 68, 69, 74, 260
param bhakta (greatest devotee), 34
Parbati, 153
parbatiya (Newari mountain community), 315
pargana (administrative region), 206
Parliament, 89, 164, 294, 307
Partition, 9

390   INDEX

Parvati, 133
Pashmina, 174
pastoralists, 102, 130
patri puja (offerings), 240, 242
patti (narrow strip of land), 261
paush, *paus* (winter months), 71, 257
peepal (*Ficus religiosa*), 114, 305, 339
Peje Nag, 60, 62
Pemble, John, 201
Penuwa, 266
Persian-Arabic, 59
phaslana, 81
pichli raunt (stale bread), 216
Poensha, 303
Pokhri, 307
Pokhu, 136
polyandry, 2, 123, 173, 291, 293, 320
polysemic symbols, 27
porous selves, 21
positivist, 175
possession, possessed, 11, 20, 49
post-colonial, 8, 29
prabhati (morning invocations), 241
Praja Mandals, 32
prasad (ritualised food offerings) 26, 326, 335
pratishtha (consecration), 339
pre-state kingship, 84
Prevention of Cruelty to Animals Act, 339
primogeniture, 75, 160
procession(s), processional ritual, 11, 12, 20, 93, 95, 100, 116, 120

pseudo-secularism, 10
Public Works Department (P.W.D.), 106
puchvai (process of seeking answers), 54
pujari (priest), 300f
Punjab Census, 220
Punjab Hill States, 198, 206
Punnath Tal, 324
Purana, Puranic (of the Puranas) 314, 354
Puri, 306
purohita (presiding priest), 325
Puttarh, 73, 76f, 188, 253–4, 255f, 256–8

Quack, Johannes, 21
Queen Elizabeth, 92
Queen Mary, 98

Raghunath, 26, 56
Ragugad, 143
Raheja, Godwin Gloria, 37, 81, 126
Raithik, 136
raj-guru, 81, 310
raj-purohit (chief priests), 260
Raja Karna, 18, 179
Raja of Tehri, 173, 178
Raja Padam Singh, 60
Rajasthan, 142
rajinama (an agreement), 168
Rajopadhyaya, 316
Rajput, 25, 42, 60, 67, 73, 75, 81, 84, 88, 90, 96, 102, 110, 140, 144, 159, 239, 246, 250–1, 254, 260, 265–6, 268, 271–2, 275, 281, 283–4, 287, 290–1, 293–4, 296, 298, 300f, 302,

304, 314, 325, 328, 353, 355, 357
rakshasa, 100
Raktabija, 132
Ram, Ganga (Jhuinya Baba), 305
Ramaserai, 254, 258
Rampur, Rampur-Bashahar, Bashahar, 36, 40–1, 53, 76f, 79, 98–99, 125, 209
Ramsay, Henry, 203
Rana, 68–9, 130, 260–1, 265, 275, 290
Rana, Jaipal Singh, 266
Rangarh, Rajmohan 179
Ranikhet, 222
Rarhu, 67, 76f
rationalisation, rationalism, rationalists, rationality, 7, 21, 86, 172, 213, 222, 226
Rawain Settlement, 187, 232
Rawain, 34, 173, 177–80, 182–5, 187, 189, 207
rawali-pand (temple kitchen), 242, 326, 338
Rawat (caste denomination), 263–4, 265–6
Rawat, Harish, 21
Rawat, Raghubir Singh, 266
reflexive, reflexivity, 223
Republic Day, 307
Rishikesh, 1
ritualisation, 281, 284, 286
rituals, ritual practices, 7, 8, 11, 19, 20, 23, 26–7, 30, 37, 49, 82, 86, 92, 95 163, 173, 249, 267–8, 272, 284, 321–2, 324, 351
Rohru, 40–1, 43, 76f

rope-sliding ritual, 347
Rose, H.A., 131, 205, 210
Ross, A. 323
Rupla, 152
Russian, 198

sadavart (kitchen at Mahasu temples), 277, 300
Sadhu Ram Sharma, 45
Saeriyaa, 263–4
Sahlins, Marshall, 37, 95, 171–2, 196–7, 222, 359
sakti (power), 106, 318
sanatana dharma (mainstream Hindu tradition), 339
sanca, sanca vidya (tantra text), 23, 54
sandaul (evening invocations), 240, 244, 251, 277, 280
sandhis (cycles of time), 240
sandhya puja (evening worship), 244
sanjayat (middle-caste order), 304
Sankrityayan, Rahul, 265, 304
Sanskrit, 145
sanskriti, 23
sathi, sathibil, 13, 14f, 15, 18, 30, 59, 65–6, 68, 70, 73–5, 76f, 84, 93, 104, 106–8, 126, 131, 143, 163, 169, 192, 251–2, 261–2, 268–73, 275–81, 283, 285, 340, 351
Sax, William S., 8, 11, 13, 25, 33–4, 58, 63, 80, 84–5, 87, 93–4, 101, 122, 165, 174–5, 327, 341, 359
sayana(s), sadr sayana, sayanacari (clan heads/elders), 16, 38, 67, 79, 83, 106–7, 120, 176, 178,

180, 251, 269–70, 292, 298–9, 302, 325, 346, 355
Scheduled Caste, 43
Scheduled Tribe, 290
Scott, James C., 233
Second Clap Regiment, 187
secular, secularism, secularists, secular age, secularising, 7–10, 21, 27, 30, 35, 37, 48, 50, 80, 88, 93, 121, 339
Sem-Mukhem, 336
Semwal, Mohanlal, 143, 253
Serhkuriya, 19, 65, 132, 216, 217
Shaant, 305, 307, 341
Shah Alpa and Sara Schneiderman, 294–5
Shah, Manvendra, 89, 294
Shah, Purtum, 183
Shah, Surendra, 210
Shakuni, 161
Shalu, 211, 215, 222, 225
Shamasastry, 57
Shamsher Singh, 209
Shatangdhar, 144
Sheodutt Mohurrur (elder from Rawain), 180, 187
shikhara (pointed temple roof), 236
Shimla, 16, 23, 40–1, 44, 99, 124, 171, 175, 198, 222
Shimla Hill States, 33, 51, 65, 89, 98, 105, 168, 173, 202, 209
Shiraji, 78, 84, 103–5, 252, 344, 353
Shirgul, Shilgur, 36, 307
Shiva, 132–6, 211, 318
Shore, John (superintendent of Dehra Dun), 203
shriphal (dried coconut), 346, 351
Sikh, 200

Singh, Diwan, 270–2, 276, 281
Singh, Gulab, 293–4
Singh, Jaipal, 270–1
Singh, Kartar, 270
Singh, Madan, 319
Singh, Virbhadra 41, 79, 355
siri (head of sacrificed goat), 336
Siridharan, Mahachakari, 307
Sirmaur, 36, 40–1, 53, 73–4, 76f, 124–5, 173, 178, 188–90, 200, 202, 260, 319–20
Sirmoor Rifles, 170, 187
Solan, 40–1, 124
Someshu, 67
soor, sur, 220, 298, 301
South Asia, 35, 37–8, 82, 174, 237
South Asian kingship/kingdoms, 49, 56–7, 87, 291
South East Asian Indic polities, 91
sovereign, sovereignty, 65, 84–5, 88, 93, 166, 174, 229
Srinagar (in Tehri Garhwal), 190
Srivijaya, 58
Stein, Burton, 342
stranger kings, 95, 141, 165, 212
structure of conjuncture, 196–7
Sub-Divisional Magistrate (S.D.M.), 446, 48, 257, 301, 304, 308–10, 313, 338, 347
subjecthood, 49
subsistence agriculture, 11
Sudarshan Shah, 179, 207
Suket (kingdom), 206–7
Sultan of Sumatra, 199
supa (vessel), 217
Suraha, Surendra Singh, 342

Surendra Shah (prince of Garhwal), 210
Suryavanshi (of solar descent), 265, 319
Sutherland, Peter, 56, 64, 95–6, 108, 123, 175, 221, 235, 296, 298, 318, 324, 342
Sutlej, 131, 170
swapaki (priests), 245
Swargarohini, 143

tamasa, 123
tamasik puja, tamasik gunas, 19, 342
Tambiah, Stanley J., 26, 56, 91, 92, 122
Tamil Nadu, 142
tandi (dancing in rows), 248
tantra, *tantrik*, 54, 265–6
Taylor, Charles, 21, 28, 63
Tehri, Tehri Garhwal, 33, 36, 60–1, 73–4, 89, 97, 179, 182–3, 185, 188–9, 191–5, 197–8, 206–7
tehsil, tehsildar, 47, 342
teleology, 11, 28, 87
Temple Entry Bill, 308
territory, 30, 35, 39f, 49–50, 58, 84–5, 93, 174, 232, 276
Thadiyar, 5, 14, 17, 104, 109–10, 268, 340, 354
Thailand, 306
Thaina, 75, 76f
thakur, etharah thakurai, 136
than, thaan, 66, 130
thani (Mahasu official), 243, 245, 254, 299, 329, 336
Tharonch, 53, 73, 78, 120, 191

Thaulna, 262
Theyyam, 143
Tibet, 170, 200, 292
tihar (practice of British grants), 207
tikke (crown prince), 136
tikoj (the throne of Kot), 265
Tiladi Kand (the outrage of Tiladi), 207
Tiuni, 44–5, 47, 176
Toffin, Gerrard, 315
Toka-Poka (mountain ranges), 319
Tomar Rajputs, 75, 261
Tons River, Tons, Tonse, 2, 13, 14f, 44–5, 51, 64–5, 76f, 93, 104–5, 111, 123, 133, 137, 139, 144, 147, 167, 170, 178, 190, 194, 264
Traill, G.W., 203
transhumant pastoralism, 11
Treaty of Sugauli, 168
tribe, tribal, tribalisation, 291, 294–5, 315, 350
Turner, Victor, 109, 282–3
tussuleenama (agreement), 180

udyapan jag (the great sacrifice), 209
Ullal, 136
Una Bhat, 74, 136–40
United Progressive Alliance, 10
United Provinces, 1, 33
universalism, 28
untouchable, 9
utpatti murti, 94
U.S.A., 8
Uttar Pradesh, 290, 292, 353
Uttarakhand, 1, 14, 26, 30, 33, 53,

55, 102–3, 105, 124f, 226, 290, 304, 336, 353
Uttarkashi, District, 6, 16, 124, 325

Vaishnavas, 181
Vajpayee, Atal Behari, 90
Van Genepp, Arnold, 283
Van Parva, 132
vazarat, vaziraiyik, 68, 73
vazir, wazir, 15, 59, 60, 63, 68–74, 97, 104, 130, 168–9, 176, 178, 188, 224, 226, 242, 252, 270–1, 273, 295, 298, 336, 346
Vidal, Denis, 145
Vijay, Tarun, 307
vikas, 23
Vir Singh Pithu, 266
Vishnu, 74, 95, 131, 141, 145, 161, 166, 181, 212, 215–17, 221, 246, 357
vote-bank politics, 11

wajib-ul-urz (land records), 168, 323
Walton, H.G., 24, 97, 131, 217
Wangtoo, 165

Weber, Max, 7, 22, 359
Western Himalayas, 88, 144–5, 160, 165, 170–2, 175, 198, 201, 204–6, 208, 211, 232, 235, 290–1, 297, 305, 353, 355
Williams, G.R.C., 24, 88, 96, 131, 175, 205

yajna, 240, 357
Yamuna, 2, 44, 123, 131
Yamunotri, 55
Yatra of Parsuram, Nirmand, 101
yatra, 101
Young, Fredrick (Major), 89, 96, 98, 173–4, 176–7, 179, 183–5, 190–3, 196–201, 217, 222, 232, 294
Yudhishthir, 160

zaildar (tax collector), 225, 226
zamindari system, 293
zamindaru geet (songs to please landlords), 296
zenana (harem), 180
Zoller, Klaus Peter, 53, 123, 142, 144, 146–7, 160
Zomia, 233